Pro Web Gadgets

Across iPhone, Android, Windows,
Mac, iGoogle and More

Sterling Udell

apress®

Pro Web Gadgets Across iPhone, Android, Windows, Mac, iGoogle and More

ISBN-13 (pbk): 978-1-4302-2551-5

ISBN-13 (electronic): 978-1-4302-2552-2

Printed and bound in the United States of America 9 8 7 6 5 4 3 2 1

Trademarked names may appear in this book. Rather than use a trademark symbol with every occurrence of a trademarked name, we use the names only in an editorial fashion and to the benefit of the trademark owner, with no intention of infringement of the trademark.

President and Publisher: Paul Manning
Lead Editor: Ben Renow-Clarke
Developmental Editors: Tony Campbell and Matthew Moodie
Technical Reviewer: Jeffrey Sambells
Editorial Board: Clay Andres, Steve Anglin, Mark Beckner, Ewan Buckingham, Gary Cornell, Jonathan Gennick, Jonathan Hassell, Michelle Lowman, Matthew Moodie, Duncan Parkes, Jeffrey Pepper, Frank Pohlmann, Douglas Pundick, Ben Renow-Clarke, Dominic Shakeshaft, Matt Wade, Tom Welsh
Coordinating Editor: Kelly Moritz
Copy Editor: Kim Wimpsett
Compositor: Mary Sudul
Indexer: Toma Mulligan
Artist: April Milne
Cover Designer: Anna Ishchenko

Distributed to the book trade worldwide by Springer-Verlag New York, Inc., 233 Spring Street, 6th Floor, New York, NY 10013. Phone 1-800-SPRINGER, fax 201-348-4505, e-mail orders-ny@springer-sbm.com, or visit http://www.springeronline.com.

For information on translations, please e-mail info@apress.com, or visit http://www.apress.com.

Apress and friends of ED books may be purchased in bulk for academic, corporate, or promotional use. eBook versions and licenses are also available for most titles. For more information, reference our Special Bulk Sales–eBook Licensing web page at http://www.apress.com/info/bulksales.

The source code for this book is available to readers at http://www.apress.com.

For Dick and Maureen, who always believed I would write

Contents at a Glance

Contents

About the Author

 **Sterling Udell** is a free-range writer of software and of books about doing so. He strives to stay at the forefront of his chosen technologies; in the last few years, these have predominantly been web mapping, gadgets, and mobile development. His programming achievements have been widely recognized both online and off, including as a Google Code Featured Project and a finalist in the Android Developer Challenge 2.

Sterling has a degree in mathematics and computer science from Drake University, followed by graduate-level computer science study at the University of Maine. Originally from Wisconsin, Sterling has lived all over the United States, including three years traveling and working full-time in an RV, before moving to his current home in the United Kingdom.

About the Technical Reviewer

 **Jeffrey Sambells** is a designer and developer of all things on the Internet. He is currently having fun with mobile and location-based technologies as the director of research and development for We-Create Inc. The title "Director of R&D" may sound flashy, but really that just means he's in charge of learning and cramming as much goodness into the products as possible so they're just awesome. Along the way, he has also managed to graduate university, write a few books (http://advanceddomscripting.com), develop some fun iPhone apps (http://tropicalpixels.com), maintain a blog (http://jeffreysambells.com), and raise a wonderful family.

Introduction

As a freelance developer, my first experience with gadgets came when a client asked me to build a miniature version of a web app I was already working on for them. To familiarize myself with the technology, I first gadgetized a web app of my own that I'd created in my spare time (http://daylightmap.com, discussed in Chapter 1). I was amazed to find that, within weeks, page views on the gadget were in the hundreds of thousands—and some percentage of that traffic was finding its way back to my main site. I was hooked.

Over the next couple of years, I built a wide variety of gadgets on various platforms, both for myself and for clients. I also participated in the developer forums associated with these platforms and noticed that beginners were repeatedly asking many of the same questions about gadget programming. At the same time, I was also realizing that each platform was fairly insular: there wasn't much crossover from one to another, even though many of the basic principles were the same. Thus, the idea for this book was born: a platform-agnostic manual to guide web developers into the rewarding world of gadget development, leveraging a single skill set onto a range of different APIs.

While the concept for this book was crystallizing, another change was taking place in software development: the popularization of smartphones and the maturation of their onboard browsers. Clients were beginning to ask me whether their gadgets could reasonably be ported to these new platforms, and I immediately recognized the inherent synergy—what is a web app for a 3-inch window if not a gadget? It's a natural fit, making smartphones an integral part of any complete gadget plan.

How This Book Is Structured

This book is split into four parts. In the first, you'll find a thorough introduction to gadget principle, design, and construction; this is required reading for any web professional starting out in gadgets. The goal here is to give you a solid foundation by building what I call the *core gadget*, a stand-alone web mini-app unaffiliated with any platform-specific API. This core gadget can be deployed on its own but more important will serve as your reference implementation as you move beyond Part 1.

The remainder of the book, then, is devoted to individual gadget platforms, one per chapter. These chapters are grouped into Parts 2, 3, and 4: web, desktop, and mobile, respectively. Each chapter gives you a complete guide to porting your core gadget to that platform, from design issues through deployment, including specific opportunities to leverage—and pitfalls to avoid.

For maximum reach, I recommend reading the entirety of Parts 2 through 4 and porting your gadget to every platform covered. However, I recognize that time constraints may preclude such an approach, so the book is structured so that you can generally read Chapters 4 through 13 in any order, based on your own priorities. Any interdependencies are clearly spelled out in the text.

Downloading the Code

You can find all the code in numbered listings throughout this book on the book's web site, http://sterlingudell.com/pwg. It is also available in zip file format in the Source Code section of the Apress web site (www.apress.com).

Contacting the Author

If you have any comments or additional questions relating to this book, I'd love to hear from you! You can find full contact information on http://sterlingudell.com, or you can e-mail me directly at sterling.udell@gmail.com.

Acknowledgments

I'd like to thank everyone at Apress who helped make this book a reality for their patience and understanding during what has been a sometimes-difficult writing process. In particular, I'd like to express my gratitude to Kelly Moritz, Ben Renow-Clarke, Tony Campbell, Kim Wimpsett, and Steve Anglin.

Jeffrey Sambells also deserves extra recognition for keeping me on the straight and narrow, questioning my approach when needed, and providing a sanity check throughout. He's performed above and beyond the requirements of a technical reviewer.

And finally, my most heartfelt gratitude goes to my nontechnical reviewer (and loving wife), Teresa Petrykowski, for her unfailing support throughout.

PART 1

Web Gadget Fundamentals

CHAPTER 1

■ ■ ■

Introducing Web Gadgets

Let's get any preconceptions out in the open right at the start. Web gadgets have been around for several years, so by now most web professionals have seen them and have perhaps dismissed them as toys or distractions.

Although these may be accurate assessments for some of the early web gadgets, writing off the entire segment on that basis is a grave mistake. Done correctly, gadgets are a powerful tool for generating huge amounts of web traffic. They can effectively deliver your web content far beyond the boundaries of your own web site, channeling visitors back to it while simultaneously increasing your visibility overall. It's a winning combination, available for relatively little development effort.

In addition, there is a new and compelling reason why web gadgets deserve serious consideration: web-enabled mobile devices, such as smartphones. There's a natural synergy between these physical "gadgets" and their web-based counterparts. With their compact yet standards-based architecture, web gadgets are the perfect entry point into this growing market.

All in all, they're worth another look.

What Is a Web Gadget?

If you're reading this book, you probably think you understand what the term *web gadget* means. Before we proceed, though, it's best to be sure that we're all speaking the same language. There's no central, standardizing body for web gadgets, so everyone involved has been free to define *gadget* as it suited them, and consequently there can be some subtle differences.

■ **Note** There's no established standard for web gadgets yet, but there is one in the works. The W3C is developing a comprehensive widgets standard; see www.w3.org/TR/widgets for more information.

For the purposes of this book, a *web gadget* is a miniature web application that distributes your web assets beyond your own site. In the following sections, I'll break down that definition and explore the power that lies within. Figure 1-1 shows an example gadget, PolyClock, in the interface of Gmail.

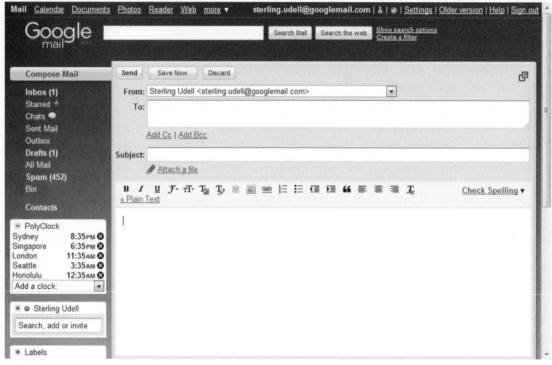

Figure 1-1. A web gadget, PolyClock, in the sidebar of Gmail

GADGETS VS. WIDGETS

Apart from defining what *web gadget* means, there's also the question of how the term relates to *web widget*. I'll make it easy for you: as far as this book is concerned, there's no difference. In truth, the only real distinction is what platform is running the miniature application in question. Some providers call their client apps *gadgets*, while others call them *widgets*.

I prefer *gadget*, because I believe its offline definition of a small, handy device is an appropriate metaphor for web gadgets. *Widget* is more nebulous, if not somewhat nonsensical, to those not well versed in the technology. You can also find more unrelated definitions for *widget*, such as the low-level user interface controls supplied by many smartphone platforms. In this book, I'll primarily use *gadget* (except when specifically discussing a platform that calls them *widgets*), but the terms are interchangeable.

A Miniature Web Application…

First and foremost, a gadget is *web-based*. All the gadgets covered in this book use standard web development technologies; as a foundation, that means XHTML, CSS, and JavaScript. So despite being small, gadgets are built using the same development techniques as any other web app, of any size. This is important, because it means that web developers don't need to learn anything intrinsically new to make good use of gadget technology.

With JavaScript and a web connection, the techniques of Ajax are open to us, creating exciting possibilities that will be covered in detail in the next chapter. Any existing CSS or JavaScript libraries you may be fond of are also fair game. Or, if you're an experienced Flash or Silverlight developer, those technologies are just as valid within a gadget as they are anywhere else online.

■ **Tip** At this writing, Flash, Silverlight, and other plug-ins have minimal support on mobile browsers, unfortunately. Although this landscape is changing, if you're hoping to deploy to smartphones, it's still best to avoid such technologies if possible.

Second, a gadget is *miniature*. Most obviously, this refers to its visual size, usually no more than a couple hundred pixels in height and width, and sometimes considerably smaller. This has obvious implications for visual design: graphics are usually kept to a minimum, and fonts are reduced to the minimum readable size. Layout is also affected; to fit more in, gadget content is frequently separated into discrete sheets or pages, unlike full-sized web apps.

Beyond presentation, the size constraint requires paring functionality down to its essence; there's no room for frippery or distractions from the gadget's main purpose. A good gadget has a single task for which it's completely optimized. It does one job and does it well. Designing a gadget requires some considerable focus, because the gadget itself needs to be completely focused on its core mission. I'll be covering key gadget design considerations in detail in Chapter 2; for now, just remember that gadgets are small, first and foremost.

Finally, a gadget is a web *application*, as distinct from a simple web page. A conventional, full-size web page is usually composed of a body of content and links to other pages. Not so a gadget. Although it may deliver static content, that's usually not its only role. And gadgets are built to be self-contained; although that doesn't mean they can't link to external pages, that's again not their usual role.

Most important, though, gadgets are never completely static. It's central to their nature that they are active, dynamic entities, responding to either user input or external stimuli. It's the difference between a book and a mobile phone: the book presents static content, while the phone provides functionality—and notice that there's only one that we would consider a *gadget*, in the traditional sense of the word.

…That Distributes Your Web Assets…

So, what might your gadget do? Most often, gadgets are part of a larger online strategy, repackaging some aspect of an existing web property in a convenient single-serving size. This is what I mean by the term *asset*, and it's the next part of our definition: what makes your web site valuable and appealing to visitors? How can that be effectively packaged as a gadget?

Again, this isn't just about content; an RSS news feed distributes content, but it's not a great gadget in itself. For an example, consider `http://weatherbug.com`, a popular weather site. WeatherBug makes its forecast content available via RSS feeds, and Figure 1-2 shows a naive gadget packaging of such a feed.

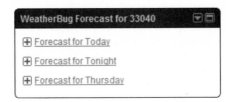

Figure 1-2. *WeatherBug RSS feed*

However, this is far from an optimal approach for a WeatherBug gadget, and WeatherBug is well aware of this fact. These are some of the important distinctions that separate the raw content from a full-fledged gadget:

- *Presentation*: The temperature, wind, and daily forecasts can all be represented graphically, and the entire gadget can be wrapped in attractive colors and backgrounds.

- *Functionality*: Alternate views on the weather, such as radar and photos, could be integrated.

- *Branding*: Cohesion with the overall marketing strategy is helped by including a clear WeatherBug logo and strapline.

Figure 1-3 shows the result, one of WeatherBug's live gadgets.

Figure 1-3. *WeatherBug web gadget*

...Beyond Your Own Site

The final aspect to the definition is that, although gadgets are web-based, they live outside your own web site. That's their real reason for being: to deliver your web assets to people who aren't specifically visiting your site. This is done by means of application programming interfaces (APIs) supplied by the vendors on whose properties the gadgets are being deployed. It's these APIs that will occupy the bulk of our attention in this book.

What sort of places are these that your gadgets will be deployed to? Broadly speaking, they fall into three categories: other web sites, desktop operating systems, and handheld devices.

Other Web Sites

The Web is where gadgets started, and it's still their native habitat. Using a browser-based API, your miniature web application can be placed on someone else's page, giving visitors *to that page* direct access to your web assets. This provides benefits for all parties involved. For the gadget owner, it broadens the distribution of their brand and substance, increasing their exposure. For the owner of the containing page, gadgets provide a ready-made way to enrich their own page; they're modules of relevant content or functionality that they can add to their page with minimal effort. And the page visitor gets a richer browsing experience.

For example, a site promoting tourism to the Florida Keys could easily add the weather gadget from Figure 1-2 to its page, giving its site visitors a live view of the local conditions. ("Look how warm and sunny it is in Key West! Let's go!") But in the process, WeatherBug gets greater exposure for its own brand, and some percentage of page visitors will click through to http://weatherbug.com.

Using gadgets as building blocks has been taken to its logical conclusion by the web API vendors themselves; they host sites that serve entirely (or primarily) as gadget containers. These allow users to create a page from scratch, selecting from the thousands of gadgets on offer to generate a home page of their own design. Note that, in this case, it's the user selecting the gadgets to see, not the webmaster, which empowers the user and builds their loyalty to the portal. Most of the major online players allow users to place gadgets in one form or another on their personalized pages; in addition, a few specialized services have sprung up solely as gadget platforms.

Part 2 of this book covers such web-site-based APIs; these platforms offer the most straightforward gadget implementations and are an appropriate place for new gadget authors to get their feet wet. Specifically, you'll learn to deploy to the following systems:

- iGoogle
- Netvibes

Desktops

Part of what makes gadgets appealing is that they're web apps that can be deployed outside a browser. This is made possible by APIs that run web gadgets directly on the Mac OS X and Windows Vista/7 desktops. Behind the scenes, these platforms are still using browser technologies to render and execute the gadget code, but that fact is not apparent to the user. They simply "install" your gadget (and receive the web assets you've enclosed) as a self-contained package on their desktop, without consciously using a browser. This enables ready access to your content and functionality, whenever their computer is on. Living directly on the user's desktop operating system, web apps packaged in this way have a reach far beyond the traditional browser (see Figure 1-4).

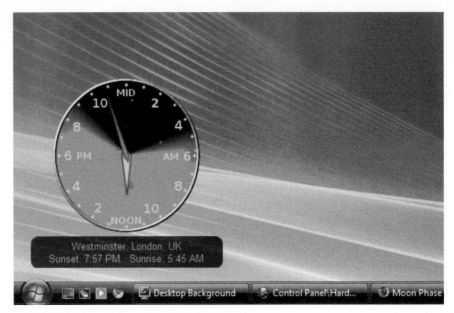

Figure 1-4. *A web gadget running on the Vista desktop*

Support for gadgets on the OS desktop comes from the two leading consumer operating systems, as well as some third parties. These gadgets are a bit more involved than pure web implementations, requiring some additional user interface elements, but the principles remain the same. In Part 3 of this book, I cover the following desktop APIs:

• Windows Vista and 7 (known as Sidebar in Vista)

• Mac OS X Dashboard

• Opera

Handheld Devices

Finally, web gadgets have the power to move off the user's PC entirely, into the palm of their hand—ready to be carried wherever they go. This is made possible by the current generation of web-enabled mobile phones and similar devices; these handheld computers have the power and connectivity to run web applications anywhere.

And gadgets are the natural medium for doing so. Designed from the ground up for minimal screen size and focused operation, web gadgets have a built-in affinity for web-enabled handsets. Develop a good web gadget, and not only can your message move beyond your own web site, but it can be conveyed into the wider world.

Deployment Techniques

There are two principal ways in which web gadgets can be deployed to mobile phones, discussed next.

In Mobile Browsers

The immediate place that all advanced handsets can display web gadgets is within their own mobile browsers. As a rule, modern smartphones support quite sophisticated and standards-compliant browsers, widely capable of running most rich web applications. You'll find that many web gadgets will "just run" on the majority of newer smartphones, with little or no modification required.

As Smartphone Applications

There are also a variety of techniques and APIs for packaging web applications as applications directly on the handset; like gadgets on a desktop OS, these allow the app to be installed directly, with no apparent browser interaction. Gadgets running in such platforms are first-class citizens of the device's operating system and can often access such lower-level hardware services as geolocation and contact lists. This is a "best of both worlds" solution, allowing access to smartphone application markets without requiring a complete code rewrite. I believe it's the future of web gadgets.

Mobile Platforms

Opportunities on the available smartphone platforms represent a mix of these two techniques. In Part 4 of this book, I cover them as a natural progression: from simple in-browser support through various widget APIs and wrapper classes to future operating systems based entirely on web technologies. These platforms are the most challenging but, looking forward, also have the potential to be the most rewarding. Here's the list:

- Windows Mobile
- Symbian S60
- iPhone
- Android
- Palm webOS

The Distributed Web

The channels described previously comprise web gadgets' participation in what is sometimes called the Distributed Web. It's a natural evolution in web development, where web content and functionality aren't confined to traditional web sites but rather are spread far and wide.

The Distributed Web got its start with the popularization of RSS feeds. As feeds came into widespread use, it was no longer necessary to visit individual web sites to receive their updates. Instead, feed aggregators allowed users to collect a variety of feeds that interested them and to see them all in one place. In the process, content suppliers saw a marked increase in their potential reach; because people could access their information with less effort, the effect was that more people did.

As Figures 1-2 and 1-3 showed, web gadgets are considerably more powerful than simple news feeds, but they share the advantage that users can access them without visiting the originating site every time. And as with RSS feeds, users of gadgets gain the power to select exactly the content they want, putting them in greater control of their daily browsing experience.

Two other, related aspects of the Distributed Web are the proliferation of APIs and the consequent rise of the web mashup. These phenomena give amateur web developers the ability to combine functionality from different sites in new and interesting ways, often creating new services that are more than the sum of their parts. Similarly, web gadgets can be seen as analogous to APIs, but for end users rather than developers. Users are able to "mix and mash" content and functionality from a variety of sources, creating precisely the home page or desktop environment they want. So again, users have greater control over their own computing experience.

In all cases, the advantage for the gadget provider is the same, and that's what I'll talk about in the next section.

Why Build Web Gadgets?

Now that we're clear exactly what web gadgets are, the next obvious question is why web professionals should be interested in building them. The following are a few answers.

Increased Exposure

As you've probably gathered by now, the primary reason for building gadgets is *exposure*. The numerous distribution channels mean that your gadget can get more page views, in more places, than you could realistically hope for with a traditional web page.

More Page Views

Even without looking beyond the traditional World Wide Web, gadgets have the potential to dramatically expand your content's visibility. This is predominantly because they can run on web sites that themselves receive huge volumes of traffic. When even a small percentage of visitors to a big-name web site install your gadget, the resulting traffic can be substantial.

An excellent example is iGoogle, the personalized start page from the search and advertising giant. Many millions of users visit iGoogle every day, so it doesn't require an exceptionally popular gadget to tap into a sizable traffic stream. Figure 1-5 shows an analytics report for a real-life example, a moderately popular gadget attracting hundreds of thousands of daily page views within three months of launch. Keep in mind that this is a single gadget on a single portal. What might your gadget accomplish?

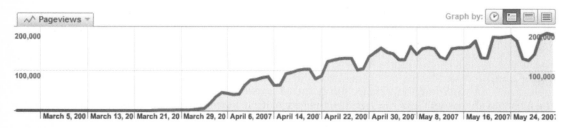

7,268,986 Pageviews

Figure 1-5. Traffic growth of an iGoogle gadget

DAYLIGHTMAP

Figure 1-5 shows the first few months of traffic from my first foray into gadget building, an iGoogle repackaging of a web application I call DaylightMap. It's a real-time display of the global day/night distribution overlaid on a Google map. Here's what the gadget looks like, essentially unchanged from that first version:

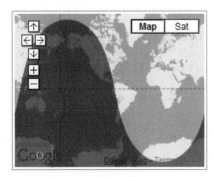

The success of this gadget raised the profile of its parent site considerably and was also largely responsible for my subsequent career shift into gadget building. You can still find the gadget (and the full-size version) at `http://daylightmap.com`.

More Places

The opportunities expand further when we move from the traditional Web to gadgets on computer desktops and handheld devices. Gadgets provide a unique opportunity to leverage your existing web assets and development skills beyond the Web itself. No other technology opens out directly from the Web in this way.

The smartphone segment in particular is one that holds enormous potential. In early 2009, it was estimated that more than 4 billion mobile phones were in use worldwide, and handsets capable of running web gadgets represent a growing percentage of that market. Traffic opportunities don't get much better than this.

Benefits of Increased Exposure

The high traffic numbers that web gadgets can generate benefit you, the developer, in a number of ways—some obvious, others less so.

Raw Traffic

The most obvious benefit is in raw traffic to the gadget itself. Since your gadget is (or should be) a distillation of your most valuable web assets, then clearly those assets are directly receiving all those page views.

For example, consider a gadget produced by a travel company that provides an interface to its booking engine. With so many distribution options, such a gadget will be seen by many times more people than would visit the travel company's web site and will be at the fingertips of far more users when the time comes to make travel plans. Gadget page views correspond directly with increased bookings.

Click-Through Traffic

A gadget's small size means that you can rarely provide all your web site's functionality within the gadget. To access what doesn't fit, visitors need to visit your main site—and a gadget on their desktop means they have a direct path to do so right in front of them. In this way, gadget traffic isn't limited to the gadget.

Returning to the example of the travel company's gadget, imagine that its booking interface won't realistically fit within the gadget. In this case, a viable alternative might be to display current fare specials or trends in the gadget instead, with a link to the main web site attached. Users are thus encouraged to click through when they see a fare of interest. Southwest Airlines has famously achieved success with its DING! gadget, implementing just such a strategy.

Viral Marketing

Finally, in certain cases, gadget traffic can build upon itself, feeding back to achieve even more growth. The term *viral marketing*, although sometimes overused, does apply in this case: the gadget medium is the message, and the very act of using the gadget promotes it.

A good example of this is a game gadget. If the game has a single-player mode, this can get users interested in playing it, and the gadget will spread on its own merits like any other. However, if a multiplayer mode is also included, users now have a motivation to get their friends to install the game as well—and the gadget spreads itself.

TOO MUCH TRAFFIC?

The phenomenal exposure that gadgets can provide has its downside. Millions of extra page views can put quite a strain on web servers, especially when your gadget is graphics-intensive or makes heavy use of server-side application code. This may not be a problem if your gadgets are hosted on enterprise-level server hardware, but for small organizations or freelance developers, it can be a real issue.

Throughout the book, I'll be revisiting this issue as appropriate, with various architectural and platform-specific mitigation techniques. For now, just be aware that the problem exists and that gadget development requires a hosting infrastructure above basic entry-level.

Small Code Footprint

A second motivator for developing gadgets comes from their small size. Although the traffic they can generate is immense, the coding effort required generally is not, yielding an excellent return on your development investment.

Quick to Build

As a rule, a gadget's small scale means that its development time can be measured in days (or weeks, at most), rather than the months or years that a full-blown web application may require. It's a rare gadget that needs more than a few hundred lines of code. This is especially true if your gadget is repackaging an existing application; it may well be able to reuse web services and code libraries from your main site. But even for new development, a gadget's single-minded focus to "do one thing and do it well" means that there tends to be less code proliferation, simply because there are fewer features to creep.

An additional benefit to this small development footprint means that gadgets don't usually require large teams of programmers. This makes them attainable for individual developers or entrepreneurs. But this fact also increases their appeal for larger organizations; not only is it easier to find the development resources, but it's well established in software engineering that small teams are more efficient, with single-person units being the best of all. Gadgets are perfectly suited to such optimizations.

Easy to Maintain

Once a gadget is deployed, the benefits of its small code base continue to be felt in terms of maintainability. It's not just that a small software unit like a gadget is less likely to contain many bugs, but (since complexity is directly related to size) they're usually much easier to find and fix.

Cross-platform Compatibility

Finally, web gadgets are probably unique in the number of different platforms—web, desktop, and handheld—that they can support from a single code base. We can thank the standardization of XHTML, CSS, and JavaScript for this, yet not even the web sites where these technologies were born can get out into the world the way gadgets can. Partner web sites, portals, desktops, and handhelds can all be targeted from one core set of source code. And, this single code base means that bug fixes and enhancements should need to be made only once, for all platforms where the gadget runs.

This benefit is especially marked on smartphones. Since no single mobile operating system has established itself as the clear leader everywhere, developing a native application for any one platform will open only a small segment of the mobile market. But the web technologies that newer handsets support are well standardized, on the other hand, so the same code base can be deployed to all web-capable devices—even ones that do not yet exist.

OUTLIERS

Inevitably, some gadget platforms aren't amenable to the web-based, cross-platform techniques that this book covers. The following platforms use proprietary markup languages and nonstandard JavaScript, and consequently, you won't learn how to develop for them here:

- Google Desktop
- Yahoo Widgets

Also, this book isn't meant to be an exhaustive catalog of every gadget or widget platform in existence. But it does include most of the major players that use standard web technologies. If you find yourself wanting to deploy a gadget to an API that isn't specifically covered here, you should still find the general design techniques and methodologies of this book helpful nonetheless.

Cross-platform Development Strategies

However, fully realizing the cross-platform advantage isn't entirely intuitive. Different APIs are supplied by the vendors that support gadgets in all these places, and on the face of it, each API requires its own development effort. Overcoming this obstacle is a central theme of this book; I present two approaches, appropriate to different circumstances.

Option 1: Self-contained

The most obvious technique for cross-platform compatibility is to keep your gadget completely self-contained, with no use of any APIs. In other words, since all platforms support the basic web technologies of XHTML, CSS, and JavaScript, a gadget that adheres strictly to these standards—and uses nothing else—will work anywhere. It's essentially the least-common-denominator approach.

I call this approach "self-contained" because it works best for gadgets that utilize few external resources. In particular, gadgets will be well suited to this technique if their functionality is embedded internally (such as in Flash or JavaScript) rather than requiring server interaction.

When this technique is possible, it's certainly the simplest approach, and for this reason, I'll use it to introduce you to gadget design and construction in Chapter 2. However, real-world requirements often dictate a more interconnected architecture than is achievable this way.

Option 2: A Middleware Layer

Because the various gadget APIs are filling a similar role, they share many functional similarities. Fundamentally, these are oriented around extending the capabilities found in generic JavaScript in ways that are especially useful for gadgets. Specifically, many of the APIs contain functions in the following areas:

- *Preference loading and saving*: It's a common requirement for gadgets to save settings from one session to the next, and cloud-oriented platforms (like iGoogle) like to make such settings persistent across sessions on different workstations.

- *Content retrieval*: This encompasses the fetching of plain-text data, XML for Ajax applications, and occasionally images.

- *Size-related functions*: The small screen footprint of gadgets makes size issues paramount.

Because these functions are broadly similar between one API and the next, it's possible to create a concise JavaScript library that abstracts them into a single pseudo-API, insulating the gadget code from dependencies on any particular platform. I'll introduce this process in Chapter 3 and continue to extend it throughout the remainder of the book, supplying you with code you can directly use when implementing your own gadgets.

Summary

Gadgets present an unequalled opportunity for web developers to leverage their existing skills well beyond traditional web sites. By deploying these mini-applications to high-traffic portals, desktop operating systems, and mobile phones, you can reach new markets and see your traffic increase.

The standards on which all web gadgets are built means that a single development effort can cover all of these bases, and their compact size means that this effort needn't be a large one. But these same factors—combined with the plethora of APIs—does mean that the effort must be focused and disciplined. In this book, I'll be supplying you with the specific guidance and code samples you'll need to make your own gadgets a success.

In the next chapter, we'll get the process underway with a nuts-and-bolts walk-through of the design, construction, and deployment of a native web gadget. Alongside the rules and guidelines of gadget development, the process will be illustrated from start to finish with the source code of a real-world example. This "case study" gadget will then be built upon for the rest of the book, readying it for release on every gadget platform I'll cover.

■ ■ ■

CHAPTER 2

Designing the Core Gadget

In this chapter, I'll introduce the fundamentals of gadget design and construction—principles that apply when creating a gadget for virtually any platform. Before you're done, you'll have a good grasp of best practices for desktop and mobile gadget development. This coverage is divided into four key areas:

- *Preliminary design decisions*: What makes a good gadget and what pitfalls to avoid

- *User interface development*: How to fit what you already know about web apps into the confines of a gadget

- *Coding considerations (and their rationales)*: Ajax, JavaScript frameworks, plug-ins, and more

- *Branding and descriptive aspects*: Title, description, icon, and screenshots

This foundation will serve you well for deploying a gadget to any of the APIs covered in this book—or ideally, one gadget to all of them.

Along the way, you'll see these concepts in action during the development of a real-world example, a gadget I'll use through the rest of the book as an extended case study. In this chapter, the first version of the gadget will be built as a self-contained miniature web application (not utilizing any APIs), ready to run in a browser on its own.

Creating the Concept

Developing a gadget begins long before the first line of code is written. It starts with the concept of what the gadget will accomplish: its goals and the functionality that will achieve them. It's generally worth spending a bit of time in this stage; because of their small size, the best gadgets are quite focused in their execution, and such focus usually doesn't happen by accident.

The following sections discuss the key attributes of a gadget. These are the criteria against which your gadget concept should be evaluated and refined.

Suitable for a Small Presentation

Small size is a primary defining characteristic of a gadget, and as such, it's paramount that your gadget concept will work within a small screen area. Be realistic, and consider how your concept would appear and function with only a couple hundred pixels of both height and width.

In fact, there is some argument in gadget design for "the smaller, the better." Some gadget platforms have width limits as small as 130 pixels. For maximum portability, your gadget should be able to function at this size. Even on platforms that don't enforce quite such stringent size constraints, it's beneficial for gadgets to be as compact as possible. In many environments, users tend to have multiple gadgets open simultaneously, so competition for space exists between gadgets. If yours is perceived as wasting space, or taking up more than is justified, its popularity will be reduced.

A useful exercise toward this end is mocking up your gadget concept with pencil and paper—but using a Post-it note or index card for the paper. Make sure that your mockup is reasonably complete, including all text and controls that the gadget will need. Multiple notes or cards are fine if your gadget will have multiple views, but any single view should fit comfortably on one. If you find that you can't achieve this, then it's probably worth revisiting your idea before you proceed.

Later in the chapter, I'll have specific recommendations for working in close quarters; at this stage, simply ensure that your concept can be made to fit.

A Single, Well-Defined Function

Primarily because of their small size, gadgets work best if they focus on a single, well-defined task. This begins now, at the conceptualization stage. For your gadget to have a clear, focused execution, its concept should be similarly clear and focused. The best gadgets are specialists.

One technique to help focus your gadget design is to list the functionality points that you envision your gadget will cover and then consider which of those functions can reasonably be integrated into a single coherent presentation. Where will each fit into the mockup that you created in the previous section? Functionality that doesn't fit at this stage should quite likely be removed from the design.

Note that this doesn't mean that the functionality shouldn't be implemented at all, just that it doesn't all belong in the same gadget. To cover the desired functionality, two (or more) gadgets may be better than one. As an example, consider Figure 2-1, a gadget containing both a clock and a weather forecast. These functions are not closely related and would probably make more sense as two separate gadgets.

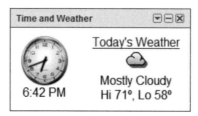

Figure 2-1. A gadget with an identity crisis

If you can creatively combine disparate types of information into a coherent whole, that's great—such innovation will help your gadget stand out from the crowd. But if this isn't possible without sacrificing the coherence, don't be afraid to partition your concept into multiple gadgets.

Dynamic Content

As mentioned in the previous chapter, true gadgets are more than simple miniature web pages displaying static content. To maintain the interest of users, there must be a dynamic element: content that changes over time or in response to user action.

As a rule of thumb, information displayed by the gadget (such as a news feed or status update) should change at least once a day, ideally more frequently. If your concept centers around conveying information that is essentially static, it may not be well suited to gadget form. Users are unlikely to devote screen space to a gadget that never changes; they're more likely to seek out your web site directly when they need the information.

Note that this isn't an issue if your gadget concept is inherently application-oriented, based on user interaction rather than simple content delivery. Examples of this sort of gadget might include a game, a to-do list, or an appointment calendar. In these cases, the user is essentially responsible for updating the information.

Immediate Usability

For a successful gadget, strive to make it usable immediately after being installed by the user. It's an unfortunate reality that many users are impatient; if the first thing they're confronted with is a complicated settings screen or Create an Account dialog box, many will simply close the gadget. Although such issues can be minimized during the development phase, it's better to start with a concept that doesn't require them in the first place.

Specifically, look at your gadget idea in light of the following recommendations, and consider whether the concept should be adjusted accordingly:

- Avoid requiring the user to log in or create an account.

- Avoid asking for personal information.

- Avoid options that must be set before the gadget is used.

- Avoid splash screens.

Note that the items in this section are simply recommendations, not unbreakable rules. Some excellent gadgets do require configuration or a user account before they can be used. If you find one or more of these areas to be completely unavoidable, that's fine—but think about whether your gadget could run in a demo or sample mode first, capturing the user's interest before requiring them to enter data.

Mobile Considerations

If you're planning to deploy your web gadget to mobile devices, you need to consider this environment when planning your concept. The major issue to keep in mind for a mobile user is that her attention is more likely to be divided; your app will be on her phone as she's riding the train or waiting for an appointment, with external distractions all around. She's also quite likely to be interrupted (and have to stop using your app): when her train arrives, her number is called, or the phone itself rings. A good mobile gadget should handle such situations gracefully.

First, make sure that at any point a user of your gadget can stop what he's doing and return to it later, picking up where he left off. As much as possible, design your process flow around small tasks that can be completed in a short span of time. State should be saved automatically when practical, even if a task is only partially complete. Ideally, your gadget should even be able to cold-boot into the middle of a half-completed task, enabling the user to pick up where he left off even if the phone has been restarted.

On a related note, try to avoid processes that require the user to act within a specific period of time. Alerts and notifications should remain until actively dismissed by the user, unless the situation they refer to has ceased to be relevant. Games and other highly interactive apps should automatically pause when they lose focus.

It's also true that user input is much less convenient on small devices than full-sized PCs; consider the impact that this will have on your process flow. I'll have specific advice for mitigating this problem later in the chapter, but it's best to start the process now, during conceptualization. Try to reduce (or make optional) areas of functionality that require a lot of text input or complicated screen interactions. Can they be simplified? Are there viable alternatives to typing?

Accommodating these aspects at the conceptual-design phase will avoid headaches (and dissatisfied users) later.

Case Study: Hello, Moon!

The best way to see the entire process of gadget development is to examine the development of a real gadget from start to finish. In "Case Study" sections like this one throughout the chapter, I'll walk you through the design, construction, and presentation of an example gadget; it's a simple one but one that has actually been deployed to thousands of users.

It's not ready for deployment yet, though. As a concept, I've decided to create a gadget that shows the current phase of the moon and perhaps tells how long since (or until) the last new moon (or next full moon). In Figure 2-2, I've mocked the idea up on an index card.

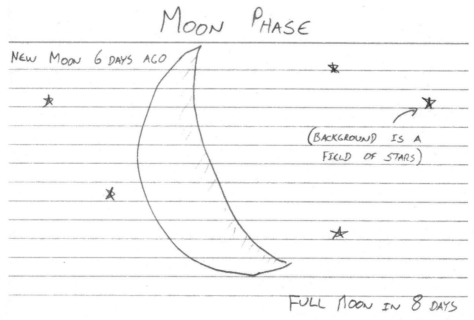

Figure 2-2. A rough mockup for the Moon Phase gadget

As a gadget, Moon Phase will primarily deliver information—there's very little interaction with the user—but the imagery and times conveyed are current and relevant. The functionality itself will be predominantly on the server side, with the moon image being created from the open source Xplanet package (http://xplanet.sourceforge.net), running as a scheduled job on the web host. The ancillary time information can be generated on demand by a PHP script and delivered as XML via HTTP—Ajax, in other words.

■ **Note** You can find further discussion of Moon Phase's Xplanet server, including source code, in Appendix C.

Designing the User Interface

With a solid gadget concept, it's time to move into the concrete visual design of the gadget. In many ways, the basic design will be determined by the concept, driven directly by the information or functionality to be presented. And in general, most basic web design rules apply as much to gadgets as to any web application.

However, you need to pay attention to a few specific areas while finalizing your gadget's appearance. The following sections outline the issues, many of which will be demonstrated in the Moon Phase case study.

Look and Feel

It's widely recommended that, when possible, a gadget should use a visual theme that corresponds to its function. For some gadgets, this trivially follows from their concept: the imagery in the case study will simply look like the moon. But in other cases, this means looking for a real-world metaphor for the gadget's functionality; for example, since timekeeping is done with clocks in the real world, a time-oriented gadget can be presented as a clock.

Many times, the correspondence may not be quite so obvious, but it's generally worth looking for. Gadgets that follow this approach will come across as more coherent and will likely gain easier acceptance by users, who will find the gadget easier to understand and more natural to use. It's a simple case of form following function.

Employing design patterns that fit the user's expectations also extends to the level of individual user interface elements within the gadget. In particular, it's a good idea to use standardized icon images wherever possible. You can see some examples in Figure 2-3. Icons like these can be styled to match your particular gadget, of course, as long as the central imagery remains recognizable.

Figure 2-3. *Some standard icons for help, configuration, refresh, power/reset, and close*

Chrome

Talk of user interface elements brings us to a discussion of *chrome*: the window borders and peripheral controls that frame a gadget on-screen. This is of special concern when developing gadgets for multiple platforms, because various systems provide varying amounts of chrome, leaving you to fill in the gaps.

Some platforms, such as iGoogle and Netvibes, provide you with a blank frame in which to build your gadget; they provide all operational controls themselves. At the other end of the spectrum, others (such as Opera and, to a slightly lesser extent, Mac OS X) simply render your gadget entirely on its own; it's up to you to provide any chrome you require. And of course, there are platforms in between the extremes (such as Windows Vista/7) that provide a partial set. Figures 2-4 and 2-5 illustrate two examples: the same StickyNote gadget on two platforms, with and without platform-supplied chrome.

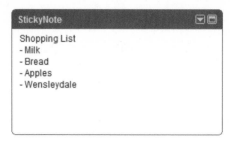

Figure 2-4. iGoogle supplies a frame, title bar, and controls to this StickyNote gadget.

Figure 2-5. On Opera, the same gadget must render its own border and control icons.

How to handle this situation? At this stage, for the self-contained gadget, I'll show how to build the core HTML/CSS as a web page without any chrome. Since this phase of the gadget will run on its own within a browser session, you can rely on the browser itself to supply the necessary chrome. Starting in the next chapter, you'll then begin to add your own chrome as needed for individual platforms, building on this foundation. Figure 2-6 shows this core version of StickyNote—running, appropriately enough, in Google Chrome.

Figure 2-6. StickyNote running stand-alone in Chrome

On mobile phones, the situation is similar. Mobile API vendors recommend that your app adopts a "full-screen" mode, filling the entire device screen with its content. This is the same appearance as would be given by a native smartphone application, leading to a more integrated presentation. In this case, the physical device provides the chrome.

Size

As discussed early in the chapter, small size is one of the most fundamental aspects of gadget design, and it's essential that your gadget is at home in a small container. Beyond that general guideline, however, it's best to have some real flexibility in terms of size, because the size requirements are different for every platform:

- Some platforms dictate a hard width limit, such as 160 pixels for Gmail and 130 for the Vista sidebar, but a variable height.

- Some have a fixed (but not preset) width. iGoogle displays gadgets in columns whose width is dependent on browser window size. They also have a variable height.

- Some platforms, such as Opera, are variable in both width and height.

- Mobile phone screens can be thought of as containers that are fixed in both width and height.

Designing a gadget to run at any possible size is not easy. It requires rearranging your content dynamically, intelligently, for any width from 130 pixels on up. On platforms where you must supply your own chrome, even more work is required, because the frame drawn around your gadget must be similarly adaptable. However, this approach can yield the most professional-looking gadgets.

At the other extreme, you can design your gadget specifically to work in the smallest platform that you intend to deploy to (specific sizes for each platform can be found in Parts 2 through 4 of this book and are collected in Appendix A). Then on other systems, your gadget will simply show some amount of empty space, ideally filled with a background color or image. This is the easiest approach, but the appearance can then be unsatisfactory on larger platforms.

As a compromise, a good solution is often to support a few discrete but fixed sizes and select between them in code. Your gadget might have a "small" mode at 130 pixels wide and a "large" mode at 250. Such a scheme will give a reasonable appearance on the vast majority of platforms, without requiring the complexity of fully dynamic sizing.

■ **Tip** For scaling content in JavaScript, you can find code for determining the screen size in Listing 2-5, later in the chapter.

As for height, more platforms are flexible in this regard, so it's less of a concern. If you're working with a concept that fits comfortably into gadget proportions, it's usually acceptable to simply assume that height won't be a problem.

In any case, it's incumbent on you as a developer to completely fill the gadget container in question. Even if your content is fixed-width, make sure that any background color or image covers the entire gadget. It may be necessary to use a style of `width: 100%` or `height: 100%` on the body (or other container element) to ensure that this occurs.

Finally, here are a few layout-specific tips to help you implement your gadget design:

- In the tight confines of a gadget, absolute positioning is often the most direct way to achieve the desired layout.

- For best use of space, user interface elements (such as tables and text inputs) should scale with your gadget, rather than remaining a fixed width.

- When you do have horizontal whitespace in a gadget, centering your content block frequently looks best.

- By convention, gadgets don't usually have scroll bars; if necessary, try to place them on a specific screen element rather than the entire content body.

GIANT GADGETS

Gadgets are typically thought of as quite small, only a couple hundred pixels on a side. However, there are instances where gadgets can be displayed much larger, and it's worth taking these into account when developing your visual design.

First, when a stand-alone gadget is opened directly in a web browser, it will be shown at the screen resolution of the client device. For conventional computers, this can be thousands of pixels on a side.

Second, the iGoogle gadget platform supports what's called *canvas view*, where a single gadget is maximized to fill the majority of the browser page (minus some chrome for iGoogle itself). This view is also finding its way into other platforms that share the iGoogle API, such as Orkut and Gmail. I'll discuss canvas view more thoroughly in Chapter 5, but for now, just be aware that it's much larger than conventional gadget presentations.

When offered so much screen real estate, many gadgets are a bit lost; they've been specifically designed for a smaller world. Here are a few options for ways your gadget might handle the big screen:

- If your content can simply scale, that's the most straightforward approach. Blocks of text, grids of data, and images can often be handled this way.

- Auxiliary content, perhaps ordinarily shown in separate tabs, can be moved to the main view. An example of this might be a weather gadget that ordinarily uses tabs for current conditions, forecast, and maps; in canvas view, all of these can be shown simultaneously.

- If your gadget is tightly tied to your main web site, consider whether a full-scale version of your main site can be shown here. This can sometimes be accomplished with an `iframe` in the gadget.

Use of Space

Within the small confines of a gadget, space is at a premium. There's usually none to waste, so particular care should be taken when laying out the gadget to use space effectively and efficiently. This often means keeping image and font sizes to a minimum. Placing small content blocks side-by-side when possible can avoid using more vertical real estate than is necessary. Generally, you may well find that fitting the content into a gadget requires all your design skills.

On the other hand, don't feel obliged to fill every pixel. A skillful use of whitespace can delineate areas of content. As with any design, excessive crowding can make the gadget seem cluttered, as well as lead to usability problems. If you find you have more content than will comfortably fit in the gadget, it's often best to split it into multiple views—perhaps accessed via tabs.

Icons and Tooltips

One way to use space effectively is to replace text buttons with icons where possible. Although this does run some risk of losing clarity, user confusion should be kept to a minimum if you stay with standard imagery (as in Figure 2-3, discussed earlier). It's also quite helpful to add tooltips for control labels. For example, a Help button might be implemented with the following code:

```
<img width="16" height="16" img="question.png" alt="Help" onclick="help()" />
```

With a technique like this, the user will see a question-mark icon (leftmost in Figure 2-3) in the gadget, and the text "Help" will appear when the mouse pointer is over the image.

Hover

A related technique is using mouse hover events to display controls or auxiliary content. This can be an effective way to reuse screen area; most of the time, the gadget shows its core content or functionality but reveals additional elements when the user's mouse pointer is over the relevant areas. In addition to making good use of space, this approach also allows you to emphasize the gadget's key elements in either state.

One easy way to show additional content on hover is via the title attribute of a link element. On most browsers, this title will display automatically on hover, as shown in Figure 2-7. The code to accomplish this is quite simple:

```
<a href="http://link.to/content" title="Hover text goes here">Link Text</a>
```

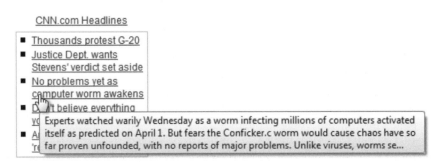

Figure 2-7. This RSS feed reader gadget shows the summary for each story using each link's title attribute.

You can achieve a more general hover-related technique with CSS. Using the opacity property, any control can be hidden until the mouse pointer is over it or its container. For example, imagine you want to apply hover effects to some command controls defined with the following HTML:

```
<div id="controls">
  <img img="wrench.png" alt="Settings" onclick="config()" />
  <img img="up_arrow.png" alt="Show More" onclick="showMore()" />
  <img img="down_arrow.png" alt="Show Less" onclick="showLess()" />
</div>
```

The basic approach is that the controls are hidden most of the time. So, you can set an opacity of 0 as a default for the controls container using CSS like this:

```
#controls {
  opacity: 0.0;
}
```

Of course, this rule will be in addition to any other CSS in place to size and position the controls container.

Then to achieve the hover effect, a simple modifier of hover is added to the #controls selector, setting the opacity to 1 as follows:

```
#controls:hover {
  opacity: 1.0;
}
```

You can see this effect in action in Figure 2-8. It's the same feed reader from Figure 2-7, but with a control panel visible under the mouse pointer. This makes the controls available to the user when required but gives the gadget a cleaner appearance the rest of the time.

Figure 2-8. Feed reader controls appearing on hover

However, there are some issues to be aware of with hover-based techniques, especially if you're planning to deploy to mobile phones. First, some handheld devices don't support the hover modifier in CSS, so the hovered state won't be visible. Similarly, touchscreen devices don't have a usable equivalent for hover (their screens can't tell when the user's finger is hovering over it). One solution for this problem is to include device-specific CSS in these instances overriding the opacity: 0.0 property. You'll see specific examples of this in the appropriate chapters later in the book.

■ **Note** Some older browsers, notably Internet Explorer 6 and earlier, also don't support hover for certain elements. Happily, IE6 also doesn't support the opacity property, so this case will usually degrade gracefully with no additional effort.

Generally, the fact that hover is not universally supported does mean that you should treat it as a supplementary technique. Since it won't be available on certain platforms, use it only to display auxiliary information or to emphasize what is already visible. Don't hide crucial controls and expect that the user will necessarily be able to see them on hover.

■ **Tip** JavaScript code for detecting the current gadget platform will be introduced in Chapter 3 and expanded on in the platform-specific chapters throughout the rest of the book.

Branding

Before you complete your design, you should consider whether and how to include branding on your gadget. Will it include your company name or logo, with a link back to your main web site? Should you reuse the colors and fonts from your other web properties to imbue some continuity?

By and large, the answer to these questions is *yes*. Since a major goal of gadget development is to increase your exposure on the Web, it would be counterproductive not to include some connection from the gadget back to your main site. A logo or site name is usually a good idea, perhaps within a "Powered By" mark. However, some restraint is called for here; unless the sole purpose of the gadget is to funnel traffic back to your site (as with a site search gadget, for example), your brand shouldn't be the dominant visual element in the gadget.

■ **Note** A few platforms (notably Mac OS X) discourage branding on the face of the gadget. It's possible to simply hide it with platform-specific CSS; this is covered in more detail in the next chapter.

Typically, it also makes sense for this brand mark to be a clickable link to your own web site. One warning, however: on web platforms, gadgets frequently run in an iframe, so a simple link will open your main site within the same iframe! To avoid this problem, open your site in a new browser tab or window by including a target="_blank" attribute in the link:

```
<a href="http://mysite.com" title="Visit My Site" target="_blank">
  Powered By MySite</a>
```

Alternately, _top instead of _blank will open the link in the topmost frame of the current window (breaking out of all frames), rather than in a new window or tab. If you're using a form, try adding target="_blank" to the form tag itself. Like so:

```
<form action="something" target="_blank">
```

Mobile Considerations

As occurred during the concept phase, a few specific design issues arise when the gadget is to be deployed on mobile platforms. These primarily have to do with the realities of user input and output on small devices; thoughtful design of the user interface can make your mobile app much easier to use on the go.

First, recall that text entry is generally less viable on handhelds than on full-size PCs. Many mobile phones have no dedicated keyboard and make do with a numeric keypad or touchscreen equivalent. Even when a full hardware QWERTY keyboard is present, it's usually miniscule and far less usable than on the desktop. To accommodate this limitation, keep text-entry elements to a minimum; try to replace them with selection lists wherever possible. Or if your app requires only limited character entry, consider supplying your own UI rather than relying on unknown hardware. An example of this might be a calculator gadget that creates its own numeric "keypad" on-screen.

Second, be aware that the precision of touchscreens is less than that of a mouse. Accommodate this reality by creating larger click areas for all controls. It's also a good idea to separate adjacent controls with as much whitespace as possible; this will help avoid the user inadvertently clicking the wrong one.

Case Study: Moon Phase's User Interface

The Moon Phase gadget I'm developing will be a simple one, so its design is correspondingly clean and simple, as shown in Figure 2-9. The moon image is centered on a black background with a field of stars, simulating the night sky. The textual information is arrayed at the corners, with the time since the last full or new phase in the upper left, the time to the next in the lower right, and branding (as a discrete link to the sponsoring web site) in the lower left.

Figure 2-9. *The Moon Phase gadget design realized*

To accomplish this design, I've implemented my mockup as the fairly basic HTML shown in Listing 2-1. It has some placeholder text (in the #last and #next elements) for the Ajax-sourced DHTML that I'll be writing later, and I've already plugged in the open source moon image from my Xplanet server.

Listing 2-1. *The Initial HTML for the Moon Phase Gadget*

```
<?xml version="1.0" encoding="UTF-8"?>
<!DOCTYPE html PUBLIC "-//W3C//DTD XHTML 1.0 Transitional//EN"
```

```
                        "http://www.w3.org/TR/xhtml1/DTD/xhtml1-transitional.dtd">
<html xmlns="http://www.w3.org/1999/xhtml">
  <head>
    <meta http-equiv="Content-Type" content="text/html;charset=UTF-8" />
    <title>Moon Phase</title>
    <link href="phase.css" type="text/css" rel="stylesheet" />
  </head>
  <body class="moonPhase">
    <div id="main">
      <p id="last" class="text">New moon 6 days ago</p>
      <p id="image_container">
        <img id="moon" alt="Current Moon Image" width="176" height="176"
             src="http://daylightmap.com/moon/images/luna_north_small.jpg" />
      </p>
      <p id="next" class="text">Full moon in 8 days</p>
      <p id="credit" class="text">
        by <a target="_top" href="http://www.daylightmap.com">DaylightMap</a>
      </p>
    </div>
  </body>
</html>
```

■ **Tip** The gadget HTML is one source file that often cannot be reused between platforms; many APIs require "wrapping" your markup in their own proprietary format. For this reason, it's best to keep your HTML as simple as possible; if practical for your gadget, consider creating markup from JavaScript with DHTML.

There's not much to it: the body contains the few HTML elements required to display the content described in the previous section. The presentation of these is controlled by the CSS of Listing 2-2.

Listing 2-2. The CSS for the Basic Moon Phase Gadget, phase.css

```
.moonPhase {
  margin: 0;
  padding: 0;
  overflow: hidden;
  font-family: sans-serif;
  color: #cccccc;
  background: black url(http://daylightmap.com/moon/images/stars_large.jpg) center;
}

/* Styling for the full content area and moon image */
.moonPhase #main {
  position: relative;
  left: 0;
  top: 0;
  width: 100%;
  font-size: 11px;
}
```

```css
.moonPhase #image_container {
  margin: 0 10px;
  padding: 10px;
  text-align: center;
}

/* Presentation of the auxiliary text blocks */
.moonPhase a,
.moonPhase a:visited {
  color: #cccccc;
  text-decoration: none;
}
.moonPhase a:hover {
  color: #ffffff;
  text-decoration: underline;
  cursor: pointer;
}
.moonPhase .text {
  width: 30%;
  position: absolute;
  line-height: 1.1em;
  margin: 5px;
}
.moonPhase #last {
  text-align: left;
  left: 0;
  top: 0;
}
.moonPhase #next {
  text-align: right;
  right: 0;
  bottom: 0;
}
.moonPhase #credit {
  text-align: left;
  left: 0;
  bottom: 0;
}
```

The most unusual aspect of this style sheet is its use of a *CSS pseudo-namespace*, namely, a class to prefix every rule, which in this case is moonPhase. The class was applied to my body element back in Listing 2-1, and here in the CSS every rule is prefaced with .moonPhase. This limits all selectors in the style sheet so that they apply only to descendants of <body class="moonPhase">. In the HTML of Listing 2-1, this has no effect; instead, it's a forward-looking technique for implementations yet to come. Some gadget platforms will render your markup within the context of a larger page, and using a container class like this will prevent CSS overlap problems from arising when you get to those platforms. You'll look more closely at namespaces in a few pages, in the context of JavaScript.

■ **Note** The first rule in Listing 2-2 uses a selector of `.moonPhase` only; this replaces a `body` selector in non-namespaced CSS.

Beyond the pseudo-namespace, there are just a few presentational items mentioned earlier in the chapter that are implemented in this CSS and that I'd like to call your attention to:

- The moon image is centered within the gadget, with a `text-align: center` rule on its container.

- The text content is absolutely positioned, ensuring it will remain in place for all supported browsers.

- The branding link has a hover effect, turning brighter and displaying an underline when the mouse pointer is over it.

To accommodate different screen sizes, I've made the design decision to support three discrete size modes within the gadget, as shown in Figure 2-10. The basic moon graphic from Xplanet that I'm using is 176 pixels square; for most applications, I'll simply use this image at its native size. For smaller screens, I'll switch to a half-size version (88 pixels), while for full-screen views on desktop monitors, I also have a high-resolution image (at 625 pixels) to use instead. The accompanying text (for the last and next phases) will also be shown adaptively, depending on the window size. All of this dynamic sizing will be implemented with JavaScript in the next section.

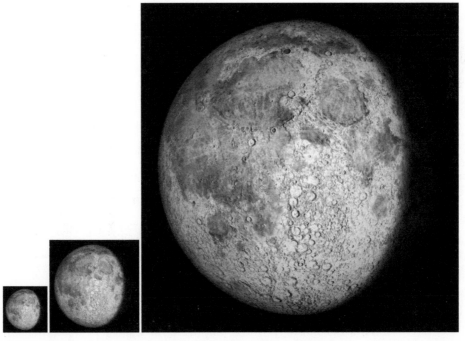

Figure 2-10. The moon phase source imagery in small, medium, and large

Architecting the Gadget

When you've finalized your visual design, you're finally ready to get your hands dirty and begin coding the functionality of the gadget proper. By and large, this is no different from writing any other web application; most of the gadget-specific issues have actually been dealt with already, during the conceptualization and design phases. This part of the chapter will acquaint you with the development topics that are of particular interest when creating gadgets.

■ **Tip** For references to external resources, you're generally better off using relative URLs; this will be compatible with more platforms. The few that require absolute URLs will be specifically called out in their respective chapters.

Structural Organization

With all web development, there is a question of (and difference of opinion on) how best to organize your code. Should everything be included in a single HTML file, with CSS and JavaScript embedded within `style` and `script` blocks? Or is it better to separate all content, presentation, and functionality by linking in external `.css` and `.js` files as necessary? Gadget development brings a couple of new twists to this old question.

The classic advantage to "monolithic" code, with everything in a single source file, is performance. Since each file downloaded by the browser requires a separate HTTP request, there's an overhead to requesting numerous files instead of one. In addition, since external `.css` and `.js` files are only known about once the browser has downloaded and parsed the base HTML file, there's an additional delay. Monolithic code has none of these slowdowns.

The performance issues with separate files can be exacerbated by multiple gadgets running on a single page, as occurs with portals like iGoogle. If there are ten gadgets on a page, each requiring ten separate files, those 100 HTTP requests introduce latency noticeable to the user. The large distribution figures for gadgets can also mean that separate files introduce a significant load increase for the web host, where, again, there's some overhead for each request. So, handling 10 million requests requires more server than 1 million, even if the amount of data transferred is similar.

The classic advantage to separate files, of course, is maintainability. CSS and JavaScript that's common to multiple pages can be kept in a single location; if a change needs to be made or a bug fixed, it can be done once and will take effect everywhere (with appropriate care being taken that changes remain compatible with existing code). So, a separate-file architecture scales to large projects much better, and if you're developing a single gadget for all the platforms mentioned in this book, you're unavoidably embarking on a project of reasonable size.

Additionally, not all gadget platforms use raw HTML; some wrap the web content in additional XML or other code. This introduces an additional strike against monolithic code for cross-platform development: it's simply impossible to use the same HTML for all gadget platforms. This means that all code embedded in the HTML must be replicated for each platform and kept in sync manually.

Therefore, I believe that it makes the most sense to split the code into separate files that *can* be reused across disparate platforms. To reduce the performance penalty, though, I try to keep the number of such files that needs to be downloaded to a minimum. It's also worth noting that most desktop (and some handheld) APIs allow you to package all the related files together on the client machine, making such downloads irrelevant.

This minimally split approach is the one that I'll be following in this book, but as with any web development, there's no single right answer. If you're only writing for a single web-based platform, it might be advisable to optimize for speed instead and include all your resources within the HTML.

Scripting and Functionality

How to write the actual code of a web application is beyond the scope of this book; I have to assume that if you're reading this, you already have that end of the business in hand. Instead, what you will find in the following sections is some specific guidance for doing so in the context of a gadget.

Ajax

You may have noticed that I keep mentioning JavaScript (also known as JScript, or officially, ECMAScript), and you may also have mentally objected that it's technically not required for web development. You'd be correct: it would be possible to write gadgets with little or no JavaScript, instead relying on server-side coding accessed through a page-based request-response model—the classic HTTP GET/POST model of the Web. However, I don't recommend it. I strongly advocate loading your gadget's page only once, on initialization; coding all functionality in JavaScript; and doing any necessary client/server interactions in the background, via XMLHttpRequest (XHR) calls.

Primarily, this is because such gadgets will appear much more responsive and interactive to the user. Although this is always the case with Ajax applications (compared to classic web sites), it's especially important in gadgets; their small size and lightweight form factor makes any sluggishness especially noticeable. Users expect such responsiveness from gadgets and will be disapproving if it's not there. A page-loading gadget will not compare well with its competition.

But also important is the fact that all the gadget platform APIs are JavaScript-based. So if you want to use any platform features, that portion of your code will need to be in JavaScript at least.

JavaScript Frameworks

If you're going to be programming in JavaScript, what about framework libraries? With the widespread deployment of Ajax-based web applications, these have proliferated in recent years; popular examples include jQuery, Dojo, Prototype, and YUI (the Yahoo! User Interface). These libraries provide some impressive functionality with easy-to-use interfaces and can greatly speed JavaScript development.

Of particular interest, most of these libraries include routines for adding autocomplete functionality to text entry fields. As mentioned earlier in the chapter, this can be a great boon to users of mobile devices with restricted typing facilities and is highly recommended.

However, in this book I'm *not* going to be using such a framework. For the purposes of a book, it's more important that the code remain general—as free from dependencies as possible. It doesn't matter very much; most of the example code herein isn't complex enough that a framework would make much difference. But in your own gadgets, please feel free to use whatever library you prefer.

■ **Note** Both jQuery and Dojo have specific recommendation for mobile web gadget development: the former has been officially adopted by Nokia as the development framework for its Web Run-Time (WRT) widget platform, and the latter forms the foundation of Mojo, the SDK for Palm's webOS. You can find more details in Chapters 10 and 13, respectively.

JavaScript Namespacing

Within the JavaScript that you will be writing (with or without a framework), I recommend that your code be structured within a *namespace*. One of the chief flaws in JavaScript is a lack of module-level scoping; all variables outside of functions are effectively global, and this can produce hard-to-find bugs when variable names collide. In fact, this is especially important when using external libraries such as frameworks—or the cross-API middleware code you'll find in this book.

To illustrate this problem, consider the following line of JavaScript code:

```
var location = 'New York, NY';
```

In isolation, it's perfectly reasonable; you're declaring a variable and storing a string in it. However, for JavaScript code running in a browser, all variables in the "global" scope are actually properties of the window object containing the script—and the window object already has a location property. If you (or your framework) want to use that predefined location object (perhaps to manage page history as part of making the Back button work), that code will be broken by simply declaring the string variable shown here. Such bugs are notoriously hard to track down and fix because the offending variable declaration is likely to be far removed from the code that actually breaks.

This difficulty also occurs with function declarations. The following code has the same problem as the variable declaration did; it overwrites a property of the window object, which is then no longer usable by any code that comes later:

```
function find(searchLocation) {
  // Find the given location
  return (location == searchLocation);
};
```

If your preferred JavaScript framework uses window.find, that functionality will be broken by this declaration. Even if it doesn't cause a problem today, there's no guarantee that it won't happen when the *next* version of the framework is released.

To minimize this problem, use a namespace. JavaScript namespaces work by declaring a single object at the beginning of the script and then declaring all module-level variables and functions as properties of that object. This way, only the namespace object itself is in the global (or window) scope, and thus there is only a single point where a name collision can occur.

There are many different approaches to implementing namespaces in JavaScript, each with their own advantages and proponents. In this book, I'll be declaring my namespace as follows:

```
var myNameSpace = window.myNameSpace || {};
```

The namespace itself is declared as an empty object literal; note that I precede it with window.myNameSpace ||. This allows me to reuse the namespace in multiple scripts, adding properties as needed by including precisely this same line of code at the top of each script. If myNameSpace is already declared, the || operator will find it as property of window, and not redeclare it—leaving existing properties and methods intact.

■ **Note** Because namespaced variables and functions are declared as object properties, it's common to use a .* notation to talk about a given namespace. So, I could refer to the example given here as myNameSpace.*.

With myNameSpace in place, I can safely declare the risky code given earlier, as shown in Listing 2-3.

Listing 2-3. myNameSpace in Action

```
var myNameSpace = window.myNameSpace || {};

myNameSpace.location = 'New York, NY';

myNameSpace.find = function (searchLocation) {
  // Find the given location
  return (myNameSpace.location == searchLocation);
};
```

You'll find more complete examples of this approach in the JavaScript listings toward the end of this chapter. And again, there are many other namespacing techniques in existence; if you prefer a different convention, that's fine. But I strongly encourage you to use one.

HOW TO NAME YOUR SPACE?

Just as there's no single accepted way to declare a namespace, there's also no single way to select the name itself. Generally, a name needs to be unique (to avoid collisions) and as short as possible (for convenience), but these two goals are somewhat at odds. The fewer characters in your name, the greater the probability that someone else will choose the same string at some point.

One path that's often taken, therefore, is to select a namespace based on company name. Google uses this approach; many of its JavaScript APIs are declared under a namespace of `google.*`. However, this can cause problems if a company doesn't have a strong coding standard in place or if the parent company is bought out or rebranded.

Another good choice is the name of the project or product for which the code is being written. Although this is less likely to be unique than the company name, it is true that project-name collisions won't occur often in the real world. Again, we can find an example at Google: it has a `gadgets.*` namespace for its iGoogle Gadgets API. Although there certainly are other `gadgets.*` namespaces in existence outside of Google, it's not likely that another will be used at the same time, in the same script. Note that this approach is less useful for common library routines (where collisions would be more likely), and it's also true that the rebranding issue can apply to products as well as entire companies.

A hybrid is even possible: declare a namespace for your company and then subspaces underneath it for projects and other logical units of code. Under its main `google.*` namespace, for example, Google uses `google.maps.*`, `google.search.*`, and others. One might wish that Google would have also used `google.gadgets.*`, but as I mentioned, coding standards within a company come into play.

As usual, there's no single right answer; consider your situation, and decide what's best for you. In this book, I'll be using two project-based namespaces (`moonPhase.*` and `crossPlatform.*`), introduced in Listings 2-4 and 2-5. Note that `moonPhase` is the same name that I used for my CSS pseudo-namespace, back in Listings 2-1 and 2-2.

Plug-Ins

Although JavaScript is the native scripting language of web browsers, it isn't the only client-side code space. A variety of other environments are in widespread use for web programming on the client; systems like Flash, Silverlight, and Flex all have their following. Although they do require browser plug-ins, there's no denying that they can provide a richer user experience that can native HTML/CSS/JavaScript, especially in graphics-intensive applications.

The use of such plug-ins is certainly possible in gadgets, but it does limit their generality. The obvious issue is that every client requires the specific plug-in. Although this is not a large hurdle on traditional web platforms, it's a somewhat bigger problem for desktop gadgets and is downright insurmountable for many mobile devices. The plug-ins just don't exist for many phones. This is becoming less true for newer, mobile-aware technologies like FlashLite, but the penetration on handhelds is still far less complete than on the desktop.

For this reason, my advice is to avoid gadgets based on plug-ins if possible; I also won't be covering them in detail in this book. If your killer app is achievable only through the use of a plug-in, I don't want to dissuade you; most of this book will still be useful to you for the parts of your gadget outside the plug-in itself. Just be aware of the trade-offs.

■ **Note** I've spent a few pages here discussing client-side scripting within gadgets. What I'm *not* going to talk about is server-side programming, because that's not strictly within the purview of gadgets. In other words, you're free to use any such tools you like!

Cross-browser Compatibility

Issues of supporting multiple browsers in gadgets are largely dictated by the breadth of platforms that you're targeting. If you're seeking the widest possible distribution by deploying to as many gadget APIs as you can, then you'll need to ensure that your gadget is as compatible as possible. This is no different from any web site or application.

However, if your gadget will be deployed only to a limited range of platforms, you may be able to ignore some cross-browser issues on that basis. For example, Mac OS X Dashboard widgets run in an embedded version of Safari, so if you're specifically building an OS X widget, you're free to use Safari-specific features. An analogous situation exists for Windows desktop gadgets, which always use Internet Explorer. And Opera widgets, of course, use their eponymous browser.

Even on web platforms, some cross-browser compatibility issues can be safely ignored. Most of the gadget containers (such as iGoogle or Netvibes) require JavaScript in order for the container to function. Therefore, in these APIs you can safely assume that the user has JavaScript enabled, and not worry about degrading your functionality gracefully.

Conversely, some mobile platforms do not include good JavaScript and full CSS support, so deploying to the widest range of handhelds *will* mean you can't rely too much on advanced browser features. These platform-specific browser issues are covered thoroughly in their respective chapters.

Security

By and large, the security issues present in gadgets are no different from in any other web application. One difference, however, is that the stakes are sometimes higher: gadgets that run on the desktop often have the same privilege level as native applications on the local machine. Therefore, a security hole in your gadget could theoretically expose all of a user's local data to an attacker; this is a heavier burden than most web applications, where exploits rarely expose more than the data stored online.

Web application security is a large and evolving topic, and one that I can't safely cover in its entirety, so I strongly encourage you to learn and follow best practices in this area before releasing your gadgets. In the remainder of this section, I'll mention a few important topics, but it's by no means an exhaustive coverage. [1]

First, I recommend that you consider using HTTPS for all network operations. This is by no means a complete security solution in itself, but it's a good foundation on which to start. Like any security plan, however, it's only as strong as its weakest link; using SSL won't help if it's not in place for all traffic or if unsecured cookies are used.

Within your gadget code itself, the primary security rule is to *never trust data from outside the gadget*, and this applies to both user input and any data transmitted over the network. Any external channel presents a possible vector for attack, potentially allowing the execution of unauthorized code and a compromise of data integrity.

Most obviously, all information entered by a user must be validated and sanitized before display. Validation is application-specific and simply means checking the input to ensure that it meets expectations. For example, numeric data passed as a string should be converted to a Number type before use; phone numbers and ZIP/postal codes can all be validated with well-known regular expressions. Any data that fails such validation should be rejected.

Sanitization is more general, and its main goal is removing executable code from data. For web applications, this usually means escaping special characters in URLs and any text to be rendered by the browser. The former can be done with JavaScript's encodeURI and encodeURIComponent functions; the latter is easily accomplished with simple code to insert HTML entities for special characters (especially angle brackets, quotation marks, and ampersands).

■ **Tip** A function to sanitize HTML content, escapeHTML, can be found in Listing 2-5.

In addition to performing these operations on data entered by any user, good practice dictates doing the same to all data transmitted "over the wire," even if it comes from a server that should be trustworthy. Doing so will guard against man-in-the-middle attacks, and although these may be less common than other exploits, they should not be ignored.

The basic goal here is to avoid executing code that you didn't write yourself. This also means that you should be restricting the use of JavaScript's eval function (as well as its cousins, setTimeout and Function). If you're transferring data via JSON, a parser like those found at www.json.org is a far safer choice than eval.

Finally, one additional step will help to ensure that the preceding measures function as expected. Web site exploits have been found that resulted from incorrect code page usage; the danger here is that special characters are only *special* in their native character set, so you need to explicitly specify which set to use. For XML (including HTML), make sure that your document starts with the following line:

```
<?xml version="1.0" encoding="UTF-8"?>
```

Obviously, if your document isn't encoded as UTF-8, substitute the correct encoding here. And additionally, for X/HTML it's a good idea to also include the corresponding meta tag:

```
<meta http-equiv="Content-Type" content="text/html;charset=UTF-8" />
```

---

[1] For a solid introduction to web application security, please see *Foundations of Security: What Every Programmer Needs to Know* (Apress, 2007).

Mobile Considerations

Just a few years ago, the mobile considerations for building web apps of any kind could be summed up in a single word: *don't*. Neither the devices, their browsers, nor the networks were up to the task. Although all three have unquestionably changed enough to make mobile web apps viable, the environment is still not as robust as that for stationary computers.

The major issue is still connectivity. In the best case, 3G (and beyond) have enabled an online experience rivaling that of most consumer broadband. However, the coverage is still far from complete—and in the gaps, speed drops considerably, sometimes to zero. Where there is coverage, it's also sometimes true that the user is paying by the byte. All of these connectivity questions should influence how you architect your mobile web gadget.

Because the connection may be nonexistent, you should build your app to function offline as much as possible. Cache as many resources as you feasibly can, both during and between sessions. This may be as simple as storing downloaded text in a local variable for later reuse or as complicated as interfacing with a middleware stack like Google Gears. The specifics will depend on your situation.

Similarly, all your data retrievals should be fault tolerant. If a connection fails midstream, the app should either fall back to cached content, show an alternate display, or politely inform the user of the situation—and then keep trying to connect.

Varying download speeds, and the possibility of chargeable data rates, both point to the same solution: minimize the data to be downloaded as much as possible. This should apply to your images, textual data, and even client-side source code.

- For images, optimize their compression and colors, and consider using multi-image glyphs (or *sprites*) whenever possible.

- For data, use efficient data formats (such as JSON instead of XML for larger data sets), and don't download more than you need.

- For source code, remove comments and extra whitespace from your production code where practical. One good automated tool for doing this to JavaScript is JSMin, available at `http://javascript.crockford.com/jsmin.html`.

In all cases, try to reduce both the number of discrete files to be sent and the size of each file. And in addition to its role in fault tolerance mentioned earlier, wise use of caching can also come into play here by reducing data transfer loads.

All of these techniques do seem somewhat contradictory to the whole idea of a web application, taking a fundamentally client-server architecture and reducing its dependence on the server. For mobile devices in the real world, however, the fact is that connectivity can't be taken for granted. The techniques in this section will make for a better user experience even on the desktop: reduced data transfer will improve performance everywhere, and all connections do occasionally go down.

Case Study: Architecture on the Moon

As discussed earlier in the chapter, I've separated the content, presentation, and functionality of the Moon Phase gadget into HTML, CSS, and JavaScript files. You can find the core JavaScript to make the gadget work in Listing 2-4. After declaring a namespace of `moonPhase` and a few module-level variables, it consists of five functions:

- `init`, called when the gadget opens, establishes links to the HTML elements and events that will be required later in the code.

- `load`, attached to the window's `resize` event, loads the text and image content appropriate for the current size mode.

- receiveNextLast is a callback for the Ajax retrieval of the next/last phase information. It *validates* the data and then *caches* it in a module variable.

- showText moves the next/last data out of the cache variable and into the on-screen display elements.

- timeDelta is a helper function that nicely formats the time difference between now and the next/last phases.

Listing 2-4. *The JavaScript for the Basic Moon Phase Gadget,* phase.js

```
// The moonPhase namespace
var moonPhase = window.moonPhase || {};

// Declare module-level variables
moonPhase.nextLast = null;
moonPhase.timeout  = null;
moonPhase.elements = {
  'moon':   null,
  'last':   null,
  'next':   null,
  'credit': null
};

// init: Initialize the gadget
moonPhase.init = function () {
  // Links to XHTML elements
  var id;
  for (id in moonPhase.elements) {
    moonPhase.elements[id] = document.getElementById(id);
  }

  // Attach (and call) the resize handler to load content
  crossPlatform.addHandler(window, 'resize', moonPhase.load);
  moonPhase.load();
};
crossPlatform.addHandler(window, 'load', moonPhase.init);

// load: Load the visible content appropriate for the current size of the gadget
moonPhase.load = function () {
  var width, size, imgSrc;

  // Get the sceen width
  width = crossPlatform.getWidth(window);

  if (width > 220) {
    // Show the ancillary text
    moonPhase.elements.last.style.display = 'inline';
    moonPhase.elements.next.style.display = 'inline';

    if (!moonPhase.nextLast ||
        (Number(new Date()) > moonPhase.nextLast.next.when)) {
      // Retrieve the next/last data
```

```
          crossPlatform.fetchXML('http://daylightmap.com/moon/next_last.xml.php',
              moonPhase.receiveNextLast);
      } else {
        // No retrieval necessary, just show it
        moonPhase.showText();
      }
    } else {
      // Hide the ancillary text
      moonPhase.elements.last.style.display = 'none';
      moonPhase.elements.next.style.display = 'none';
    }

    if (width < 180) {
      size = 'small';
    } else if (width < 800) {
      size = 'medium';
    } else {
      size = 'large';
    }
    if (size === 'large') {
      // Large display (for full-sized monitors)
      imgSrc = 'luna_north_large.jpg';
      document.body.style.overflow = 'auto';
      moonPhase.elements.moon.height = 625;
      moonPhase.elements.moon.width  = 625;
    } else {
      // Ordinary gadget-sized siaplay
      imgSrc = 'luna_north_small.jpg';
      document.body.style.overflow = '';

      if (size === 'small') {
        // Small display
        moonPhase.elements.moon.height = 88;
        moonPhase.elements.moon.width  = 88;
      } else {
        // Medium-sized display
        moonPhase.elements.moon.height = 176;
        moonPhase.elements.moon.width  = 176;
      }
    }

    // Set the source for the main moon image
    moonPhase.elements.moon.src = 'http://daylightmap.com/moon/images/' + imgSrc;
};

// receiveNextLast: Callback for the next/last XML retrieval
moonPhase.receiveNextLast = function (responseXML) {
    var nodes;
    if (!responseXML) {
      // Error retrieving the data - try again, using exponential back-off with jitter
      moonPhase.delay = moonPhase.delay || 5 * 1000;
      // Give up after 4 failures.
      if (moonPhase.delay <= 40 * 1000) {
```

```
      moonPhase.delay *= 2;
      window.setTimeout(moonPhase.load, moonPhase.delay);
    }
  } else {
    // Cache the retrieved data into a JS variable and show it on screen
    nodes = responseXML.getElementsByTagName('phase');
    try {
      moonPhase.nextLast = {
        'last': {'type': crossPlatform.escapeHTML(nodes[0].getAttribute('type')),
                 'when': crossPlatform.nodeValue(nodes[0])},
        'next': {'type': crossPlatform.escapeHTML(nodes[1].getAttribute('type')),
                 'when': crossPlatform.nodeValue(nodes[1])}
      };
    } catch (e) {
      moonPhase.nextLast = null;
    }
    moonPhase.showText();
  }
};

// showText: Extract the next/last data from the local cache to the visible HTML
moonPhase.showText = function () {
  if (!!moonPhase.nextLast) {
    // Cache has been filled - go ahead!
    moonPhase.elements.last.innerHTML = moonPhase.nextLast.last.type + ' moon ' +
      moonPhase.timeDelta(moonPhase.nextLast.last.when) + ' ago';
    moonPhase.elements.next.innerHTML = moonPhase.nextLast.next.type + ' moon in ' +
      moonPhase.timeDelta(moonPhase.nextLast.next.when);

    // Refresh the text display in 1 hour
    if (!!moonPhase.timeout) {
      window.clearTimeout(moonPhase.timeout);
    }
    moonPhase.timeout = window.setTimeout(moonPhase.load, 60 * 60 * 1000);
  }
};

// timeDelta: Generate a human-readable string showing the difference between the
//            current time and the given JS Date object, as in "3 days, 22 hours"
moonPhase.timeDelta = function (date)
{
  var days = Math.abs(date - Number(new Date())) / (24 * 60 * 60 * 1000),
      hours = Math.round((days - Math.floor(days)) * 24),
      result = '';

  if (Math.floor(hours) === 24) {
    days += 1;
    hours = 0;
  }

  if (days >= 1) {
    result = result + Math.floor(days) + ' day';
    if (days >= 2) {
```

```
      result = result + 's';
    }
    result = result + ', ';
  }

  result = result + Math.floor(hours) + ' hour';
  if (hours !== 1) {
    result = result + 's';
  }

  return result;
};
```

I'd like to particularly call your attention to the following aspects:

- The load function is predominantly composed of code to handle the three image sizes supported by the gadget, as described earlier in the chapter.

- The ancillary phase data is retrieved from the server once, when the gadget opens, and cached thereafter in the moonPhase.nextLast variable. It's retrieved again only if it becomes stale.

- The receiveNextLast function (as the XHR callback for the ancillary data) contains code to retry the retrieval if it fails.

- The same function validates and sanitizes the data before caching it.

Note that one recommendation I'm *not* following here is to use JSON rather than XML for data transfer. Often, this is a good idea, because JSON is more compact. However, the data in this case is tiny (104 bytes), so it's not worth the additional overhead of downloading a JSON parser.

You'll also notice several references here to functions that aren't in this listing but are in a different namespace, crossPlatform. This is a small library of routines that I've abstracted out of Listing 2-4 for reuse elsewhere; as the name implies, they're predominantly for implementing common functionality in a platform-agnostic way. You can find the code for these in Listing 2-5.

Listing 2-5. Cross-platform Library Routines, the Initial platform.js

```
// The crossPlatform namespace
var crossPlatform = window.crossPlatform || {};

// Initialize an XHR object for later use
if (!!window.XMLHttpRequest) {
  crossPlatform.xhrFetcher = new XMLHttpRequest(); // Most browsers
} else if (!!window.ActiveXObject) {
  crossPlatform.xhrFetcher = new ActiveXObject('Microsoft.XMLHTTP'); // Some IE
}

// fetchXML: Retrieve an XML resource asynchronously
crossPlatform.fetchXML = function (url, callback) {
  if (!!crossPlatform.xhrFetcher) {
    crossPlatform.xhrFetcher.open('GET', url, true);
    crossPlatform.xhrFetcher.onreadystatechange = function () {
      if (crossPlatform.xhrFetcher.readyState === 4) {
        // Retrieval complete
```

```
      if (crossPlatform.xhrFetcher.status >= 400) {
        // Returned an HTTP error
        callback(null);
      } else {
        // Returned successfully
        callback(crossPlatform.xhrFetcher.responseXML);
      }
    }
  };
  crossPlatform.xhrFetcher.send(null);
} else {
  // We were unable to create the XHR object
  callback(null);
}
};

// nodeValue: Extract the text value of a DOM node
crossPlatform.nodeValue = function(node) {
  return (node.innerText || node.text || node.textContent ||
          node.childNodes.length ? node.childNodes[0].data : null);

};

// getWidth/getHeight: Return the size in pixels of the window or a DOM element
crossPlatform.getWidth = function (element) {
  if (element === window) {
    return document.body.offsetWidth || document.body.parentNode.clientWidth;
  } else {
    return element.offsetWidth || element.innerWidth;
  }
};
crossPlatform.getHeight = function (element) {
  if (element === window) {
    return document.body.offsetHeight || document.body.parentNode.clientHeight;
  } else {
    return element.offsetHeight || element.innerHeight || element.clientHeight;
  }
};

// addHandler: Attach a function as a handler to a DOM event
crossPlatform.addHandler = function (element, event, handler) {
  if (!!element.addEventListener) {
    // W3C DOM Level 2 compliant
    element.addEventListener(event, handler, false);
  } else {
    // Other browsers
    var oldHandler = element['on' + event];
    element['on' + event] = function() {
      if (!!oldHandler) {
        oldHandler();
      }
      handler();
    };
```

```
  }
};

// escapeHTML: Make a string safe for display within page content
crossPlatform.escapeHTML = function (text)
{
  if (!!text) {
    text = String(text).replace(/'/g, '&apos;').replace(/"/g, '&quot;');
    text = text.replace(/&/g, '&amp;').replace(/</g, '&lt;').replace(/>/g, '&gt;');
  }
  return text;
};
```

■ **Note** Although the routines in Listing 2-5 are complete and functional, be aware I'll be expanding on them throughout the rest of the book. In particular, Chapter 3 will dive into them in much more detail. The complete, final code for Moon Phase (including its Ajax server) can be found in Appendix C.

That's the entirety of the code for the stand-alone Moon Phase gadget, ready to run in a browser at nearly any resolution. We'll be doing the final assembly in the next few sections of the chapter, but for a preview, flip forward to Figure 2-13.

Considering External Design Issues

Architectural issues also extend beyond the boundaries of your gadget; for virtually all platforms, the gadget itself is just part of a larger package. Much of the packaging is presentational and represents your gadget's face to the world. In the following sections, you'll explore the concepts and practicalities of putting on the best face.

Title

The *title* of a gadget should be short and effective. It's your best description of what the gadget does, in as few words as you can manage. This is effectively your gadget's name, and it should rarely be more than two or three words; make those words count.

Ideally, your gadget concept is relatively unique, and as a result, its title will be too. If not, make it so: what sets your calculator or to-do list apart from all the others? Try to capture that distinction in the title. Your goal is to stand out and to catch the attention of the prospective user browsing a gadget directory.

Don't feel compelled to include your company name or other branding information in the title unless it's intrinsically part of what the gadget does or the brand is extremely well known and will help "sell" the gadget just on its own. A good example of this might be "eBay Search," while an example of what to avoid might be "Auction Search Gadget by GadgetMaker."

Description

A gadget's *description* is the slightly longer version of what it is and does. If the title is your gadget's name, the description is its elevator pitch. It usually appears on your gadget's detail page in the various directories. You can't write a novel here, but you do have a few sentences in which to convince a prospective user that your gadget is worth installing. She has already clicked into this page; you've gotten that much of her interest. This is your chance to make your pitch and seal the deal. Clearly and concisely describe what makes your gadget unique, useful, interesting, and fun.

Simultaneously, once you've convinced her that it's worth a try, this is also your only opportunity to communicate with the new user before she installs your gadget. If it has any prerequisites or requires any nonobvious installation instructions, this is where you need to state them—without contravening your sales pitch.

Most gadget directories are searchable; search results will be weighted toward gadget titles but will draw from descriptions as well. As a result, you should aim to work any important keywords into the description that aren't in the title.

It's also worth noting that the description is almost always plain text. If you have a URL in your description—for instance, a link to full installation instructions or other information on your web site—endeavor to make it as short as possible. Users will generally have to transcribe it manually, rather than being able to click it directly. So, it's much better to include an address like `www.mysite.com/clockguide` than `www.mysite.com/en/27/Projects/gadgets/ClockGadget/Instruction_Guide_New.html`, even if you need to set up a redirect from your web root to make it happen. Alternatively, consider a good TinyURL (`www.tinyurl.com`).

Icons and Thumbnails

Virtually all platforms support (if not require) an *icon*, which is a small graphic to accompany your gadget. These are some of the ways that this image may be used:

- Accompanying your listing in a directory or app store

- On your gadget's detail page, as a thumbnail view alongside its description

- As a favicon when your gadget is shown as a stand-alone web page in a browser

- As a desktop shortcut

- As an icon in an operating system's list of running applications (such as Windows' taskbar)

The image itself should be as clear, simple, and distinct as possible, embodying the central concept of your gadget in a nutshell. I suggest brainstorming a number of possibilities, evaluating each on how well it conveys the idea of your gadget, as well as its suitability for sizes as small as 16 pixels square. For a major gadget project, it's often worth consulting a professional designer to get the icon right.

It's generally a good bet to use an image with a square aspect ratio; many platforms require a square icon, and it will usually look acceptable even on those that don't. If your preferred icon doesn't start out square, you will still need a square version of it at times, either as a judicious crop or by adding margins.

Because this graphic is used in so many places by so many platforms, you'll need to have versions of it many different sizes. Depending on your image, you may be able to simply resample it at a different size, or you may need to manually tweak it in a graphics application. If you're going to be simply resizing your icon, I recommend starting with the largest size (128×128 pixels) and always sampling down from there. In other words, for each discrete size required, open the 128×128 version fresh in your graphics app, and scale it to the desired size.

■ **Note** You can find a table of the icon/thumbnail sizes required by all the platforms in the book in Appendix A.

If possible, use a semitransparent PNG and generate the different-sized icons against a transparent background. If this isn't practical for your image, try to create separate versions that will work on both black and white backgrounds; this should cover most cases.

Screenshot

In addition to an icon, a few platforms support a gadget *screenshot*. This is a larger image of your gadget in action that is typically displayed instead of its icon on the directory detail page for these platforms.

Depending on your app, you may be able to simply screen-capture the gadget in its entirety (see Figures 2-4 and 2-5 for examples) or a portion of the gadget showing its primary functionality. Alternately, it may be best to create a composite image showing several key aspects, as shown in Figure 2-11.

Figure 2-11. *A composite screenshot*

Case Study: The Face of the Moon

Since this version of the Moon Phase gadget is simply an HTML page, the external design elements are referenced from the head section. Looking at Listing 2-6 (the final HTML for the gadget in this chapter), you'll find the gadget's title, description, and icon in their appropriate `meta` and `link` elements.

Listing 2-6. The Complete phase.html for the Basic Moon Phase Gadget

```
<?xml version="1.0" encoding="UTF-8"?>
<!DOCTYPE html PUBLIC "-//W3C//DTD XHTML 1.0 Transitional//EN"
                      "http://www.w3.org/TR/xhtml1/DTD/xhtml1-transitional.dtd">
<html xmlns="http://www.w3.org/1999/xhtml">
  <head>
    <meta http-equiv="Content-Type" content="text/html;charset=UTF-8" />
    <meta name="description"
```

```
      content="Shows the current phase of the moon on a field of stars." />
  <title>Moon Phase</title>
  <link href="moon_32.png" type="image/png" rel="icon" />
  <link href="phase.css"   type="text/css"  rel="stylesheet" />
</head>
<body class="moonPhase">
  <div id="main">
    <p id="last" class="text"></p>
    <p id="image_container">
      <img id="moon" alt="Current Moon Image" width="176" height="176"
           src="http://daylightmap.com/moon/images/luna_north_small.jpg" />
    </p>
    <p id="next" class="text"></p>
    <p id="credit" class="text">
      by <a target="_top" href="http://www.daylightmap.com">DaylightMap</a>
    </p>
  </div>

  <script src="platform.js" type="text/javascript"></script>
  <script src="phase.js"    type="text/javascript"></script>
</body>
</html>
```

The title is simply "Moon Phase," and has been in the HTML since Listing 2-1. The description has been kept especially brief because of the formatting constraints of this book. The icon here is a 32-pixel square PNG, shown in Figure 2-12; it's simply a typical crescent-moon image from the server-side Xplanet job, enhanced slightly in a graphics application. I've then attached it to the page as a favicon. You can also see it in place back in Figure 2-10, in the Firefox address bar and page tab.

Figure 2-12. The Moon Phase gadget's 32×32 favicon

■ **Tip** Favicons should typically be either 16 or 32 pixels square and are of type `.ico`, `.png`, or `.gif`.

Deploying the Core Gadget

The stand-alone gadget is now complete; it's ready to face the world. Although the major purpose in building the core gadget is to lay a foundation for the various gadget APIs discussed in Parts 2 through 4 of this book, it is nonetheless a self-contained web application. As such, it can be "deployed" by simply displaying it in a browser: enter the gadget's URL in the address bar and go, as shown in Figure 2-13. There are also other, more specialized uses for the core gadget you've built; this part of the chapter explores a few such ways in which you can use the existing gadget on its own.

Figure 2-13. *The basic Moon Phase gadget, running stand-alone in Firefox*

Your Gadget As a Mobile Version of Your Site

If the gadget you've built is a miniature version of your web site's primary functionality, an excellent way to deploy it is as the mobile face of your web application. The idea here is that visitors on conventional computers will continue use the full-size version of your web application, while those on handhelds are better off receiving the miniaturized version.

One way to accomplish this is with a mobile-specific URL. Although there's no universal standard for doing so, several common techniques are emerging. Using one of the following approaches will help your mobile content to be readily discoverable.

The easiest approach is to simply place your mobile-specific version in a subdirectory named /m (for mobile) off your web root so that the mobile content is delivered from a URL like http://mydomain.com/m.

A similar approach is to use a subdomain of m, such as http://m.mydomain.com. This works nicely with the first approach, because many commercial hosting providers set subdomains up as root directories by default. In other words, if you create a subdomain of m, you may find that its content is placed in a directory named /m automatically.

Or, a different tack is to register a .mobi domain for your application, such as http://mydomain.mobi. The .mobi top-level domain is specifically intended for mobile devices; some users will look there first for handheld-optimized content, and search engines will favor it if they know the searcher is using a mobile phone.

In all these cases, you should be aware that some mobile visitors will be using older, "dumb" handsets (so-called feature phones), without good JavaScript or CSS support. Consequently, you should ensure that gadget code placed in these locations degrades gracefully, or you should provide a static landing page with equivalent content for these devices.

It's also true that not all mobile users will automatically gravitate toward mobile-specific URLs like these. As the mobile web grows more pervasive, there will be less of a split in users' consciousness between the "mobile" and "conventional" web; the first point of arrival for most of your visitors will continue to be your primary URL, whatever device they're using. To help guide mobile users in the right direction (if they so choose), it may be helpful to include a link in your main page or web application:

```
<a href="/m" id="mobile_link">Mobile users, click here for compact version</a>
```

If you want, you can make this link only be visible for users with a small screen by including JavaScript like the following in your page initialization code. Note that it uses a method from the `crossPlatform` library introduced earlier in the chapter.

```
if (crossPlatform.getWidth(window) > 480) {
  document.getElementById('mobile_link').style.display = 'none';
}
```

■ **Note** It's probably *not* a good idea to browser-sniff mobile devices and automatically forward them to the mobile version of your site. The better mobile browsers can probably handle the full version of your site, and users of these will appreciate the option.

Embedding Your Gadget Within Another Page

Rather than your gadget standing completely on its own, you can display it within another page on your web site, in the manner conventionally associated with gadgets. If your gadget is complementary to your site's main function, rather than duplicating it in a smaller package, this may be the most appropriate way to use it on your site. Or, if it *is* essentially a repackaging, you can use your new gadget to place the bite-sized view on other pages within your site or perhaps other affiliated sites that you also own.

The most straightforward technique to display a gadget within another page is to embed it in an `iframe` element of the desired dimensions, with the `src` attribute pointing to the gadget's URL. For example, to embed the Moon Phase example gadget in a page, you could use the following HTML fragment:

```
<iframe style="width: 300px; height: 200px; border: 1px solid black"
        src="http://daylightmap.com/moon/phase.html"></iframe>
```

Note that I've included the dimensions and border style inline here. This is partially for brevity, to avoid the complexity of separate CSS, but I'll also make specific use of this in the next section.

Supplying Your Gadget to Other Webmasters

Embedding your gadget on a page of your own web site is typically of limited usefulness, because it does little to expand your content's reach—a major purpose of gadget development. But the same technique can be used to supply your core gadget to other webmasters, allowing them to embed it in *their* web sites.

Essentially, all they need is the `iframe` code from the previous section. You can simply place it in your page, with text instructions for its use, like the following:

```
<p>Copy the following code into your web page source to embed the gadget.</p>
<textarea readonly="readonly" onfocus="select()">
&lt;iframe style=&quot;width: 300px; height: 200px; border: 1px solid black&quot;
src=&quot;http://daylightmap.com/moon/phase.html&quot;&gt;
&lt;/iframe&gt;
</textarea>
```

Observe that I've HTML-encoded the `iframe` source into a `textarea` element for easy copying by the user; otherwise, the code is unchanged. And tying up a loose end from the previous section, it should also be clear now why the style was included inline for the `iframe`.

This basic technique is used by many well-known web sites, such as Amazon.com and the Weather Channel, for distributing their content in gadget form. Although many of the web gadget APIs covered later in this book offer a similar capability, using their APIs to place your gadget on third-party sites, this simple `iframe` wrapper supports the same functionality while keeping you in full control.

Summary

As a web development professional, gadgets shouldn't hold any large surprises for you; most of your experience is directly transferable. But with their size and functionality constraints, they do bring the usual issues into sharper focus, requiring an equally focused effort from you.

In general, the gadget development process usually goes something like this:

1. *Conceptualize* precisely what your gadget will do, keeping your eye on its core mission.

2. *Design* the gadget's user interface, making optimal use of the space available.

3. *Build* the gadget code. With a good concept and design, this should be fairly straightforward.

4. *Present* your gadget's best face to the world, with a well-polished icon, title, and description.

5. *Deploy* your gadget, possibly as standalone HTML, or to the other APIs covered in later chapters.

With the stand-alone gadget now complete, the next chapter will begin the process of extending it to use the platform-specific features of gadget APIs—but in a non-platform-specific manner, reusing as much code as possible throughout the book.

CHAPTER 3

■ ■ ■

Developing for Multiple Platforms

The self-contained web gadget I showed how to develop in the previous chapter was perfectly functional, but to fully use the power of gadgets, you need more. The core gadget is constrained by its very self-contained nature: by definition, it's plain-vanilla HTML and can't use any of the more advanced features that gadget platforms offer. But if your gadget uses a feature from a specific API, how can you avoid being locked into that API?

This chapter is all about addressing that question; it's about using platform features while maintaining the platform independence that allows you to deploy your gadgets to the widest possible audience. Toward that end, I'll be introducing a JavaScript abstraction technique that will access APIs' most useful features but still isolate your gadgets from dependency on any single API. The major functionality areas to be abstracted include the following:

- *Platform detection*, allowing the code (both crossPlatform and your own) to dynamically adjust to different platforms

- *Content retrieval*, for dynamic loading of data from outside the gadget

- *Data loading and saving*, for storing gadget state in a clean, object-oriented fashion

- *Size-related functions*, always handy within the small confines of a gadget

The abstraction layer will be built within the crossPlatform.* namespace introduced in the previous chapter in Listing 2-5, where some of the previous functionality was encapsulated to isolate your gadget code from browser dependencies. Now, the crossPlatform module is being extended to also isolate you from gadget API dependencies. In this chapter, I'll be generalizing the cross-browser support into a more general-purpose code base, and in the following chapters, I'll build on that foundation to integrate with each specific API.

In addition, I'll be extending the Moon Phase example gadget from the previous chapter here, demonstrating the use of the abstraction layer in the process. This gadget will then also be ready to deploy to each of the platforms covered in the rest of the book.

Platform Detection

The cornerstone of the crossPlatform abstraction layer is platform detection; the goal is to determine which gadget platform (if any) is in place at runtime. This allows the crossPlatform code to invoke routines and instantiate objects appropriate to that platform and to utilize as much of that platform's specific functionality as possible.

The result of the platform detection will be a simple string, naming the API, placed in a variable named api (within the crossPlatform namespace). As a default, I'll simply initialize this as follows near the start of my JavaScript:

```
crossPlatform.api = 'none';
```

The actual detection will occur later in the code and will override this value as appropriate. For example, if the detector code determines the environment to be a Mac OS X widget, it will set crossPlatform.api to 'mac'.

Detecting the API

How will this detection occur? The primary method will be checking for the existence of key *global objects*. Most of the gadget and widget APIs supply their additional functionality to client code (like yours) in the form of JavaScript objects; by checking to see which of these objects is defined, the detector can ascertain which API is in effect.

For example, the Windows Desktop Gadget API defines a namespace object of System, under which its API methods reside. It's the only gadget platform to use the System object, so its existence is a sure indication that code is running as a Windows gadget. Thus, the following code will detect the Windows Desktop API:

```
if (!!window.System) {
  crossPlatform.api = 'windows';
}
```

■ **Note** The !! notation in the previous test safely converts the System object (or lack thereof) to a Boolean value. Referring to System as a property of the browser's window object instead of a top-level global is also safer on certain browsers, because it avoids any possible "variable not defined" errors.

The specific detector code for each API will be presented in the following chapters; for now, it's sufficient that you have a general idea of how it's going to work.

PLATFORM DETECTION VS. COMPATIBILITY TESTING

Some readers will find my usage of generic platform detection objectionable, preferring instead to test for compatibility by checking for object definitions at the time of use. For example, rather than testing for the existence of System (as on the previous page) and setting an api variable to 'windows', this approach would instead wait until some Windows-specific object needed to be used—say, the System.Gadget object (which you'll see in Chapter 6)—and test for it just in time:

```
if (!!window.System && !!System.Gadget && !!System.Gadget.Settings &&

    !!System.Gadget.Settings.readString) {

  myValue = System.Gadget.Settings.readString(name);

}
```

Note that there's no reference to api === 'windows' here at all. In a way, the code neither knows nor cares that the platform is Windows; it just knows that System.Gadget.Settings.readString is available for use.

It's generally agreed that direct object detection is more robust than platform-wide "sniffing," as I'm doing in this chapter. The reasoning is that some other API may someday decide to define a System object; my code would then misidentify it as Windows and misbehave accordingly. Checking for specific objects means that this hypothetical API would need to duplicate Windows' object structure, right down to readString, before my code would break.

Although I concur that object detection is superior in this regard (and I use it for the non-platform-specific XHR code of Listing 3-1), I've found that it's not sufficiently flexible for my needs in crossPlatform. Specifically, I frequently need to run platform-specific code that *isn't* tied to a specific object but rather to more nebulous characteristics of the API, ones that aren't possible to test for directly. One example will occur later in this chapter: the emptyPref property described in the section "The Storage Class." Consequently, I've had no choice but to detect at the platform level and accept the risk that changes to one of the supported APIs could break my code in the future. But don't API coders always run such a risk?

Using the Results

Once detected, the api value will be useful any time you need to execute different code for different platforms. You can simply test for the appropriate values of api in the JavaScript and branch the code accordingly.

For example, gadgets running on the Windows desktop have a fixed width of 130 pixels. If your gadget needs to fix its own width accordingly, you might use code like the following to do so:

```
if (crossPlatform.api === 'windows') {
  body.style.width = '130px';
}
```

Within the crossPlatform middleware layer, I use such code extensively to call API-specific interface routines for most of the specialized functionality described in this chapter. But keep in mind that crossPlatform.api isn't just for my use; you'll find it handy too on the occasions when the ideal of platform-independent coding breaks down.

Retrieving Content

The need to pull data from a remote server is extremely common in gadgets. This a fundamental component of Ajax development: any time your gadget needs information that has been updated since it first loaded, or in response to some user action, content retrieval will be called for. This content may be generated from your own server, or it may be from an external source as part of a web mashup. So, a robust, versatile content retrieval infrastructure will be a crucial part of your gadget tool set.

As you may recall from the previous chapter, even the simple Moon Phase gadget relied on remote content for some of its functionality, retrieving and parsing XML data for full and new moon times bracketing the present. In that chapter, I introduced some very basic content retrieval code in the first version of crossPlatform. Now it's time to get it ready for building on, and Listing 3-1 shows the way.

Listing 3-1. The Content Retrieval Foundation

```
// fetchXML: Retrieve an XML document from url and pass it to callback as a DOM
crossPlatform.fetchXML = function (url, callback) {
  crossPlatform.fetch(url, callback, 'responseXML');
};

// fetchText: Retrieve a text document from url and pass it to callback as a string
crossPlatform.fetchText = function (url, callback) {
  crossPlatform.fetch(url, callback, 'responseText');
};

// Helper code for content-fetching routines
crossPlatform.fetch = function (url, callback, propertyName) {
  var xhrFetcher = crossPlatform.getFetcher();
  if (!xhrFetcher) {
    // We were unable to create the XHR object
    callback(null);
  } else {
    xhrFetcher.open('GET', url, true);
    xhrFetcher.onreadystatechange = function () {
      if (xhrFetcher.readyState === 4) {
        // Retrieval complete
        if (!!xhrFetcher.timeout) {
          clearTimeout(xhrFetcher.timeout);
        }
        if (xhrFetcher.status >= 400) {
          // Returned an HTTP error
          callback(null);
        } else {
          // Returned successfully
          callback(xhrFetcher[propertyName]);
        }
        // We're done with this fetcher object
        crossPlatform.fetchers.push(xhrFetcher);
      }
    };
    xhrFetcher.timeout = setTimeout(callback, 60000);
    xhrFetcher.send(null);
  }
```

```
};
crossPlatform.fetchers = [];
crossPlatform.getFetcher = function () {
  if (!!crossPlatform.fetchers.length) {
    return crossPlatform.fetchers.pop();
  } else {
    if (!!window.XMLHttpRequest) {
      return new XMLHttpRequest(); // Most browsers
    } else if (!!window.ActiveXObject) {
      return new ActiveXObject('Microsoft.XMLHTTP'); // Some IE
    } else {
      return null;  // Really old browser
    }
  }
};

// nodeValue: Extract the text value of a DOM node
crossPlatform.nodeValue = function(node) {
  return (node.innerText || node.text || node.textContent ||
          node.childNodes.length ? node.childNodes[0].data : null);
};
```

You'll note that the fetchXML function used by Moon Phase in the previous chapter is now accompanied by fetchText, which is for retrieving plain-text content as a string. Both of these are wrappers for a generic fetch routine, where the real work happens in this listing (as opposed to directly in the fetchXML function of Listing 2-5). Although fetch bears a strong resemblance to its forebear from Chapter 2, it's been rearchitected slightly to support multiple concurrent retrievals. This is a safer way to proceed when dealing with asynchronous processing. Rounding out the listing is the nodeValue function, unchanged from Chapter 2, which merely provides a cross-browser method for extracting the text content of a DOM node.

■ **Tip** Note that nodeValue will work on any DOM node, from the HTML of a web page as well as the XML of some remote content. Handy!

Using this code is essentially unchanged from the previous chapter: simply call fetchText or fetchXML with the URL of the desired content and a pointer to the callback function that will handle it.

```
crossPlatform.fetchXML('last_next.xml.php', moonPhase.receiveNextLast);
```

When the resource is retrieved, your callback function will be invoked, with a single parameter. This will be a string in the case of fetchText or a DOM document object in the case of fetchXML. In either case, if an error occurred during retrieval, a null value will be passed to the callback (where it's up to you to handle it further). Such an error could be an HTTP failure, a timeout, or a browser that doesn't support XHR; crossPlatform.fetch* doesn't distinguish, so if you need to, it's up to you to extend this code accordingly.

Cross-domain Issues

Sharp-eyed readers will have noticed a flaw in the code description of the previous section, where I glossed over restrictions on the url parameter to fetch*. The restriction I'm referring to is the *same-origin policy* coded into all modern browsers, which states that XHR can retrieve content only from the same domain, port, and protocol as the containing page. This is indeed a thorny issue, handicapping many a prospective mashup: how do you mash up content from multiple sources if you can retrieve only from your own domain?

The usual answer is by employing an *HTTP proxy*, a server-side script that circumvents the policy. Because they're running on a server, not within a browser, such proxies are free to access any domain they like. I'm not going to go into how to build such a proxy—it's not the topic of this book, and there are many relevant resources online for every server-side language—but basically, they function by running on the same domain as your gadget's page but relaying all requests to another domain. They're relatively easy to build, and they let your gadget mash up content from anywhere you please.

On the other hand, you might not need to build your own. Many web gadget APIs supply their own content proxies, and when you deploy to these platforms, you'll simply use theirs. The truth is, gadget platforms on the Web usually *need* to supply an HTTP proxy, because the gadgets they host are served from the platform's own domain. As a result, a proxy is required for *any* remote content to be displayed in a gadget, even content coming from the gadget's "home" domain: *every* request would otherwise run afoul of the same-origin policy. In Part 2 of this book, I'll be extending crossPlatform.fetch* to transparently use the API-supplied proxies for each platform I cover.

Desktop (and some mobile) gadget platforms have a similar issue but a different solution. Their gadgets are served locally, from packaged source, rather than directly from your server—so again, all XHR requests to the Web would seemingly be to a different domain. Like web gadget platforms, however, the vendors recognize this issue. But their solution is to simply relax the policy in the embedded browsers that run their desktop gadgets. So generally, you can go ahead and request whatever content you like. In a few cases, you'll need to take the additional step of informing the API ahead of time; I cover these in the appropriate chapters in Parts 3 and 4.

Caching

Another issue that developers need to be aware of when working with any web content is caching. Instead of always retrieving content from its original source, browsers will often fulfill their request from a cache that's closer in terms of network topology, saving bandwidth (and often download time). This cache may be within the browser itself, it may be supplied by the platform vendor, or it may be on some intermediate server such as the user's ISP or a third-party content delivery network (CDN).

For the developer, caching is a double-edged sword. On the upside, serving content from cache (especially in the local browser) can provide significant performance gains. In addition, API-supplied caches are a key factor in the scalability of gadgets. Platforms like iGoogle can be made to cache virtually all of your content on their own servers, meaning that your own host needs to bear very little traffic, even if your gadget is receiving many thousands of page views per day. Every one of these users will draw from the same iGoogle cache, so that Google bears the traffic load instead of you.

On the downside, however, caching can lead to stale content. If your gadget is displaying a news feed, for example, a cache that's refreshed only once per week will cause the "news" that's displayed to be very old indeed. And some highly dynamic content should never be cached, such as the current bids in an online auction. In cases such as these, inappropriate caching will greatly decrease the usefulness of the gadget and, correspondingly, the satisfaction of its user base. You need to look at your own content and decide what level of caching is appropriate.

Because you (the gadget developer) don't know what caching may be in place for any particular user, you should always assume that it might occur and architect your code accordingly. This means considering both sides of the caching equation: enabling caching when it's to your benefit and preventing it when not.

Server-Side Cache Control

Developers can control caching in a couple of ways. The first is by sending appropriate HTTP headers in your responses, mostly Cache-Control and Expires, which allow you to specify exactly how long resources of a given type should be kept in any cache along the route. If your web server is using Apache, one easy place to specify these headers is in an .htaccess file for the directory containing the resources you want to control. For example, the following commands will disable all caching for the affected directory by setting the expiration time to zero seconds:

```
ExpiresActive On
ExpiresDefault "access plus 0 seconds"
```

A much finer level of control is also possible. For instance, on many RSS news feeds, a one-hour maximum cache strikes a good balance between freshness and performance. To implement this for a feed on your server, simply add the following directives in the appropriate .htaccess file:

```
ExpiresActive On
ExpiresByType application/rss+xml "access plus 1 hours"
```

Although you can't guarantee that your RSS feeds will indeed be cached for any particular user, a header like this will at least ensure that caching is possible, while simultaneously preventing the feed from being stored too long. Please see the documentation for mod_expires and .htaccess at http://httpd.apache.org/docs/ for more details on how to use such commands. Or, if you're using a different web server (such as Microsoft IIS), refer to its documentation instead.

Client-Side Cache Control

Although server-side cache control is the easiest approach, allowing you to specify cache parameters for broad areas of content at a stroke, the unfortunate reality is that not every cache obeys these HTTP headers. If cache control is vital to the correct functioning of your gadget, you'll need to take matters into your own hands by coding the controls directly into your JavaScript.

The primary technique for doing this is to modify the URLs of retrieved content with parameters added purely for cache control. To see how this works, consider the following URLs for an XML content feed:

```
http://mydomain.com/path/to/content.xml?cache=1
http://mydomain.com/path/to/content.xml?cache=2
```

The base URL is the same, so in both cases it's loading the same resource from mydomain.com. But if the cache parameter changes every hour, for example, this means that the resulting URL is different every hour, and any cache on the network will reload the resource—because its URL has changed. Within any given hour, however, the URL will be unchanged and available to be cached.

To implement such a technique, JavaScript code like the following can be used:

```
var now = new Date(),
    url = 'http://mydomain.com/path/to/content.xml?cache=' +
          now.getMonth() + now.getDate() + now.getHours();
crossPlatform.fetchXML(url, callback);
```

The idea is simple: every time this code runs, the now variable gets initialized to the current date and time, and then its date and hour components are appended to the content url. You can adapt this code to craft any degree of cache control you may require; the JavaScript Date object has a full range of component-extracting functions, from getMilliseconds to getFullYear.

■ **Note** You can find a working example of this technique in Moon Phase's image retrieval code; see Listing C-3 in Appendix C.

Variations on this technique are also possible if the cache control you need isn't directly time-related. The principle remains the same, however: include a dynamic URL parameter whose value corresponds to your specific caching needs. This will ensure that your content URLs are unique exactly when they need to be, taking advantage of any possible caching in the network while also avoiding stale content problems.

CACHE CONTROL FOR DEVELOPERS

As with any web application, testing/debugging gadgets requires a good awareness of the caching that affects your environment. As you're uploading and reloading new versions of gadget code in a typical development cycle, viewing cached content means that you're not viewing your latest modifications—and you're not testing the code that you think you are. So, in addition to the content cache control discussed in this section, you need to take control of source code caching.

Typically, this breaks down into the following three areas:

- *Browser cache*: The instructions for clearing or disabling page cache vary by browser. Consult `http://wikipedia.org/wiki/Bypass_your_cache` (or your browser vendor) for comprehensive instructions.

- *Gadget platform cache*: Different platforms utilize different levels of caching. You can find specific recommendations in the chapters on the various APIs in Parts 2 through 4 of this book.

- *Other network cache*: Your web server may have caching of its own or be routed through a CDN, or your ISP may implement some degree of caching. In these cases, you'll need to investigate the cache supplier for more instructions.

Note that client-side cache controls similar to those described in this chapter can also be applied to source code. For example, to ensure that a given source file *never* gets cached, you could append a pseudorandom value to its URL with code like the following:

```
var url = 'http://mydomain.com/uncacheable_source.js?cache=' + Math.random();

document.write('<script type="text/javascript" src="' + url + '"><\/script>');
```

Barring extremely improbable random-number-generator collisions, this should result in a fresh copy of `uncacheable_source.js` being retrieved directly from your server on every page load.

Saving State

Another key area of functionality for most gadgets is the ability to save information from one session to another. Saving data is usually required for all but the most trivial gadgets; common uses include remembering user preferences and saving the state of a gadget as it changes during a session. Virtually any gadget with which a user interacts will benefit from saving the current state of those interactions; it's the behavior that users expect.

Because it has no user interaction, the basic Moon Phase gadget from Chapter 2 does not save any information from one session to the next. However, that doesn't mean it might not benefit from doing so. The following settings could be useful as user-selectable preferences (which the gadget would then remember for subsequent sessions):

- Although the gadget automatically sizes itself based on its container, some users might specifically prefer the compact version so that it doesn't take up more room than it needs. While we're at it, I'll allow them to always have the large version, too.

- Some users may also not care about the number of days until the new or full moon but would rather have a clean display of just the moon image.

- The crescent moon images generated by Xplanet are calibrated for Earth's northern hemisphere and are backward from the phases seen by users south of the equator. It would be good to allow users to select which hemisphere they're in.

User Interfaces for Configuration

Before you can save preferences, you need controls to allow the user to set them. You need a user interface for gadget configuration—and as it turns out, this is an extremely common need among gadgets. So, I'll add such a user interface to Moon Phase, as depicted in Figure 3-1.

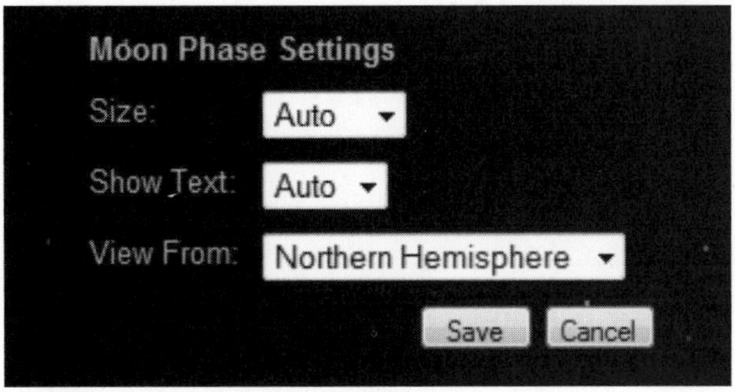

Figure 3-1. The configuration pane for the Moon Phase gadget

Listing 3-2 presents the required markup; it's a simple HTML form that will be added to the page source alongside the main content. As you can see, I have a select for each preference item, along with appropriate labels and buttons to make it usable. I'll be discussing the functions referenced from the buttons in just a few pages.

Listing 3-2. The HTML Fragment for the config Pane

```
<div id="config" style="display: none">
  <p><strong>Moon Phase Settings</strong></p>
  <p>
    <label for="size">Size:</label>
    <select id="size" name="size">
      <option value="small">Small</option>
      <option value="large">Large</option>
      <option value="auto">Auto</option>
    </select>
  </p>
  <p>
    <label for="text">Show Text:</label>
    <select id="text" name="text">
      <option value="yes">Yes</option>
      <option value="no">No</option>
      <option value="auto">Auto</option>
    </select>
  </p>
  <p>
    <label for="hemisphere">View From:</label>
    <select id="hemisphere" name="hemisphere">
      <option value="north">Northern Hemisphere</option>
      <option value="south">Southern Hemisphere</option>
    </select>
  </p>
  <p id="config_buttons">
    <input type="submit" value="Save" id="save_button"
           onclick="moonPhase.saveConfig(); return false;" />
    <input type="button" value="Cancel" id="cancel_button"
           onclick="moonPhase.hideConfig();" />
  </p>
</div>
```

■ **Note** For brevity, many listings in this chapter are just relevant fragments of the full source. You can find the full, final source code for the Moon Phase gadget in Appendix C, or you can download it from `http://sterlingudell.com/pwg`.

Accompanying the new markup is a small amount of CSS, shown in Listing 3-3, to tidy up the appearance a bit. Note in particular the display="none" rule on the main config div so that the configuration pane is not visible when the gadget first opens; also note that I'm still working within the .moonPhase CSS pseudo-namespace class introduced in Listing 2-2.

Listing 3-3. Style for the config Pane

```css
.moonPhase #config {
  display: none;
  padding: 3%;
  font-size:12px;
  max-width: 250px;
  margin: auto;
  background-color: black;
}
.moonPhase #config p {
  margin: 0 0 0.8em 0;
}
.moonPhase #config p {
  padding-left: 3px;
}

.moonPhase label {
  float: left;
  clear: left;
  width: 6em;
}
.moonPhase input {
  vertical-align: top;
  color: black;
}
.moonPhase #config_buttons {
  text-align: right;
}
.moonPhase #config_buttons input {
  height: 20px;
  width: 50px;
  font-size: 11px;
}
```

■ **Tip** When designing your gadget, make sure that it's obvious to the user that a configuration pane isn't your gadget's main view. Give it a clear title, and consider giving it a different background color, ideally one that's darker or more subdued than your ordinary gadget view.

Given that the pane is initially hidden, I'll also need to add a control to the main face of the gadget to enable user access to it. I've chosen to use a standard icon—a wrench image, for configuration—and position it in the unused upper-right corner of the gadget. You can see it in Figure 3-2 (note the "Settings" hint), and the minimal HTML required is as follows:

```html
<div id="main_icons">
  <a id="config_icon" class="control_icon" title="Settings"
     onclick="moonPhase.showConfig()"></a>
</div>
```

61

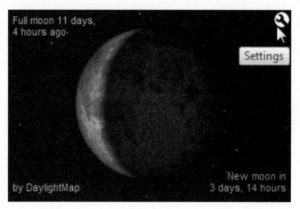

Figure 3-2. *The Settings icon in action*

The CSS is a bit more involved but still quite straightforward; see Listing 3-4. I reuse this icon placement code in a number of gadgets, so the CSS is split among a container div, a `.control_icon` class (for all such icons in the gadget), and the #config_icon itself, even though this gadget has only one icon.

■ **Note** This icon also uses the hover opacity technique outlined in Chapter 2.

Listing 3-4. *CSS to Control the Appearance of the Settings Icon*

```
.moonPhase #main_icons {
  opacity: 0;
  display: block;
  position: absolute;
  right: 0px;
  top: 0px;
  height: 18px;
  width: 18px;
  z-index: 99999;
  overflow: visible;
}
.moonPhase .control_icon {
  overflow: hidden;
  position: absolute;
  right: 2px;
  height: 16px;
  width: 16px;
  border: none;
  cursor: pointer;
}
.moonPhase #config_icon {
  top: 2px;
}
```

```
.moonPhase #main:hover #main_icons {
  opacity: 0.5;
}
.moonPhase #main #main_icons:hover {
  opacity: 1.0;
}
```

Toggling between the two views is accomplished with two very simple JavaScript functions, showConfig and hideConfig, called from the onclick events of the appropriate buttons. Their implementation is predominantly a matter of dynamically hiding and revealing the correct divs with dynamic CSS, as shown in Listing 3-5.

Listing 3-5. Showing and Hiding the Configuration Pane in JavaScript

```
moonPhase.showConfig = function () {
  moonPhase.loadConfig();
  moonPhase.elements.main.style.display   = 'none';
  moonPhase.elements.config.style.display = 'block';
  crossPlatform.adjustSize();
};

moonPhase.hideConfig = function () {
  moonPhase.elements.config.style.display = 'none';
  moonPhase.elements.main.style.display   = 'block';
  crossPlatform.adjustSize();
};
```

■ **Note** The other functions referenced in Listings 3-2 and 3-5 (saveConfig, loadConfig, and adjustSize) will be covered slightly later in the chapter, along with a full explanation of the elements object.

User Interface Alternatives

The approach I've described here for configuring Moon Phase, a separate configuration pane as a completely different view on the gadget, is just one possible way to support a gadget settings user interface. This paradigm is encouraged by several major gadget platforms, including Mac OS X and Opera, so it's a reasonable option to take, but it's by no means the only way forward.

If all the required controls can be comfortably worked into the main view of your gadget, you don't necessarily need a configuration pane at all. This technique often makes for a design that's both more natural for the user and simpler to program than a separate settings pane. Figure 3-3 shows an example, a clock with multiple time zones and a user interface for adding, deleting, and renaming zones right on the face of the gadget.

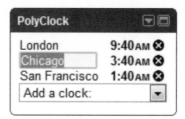

Figure 3-3. *The PolyClock gadget's configuration UI is integrated into its design.*

A hybrid approach is also possible. Figure 3-4 shows a game gadget with controls on its face for selecting the difficulty level of the game (the left and right arrows near the top). However, the game also has broader difficulty ranges; these are selected by clicking the levels button, which opens an appropriate configuration pane.

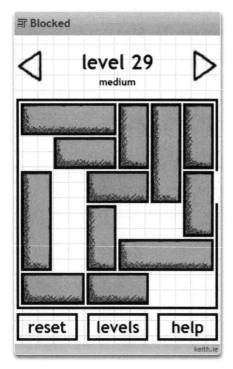
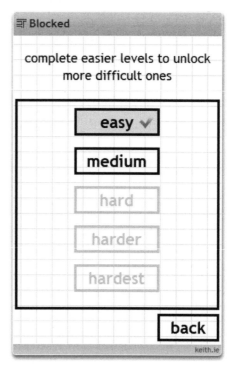

Figure 3-4. *The Blocked gadget has configuration controls both on its main view and within a settings pane.*

Finally, there are also two web gadget platforms, Netvibes and iGoogle, that will supply the configuration user interface for you if you prefer. I'll be covering the details in Chapters 4 and 5, respectively, but the idea is that you denote your settings in the gadget specification, and the API generates a user interface on your behalf, as shown in Figure 3-5. You won't have the same degree of control as when you build your own UI, but if your deployment plans don't extend beyond these two platforms, this approach can reduce your gadget's development time.

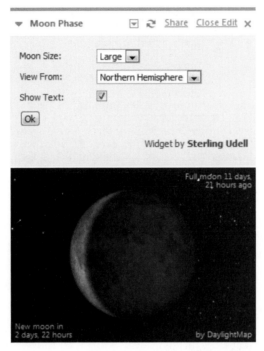

Figure 3-5. *The integrated settings UI of the Netvibes platform (compare with Figure 3-2)*

Storage Mechanisms

Regardless of the user interface, some mechanism will need to be employed to actually save the settings from one session to the next. In the fundamentally stateless environment of the Web, *where* to store this information presents something of a challenge. Ideally, we'd like such a mechanism to be fast, secure, and transparent to the user, even if the user accesses your gadget from different clients or platforms. Not surprisingly, this is a tall order.

Within the web client, the only viable option is to use cookies, the classic browser data storage technology.[1] Cookies are accessible from JavaScript in virtually every browser; they store data as simple name/value pairs, where each piece of information is assigned a unique name and stored as a text string. These named values can be used to store individual user preferences, blocks of typed text, data retrieved from remote sources, or nearly any other information. Although cookies aren't the most glamorous technology, they are generally sufficient for most needs. Listing 3-6 shows a simple JavaScript wrapper for cookie access.

---

[1] Many newer browsers support client-side storage technologies more advanced than cookies, such as HTML5's Structured Storage. Although you'll have opportunities to take advantage of this on certain platforms where a modern browser is assured (like Safari in Chapter 7), at this writing there isn't wide enough adoption to use it in crossPlatform's base layer. Fortunately, cookies are sufficient for our needs.

Listing 3-6. JavaScript Functions to Save and Retrieve Cookie Values

```javascript
crossPlatform.setCookie = function (name, value) {
  var mSecPerYear = 1000 * 60 * 60 * 24 * 365,
      cookieExpire;

  if (!value) {
    // Delete the cookie by setting an expiration date in the past
    cookieExpire = 'Sun, 24-Apr-05 00:00:00 GMT';
  } else {
    // Upsert the cookie by setting an expiration date one year from now
    cookieExpire = (new Date(Number(new Date()) + mSecPerYear)).toUTCString();
  }

  document.cookie = name + '=' + value + ';expires=' + cookieExpire +
                    ';path=' + window.location.pathname;
};

crossPlatform.getCookie = function (name) {
  var cookies = document.cookie.split(';'),
      thisCookie,
      c;

  // Iterate through the cookie list, returning the value associated with "name"
  name = name + '=';
  for (c = 0; c < cookies.length; c += 1) {
    thisCookie = cookies[c].replace(/^\s+/, '');
    if (thisCookie.indexOf(name) === 0) {
      return thisCookie.substring(name.length, thisCookie.length);
    }
  }
  // Target "name" not found
  return null;
};
```

Its usage is quite straightforward, consisting of two functions that set and get cookie values by name. Although these functions are ready for use, they do come with a couple of caveats:

- The cookies they set are *path-specific*. So, if you have two gadgets both served from the same path, such as http://mydomain.com/gadgets/, the potential exists for cookie name collisions between them.

- Conversely, subdomains that resolve to the same location are seen by cookies as different locations, with different sets of cookies. So, a cookie set by a gadget at http://mydomain.com won't be available to one at http://www.mydomain.com.

This second limitation is similar to a larger issue with cookies generally, and that is their client-specific nature. In other words, any data that is stored in cookies on one computer will be unavailable on any other computer, even if both are accessing the same gadget. Although this may not be a big issue for desktop gadgets, it is quite limiting on web and mobile platforms. The emerging paradigm for these environments is one of cloud computing, where users expect their data and settings to persist independently of device or browser—in effect, for their virtual environment to follow them around.

Supporting this capability would require saving state on the server instead, but even in this case, you probably would not be completely freed from saving state on the client anyway. If you don't save some identification data (such as user ID and password) locally, your users will be faced with having to log into the gadget every time they use it in order to access their server-side data.

Fortunately, many gadget platforms supply a solution themselves in the form of a storage infrastructure. They provide the storage and the transport mechanisms, as well as a user ID infrastructure built into their platforms. Naturally, every gadget API does this differently—but that's exactly what the crossPlatform abstraction layer is all about.

So, in the following chapters, I'll be extending crossPlatform to use the storage mechanism of each platform that provides one. When no platform-specific storage is available, it will fall back to using the cookie functions from Listing 3-6 so that your code can transparently use the best form of persistent storage that's available. If you want to extend it yourself to use your own server-based storage, that option is also open to you, of course.

STATE SECURITY

If you're developing a gadget to handle sensitive information, you'll need to take particular care with the security of its saved state. As with all web app security, this is a specialist subject, but here are a few points to get you started:

- Cookies should be limited to HTTPS pages; this can be done by appending ';secure' to the cookie string set by crossPlatform.setCookie in Listing 3-6.

- Sensitive data should also be encrypted before storing in cookies, because they are often saved on the user's PC as plain text.

- All server communication should be secured with SSL; this includes all settings saved at the server, as well as the gadget source and content.

Note that this last item may preclude being able to deploy a secure gadget to some platforms at all, because there is no way to ensure the use of SSL for all your gadget's traffic there.

The Storage Class

To encapsulate the functionality of saving gadget state, I've created a persistent storage class in the crossPlatform layer, named Storage. You can find the basic class declaration in Listing 3-7; note that it calls the setCookie and getCookie methods defined earlier. Also notice that the object constructor takes an optional second parameter containing the default value for the named storage location; this value will be used if no stored value is found. This condition occurs when the retrieved myValue is equal to the namespace-level variable emptyPref; this will be used to handle the different values for "empty" storage on different APIs. In stand-alone mode, an empty cookie is null.

Listing 3-7. The Persistent Storage Class

```
crossPlatform.emptyPref = null;

crossPlatform.Storage = function (name, defaultValue) {
  var myName = name,
      myValue;
  myValue = crossPlatform.getCookie(name);
```

```
if (myValue === crossPlatform.emptyPref) {
  myValue = defaultValue.toString();
}

// Retrieve the value
this.get = function () {
  return myValue;
};

// Save a value
this.set = function (value) {
  if (myValue !== value) {
    myValue = value.toString();
    crossPlatform.setCookie(myName, myValue);
  }
};
};
```

Within the JavaScript code, you can use this class by simply instantiating it for each name/value pair you'll need to store, supplying the name (and optionally, the default initial value):

```
var highScore = new crossPlatform.Storage('score', '0');
```

■ **Note** All `Storage` values are text strings, even if the data may be natively of another type or the platform on which it's running has the capability to store other types.

In the Moon Phase gadget, I have three user preferences I want to store: the preferred text display, the image size, and the hemisphere (refer to Figure 3-2). For generality, I'm going to follow a pattern of containing all my preferences in a single JavaScript object, with the name and default value for each preference as properties of that object. So, I declare the object as such:

```
moonPhase.prefs = {
  'text':       'auto',
  'size':       'auto',
  'hemisphere': 'north'
};
```

This keeps all my gadget preferences (and their default values) in one location, which is easy to find and work with. It also enables me to initialize them with a simple for...in loop, as follows:

```
for (name in moonPhase.prefs) {
  moonPhase.prefs[name] =
    new crossPlatform.Storage(name, moonPhase.prefs[name]);
}
```

I find this to be an extremely useful approach, because if I later add a new preference (or remove an existing one), I don't need to touch the for...in loop: it's sufficient to just add another property to the prefs object. However, I want to stress that the Storage class works just as well with simple variables, as shown in the earlier highScore example.

With my Storage objects instantiated, I can finally implement the saveConfig (from Listing 3-2) and loadConfig (from Listing 3-5) methods of moonPhase. You'll find their source in Listing 3-8; like the instantiation, I have been able to simplify the code by looping through the properties of prefs. The only additional functionality is a call to moonPhase.load in saveConfig to refresh the gadget's display with the latest settings.

Listing 3-8. Loading and Saving the Configuration Pane for Moon Phase

```
moonPhase.saveConfig = function () {
  var name, selector;

  try {
    for (name in moonPhase.prefs) {
      selector = moonPhase.elements[name];
      moonPhase.prefs[name].set(selector.options[selector.selectedIndex].value);
    }

    moonPhase.load();
  } catch (e) {
    alert('Unable to save settings: ' + e.message);
    if (!!window.console && !!console.log) {
      console.log(e.message);
    }
  }
  moonPhase.hideConfig();
};

moonPhase.loadConfig = function () {
  var name, value, selector, s;

  for (name in moonPhase.prefs) {
    value = moonPhase.prefs[name].get();
    selector = moonPhase.elements[name];
    for (s = 0; s < selector.length; s += 1) {
      selector.options[s].selected = (selector.options[s].value === value);
    }
  }
};
```

ACCESSING PAGE ELEMENTS

As with user preferences, I find it convenient to follow a consistent pattern for accessing HTML elements from within my JavaScript. So, alongside the `prefs` object, I also declare one for `elements`, whose property names mirror the HTML `id` attributes of elements I'm going to want to access in code. The relevant object declaration for Moon Phase looks like this:

```
moonPhase.elements = {
  'main':        null,
  'config_icon': null,
  'moon':        null,
  'last':        null,
  'next':        null,
  'credit':      null,
  'config':      null,
  'size':        null,
  'text':        null,
  'hemisphere':  null
};
```

If you compare these object properties with Listings 2-6 and 3-2, you'll find that each matches up with an HTML element, such as `<div id="main">`. This means that I can again initialize the entire object with a single `for...in` loop, much as I did for `prefs`:

```
var id;
for (id in elements) {
  elements[id] = document.getElementById(id);
}
```

Then, any time I need to modify a page element later in the code, I can simply reference the appropriate property of `elements` (as opposed to making a verbose, and potentially slow, call to `getElementById` each time):

```
moonPhase.elements.main.style.display = 'none';
```

Like `prefs`, there's no requirement for you to follow a pattern like this in your own code, but this explanation should help you make more sense of mine.

Size-Related Functions

The bulk of the core `crossPlatform` code is now behind us; what remains are a few utility functions, which I'll cover in this section and the next. The first three of these all have to do with screen real estate; as discussed in the previous chapter, this takes on a good deal of importance within the tight confines of a gadget.

Accordingly, the first two functions were also introduced in the previous chapter, toward the end of Listing 2-5. They're named `getHeight` and `getWidth`, and their job is to return the size (in pixels) of any DOM element, including `window`, in a cross-browser compatible fashion. You can see `getWidth` in action in the following line from Listing 2-4:

```
width = crossPlatform.getWidth(window);
```

It simply returns the pixel width of the browser window, and the width variable set from it is then used to adapt the Moon Phase display. You should find these functions handy in any situation where size-specific coding is necessary. A word of caution, however: although getHeight and getWidth are cross-browser compatible, differences in browser rendering models mean that you won't always get precisely the same pixel dimensions for a given object. In particular, getHeight(window) returns the full window height only in WebKit-based browsers (currently Safari and Chrome); other browsers will give the height of rendered content only. So, use these functions with a bit of care, and allow some leeway for variance in their return values.

The third size-related function is a bit more esoteric; it's named adjustSize and is actually only being declared as a stub right now:

```
crossPlatform.adjustSize = function () {
};
```

Its future purpose is as follows. On many gadget platforms, the size of the gadget is relatively static, and if the amount of content in your gadget changes, a special API function must be called to adjust the size of the gadget to match the new content. That's why adjustSize is there; it will serve as the crossPlatform abstraction point for such API calls.

You can see it in use in the showConfig and hideConfig functions in Listing 3-4. After setting the style.display of the content divs, both functions call crossPlatform.adjustSize. The configuration pane is likely to be of different proportion than the main Moon Phase view, and this call should sort out the gadget boundaries if necessary.

Of course, no such adjustment is needed with the core native HTML gadget we're working with in this chapter, so for now, adjustSize is just a stub. It will be filled as needed in later chapters.

■ **Caution** Do not call adjustSize from an onresize event handler! On platforms where adjustSize is implemented, it will often change the size of the gadget's containing window (or frame), triggering another resize event. Calling it from the handler will thus usually result in an infinite loop.

Utility Functions

The last two crossPlatform methods are general utility functions, of sufficient use to gadget developers to warrant their inclusion in the library. Like the size-related functions, these were both introduced in the previous chapter, at the end of Listing 2-5.

The first of these is addHandler, a function for attaching a JavaScript function to any DOM event. A typical usage occurs in the Moon Phase gadget, where the init function is attached to the window's load event:

```
crossPlatform.addHandler(window, 'load', moonPhase.init);
```

The three parameters to addHandler are as follows:

- The DOM object to which the event belongs, passed as a JavaScript reference. This may be window or any DOM element returned from a function such as document.getElementbyId.

- The event name to attach to, passed as a String. Any standard DOM event may be passed, but note that the name should not be prepended with on (for example, use 'load' rather than 'onload').

- The function to attach to the event. This may be passed as either the name of the function (as moonPhase.init shown previous) or a function literal defined inline.

Finally, the last utility function in crossPlatform is escapeHTML. Its use, to sanitize text for display in the browser, was mentioned in the previous chapter's "Security" section. To recap, here it is in action in moonPhase.receiveNextLast, which is the function that loads text data from the retrieved XML:

```
moonPhase.nextLast = {
  'last': {'type': crossPlatform.escapeHTML(nodes[0].getAttribute('type')),
            'when': crossPlatform.nodeValue(nodes[0])},
  'next': {'type': crossPlatform.escapeHTML(nodes[1].getAttribute('type')),
            'when': crossPlatform.nodeValue(nodes[1])}
};
```

Its usage is quite simple: pass crossPlatform.escapeHTML any text that has originated from outside your gadget, and it will return the same text with applicable characters converted to their HTML entities. You can find the characters converted (and their entities) in Table 3-1.

Table 3-1. *Characters Converted by* crossPlatform.escapeHTML

Character	Entity
<	<
>	>
"	"
'	'
&	&

If you find you need to escape any other characters, you can easily extend escapeHTML yourself to include them.

Summary

The key to efficiently deploying a gadget to multiple platforms is to not program dependence on any single platform into your gadget. This allows you to deploy most of the same source code to every platform, greatly simplifying your development and maintenance loads. One approach to this (used in Chapter 2) is to simply avoid using any API functions at all; however, this severely limits your gadget's capabilities.

In this chapter, you've seen another way to isolate the API dependencies in a middle layer of software. This layer can be reused from one gadget to another, and when an API changes or a bug is found, the change need be made only once. At the same time, your gadgets can use all the most useful features from every platform they run on, without having to delve into the messy details.

In the crossPlatform layer presented here, those features include platform detection, content retrieval, loading and saving of gadget state, and size-related functions, as well as a couple of miscellaneous utility methods. In this chapter, they've all been fully implemented for native HTML gadgets, and the Moon Phase gadget has been usefully extended to take advantage of them. This new version is still ready to deploy to all the places described in Chapter 2.

In all the following chapters of this book, I'll cover a different gadget platform for web, desktop, or mobile environments. For each, I'll discuss the important issues you need to know and extend `crossPlatform` as needed to fully support the API in question. I'll also demonstrate its use by porting Moon Phase to every platform—with absolutely minimal source code changes.

PART 2

∎∎∎

Web Platforms

■ ■ ■

CHAPTER 4

Netvibes

In this chapter, I'll introduce you to the process of rolling your gadget out to a real platform, and the place we'll start is Netvibes. As a fairly representative web-based platform, it's a natural place to get your web gadget underway. The Netvibes API provides you with a good level of functionality and visibility and doesn't require a great deal of modification to your core gadget code.

Introducing Netvibes

Netvibes is an independent web portal and API provider from Netvibes Limited, one of several that choose the term *widget* for what this book calls web gadgets. As an business entity, Netvibes Limited is entirely focused on widgets; in addition to the developer API and end user gadget aggregation pages (such as Figure 4-1), it also provides a widget directory (called the *Ecosystem*) and a selection of prepackaged widget collections (called *Universes*). All of these are hosted at www.netvibes.com.

 Of most interest to us, of course, is the gadget platform. Netvibes calls its platform the *Universal Widget API*, or UWA, and the "Universal" claim refers to the intent that widgets written for this API can also be deployed to a host of other platforms: iGoogle, Mac OS X, Opera, Windows, and more. Although this sounds promising, especially to a cross-platform evangelist like myself, there's a catch: when a UWA widget is used on any of these other platforms, it comes with a "Powered by Netvibes" imprint. My preference is to retain control over the branding on the face of my gadgets, rather than devoting valuable screen real estate to someone else's link, so I don't advocate following this course. Instead, I'll show how to deploy to Netvibes on its own and (in subsequent chapters) to the other platforms directly.

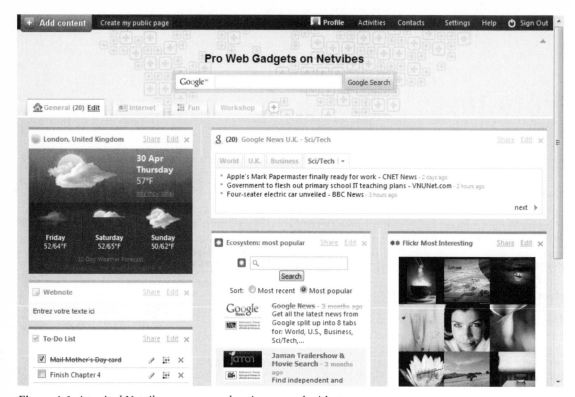

Figure 4-1. *A typical Netvibes user page, showing several widgets*

Developing for Netvibes

Netvibes' widget architecture is slightly unusual. While most platforms package a web gadget with additional files for the platform, Netvibes has instead chosen to extend the widget's HTML itself, with additional `meta` tags and other elements. Consequently, developing a Netvibes widget closely mirrors an ordinary (nongadget) web development process: you'll be editing the same `.html`, `.js`, and `.css` files and uploading them to your server as you would for any other page.

Netvibes is also unique in that it embeds your widget code directly within the user's page at `netvibes.com`; no `iframe` or other technique is used to isolate your widget from the rest of the page. This is when the JavaScript and CSS namespaces that you've built into your gadgets will stand you in good stead: without them, serious issues would arise of colliding with others' code.

So, the basic Netvibes architecture is that widget metadata is contained in the `head` section of the `.html` file; this is parsed by the widget engine at Netvibes and used to invoke various platform-level code. The widget itself is simply copied from the body of your source HTML to a container `div` on the Netvibes page. You'll see this in action in the next section.

On the Netvibes page, widgets are shown in columns whose width is static but not fixed. In other words, the columns are a fixed *percentage* of the browser window width, but not a fixed width in pixels. Your gadget must operate within that column width but is free to use as much height as desired (within reason).

Netvibes is also a platform that supplies virtually all chrome external to your gadget proper, creating the visual interface between your gadget and the user's page. In other words, Netvibes draws the box, and it's up to you to fill it.

Adapting the Core Gadget

Starting from a native web gadget as described in Chapters 2 and 3, your modifications should all be within the HTML. Essentially, you'll be creating a Netvibes-specific version of your `.html` file, extending the core gadget's `.html` file with Netvibes code.

■ **Note** You will want to keep these modifications separate from your core gadget; I recommend making a copy of your HTML and renaming it (or branching it in your version control system). In my case, I've created a new copy named `phase_netvibes.html`.

Listing 4-1 shows the way, using the Moon Phase gadget as an example. Take a look, and then I'll go through the changes one by one. As you can see, the modifications are almost entirely in the head section, sufficiently so that I've omitted the body content from this listing for brevity.

Listing 4-1. Modifications to Moon Phase for Netvibes

```
<?xml version="1.0" encoding="UTF-8"?>
<!DOCTYPE html PUBLIC "-//W3C//DTD XHTML 1.0 Transitional//EN"
                      "http://www.w3.org/TR/xhtml1/DTD/xhtml1-transitional.dtd">
<html xmlns="http://www.w3.org/1999/xhtml"
      xmlns:widget="http://www.netvibes.com/ns/">
  <head>
    <meta http-equiv="Content-Type" content="text/html;charset=UTF-8" />
    <meta name="description"
        content="Shows the current phase of the moon on a field of stars." />
    <title>Moon Phase</title>
    <link href="http://daylightmap.com/moon/images/moon_32.png"
        rel="icon" type="image/png" />

    <!-- head elements below here are Netvibes-specific -->

    <style type="text/css">
      @import url('http://daylightmap.com/moon/phase.css');
    </style>

    <meta name="keywords"   content="moon, phase, science, astronomy, tide" />
    <meta name="author"     content="Sterling Udell" />
    <meta name="website"    content="http://www.daylightmap.com" />
    <meta name="version"    content="2.0.0" />
    <meta name="apiVersion" content="1.2" />
```

```
    <widget:preferences>
      <preference type="hidden" name="text" />
      <preference type="hidden" name="size" />
      <preference type="hidden" name="hemisphere" />
    </widget:preferences>

    <script type="text/javascript">
      widget.onLoad = function () {
        widget.body.addClassName('moonPhase');
        widget.body.style.backgroundImage =
          'url(http://daylightmap.com/moon/images/stars_small.jpg)';
      };
    </script>
  </head>
  <body class="moonPhase">

    <!-- body content goes here -->

    <script src="http://daylightmap.com/moon/platform.js"
            type="text/javascript"></script>
    <script src="http://daylightmap.com/moon/phase.js"
            type="text/javascript"></script>
  </body>
</html>
```

■ **Caution** Do not place other standard HTML elements, such as `link` or `script`, in the `head` of a Netvibes widget. Because the platform itself (rather than the browser) processes the `head` and loads only the `body` into the final page, elements that Netvibes isn't expecting will be ignored. See the "External Resources" sidebar (a few pages hence) for alternatives.

HTML Namespace

Because the Netvibes widget architecture works by adding elements to the source HTML, you'll need a new namespace on your root `html` element. Simply add an attribute of `xmlns:widget="http://www.netvibes.com/ns/"`, as shown near the top of Listing 4-1. Not only is this required for the source to be valid HTML, but it must be in place before your widget can be uploaded to Netvibes' Ecosystem.

In addition, Netvibes requires that the source HTML document be UTF-8 encoded.

Absolute URLs

Netvibes widgets are served directly from `netvibes.com`, so all URLs referenced by your gadget must include the global path to the resource; no relative URLs are possible. You can see this in the `script` and favicon `link` elements of Listing 4-1, among other places.

■ **Caution** Don't forget to confirm that you're using absolute URLs for any resources referenced in other files your gadget may include, such as CSS and JavaScript.

As a fully web-based service, Netvibes adheres to a cloud computing model, so your Netvibes page and widgets will be available from wherever you might log in. They're not tied to any specific client computer or browser. But as a result, your widget source files will need to be on a publicly accessible web server for deployment on Netvibes.

Importing Style Sheets

When porting a generic web gadget to a Netvibes widget, it's necessary to convert all `link` elements that reference style sheets to a `style/@import` syntax. In other words, the following element from the original Moon Phase gadget:

```
<link type="text/css" rel="stylesheet"
    href="'http://daylightmap.com/moon/phase.css'" />
```

has been to be converted to this syntax in Listing 4-1:

```
<style type="text/css">
  @import url('http://daylightmap.com/moon/phase.css');
</style>
```

This is because of a minor peculiarity in the Netvibes process that embeds your gadget within the page. It appears that `link` elements (like the first syntax shown earlier) are not processed, while `style` elements are. It's a minor change but one you need to be aware of.

■ **Tip** If you find you need any other CSS specifically for Netvibes, you can add it directly in this style block or create another `@import` statement to link it in.

---

meta Tags

In a logical extension to the HTML standard, most of a Netvibes widget's metadata is placed in `meta` elements in the head section. These will be read by the platform when it's assembling both your widget's directory entry and its display on a user's page. The following sections describe the meta tags used by Netvibes; the first two are reused from standard HTML, while the rest are platform-specific.

description

This is a short description of your gadget (see Chapter 2).

keywords

This consists of up to six descriptive words to help users find your widget in the Ecosystem, separated by spaces.

The meta keywords tag has largely fallen into disuse on the wider Web because of its abuse in search engine placement. However, the Ecosystem directory is monitored closely enough to discourage fraud, so it's still worth using keywords in a Netvibes widget.

author

This is your name or organization name.

website

This is the URL of your web site.

version

This is the version number of your widget (free form).

apiVersion

This is the version of the Netvibes platform that your widget was developed for. As of May 2009, the current version is 1.2.

title Element

In a similar manner to the meta tags, Netvibes reuses the HTML title element to contain the gadget's title. Like the meta element's description, your gadget's name should already be in place here.

■ **Note** Netvibes also uses the standard HTML favicon that I already had in place in this gadget.

Preferences

Netvibes provides widgets with persistent storage in the cloud, allowing them to save state across sessions on different client computers. To use this storage, however, it needs to be declared, and this occurs in the Netvibes-specific widget.preferences element. Your widget will need one such element in its head, containing a child preference element for each storage location you plan to use.

Let's look at an example. Recall from Chapter 3 that the Moon Phase gadget uses three storage fields, containing the user preferences for size, hemisphere, and text. Storing these on the Netvibes platform requires the following custom XML block in the gadget's head section (from Listing 4-1):

```
<widget:preferences>
  <preference type="hidden" name="text" />
  <preference type="hidden" name="size" />
```

```
    <preference type="hidden" name="hemisphere" />
</widget:preferences>
```

Each preference tag contains two attributes: the name of the storage field and a type of hidden. The name will need to match the name used in the JavaScript code to access each storage field; I'll be completing that link by extending the crossPlatform.Storage object a bit later in the chapter. And for our purposes, the type is always hidden; because I'm providing my own preference-setting user interface, as detailed in Chapter 3, I use Netvibes' preferences only for the actual data storage.

■ **Note** If your gadget is being deployed only to Netvibes (and possibly iGoogle; see Chapter 5), there are other type values you can use, discussed later in the chapter.

The Inline script Element

The final addition to the gadget's head element is a block of inline JavaScript; because this is in the Netvibes-specific area of the head, code in this script element will execute only when your gadget is running on Netvibes.

You can use this to your advantage to work around peculiarities arising from Netvibes' embedded-HTML architecture. This workaround is based on a function named onLoad in Netvibes' widget namespace, which will be called by the platform when the widget loads, similar to a body onload handler in standard HTML. The code in question looks like this:

```
<script type="text/javascript">
  widget.onLoad = function () {
    widget.body.addClassName('moonPhase');
    widget.body.style.backgroundImage =
      'url(http://daylightmap.com/moon/images/stars_small.jpg)';
  };
</script>
```

Inside the onLoad handler, the workaround itself also utilizes the widget namespace—or more accurately, the widget.body subnamespace. This object is a code construct used to refer to your widget's container div inside the Netvibes page, which (as you'll recall) takes the place of a body element for your widget. Herein lies the heart of the workaround: you call the addClassName function to apply a class attribute to this container div, and the class you apply is the CSS pseudo-namespace from Chapter 2.

This is the primary reason why I recommended using a pseudo-namespace class in your CSS: you need to call addClassName with your chosen name. If this doesn't occur, your namespaced CSS won't be applied to your widget. This is the only practical way to target CSS in Netvibes.

The rest of the workaround is more flexible: in addition to addClassName, you may also be required to set some widget.body.style properties explicitly. Netvibes' pseudo-body architecture generally works quite well, but nonetheless, some body-level style often doesn't get applied correctly—even when using a namespace class instead of body in your CSS. If you find this is happening to your gadget, you'll need to replicate the offending rules here, using JavaScript. In the previous example, the body background image for Moon Phase needed this treatment. And unfortunately, trial and error is the only real way to discover which CSS rules must be reapplied here.

■ **Tip** If your gadget requires any other Netvibes-specific JavaScript, this inline `script` element is the best place for it.

EXTERNAL RESOURCES

The Netvibes documentation recommends avoiding external CSS and JavaScript and instead including them inline in your HTML. I suspect this is for reasons of performance: as discussed in Chapter 2, dozens of widgets on a page, each loading dozens of external resources, could result in hundreds of HTTP requests and a very slow page. And if you were to follow the UWA path and deploy to other platforms from within Netvibes, inline resources would probably work fine.

However, for a true cross-platform gadget, such as deploying natively to more platforms than UWA supports, I still believe that separate files are the only practical course for a maintainable gadget—no more files than you need, granted, but separate files nonetheless.

The problem is that Netvibes tries to enforce its recommendation by ignoring `<link rel="stylesheet">` and `<script src="…">` elements within the document's `head`. So, to use separate files, you need to follow these guidelines:

- For CSS, convert any `<link rel="stylesheet">` elements to `style/@include` syntax, as described in "Importing Stylesheets" earlier in the chapter.

- For JavaScript, ensure that all `<script src="…">` elements are in the `body`, not the `head`, as shown in Listing 4-1.

Adding to crossPlatform

To make your general-purpose gadgets work correctly on Netvibes, you'll also need to extend the crossPlatform middleware layer to support the UWA. This straightforward process is outlined in the following sections and can be found in its entirety in Appendix B.

Platform Detection

Detecting the presence of the Netvibes API is quite easy: it has a global namespace of UWA that no other platform declares. Therefore, Netvibes can be tested for as follows:

```
if (!!window.UWA) {
  // Netvibes Universal Widget API
  crossPlatform.api = 'netvibes';
  crossPlatform.emptyPref = undefined;
}
```

In addition to setting the `crossPlatform.api` property, note that I also initialize `emptyPref` (introduced in Listing 3-7) to undefined, the value that Netvibes returns for an uninitialized preference field.

Persistent Storage

The Netvibes preference interface introduced earlier in the chapter has an extremely straightforward API; wrapping it in the `crossPlatform.Storage` class is thus quite simple. Retrieving a preference by name is accomplished by `widget.getValue`:

```
switch (crossPlatform.api) {
  case 'netvibes':
    myValue = widget.getValue(name);
    break;
  ...
}
```

and saving a preference uses `widget.setValue`:

```
switch (crossPlatform.api) {
  case 'netvibes':
    widget.setValue(myName, myValue);
    break;
  ...
}
```

These code snippets will fit directly into the `Storage` interface defined in Listing 3-7.

Content Retrieval

As with persistent storage, Netvibes' remote content API is an extremely good fit for `crossPlatform`. It has a built-in method, `UWA.Data.getXml`, for retrieving XML data:

```
switch (crossPlatform.api) {
  case 'netvibes':
    UWA.Data.getXml(url, callback);
    break;
  ...
}
```

and for plain-text data, `UWA.Data.getText`:

```
switch (crossPlatform.api) {
  case 'netvibes':
    UWA.Data.getText(url, callback);
    break;
  ...
}
```

Again, these cases will slot right into `crossPlatform.fetchXML` and `fetchText` (from Listing 3-1), respectively.

Testing and Debugging

With the basic code changes in place, it's time to see how well they work, and this means running your repackaged gadget on Netvibes. The first step is to sign up for the service at www.netvibes.com; after registration, you'll be presented with a new Netvibes home page (similar to Figure 4-1). For gadget development, I recommend creating a new tab uncluttered by the various default widgets, where you can more easily work on your own creations. You can see mine, labeled Workshop, also back in Figure 4-1.

■ **Note** In the Netvibes developer documentation, you may see reference to "Standalone mode," a method for running widgets outside www.netvibes.com. Feel free to try it if you want—many developers swear by it—but I've never found it to be an accurate representation of how my widgets will operate on Netvibes.

The only way to add a widget to your page is through the Ecosystem directory, so to test your gadget prior to directory submission, you need an intermediary: the UWA Test Module. This is a generic container widget, created for developers by Netvibes, that allows unlisted gadgets to be shown by URL. To add the Test Module, log into Netvibes, and then browse to www.netvibes.com/subscribe.php?module=UWA. After confirmation, you'll be returned to your Netvibes user page with the Test Module in place; click its Edit link to open the settings pane (Figure 4-2).

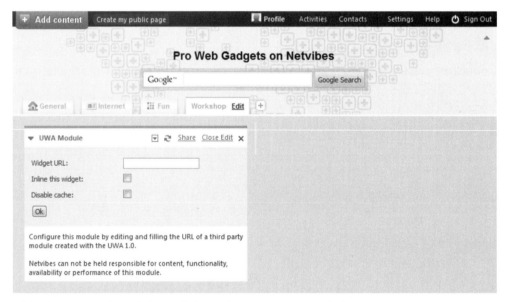

Figure 4-2. The UWA Test Module, ready to display an arbitrary widget

From this point, you simply need to enter the URL of your converted gadget's main HTML page. For current versions of Netvibes, you can safely ignore the "Inline this widget" check box. However, I do recommend that you select the "Disable cache" box. Netvibes will ordinarily cache your source within its CDN, but this control should ensure that your latest source changes will be shown on the page.

With the Test Module configured, you should now see your own gadget on the Netvibes page, just as if you had added it natively from the Ecosystem directory. All functionality should be in place and ready for debugging, though it's not uncommon for a gadget to require some small changes to get it working properly on a new platform. It's up to you to fully unit test your gadget within the Netvibes environment, using your usual web debugging tools and techniques, until your gadget is fully functional.

Deploying to Netvibes

When you're satisfied that your new Netvibes widget is working as intended, it's time to submit it to the Ecosystem for public consumption, publishing it to the wider world of Netvibes users.

Listing in the Ecosystem

The first place to deploy a Netvibes widget is its own Ecosystem directory. To get started, log in to Netvibes, navigate to `http://eco.netvibes.com/widgets`, and click the "Submit widget" button. You'll be asked to enter the URL of your widget's main HTML page and then taken to an "Add information to your widget" page like that shown in Figure 4-3.

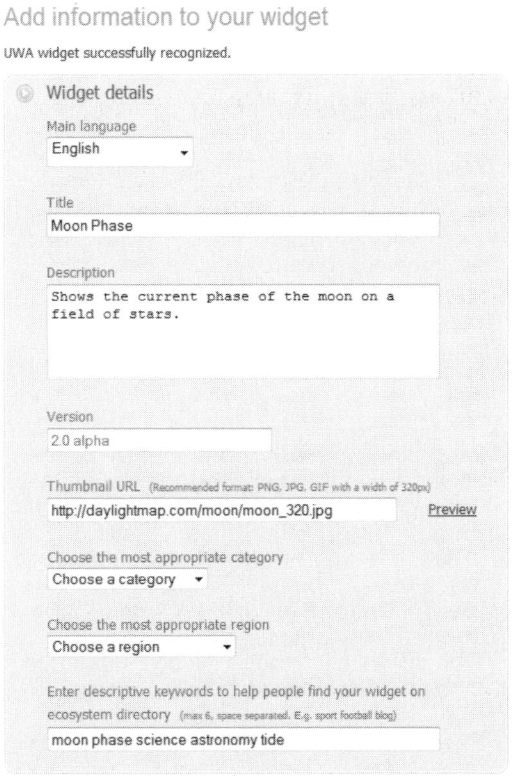

Figure 4-3. Adding information for your widget's listing in the Netvibes Ecosystem

On this page, the title, description, version, and keywords are all taken from your HTML head section (as discussed earlier in the chapter). You can change most of this information here, and it will override the values in your source code. This is an important distinction: the values in your HTML are used for *the widget itself*, while values on this page are for *the directory listing*.

In addition, you have the opportunity to include an image of your gadget, which will be used alongside your widget's entry in Ecosystem listings and search results. Although the official recommendation is for an image 320 pixels wide, the current directory shows only a 64×48-pixel version; other sizes will be scaled to fit by the platform. Therefore, my recommendation is to make sure your screenshot thumbnail has a 4:3 aspect ratio and not concern yourself with trying to exactly meet a 320-pixel width.

Finally, you're required to choose a category and optionally a country (labeled "region" here). These fields help the Ecosystem classify your gadget in its directory.

■ **Tip** Don't worry if you make a mistake on the "Add information to your widget" page; all of these details can be changed later.

You will also be given a "Widget privacy" selection, as in Figure 4-4. In addition to the obligatory terms-of-service agreement, this controls whether your widget is included in the public Ecosystem listings. Although that is the eventual goal, and in theory it should be ready by now, I recommend keeping it unpublished for the time being while you double-check that everything is to your liking. You'll come back and change this setting in a little while, after final testing.

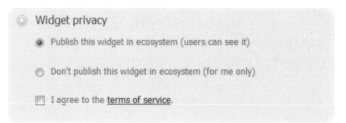

Figure 4-4. Widget privacy controls

After submitting the "Add information to your widget" page, Netvibes will evaluate your entry before they include it in the directory. Assuming your widget works and doesn't contain objectionable content (as described in its terms of service at www.netvibes.com/static.php?show=tos), this should happen quite quickly; the guidelines say to allow three to four hours, but my experience is that it's often complete within minutes. If they do find a problem, Netvibes should contact you directly about resolving it.

Once your widget is approved, it will appear on your developer page of the Ecosystem. To see this page, navigate to http://eco.netvibes.com/widgets again; you should see a "My widgets" link near the top of the page. Clicking this will open a list of all widgets you've submitted to Netvibes. You can open an individual widget's detail page by clicking its name or thumbnail image.

■ **Tip** To see "My widgets," you may need to log in to the Ecosystem separately from your main Netvibes page, though your user ID and password are the same.

Figure 4-5 shows a typical detail page. This is similar to the directory-detail page that any Netvibes user will see for your widget; in addition to a live preview of the widget, it includes installation links and statistics about its use. You can add it to your own page by clicking the "Add to Netvibes" button; I encourage you to do so and test the gadget once more, in its live state, before proceeding.

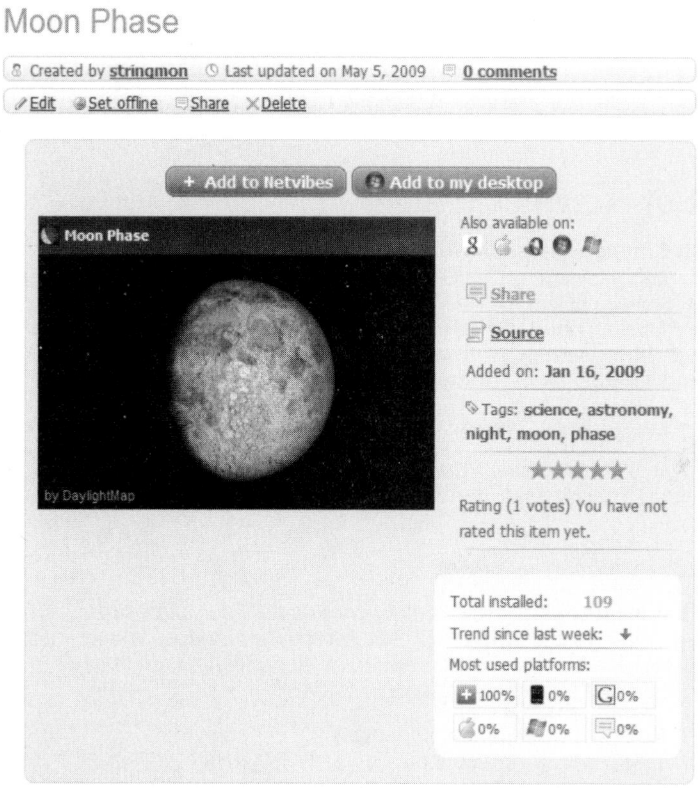

Figure 4-5. A widget detail page in the Ecosystem (widget developer's view)

■ **Note** As mentioned earlier, Netvibes caches the source for live widgets shown on user pages. So if you find a problem at this stage, changes you make to your gadget's source will take up to five minutes to propagate to www.netvibes.com.

As the widget owner, you have a few additional controls on the detail page, in the second toolbar under the main title. Here's what they do:

- *Edit* reopens the "Add information to your widget" page from Figures 4-2 and 4-3, allowing you to modify the directory listing data.

- *Set Offline* hides your widget's directory listing and prevents users from adding it to their Netvibes pages (or other location).

- *Share* opens a configuration page for deploying your widget outside of Netvibes (discussed in the next section).

- *Delete* removes your widget from the Ecosystem directory and should obviously be used with care. Note, however, that it does not delete your widget from user pages where it's already installed.

Once you've tested your live Ecosystem widget and you're happy with both its operation and the appearance of its directory listing, use the Edit button to return to the "Privacy settings" (shown in Figure 4-4), and select Publish.

Promoting Your Netvibes Widget

With your widget listed in the Ecosystem, you'll want to promote its use. It's easy to add a direct link to your widget on your main web site so that site visitors who are also Netvibes users can add your widget to their own page with just a click.

The first step is to locate your widget's unique code in the Ecosystem, usually a six-digit number. You can find your code by navigating to your widget's detail page from `http://eco.netvibes.com/mine`; once there, the code will be visible in the detail page's URL, like this:

`http://eco.netvibes.com/widgets/`**299402**`/moon-phase`

In this example, the code for Moon Phase is 299402. This code is used to build a unique link for installing your widget on a user's page; continuing the example, the URL for installing Moon Phase is as follows:

`http://eco.netvibes.com/subscribe/`**299402**

Obviously, you'll substitute your own six-digit code at the end of this link.

With your code in hand, you're ready to build a link to the Netvibes widget installer from your own site. One approach is to use a button image supplied by Netvibes, as shown in Figure 4-6; this is simply built into a link to your widget's installation page as follows:

```
<a href="http://eco.netvibes.com/subscribe/299402">
  <img width="91" height="20" alt="Add to Netvibes" style="border:none"
      src="http://dev.netvibes.com/forum/style/netvibes/subscribe.png" />
</a>
```

Figure 4-6. The button supplied by Netvibes for adding widgets

Deploying Beyond Netvibes

The first letter of UWA stands for "Universal," and in support of that idea, Netvibes encourages the use of its widgets beyond its borders. This takes two basic forms: a generic container for webmasters and a set of UWA wrappers for other gadget APIs.

The generic widget container is accessed from the Share link mentioned on the Ecosystem detail page (among other places), and it opens a page that allows the user to configure basic gadget parameters and then copy a snippet of HTML code that they can place in their own page. Netvibes calls this *blog distribution*, presumably because that's the dominant type of page such widgets get installed on. In theory, it should work on any web site, with the end result being little different from the `iframe` code technique in Chapter 2.

To implement a UWA widget on other gadget platforms, on the other hand, the user clicks one of the icons located on the Ecosystem detail page under "Also available on" (see Figure 4-5). The available platforms for most widgets are as follows:

- iGoogle
- Mac OS X Dashboard
- Opera
- Windows Vista/7 desktop
- Windows Live.com

Clicking one of these will launch a gadget installation process appropriate to the platform in question.

However, as mentioned earlier, I'm not a strong advocate of either of these techniques for distributing gadgets beyond Netvibes. First, the installed widget comes with Netvibes branding and link, distracting from your own message. And second, the additional Netvibes layer usually means that gadgets distributed in this fashion don't work quite as well as native implementations do. Small bugs frequently creep in that can be hard to find among all the API layers. On the other hand, if you follow the techniques laid out in this book, you'll be positioned to deploy your gadget to each of these platforms directly.

Because there's no way to disable this functionality in the Ecosystem, though, it's always possible that users will take this initiative themselves and install your UWA widget on another platform—even if you have deployed your own version to that platform directly. For this reason, you should ideally test your widget in each of the UWA-wrapper forms and ensure that it is as operational as possible. But in practice, the number of these cross-platform installations seems to be quite low, so such testing is not a top priority.

Using Netvibes-Specific Extensions

If you are deploying a widget only to Netvibes and no other platform, for whatever reason, there are a number of extensions to the core gadget that you can implement. Because such techniques are not portable, they run counter to the cross-platform philosophy that underlies this book, but they can make for a slightly better UWA widget.

Inline Style and Script

The first change is less of an extension, more of an optimization: move your CSS and JavaScript out of external `.css` and `.js` files and into inline `style` and `script` elements in your HTML. This is the technique that Netvibes recommends, and if you're not attempting to support multiple platforms, there's no good reason not to follow Netvibes' advice. Your widget will load somewhat faster, and since the HTML is cached and delivered by Netvibes' CDN, these resources will no longer need to be drawn directly from your server.

Additional Preference Types

As mentioned in Chapter 3, Netvibes provides a user interface for setting preferences, and if you're not deploying to other platforms, you're free to pursue this option. There are a number of advantages:

- Your widget will be a slightly better fit into the user's page, because preferences will be set in a consistent manner with all its other widgets.

- There's no need for you to design and build your own user interface (such as the settings pane from Chapter 3), reducing the complexity of your gadget development effort.

- When installed on blogs (and other independent web pages), your widget will give more control to the webmaster. See the sidebar "Gadget Owners vs. Users" for more details on this issue.

Within your widget, this technique is implemented by changing the `type` attribute of the `preference` elements in the HTML head section. Table 4-1 lists the available preference types, along with the HTML user interface element Netvibes supplies for each. You can see an example of `text` and `boolean` in use in Figure 3-5.

Table 4-1. Supported UWA Preference Types

Type	Description	User Interface
text	An ordinary string value	`<input type="text" />`
password	A concealed string value	`<input type="password" />`
boolean	true or false	`<input type="checkbox" />`
range	An integer within supplied limits	`<select>`
list	A string from a supplied list of values	`<select>`
hidden	A string value used for storage behind the scenes	None

The first three (`text`, `password`, and `boolean`) are quite easy to specify, but `range` and `list` require a bit more XML code within the `preference` element. Since platform-specific features like this aren't the main focus of this book, I won't delve further into the details here, but you can find full information in the UWA documentation (see the next section).

■ **Tip** If you choose to employ these other preference types, you can still use the `crossPlatform.Storage` class to `get` and `set` their values in your JavaScript code.

In addition to making your widget platform-specific, one other drawback to using these preference types is that you lose virtually all control over the user interface. If you want anything more sophisticated than the basic HTML elements of Table 4-1—an autocomplete field, for example, or one field whose possible values depend on another, such as city and state—you will still need to create your own settings pane and store the values in `hidden` preferences.

■ **Note** The Google Gadgets API, covered in Chapter 5, implements preferences in a similar way to Netvibes. Therefore, it is possible to use most of the preference types described in this section (all except `range`) and still deploy to both of these platforms.

GADGET OWNERS VS. USERS

The concept of gadgets being deployed to third-party web sites (such as blogs) raises a subtle issue concerning user preferences: whose preferences should the gadget be using? The distinction is between the gadget *owner* (the webmaster or blogger) and the *user* (the site visitor who is viewing the gadget on her screen).

In most situations, where a gadget is deployed directly to a user's portal page (like Netvibes), desktop, or handheld, there's no difference. The page owner is the same person as the end user, so when that person sets his preferences in your gadget, it's appropriate that the gadget remember them for the next time the page opens.

When the page owner isn't the same person as the user, however, the circumstances become murky. Should the owner be able to preset the preferences so that every site visitor has the same experience from the gadget? Or should the user be able to personalize their own visit and have those preferences remembered when she returns to the site? There's no clear, correct answer that's consistent for all gadgets.

A settings pane within the gadget (as implemented in Chapter 3) takes the latter course, allowing the gadget user (or site visitor) to set preferences. Netvibes' and iGoogle's built-in user interfaces take the former, allowing the webmaster to set the preferences before deploying the gadget to his page.

Unfortunately, there's no especially good cross-platform way to implement preference setting by the page owner. Cross-platform code runs within the gadget itself and therefore is always accessible to the user, the page visitor. If owner-level settings are important to your gadget, one option might be to use the Netvibes user interface described in this section, combined with an in-gadget settings pane for other platforms. Then, hide the control that opens that pane with Netvibes-specific CSS. This should be manageable on both Netvibes and iGoogle, the only two platforms that support third-party web site deployment.

Learning More About Netvibes

This completes my coverage of the UWA, and although the information in this chapter is sufficient to deploy most cross-platform gadgets to Netvibes, there will often be issues that I haven't anticipated. For further information, your best resources are those hosted by Netvibes, in its developer area at `http://dev.netvibes.com`. These are of particular interest:

- Current and complete documentation on the UWA is available at `http://dev.netvibes.com/doc/uwa`.

- News and announcements pertaining to the Netvibes platform appear on the official weblog at `http://dev.netvibes.com/blog`.

- A community of UWA developers, including a good contingent of Netvibes staff, is on the discussion forums at `http://dev.netvibes.com/forum`.

Summary

Netvibes isn't the biggest name in web gadgets, but gadgets are its main business focus, and its solid API is an excellent place to get your first taste of deploying miniature web apps in the real world. In this chapter, you've learned to extend your gadget's HTML to run on `http://netvibes.com`, to debug with the UWA Test Module, and to publish to the Ecosystem. You've also seen the pros and cons of Netvibes' own cross-platform support and preferences user interface.

In Chapter 5, you'll raise your game by setting your sights on the largest web platform, the Google Gadgets API, enabling your gadget to run on a host of Google properties, from iGoogle to Gmail and beyond.

CHAPTER 5

■ ■ ■

iGoogle

There's little doubt that Google is the dominant player in the traditional web gadget space, not only in the number of users reached but also in both the depth and the breadth of its offerings. Google gadgets are unparalleled in the richness of their API, offering greater functionality than any competitor. They are also natively deployable across a host of Google's premium locations, from Gmail to Blogger to Google Maps, giving this platform one of the highest rates of return for your development investment. And not incidentally, this platform has the full might of Google behind it, with active support and development from the web giant. It's the premium web gadget platform.

In this chapter, you'll learn to port your core gadget to this important platform and then deploy it to iGoogle and beyond.

Introducing iGoogle Gadgets

The personalized start page called iGoogle is accessed by users at `www.google.com/ig`; you can see a typical example in Figure 5-1. iGoogle was first introduced in 2005, with an accompanying API for the gadgets it contains. Officially, the platform is known as the Google Gadgets API; however, Google also has an entirely separate Desktop Gadgets API, so to avoid confusion, I'll refer to the subject of this chapter specifically as *iGoogle gadgets*. Although iGoogle gadgets are now supported on a wide variety of Google properties, iGoogle is still their home base. Later in the chapter, I'll discuss in detail all the places you can deploy these gadgets.

There are actually two distinct versions of the iGoogle gadget API. The original API that launched with iGoogle, though much improved since 2005, has been officially deprecated and is on its way out. It's now referred to as the Legacy Gadgets API.

Moving forward, a newer version has been introduced; it doesn't have a specific name, but when developers talk about it, they refer to it as the `gadgets.*` API (from its JavaScript namespace). It essentially contains a superset of the functionality in the Legacy API, but provided in a more organized and consistent package. It's also the basis for OpenSocial, Google's foray into social networking. As of this writing, however, the consumer-facing iGoogle has only just begun to support the `gadgets.*` API, and some other Google gadget containers still do not.

In this chapter, you'll largely be isolated from the specific API implementations by the `crossPlatform` layer, but it's still important to have some idea what's going on beneath the surface. Gadgets built on top of `crossPlatform` are invisibly compatible with both the Legacy and `gadgets.*` APIs, and so they will happily run on all Google containers.

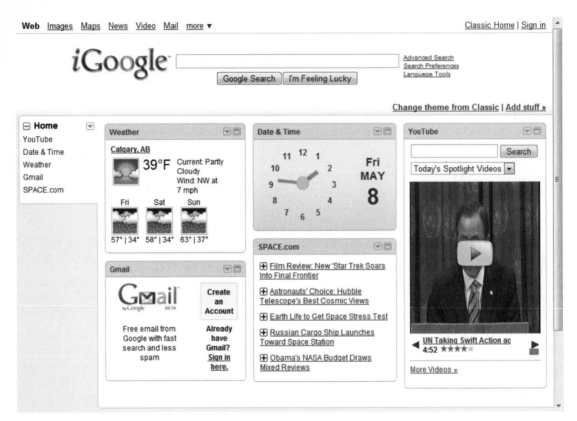

Figure 5-1. *A basic iGoogle user page*

Developing an iGoogle Gadget

The iGoogle API takes the approach of packaging each gadget within an XML document of Google's own specification; in effect, this document takes the place of your own HTML on the platform. Listing 5-1 shows the structure of an extremely simple iGoogle gadget XML document. At a high level, it consists of two primary sections: a *metadata* area, containing the specifications for the gadget, and a *content* area, containing the executable code of the gadget itself.

Listing 5-1. *The "Hello, World" of iGoogle Gadgets*

```
<?xml version="1.0" encoding="UTF-8" ?>
<Module>
  <ModulePrefs title="Hello, World" />
  <Content type="html">
    <![CDATA[
    <p>
      Hello, World!
    </p>
```

```
  ]]>
  </Content>
</Module>
```

In this simple gadget, the metadata area consists solely of a `ModulePrefs` element with a single attribute, `title`. In later examples, you'll see additional attributes for `ModulePrefs`, as well as other metadata elements for the gadget. Google uses these metadata tags both to build the XHMTL page for your gadget and to define your entries in their various gadget directories.

The content area of the gadget is contained in the `Content` element, logically enough, and it holds the HTML that makes your gadget work. Within it, you will generally place the following code from your core gadget's HTML file:

- Any `link`, `style`, or `script` elements from the `head` section that add CSS or JavaScript to your gadget

- The entire contents of the `body` section (but not the body tags themselves)

■ **Note** Because `Content` is an XML element that itself contains XML (in the form of HTML), the whole of its content needs to be wrapped in `<![CDATA[` and `]]>`, as shown in Listing 5-1.

With the metadata and content in place, the gadget is now ready to be rendered. The Google servers will generate HTML for it on the fly, with appropriate `head` elements from the metadata and a body containing the specified content, and place it in an `iframe` on the user's iGoogle page (Figure 5-2). We'll get further into the specifics of structuring the metadata and content areas in the next section of the chapter.

Figure 5-2. The "Hello, World" gadget on iGoogle

From a design standpoint, iGoogle gadgets are much like Netvibes widgets: they're supplied with chrome by the platform, and they're displayed within columns of fixed-percentage width on the page. As a result, gadgets on iGoogle operate within a static width but may determine their own height (note that "Hello, World" could benefit from doing so). A few Google gadget containers impose more stringent width limits, but those will be discussed later in the chapter.

Adapting the Core Gadget

With the broad framework in place, let's look at the specifics of converting a real gadget to work on iGoogle. The foundation is the core HTML gadget from Chapters 2 and 3; on the following pages, I'll detail the steps involved in converting that gadget source to iGoogle XML. As a reference (and a template for your own conversions), Listing 5-2 shows the converted Moon Phase case-study gadget.

Listing 5-2. *The Moon Phase iGoogle Gadget Specification*

```
<?xml version="1.0" encoding="UTF-8"?>
<Module>
  <ModulePrefs title="Moon Phase"
               title_url="http://www.daylightmap.com"
               height="210"
               width="300"
               description="Shows the phase of the moon on a field of stars."
               category="tools"
               screenshot="http://daylightmap.com/moon/images/moon_280.jpg"
               thumbnail="http://daylightmap.com/moon/images/moon_120.jpg"
               directory_title="Moon Phase"
               author="Sterling Udell"
               author_email="sterling.udell+gadgets@gmail.com"
               author_location="North Wales, UK"
               author_affiliation="Udell Enterprises, Inc"
               author_photo="http://gad.getpla.net/images/my_photo.jpg"
               author_aboutme="Free range writer of books and software"
               author_link="http://sterlingudell.com">
    <Icon>http://daylightmap.com/moon/images/moon_16.ico</Icon>
    <Require feature="dynamic-height" />
    <Require feature="setprefs" />
  </ModulePrefs>

  <UserPref datatype="hidden" name="text" />
  <UserPref datatype="hidden" name="size" />
  <UserPref datatype="hidden" name="hemisphere" />

  <Content type="html" view="default,home,profile,preview,canvas">
    <![CDATA[
    <link href="http://daylightmap.com/moon/phase.css"
          type="text/css" rel="stylesheet" />
    <script type="text/javascript">
      document.body.className += ' moonPhase';
    </script>

    <!-- body content goes here -->

    <script src="http://daylightmap.com/moon/platform.js"
            type="text/javascript"></script>
    <script src="http://daylightmap.com/moon/phase.js"
            type="text/javascript"></script>
    ]]>
  </Content>
</Module>
```

The ModulePrefs Element

The bulk of the gadget's metadata is contained in one large element, `ModulePrefs` (short for "module preferences"), traditionally the first tag under the gadget's XML root. As described earlier, `ModulePrefs` contains virtually all the descriptive information *about* your gadget, which Google will use to generate the gadget's container, directory entries, and detail pages.

Attributes

Within the `ModulePrefs` tag itself, a number of attributes contain textual information about the gadget. Strictly speaking, none of the attributes is required, but as a practical matter, several are essential (such as `title`, `description`, and `author`), and you should try to leave out as few of the rest as possible:

title

This is the name of your gadget as it will appear in its header on iGoogle.

directory_title

If supplied, this replaces `title` as your gadget's name in the iGoogle gadget directory.

title_url

This is a web address that `title` (in the gadget's header) will link to. This should be a page related to the gadget.

■ **Note** All URLs in an iGoogle gadget need to be fully qualified (not relative), whether in `ModulePrefs` attributes or elsewhere.

---

height

This is your gadget's preferred height, in pixels.

width

This is your gadget's preferred width, in pixels. It is not often used; width is usually determined by the container.

description

This is a short description of your gadget (see Chapter 2).

category and category2

These two are the classification for your gadget in the directory. Permitted values are `news`, `tools`, `communication`, `funandgames`, `finance`, `sports`, `lifestyle`, `technology`, and `politics`. If your gadget doesn't fit neatly into a single category, you may supply a second in `category2`.

author

This is your name.

author_email

This is your e-mail address. Note that this isn't protected against spam harvesters in directory listings. Google recommends that you use a Gmail address with +some_string appended to your login name, such as sterling.udell+gadgets@gmail.com; this affords some protection against spam.

author_location

This is a string describing your locale.

author_affiliation

This is your employer or other group you represent.

author_photo

This is a URL of a photo online, used on your iGoogle developer page.

author_aboutme

This is a sentence or two describing who you are.

author_link

This is the URL of your home page or other website, used on your iGoogle developer page.

screenshot and thumbnail

These are two URLs of images to be associated with your gadget in the iGoogle directory (see the next section).

Gadget Graphics

An iGoogle gadget is represented by up to three different graphics in various contexts, all specified within the ModulePrefs element. Table 5-1 lists the comparative details for each.

Table 5-1. iGoogle Gadget Metagraphics

	Location	Width	Height	Usage
screenshot	Attribute	280px	Variable	Directory detail page
thumbnail	Attribute	120px	60px	Directory listings (visible in Figure 5-4)
Icon	Subelement	16–64px	16–64px	Gadget page on certain containers

All of these graphics are specified as full URLs to files on a publicly available web server that is not blocked by a `robots.txt` file. The files may be of type png (preferred), jpg, or gif; Icon may also be of type ico.

■ **Note** The `Icon` element is not yet widely supported in the Google ecosystem; it's primarily for future use.

Require Elements

After `Icon`, the remaining subelements within `ModulePrefs` are `Require` tags. In the API definition, these elements specify optional libraries that your gadget can choose to include for additional functionality, beyond the core Gadgets API.

For gadgets using the `crossPlatform` layer described in this book, the following two `Require` elements are needed and should always be included in the XML:

```
<Require feature="dynamic-height" />
<Require feature="setprefs" />
```

There are other libraries available for specific functionality, but because they only exist in the iGoogle API, they're of little use when building a cross-platform gadget.

The UserPref Elements

After the `ModulePrefs` element, there's one last metadata section required for most gadgets. This is comprised of one or more `UserPref` elements, and as their name implies, they're employed to specify user preferences. Your gadget will need one `UserPref` element for each `crossPlatform.Storage` object that it instantiates in JavaScript; these instruct the Google platform to create the required mechanisms for persisting your data between sessions.

As an example, Moon Phase creates three `Storage` objects, for size, hemisphere, and text visibility. Correspondingly, the Moon Phase iGoogle gadget needs to specify three `UserPrefs` elements in its XML (from Listing 5-2):

```
<UserPref datatype="hidden" name="text" />
<UserPref datatype="hidden" name="size" />
<UserPref datatype="hidden" name="hemisphere" />
```

The `name` attribute here must equal the `name` parameter supplied to each `Storage` object, and for our purposes, the `datatype` attribute will always be hidden. With these declarations in your XML and the appropriate extensions made to `crossPlatform` (discussed later in the chapter), the `Storage` class should be ready for use.

The Content Element

The metadata is now behind us, so what remains is the gadget proper, the code that actually makes your mini web app work. This is all contained within the XML's `Content` element and is described in the following sections. Before we get to that, however, the opening `Content` tag has a couple of attributes that deserve a mention.

```
<Content type="html" view="default,home,profile,preview,canvas">
```

The first is type, and for gadgets following the cross-platform guidelines in this book, this will usually be html. See the "type="url" Gadgets" sidebar (in a couple of pages) for details on the other type, url, which you may occasionally find to be a useful alternative.

The other Content attribute is view, and it specifies which presentation modes the gadget supports. A cross-platform gadget should almost always include the first four listed here: default, home, profile, and preview. These are the common views supported across most Google properties and OpenSocial containers; supplying this list should ensure that your gadget renders properly in all locations.

There is one additional view, however, that merits special consideration: canvas. This is a maximized, "giant gadget" view supported by iGoogle and a few other containers; when selected, your gadget is allowed to display across nearly all of the user's browser window. It's essentially a full-screen view for your gadget.

If such a full-screen mode doesn't make sense for your particular gadget—if its content can't realistically scale to utilize many hundreds of pixels in each direction—then it's best to leave canvas out of the view attribute. iGoogle will disable canvas mode accordingly, simply showing a slightly larger view when the user clicks Maximize. However, if your gadget is coded to detect size changes and scale appropriately, include canvas in the view list (as shown in the Content tag earlier, and in Listing 5-2). This will enable canvas mode and allow your gadget users to interact with your content on a grand scale, as shown in Figure 5-3.

Figure 5-3. Moon Phase in canvas mode

■ **Tip** To invoke canvas mode, click the rectangular icon in the upper-right corner of a gadget's frame.

There's also one additional option here. It's possible to specify multiple Content elements for different views, and with this approach, an entirely different set of content can be served in canvas mode. Listing 5-3 shows how this is done, in outline form. The rules for each Content element are the same as for a single one; any legal HTML content can be used. I don't generally recommend this approach, because your maintenance burden is multiplied by having multiple Content elements. But if your gadget can't scale internally, delivering different content altogether is an option to consider.

Listing 5-3. A Gadget with Multiple Content Elements

```
<?xml version="1.0" encoding="UTF-8" ?>
<Module>
  <ModulePrefs title="Multiple Views" />
  <Content type="html" view="default,home,profile,preview ">
    <!-- HTML for small mode (ordinary gadget size) goes here -->
  </Content>
  <Content type="html" view="canvas">
    <!-- HTML for canvas mode (full-screen size) goes here -->
  </Content>
</Module>
```

TYPE="URL" GADGETS

Google provides an additional content type, url, primarily as a shortcut for migrating native HTML web pages and applications to iGoogle gadgets. In essence, the url type creates an additional iframe layer, containing any page whose URL you supply. No conversion to XML (or other manipulation) is required of you.

For example, to package the native Moon Phase gadget from Chapter 2 as a type="url" gadget, the following code would be required (leaving out the cosmetic metadata for brevity):

```
<?xml version="1.0" encoding="UTF-8"?>

<Module>

   <ModulePrefs title="Moon Phase"

             height="210"

             width="300" />

   <Content type="url" view="default,home,profile,preview,canvas"

             href="daylightmap.com/moon/phase.html" />

</Module>
```

That's it! It's extremely simple—you supply the href attribute, and Google does the rest.

Unfortunately, it's a bit too simple. The problem is that many of the best features of the iGoogle platform, most noticeably persistent storage and content retrieval, are not available to `type="url"` gadgets. So, for such a gadget to be practical, it needs to be fully self-contained, like the Moon Phase of Chapter 2 was.

One circumstance where `type="url"` can be quite useful, however, is in conjunction with canvas mode. If your native gadget doesn't scale well to full-screen, one option is to create a second `Content` element that points canvas mode back to your main web site. The code to do so would be structured like this (compare with Listing 5-3):

```
<?xml version="1.0" encoding="UTF-8" ?>

<Module>

  <ModulePrefs title="Multiple Views" />

  <Content type="html" view="default,home,profile,preview ">

    <!-- HTML for small mode (ordinary gadget size) goes here -->

  </Content>

  <Content type="url" view="canvas"

          href="http://mydomain.com/path/to/web.app" />

</Module>
```

The underlying rationale is that if your gadget is a miniaturized view of your main web app and in canvas mode it's no longer miniaturized, you might as well redirect it back to your main web app. This won't work in all circumstances, of course—issues such as persistent storage are still problematic—but it can be a useful tool to have at your disposal.

Linked Resources

The bulk of the code within the `Content` element of Listing 5-2 is lifted directly from your core gadget's body, but first we need to bring in a bit from its head. Generally, what's required are any `link`, `style`, or `script` elements that apply CSS or JavaScript to the gadget. These should be copied directly into the Content section of the iGoogle gadget's XML.

For the Moon Phase gadget of Listing 5-2, this means only a single `link` tag:

```
<link type="text/css" rel="stylesheet"
      href="http://daylightmap.com/moon/phase.css" />
```

■ **Note** Observe that the style sheet's URL is fully qualified, as all network addresses in an iGoogle gadget must be.

If your gadget has any other head content, apart from metadata that went into `ModulePrefs`, you'll probably need to import those elements here as well.

The Inline script Element

While I'm on the subject of CSS, there's one additional bit of markup required to make this iGoogle gadget function correctly with the existing core HTML code. Recall that in Chapter 2, I recommended that you use a CSS pseudo-namespace, applied as a class for your body tag:

```
<body class="moonPhase">
```

However, the iGoogle platform creates its own body tag for you, and by default it won't have the class name you require. So in order for the CSS to be applied, you need to rectify this situation. A single line of JavaScript is sufficient:

```
<script type="text/javascript">
  document.body.className += ' moonPhase';
</script>
```

■ **Caution** Take careful note of the syntax here: the += operator and the extra space at the beginning of the string (before moonPhase). These will ensure that your namespace class is added to any class name that iGoogle may have already applied to the body, rather than replacing it.

As you can see, it simply applies the CSS namespace class to the body element created by the platform. Obviously, you'll need to substitute your own CSS namespace for moonPhase when you insert this code into your own gadget.

■ **Tip** If your gadget requires any iGoogle-specific JavaScript of its own, this inline script element is an excellent place for it.

---

body Content

After the inline script, you're finally ready to import the gadget's main HTML code. This should be a simple matter of copying all content from your core gadget's body element into the bottom of your iGoogle gadget's Content section. Don't forget to ensure that any relative URLs are converted to absolute!

Completing Your XML

The structure of your gadget XML should now be finished; there are just a couple of housekeeping items to verify before continuing.

The first has to do with your XML file's character encoding. Google requires that your gadget specification be encoded as UTF-8, so you'll need to ensure that your text editor, version control system, and any other software that touches your XML source is configured accordingly. Related to this, make sure that you don't have any characters in your XML with the wrong encoding or that aren't properly represented as XML entities. Your gadget can fail the iGoogle directory submission in either case.

And second, if you're having trouble at any point trying to display or list your gadget on iGoogle, it's worth checking that your XML is valid. One good tool for doing so is the W3C's markup validation service at http://validator.w3.org; another (the Gadget Checker) will be discussed later in the chapter.

Additions to crossPlatform

For the converted gadget to fully work on all of Google's gadget containers, the crossPlatform interface layer will also need extending. For the most part, this is quite straightforward, but there are a few aspects that will keep you on your toes.

The next section, "Platform Detection," will be beneficial for all developers using crossPlatform to target iGoogle; it contains important details for determining which container your gadget is running within. The latter sections here are primarily of interest if you're implementing (or troubleshooting) your own crossPlatform equivalent or are especially interested in the internals. If you're simply using crossPlatform as is, they're not required reading.

Platform Detection

The biggest challenge in modifying the middleware layer for Google compatibility is sifting through the intricacies of exactly which platform we're running on. This is the job of the platform-detection code, and for this chapter it will need a considerable extension.

Because the iGoogle gadget platform is really two APIs in one, we first have the double task of detecting (and differentiating) the two of them. Listing 5-4 contains the initial code to do so.

Listing 5-4. Platform-Detection Code for the Two iGoogle Gadget APIs

```
if (!!window.gadgets && !!window.gadgets.util) {
  crossPlatform.api     = 'igoogle';
  crossPlatform.version = 'gadgets.*';
  crossPlatform.prefs   = new gadgets.Prefs();
} else if (!!window._gel) {
  crossPlatform.api     = 'igoogle';
  crossPlatform.version = 'legacy';
  crossPlatform.prefs   = new _IG_Prefs();
}
```

As usual, we accomplish the detection by looking for the existence of API-specific objects—two in this case, one for each API—and because the gadgets.* API is a superset of the Legacy API, it's important that the tests be done in this order, because this means that any Legacy object (such as _gel) exists in gadgets.* as well.

Also note that I'm setting a couple of new variables in the crossPlatform namespace, version and prefs. The former simply denotes which iGoogle API version is in use, while the latter is an intermediate object that will be used for saving state. I'll discuss it further in the next section.

We're not done yet, though. Gadgets built to Google's API can run in many different places, and although the fundamental platform is the same, there are still subtle differences that sometimes require container-specific coding. To enable this, I set an additional variable of container to a string describing the current gadget host container. You can see this additional "container detection" in Listing 5-5.

Listing 5-5. Detecting the Google Gadget Host

```
if (crossPlatform.api === 'igoogle') {
  crossPlatform.emptyPref = '';
  crossPlatform.host = '';
  if (window._args instanceof Function) {
    crossPlatform.container = _args().synd || _args().container;
  }
  switch (crossPlatform.container) {
    case 'calendar':     break;
    case 'spreadsheets': break;
    case 'ig':           crossPlatform.container = 'igoogle';  break;
    case 'gm':           crossPlatform.container = 'mail';     break;
    case 'mpl':          crossPlatform.container = 'maps';     break;
    case 'gd':           crossPlatform.container = 'desktop';  break;
    case 'myaolgrs':     crossPlatform.container = 'my.aol';   break;
    case 'gasp2':
      crossPlatform.container = 'start';
      crossPlatform.host      = _args().pid;
      break;
    case 'enterprise':
      crossPlatform.container = 'sites';
      crossPlatform.host      = document.referrer.split('/').splice(0, 2).join('/');
      break;
    default:
      if (/^navclient/.test(crossPlatform.host)) {
        // Catches any 'navclient_xx' hosts, known (ff, ie) or unknown
        crossPlatform.container = 'toolbar';
      } else {
        // Catches blank container strings, 'blogger', 'open', and any new ones
        crossPlatform.container = (crossPlatform.container || 'unknown');
        crossPlatform.host      = document.referrer.split('/')[2];
      }
  }
}
```

It relies on a couple of API internals; first, it looks for a function named _args(), which returns URL arguments. This function is used to test for URL arguments of synd and container; every Google gadget container supplies one of these two parameters, containing a unique string identifying the host container. I then test for key values of this string in a switch statement and set my own container variable to a more user-friendly string. Most of the possible values for crossPlatform.container are highlighted in Listing 5-5, but be aware that new ones will appear if Google adds more gadget containers. The specific containers associated with each of these strings are described later in the chapter in the "Deploying iGoogle Gadgets" section.

In some cases (start, sites, toolbar, open, blogger, and unknown), the named host container is just an intermediary, displaying your gadget for a different top-level page. In these cases, I also extract the top-level host and save it in another variable: crossPlatform.host. Note that, in many cases, host will be a domain name and so will not be limited to a few discrete, predictable values as container is.

To use the container variable, simply test it against one of the highlighted values in Listing 5-4. For example, for code specific to a mapplet (which runs on Google Maps, with a container value of maps), you could use a test like this:

```
if (crossPlatform.host === 'maps') {
  // Mapplet-specific code goes here
}
```

Persistent Storage

The dual nature of the iGoogle gadgets API that made platform detection more difficult also complicates the interface to the platform's persistent storage mechanism. As noted for Listing 5-4, crossPlatform actually instantiates a different internal object for each API: _IG_Prefs for the Legacy API and gadgets.Prefs for the newer gadgets.* namespace.

■ **Note** In the Legacy API, the prefix of _IG_ functioned as a primitive pseudo-namespace, before the real gadgets.* namespace was introduced.

After these objects are created, however, fortune swings in our direction: Google didn't change the preference programming interface when it renamespaced the API. In other words, the _IG_Prefs and gadgets.Prefs objects use identical methods for getting and setting preferences. So, the crossPlatform code to retrieve a preference value looks like this:

```
switch (crossPlatform.api) {
  case 'igoogle':
    myValue = crossPlatform.prefs.getString(name);
    break;
  ...
}
```

and because both APIs' preference objects have a getString method, this call works in both cases. Similarly, both objects use a simple set method, so the call to save a preference can be unified as follows:

```
switch (crossPlatform.api) {
  case 'igoogle':
    crossPlatform.prefs.set(myName, myValue);
    break;
  ...
}
```

■ **Caution** Google sends prefs values to the gadget as URL parameters—so if the amount of data is too large, the URL can get corrupted, and the client gadget can cease to work. So, try to keep your Storage values under 2KB.

Content Retrieval

We're less fortunate when it comes to content retrieval; here, the programming interface was completely rewritten when Google introduced the gadgets.* namespace. As a result, the crossPlatform.fetchXML and fetchText methods need to branch for the two APIs; the code for this is outlined in Listing 5-6.

Listing 5-6. crossPlatform Content Retrieval Functions for iGoogle

```
crossPlatform.fetchXML = function (url, callback) {
  switch (crossPlatform.api) {
    case 'igoogle':
      if (crossPlatform.version === 'legacy') {
        _IG_FetchXmlContent(url, callback);
      } else {
        gadgets.io.makeRequest(url, function (response) {callback(response.data);},
          {'CONTENT_TYPE': gadgets.io.ContentType.DOM});
      }
      break;
    ...
  }
};

crossPlatform.fetchText = function (url, callback) {
  switch (crossPlatform.api) {
    case 'igoogle':
      if (crossPlatform.version === 'legacy') {
        _IG_FetchContent(url, callback);
      } else {
        gadgets.io.makeRequest(url, callback);
      }
      break;
    ...
  }
};
```

Resizing

Since iGoogle gadgets are contained in iframes, any change to their content size requires some special handling; without it, the containing iframe wouldn't change size, and the new content wouldn't fit correctly. Google accounts for this by supplying height-adjusting functions in its APIs; these get linked into your gadget page, and when called, they relay the current size of the content up to the container page, where a companion function resizes the iframe to fit.

■ **Note** Remember that iGoogle gadgets have a fixed width, so height is the only dimension that can be adjusted by the gadget.

In the context of `crossPlatform`, these functions will be encapsulated in the `adjustSize` method, as such:

```
crossPlatform.adjustSize = function () {
  switch (crossPlatform.api) {
    case 'igoogle':
      if (crossPlatform.version === 'legacy') {
        _IG_AdjustIFrameHeight();
      } else if (!!gadgets.window) {
        gadgets.window.adjustHeight();
      }
      break;
    ...
  }
};
```

As described in the "Size-Related Functions" section of Chapter 3, `crossPlatform.adjustSize` should be called by your gadget code whenever a change to its content affects the screen area it consumes.

■ **Caution** Don't forget, a call to `adjustSize` should never be placed in an `onresize` event handler, or unbounded recursion is likely to result.

Testing and Debugging

The first version of the iGoogle gadget code should now be ready to test. Although it may eventually be deployed to many different containers, its native habitat is iGoogle, and that's the best place to begin testing. You'll likely want to check it on other platforms also, as described later in the chapter, but start here first. Not only is iGoogle the reference container for the APIs, but it has the most comprehensive set of debugging tools.

Using iGoogle requires a Google account. If you already have one (for Gmail, Docs, or other services), sign into it and navigate to www.google.com/ig. If you don't yet have an account, a link at that same URL should get you started. In either case, I recommend creating a dedicated tab on your iGoogle page for gadget development.

Adding Gadgets to iGoogle

The primary way to add a gadget to your iGoogle page is through the content directory; this is accessed via the Add Stuff link toward the upper-right of your iGoogle home page. This link, and the directory it accesses, is even used for gadgets that aren't listed in the directory, such as gadgets under development. Figure 5-4 shows a typical view of the gadget directory.

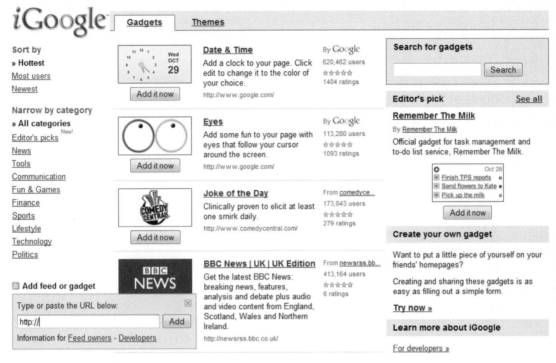

Figure 5-4. *The iGoogle gadget directory*

To add a listed gadget, the usual route is to search or browse to it in the directory and then click the Add It Now button attached to the gadget's listing. However, it's also possible to add any gadget (listed or not) if you have the URL of its XML source file; simply click the Add Feed or Gadget link at the lower left of the directory page, and enter the desired gadget's URL in the box provided. This is generally how you'll add your gadget for testing: upload its XML (and any other source files, such as JavaScript and CSS files) to a public web server, and enter its URL here.

■ **Note** Whenever you add a gadget to iGoogle, you'll see a brief warning about risks of installing a third-party gadget; this is an acknowledgment by Google that security is not fundamental to the gadget ecosystem.

Once you have your prototype gadget installed on your iGoogle, a useful debugging technique is to load it independently. This allows you to refresh the gadget and inspect its code without the overhead of the iGoogle infrastructure, and it's possible because each gadget is loaded in a iframe. To do this, you'll need the iframe's source URL; this is easiest in Firefox and Chrome, where you can right-click in the gadget on iGoogle for options like "Open frame in new tab" or "Display only this frame."

■ **Caution** Make sure you disable caching (using the iGoogle Developer Gadget; see the next section) *before* opening it independently.

Utilizing the Developer Gadgets

Before you get too deep into debugging *your* gadget, however, there are a few *other* gadgets that I suggest you also add to your iGoogle page. The following have all been produced by Google to ease the process of developing gadgets; you can add them by either of the methods described earlier.

My Gadgets

`http://www.google.com/ig/modules/developer.xml`

Also known as the Developer Gadget, this must-have module's main function is to disable the gadget caching built into iGoogle. Without this gadget, any changes you make to your XML will have to filter through the iGoogle cache before they appear on your page, which typically takes one to two hours. It's no overstatement that the Developer Gadget makes gadget development possible.

When you add this gadget to your page, it will show a list of all the gadgets on that tab, with a Cached check box for each (see Figure 5-5). Deselect the box for all gadgets you're actively working on, and every time you refresh the page, iGoogle will also refresh your gadgets' source.

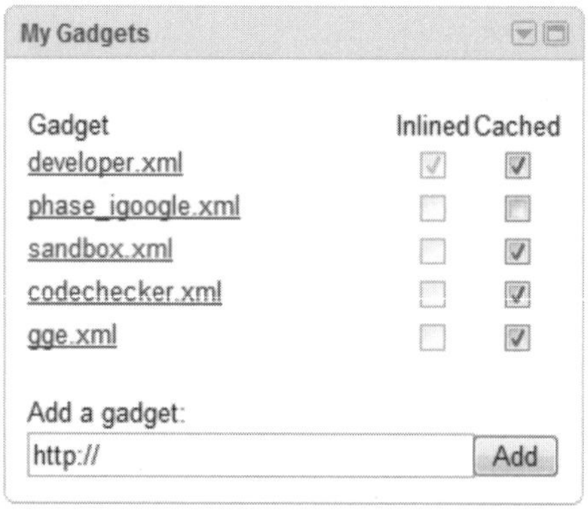

Figure 5-5. *My Gadgets, also known as the iGoogle Developer Gadget*

The Developer Gadget also has a few other tricks. The gadget file names shown in its list are links to the XML being shown on iGoogle, which allows you to directly click through to an XML source file and confirm that it's the one you were expecting. Also, when you hover your mouse pointer over one of these links, the corresponding gadget is highlighted on your page. Finally, there's a control at the bottom for adding any gadget to your page by entering its URL; this saves you a few clicks when you have a new gadget to test.

Google Gadget Editor

`http://www.google.com/ig/modules/gge.xml`

The Gadget Editor, shown in Figure 5-6, is basically a small text editor built directly into a gadget. As such, it supports all the common editor functions, such as cut, copy, and paste, as well as file operations such as load and save. What makes it useful to developers, however, is its Preview tab; enter the XML source for any gadget into the editor, and you can instantly see that gadget in action just by changing tabs.

In addition, the Gadget Editor has capabilities to upload files from your local computer, to open gadget source files by URL, and to use popular examples as templates when creating new gadgets. Taken together, these features make the Gadget Editor extremely useful for rapid prototyping of gadget modifications and new concepts; with just a few clicks, you can try a new gadget idea in a live environment. During this prototyping stage, the Gadget Editor also removes the need for uploading source after every code change.

■ **Caution** The Google Gadget Editor can be flaky on minority browsers such as Opera, and specifically doesn't support WebKit-based browsers like Safari and Chrome. I recommend that you use it primarily from Firefox or Internet Explorer.

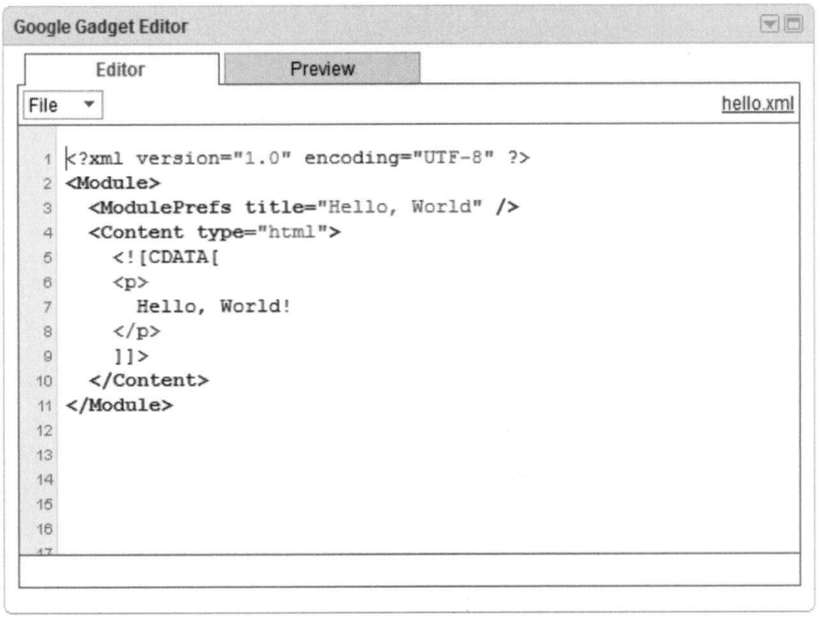

Figure 5-6. The Google Gadget Editor

Gadget Checker

http://www.google.com/ig/modules/codechecker/codechecker.xml

This new addition to Google's developer gadget line-up is a sort of validator for gadget source code (Figure 5-7). In addition to running basic tests for well-formed XML, it also checks your code for many common gadget problems and issues errors or warnings as appropriate. It even offers links to the appropriate API documentation for most problems that it flags.

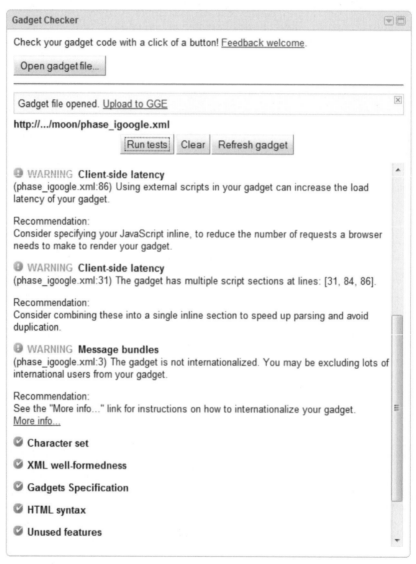

Figure 5-7. *The Gadget Checker*

As with all validators, however, results from the Gadget Checker should be taken with a grain of salt. Many excellent gadgets (with thousands of users) will display a host of "problems" when the Gadget Checker runs its tests; by the same token, not every "problem" it flags is worth "fixing" for every gadget. As an example, gadgets written to my recommendations in this book will generate the warnings about client-side latency shown in Figure 5-7; these result from the use of external JavaScript and CSS resources. As discussed in Chapter 2, my opinion is that the trade-off of latency vs. maintainability is worthwhile, but the Gadget Checker does not agree.

Deploying iGoogle Gadgets

Once your gadget is working well on iGoogle, the logical next step is to submit it to Google's gadgets directory, the location from which the majority of gadgets are installed. The actual submission process is quite simple: navigate to `www.google.com/ig/submit`, enter the URL of your gadget's XML specification, and click the Send button. Assuming you have included all the recommended `ModulePrefs` metadata attributes and worked out any major problems flagged by the Gadget Checker, all that's left for you to do is wait.

Unfortunately, there's quite a lot of waiting. Google updates its directory only every one to two weeks, so at a minimum, it will probably be that long before you see your gadget appear. There's also no feedback mechanism, so the only way to know if your gadget has been listed is to manually look for it yourself.

■ **Note** The same time frame—one to two weeks—applies to any changes made to your gadget metadata after it has been listed in the directory, so modifications to your `author*` attributes (and so forth) will take that long to be applied.

When it does appear, in addition to listing it in the general directory, Google will create a developer page for you; your listed gadgets will also be shown there. Developer pages have a URL like this:

`http://www.google.com/ig/directory?type=authors&url=`**`sterling.udell@gmail.com`**

with your own e-mail address (from your gadget's `author_email` ModulePrefs attribute) in the `url` parameter.

■ **Tip** It's important that all your gadgets have the same `author_email` value, or you'll end up with multiple developer pages.

Additionally, Google warns that it doesn't list all gadgets in its directory, but only those that exceed an undisclosed threshold number of users. My experience is that this number is fairly small—probably no more than 10 or 20 users—but nonetheless, this means that you'll need to promote your gadget externally before it will be listed in the iGoogle directory.

The primary way to do this is by placing a link to your gadget in places where your existing visitors will see it, enabling them to add the new gadget to their own iGoogle pages with just a click. The basic link looks like this:

`http://www.google.com/ig/adde?moduleurl=`**`http://yourdomain.com/path/to/gadget.xml`**

with the actual URL of your gadget substituted into the `moduleurl` parameter, of course.

A good way to include this link on your own page is with an Add to Google button. Google supplies an image for your use in constructing such a button (see Figure 5-8); to use it, place HTML code like the following on your web site:

```
<a href="http://www.google.com/ig/adde?moduleurl=your_gadget_url">
  <img width="104" height="17" alt="Add to iGoogle" style="border:none"
      src="http://buttons.googlesyndication.com/fusion/add.gif" />
</a>
```

Figure 5-8. *The Add to Google button*

Other Gadget Containers

One of the main attractions to Google gadgets is that they can be rolled out to many more locations than iGoogle. The following sections detail the major Google gadget containers at the time of this writing. Although new containers are added fairly frequently, if your gadget works well on a majority of those listed here, it should be well positioned to move onto new properties. However, don't lose sight of the fact that iGoogle accounts for the vast majority of gadget installs and thus should remain your primary focus.

■ **Note** For each container, I've included the value of `crossPlatform.container`, as discussed in relation to Listing 5-5.

Branded Start Pages

`crossPlatform.container = 'start'`

Closely related to iGoogle is a series of custom-branded start pages that Google has produced in partnership with various computer retailers. As part of joint marketing agreements, these vendors ship systems with their default browser home page set to this branded version of iGoogle. Current examples of this include www.google.com/ig/dell and www.google.com/ig/gateway.

■ **Note** For gadgets running on a branded start page, my middleware layer places the name of the partner (such as `dell` or `gateway`) into the `crossPlatform.host` variable.

Essentially, these start pages are nothing more than re-skinned versions of iGoogle; they don't have independent logins but share the same Google account as the search giant's other services. This means that you don't need to have purchased a Dell or Gateway computer to access them; you can simply browse to the appropriate URL, and your existing Google account will be used.

Because they're so similar to iGoogle, the functionality of gadgets is usually no different. They also draw from the same gadget directory as iGoogle; since users of these pages can therefore add your gadget, you should at least confirm that your gadgets work properly on them. You can do so by clicking a link labeled Add by URL, which you'll find near the top of their directory pages, and entering the address of your gadget's XML.

■ **Tip** If you find that some container-specific debugging is necessary here, the same iGoogle developer gadgets described earlier in the chapter can also be added to branded start pages.

If you have need to build a link that will install your gadget directly onto one of these branded start pages, you can do so with a link like this:

```
http://www.google.com/ig/adde?pid=dell&synd=dell&moduleurl=your_gadget_url
```

Naturally, you'll need to substitute your actual gadget address your_gadget_url and the name of the partner page in question for dell.

MyAOL

```
crossPlatform.container = 'my.aol'
```

Another twist on the branded start page is myAOL, a custom portal for AOL users that's also powered by Google. Located at http://my.aol.com, it's visually similar to the branded start pages of hardware vendors, and it serves a similar purpose in the marketplace.

However, behind the scenes, it uses a significantly different gadget engine. MyAOL is based on the gadgets.* namespace and integrates a much higher degree of caching for external resources (like JavaScript, CSS, and images). I'll be discussing such caching in more depth later in the chapter, but for now be aware that myAOL is actually further along this curve than other Google-based containers, and some of my advanced caching techniques actually conflict with this host.[1]

MyAOL is primarily intended for AOL members, so to fully explore this platform, you'll need to sign up for a free AOL account on its web site. However, it's possible to test some basic features of myAOL without a membership; simply go ahead and add your gadget by its URL. Unfortunately, the standard developer gadgets don't work here (and AOL hasn't provided equivalents), so you're somewhat on your own for debugging gadget problems.

This portal also draws its gadgets from the independent myAOL Gallery, rather than the default iGoogle directory, so if you want your gadget to be listed for myAOL users, you'll need to submit it at http://dev.my.aol.com.

Google Sites and Apps

```
crossPlatform.container = 'sites'
```

Hardware and software vendors aren't the only ones that can have custom start pages powered by Google; with Google Sites, the facility to create a custom web site in the cloud is open to everyone. Users

---

[1] It's worth noting that several aspects of the MyAOL architecture are newer than the iGoogle mainstream, such as its use of the gadgets.* namespace and also certain details of its iframe hosting infrastructure. As such, MyAOL may be a harbinger of things to come in the iGoogle ecosystem; issues that occur now in MyAOL (such as caching conflicts) may crop up elsewhere with time.

of Google Sites can add a variety of content to their pages—including iGoogle gadgets—and then publish them, either under `http://sites.google.com/sites` or a domain of their choosing.

Closely related to Google Sites is Google Apps (formerly known as Google Apps For Your Domain, abbreviated GAFYD). Essentially, Google Apps is Google Sites for organizations rather than individuals, targeted mainly at nonprofits and SMEs. The sign-up and access policies are slightly different, but the content hosting functionality is all but identical.

■ **Note** As with the branded start pages in the previous section, I use `crossPlatform.host` with Google Sites, this time to store the domain from which the page is being served.

In both cases, gadgets are installed when the site owner is editing a page by clicking the More link under the Gadgets section of the Insert menu (see Figure 5-9). This accesses the same gadget directory as iGoogle (albeit with a different user interface), including an "Add gadget by URL" link that you can use for testing your own gadgets.

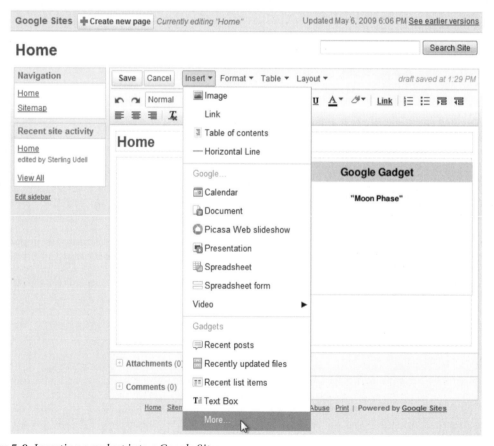

Figure 5-9. Inserting a gadget into a Google Sites page

Most gadgets won't require any special handling to function on Google Sites and Apps, but if your testing does turn up problems, they can be somewhat difficult to resolve. This is because there's no built-in way to disable the Google gadget cache for these containers, as the Developer Gadget will for iGoogle. Your best bet is to take control of the cache from the client side yourself; see the "Caching" section in Chapter 3 for more details.

Blogger

`crossPlatform.container = `**`'blogger'`**

Of course, one of the most popular types of web site is the blog, and Google makes gadgets available to webmasters here as well. This can be a great way to get substantial traffic for your gadget; popular blogs have many thousands of readers, so if your gadget adds value for the blog author, Blogger can be an effective springboard for your content.

As with Google Sites, Apps, and branded start pages, Blogger draws from the same gadget directory as iGoogle. When editing the page layout, the author simply clicks the Add a Gadget link in the sidebar and can then select a gadget either by browsing the directory or by entering its URL directly.

■ **Note** For gadgets on Blogger, `crossPlatform.host` has the domain from which the page is being served, such as `sterlingudell.blogspot.com`.

Blogger is a bit of a challenging environment for iGoogle gadgets, however. For a start, it's far less accepting of minor irregularities in the XML source code than most of Google's other gadget containers. Before even attempting to deploy a gadget to Blogger, ensure that your XML is well-formed and properly encoded, using the Gadget Checker and an XML validator. It's also mandatory here that your `Content` elements contain all five `view` attributes (`default,home,profile,preview,canvas`) as described earlier in the chapter. If a gadget is perceived by Blogger as deficient in either of these areas, attempting to add it from the directory will only result in a message saying, "We are sorry, this gadget appears to be broken." So if you get this error, check your XML and your `Content view` attribute(s).

In addition, Blogger doesn't provide gadgets with the persistent-storage infrastructure that most other Google containers do. As a result, page visitors will be unable to save any gadget settings from one visit to the next. The result is to give more control to the owner of the blog (and hence the gadget) and less to the site visitor; for more information on this issue, see the "Gadget Owner vs. User" sidebar in Chapter 4. The general workaround described in that sidebar is applicable here, and I'll be covering its implementation later in this chapter.

Open Syndication

`crossPlatform.container = `**`'open'`**

Continuing the trend of deploying gadgets to third-party web sites, iGoogle gadgets can also be installed on any web page by inserting a snippet of HTML. Again, these pull from the same directory as iGoogle itself; to reach the open syndication directory yourself, browse to `www.google.com/ig/directory?synd=open`. From this directory, listings lead to a page where the gadget can be configured and the appropriate HTML snippet generated.

Google doesn't promote open syndication gadgets much, but you can encourage this use of your own gadget by linking to its configuration page from your own site. If you'd like to do so, all that's required is a link containing your gadget's URL (much like the Add to iGoogle link described earlier):

```
<a href="http://www.gmodules.com/ig/creator?synd=open&url=your_gadget_url">
  Add our gadget to your web page.
</a>
```

Although open syndication can be a good way to extend the reach of an iGoogle gadget, it will include a Google logo and "Gadgets by Google" tag line on the destination page. If you'd rather not have the Google brand attached to your gadgets, you're better off using the generic `iframe` distribution approach described in Chapter 2.

■ **Tip** One advantage that iGoogle gadgets in open syndication *do* have over generic `iframe`s is the ability to change the height of their frame dynamically, using the `crossPlatform.adjustSize` call described earlier.

There's one other issue to be aware of: the same divide between gadget owner and user described for Blogger also applies to gadgets in open syndication, so it's not possible to save settings from gadgets on third-party web sites. Again, I'll discuss an alternate approach to this issue later in the chapter.

Google Desktop Sidebar

```
crossPlatform.container = 'desktop'
```

As mentioned at the beginning of the chapter, Google maintains a separate API for gadgets directly on Windows and Mac desktops; these gadgets run outside of the traditional web-browser environment. However, this platform also includes partial support for iGoogle web gadgets—so there may be no need for you to build another version.

Google desktop gadgets run in a sidebar, an area along one vertical edge of the user's desktop. This sidebar is a feature of Google Desktop, which the user must first download and install from `http://desktop.google.com`. With Desktop installed, iGoogle gadgets are added by entering the URL of their XML specification into the search box of the Add Gadgets window, as shown in Figure 5-10 (note the *phase_igoogle.xml* in the search box).

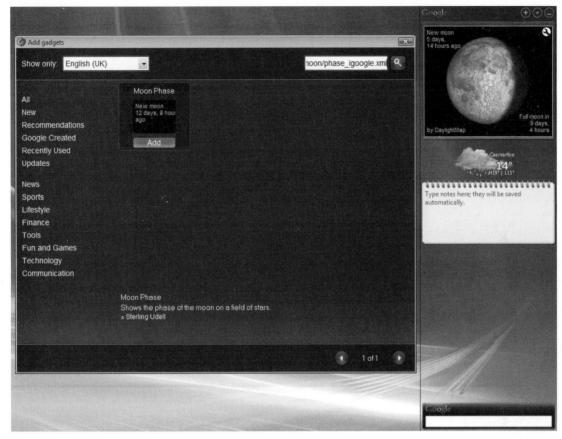

Figure 5-10. Adding an iGoogle gadget to the Desktop sidebar

This is where Desktop's *partial* support for iGoogle gadgets begins to become apparent: the only way to add a gadget is by typing (or pasting) its URL. Google claims that "selected" iGoogle gadgets are included in the Desktop gadgets directory, but in my experience, these are few indeed. And the gaps in iGoogle support continue once your gadget is installed: as with the previous two containers, persistent storage is not implemented for iGoogle gadgets on Desktop, so you'll need to implement the same workaround here.

■ **Tip** Google Desktop uses miniature instances of the operating system's "native" browser—IE for Windows, Safari for Mac—so if you run into problems on Desktop, a good approach is to debug your gadget directly in the appropriate browser instead.

Gmail

`crossPlatform.container = `**`'mail'`**

One of the more recent additions to the container line-up is Google Mail; since late 2008, it's possible to add up to five gadgets to the sidebar at `http://mail.google.com`. Although the platform is not yet well developed, the potential for reaching a huge audience of Gmail users makes it worth pursuing nonetheless.

■ **Caution** As of this writing, gadgets in Gmail are still considered by Google to be a "Labs" feature—meaning that support for them may be inconsistent and might even be withdrawn with little notice.

The complexity of the process for enabling and installing gadgets is a good indication of this primitive level of support:

1. In Gmail, click the Settings link, and go to the Labs tab.

2. In Labs, turn on the "Add any gadget by URL" feature, and save your changes.

3. Back in Settings, go to the Gadgets tab.

4. Enter the URL of your gadget's XML specification in the box provided.

Note that you'll need instructions similar to this on your own web site to guide your users through the process of installing your gadgets; currently, there is no gadget directory for Gmail.

Once the gadget is installed, there are some additional caveats. First, the containing sidebar is quite narrow; your gadget will have only between 158 and 162 pixels of width to display in (depending on the user's Gmail theme). And second, Gmail supplies no user interface for setting preferences. If you've created your own (as described in Chapter 2), this won't be a concern, but if your gadget is being deployed only to Google and you've been relying on their user interface, Gmail won't work for you.

One last concern here has to do with security. Gmail has a user option to always display the page via SSL; when selected, non-SSL gadgets (those whose URLs begin with HTTP rather than HTTPS) will cause a mixed-content warning on Internet Explorer. Currently, the only solution for this is to deploy your gadget via both the HTTP and HTTPS protocols and guide your users to the appropriate version based on their Gmail settings. Again, this is less than an ideal solution, but it's the best available currently.

Since this container is so new and since Gmail is such a high-profile product for Google, it's likely that most of these wrinkles will be ironed out with time—quite possibly before you read this. But in any case, Gmail's large user base makes it worth some sacrifice.

Specialized Gadget Containers

Gadgets in the containers described previously in this chapter all perform essentially the same task as a web gadget anywhere, functioning as miniature, self-contained web applications. By contrast, the following gadget containers all *extend* the core iGoogle functionality by enabling their gadgets to interact with other content on the page. In these cases, the basic Gadgets API has been used by Google as a foundation for creating new APIs, which then allow external developers to incorporate their own functionality into high-profile Google properties. And the result is that gadgets on these containers are no longer self-contained but become an integrated part of the larger web page.

Consequently, a generic web gadget is less likely to be of use in these containers than on those covered previously. It's possible that your gadget won't be applicable here at all. However, there are still a couple of good reasons for discussing these containers. First, it's likely that your generic gadget *will* still be useful on one or more of them; most gadgets make good toolbar buttons, and a currency converter gadget, for example, could be as handy on a spreadsheet or alongside a map as it is on iGoogle. Second, it's a good idea for you to know what the possibilities for gadgets are, to decide for yourself whether it might be worth the effort of developing a specialized version for one of the following containers.

Google Browser Toolbar

`crossPlatform.container = '`**`toolbar`**`'`

Google supplies a toolbar as a browser plug-in for Firefox and Internet Explorer on Windows, and it's possible to add gadgets as buttons on that toolbar. Such gadgets appear when their button is dropped down, as shown in Figure 5-11. Overall, the toolbar gadget implementation is quite good, better than many of the niche web containers discussed earlier in the chapter.

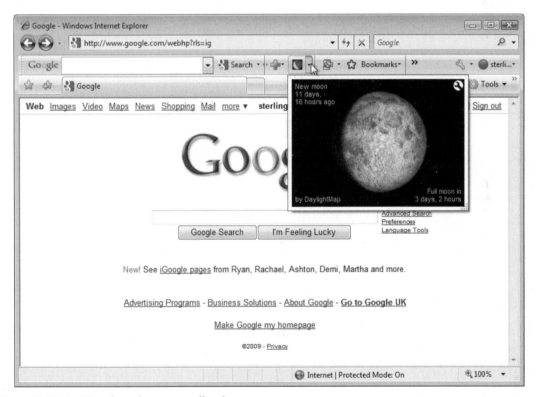

Figure 5-11. An iGoogle gadget as a toolbar button

■ **Note** My middleware layer stores a two-character abbreviation (supplied by Google) of the host browser in `crossPlatform.host`. Currently, the possible values are `ff` and `ie`, but if more browsers are supported in the future, their abbreviations should get included automatically.

Users can install your gadgets to their toolbar from a built-in gallery (which again shares its content with the iGoogle gadget directory), but if your gadget is not yet listed, you'll need to take a few additional steps to test your gadget as a toolbar button.

First, install the toolbar: using one of the supported browsers, visit `toolbar.google.com`, and follow the instructions there.

Second, create a temporary *button definition* file, which wraps your gadget specification with additional XML from the Toolbar Button API. Listing 5-7 shows a button definition file for Moon Phase.

Listing 5-7. A Browser Toolbar Button Definition for an iGoogle Gadget

```
<?xml version="1.0" encoding="UTF-8"?>
<custombuttons xmlns="http://toolbar.google.com/custombuttons/">
  <button>
    <title>Moon Phase</title>
    <site>http://www.daylightmap.com</site>
    <gadget height="200">http://daylightmap.com/moon/phase_igoogle.xml</gadget>
  </button>
</custombuttons>
```

The only critical element you must set in this XML is gadget; this contains the URL of your gadget specification, as used in all other Google gadget containers. The other two elements, `title` and `site`, are optional.

When you've created the button XML file, installing it to the toolbar is a matter of saving it to a specific location on your hard disk. In Windows Vista and 7, the path to use is as follows:

```
C:\Users\username\AppData\Local\Google\Custom Buttons\filename.xml
```

where *username* is your Windows login name and *filename*.xml is the name you choose to give the XML file. For Moon Phase, I named it `phase_button.xml`. With the XML file saved, your gadget's button should be visible on the toolbar after you restart the appropriate browser.

■ **Note** Button definition files are only needed for installing gadgets that aren't listed in the iGoogle directory. When your live gadget is installed by a user, all of the button's attributes (such as title, icon, and so on) are generated automatically from the gadget XML file.

As mentioned earlier, the Toolbar API is an extension of the Gadgets API, meaning that there are additional capabilities that can be built into toolbar-specific gadgets. In this case, the extensions have to do with the page currently being displayed in the main browser window: the gadget can receive information about the host, URL, search string, and more. Toolbar-specific gadgets using this data will require their own button XML, tailored for their specific tasks, and this button XML will then be submitted to the toolbar button directory, rather than using the iGoogle directory for the gadget XML. Full coverage of gadget buttons is off-topic for this book, but I encourage you to pursue it at toolbar.google.com/buttons/apis if you're interested.

Google Maps (Mapplets)

```
crossPlatform.container = 'maps'
```

A *mapplet* is a gadget for Google Maps. This platform is something of a hybrid of Google's Maps and Gadgets APIs; in addition to full gadget functionality, mapplets can interact with the map displayed on http://maps.google.com, rendering (or extracting) geographic data for the user. As with all the platforms in this section, the API for mapplets is a superset of iGoogle's, meaning that virtually any gadget can be installed in the sidebar of Google Maps. Although many gadgets won't be useful here, it's worth considering whether yours might be.

If you think it is, you can test it by browsing to http://maps.google.com and clicking the Browse the Directory link you'll find at the top of the My Maps tab. Within the directory is a Add by URL link; enter your gadget's XML address in the box that follows. When you return to Google Maps, you should find your gadget displayed in the sidebar, as shown in Figure 5-12.

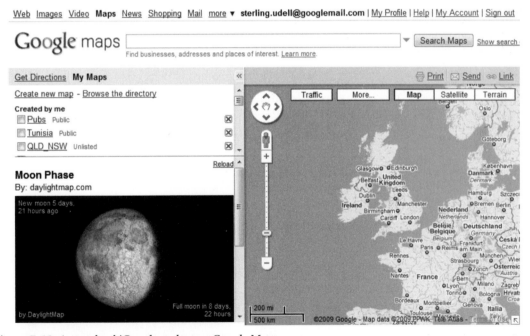

Figure 5-12. A standard iGoogle gadget on Google Maps

If you are going to deploy your gadget here, there's a developer mapplet that's worth installing; its URL is www.google.com/ig/modules/geodeveloper.xml. It will add a Reload link to your mapplet (visible in Figure 5-12) that speeds iterative development; simply click that link to refresh your gadget, rather than refreshing the entire Google Maps page.

And if you think that your gadget does have value to Maps users, you'll need to submit it to the mapplet directory in order for them to find it. When you've completed your debugging, open the Mapplets API documentation (at the address in the next paragraph), click the Submit a Mapplet link in the sidebar, and enter your gadget's URL. The time frame for listing is similar to that for the main Gadgets directory, although there's no indication that a minimum-usage threshold is in place here.

Of course, most mapplets are much more specialized than generic iGoogle gadgets, entailing a shift from ordinary web apps into the geographic Web. As such, full-fledged mapplet development is well beyond the scope of this book, but you can find information to get you started at http://code.google.com/apis/maps/documentation/mapplets.[2]

Google Docs Spreadsheets

`crossPlatform.container = '`**`spreadsheets`**`'`

Spreadsheet gadgets, which reside at http://spreadsheets.google.com, are another example of Google using gadgets to add external functionality to its own web applications. They're placed on the surface of a Google Docs spreadsheet, and fully functional examples are able to read and display data from within the spreadsheet cells. They do this by using the Data Visualization API, a Google product whose main function is to produce charts and graphs from spreadsheet data.

But what makes spreadsheet gadgets interesting to developers is that the Visualization API is optional; any iGoogle gadget can be placed within a spreadsheet, including the ones covered in this chapter. To do so, open a Google Docs spreadsheet, select Insert → Gadget, click the Custom link, and enter your gadget's URL. It should appear on the spreadsheet immediately.

More generally, the dialog box that opens when you select Insert → Gadget draws from a special directory—the Visualization Gadgets Gallery—and it's this list of gadgets that ordinary Spreadsheets users will draw from. In other words, if you have a generic gadget (not using Visualizations) that is nonetheless useful on a spreadsheet, you'll be unable to list it in the Gallery, and a Custom link will be the only way for your users to install it. So, if you have a gadget that you'd like to be generally available to Spreadsheets users, you will need to integrate the Visualizations API—and this means departing from the generic gadgets that are the subject of this book. For information on doing so, please see http://code.google.com/apis/visualization.

Google Calendar

`crossPlatform.container = '`**`calendar`**`'`

In August 2007, Google announced support for gadgets on its popular online Calendar. Like Mail and Spreadsheets, this is potentially a way to get your gadget out to thousands of people by adding it to a web app they use every day—but unfortunately, Google has never developed the platform to its full potential or even documented its use fully for developers. As a result, deploying gadgets to Google Calendar remains a challenge.

The first obstacle is simply installing a given gadget on Calendar. Although Google has provided documentation for several advanced installation techniques, such as the iCal and GData formats, it hasn't done so for the simple, straightforward route of installing a gadget directly. But it is possible: as with many other Google properties, installing a gadget on Calendar is done with a specially formed link containing the gadget's URL, but the format here is particularly obtuse. To ease the process, I've created

---

[2] A good guide for the experienced web developer is Michael Young's *Google Maps Mashups with Google Mapplets* (Apress, 2008).

a wizard for generating such links—and I've built it into an iGoogle gadget for you to use. You simply need to add the following to your iGoogle page (following the instructions earlier in the chapter):

```
http://sterlingudell.com/pwg/gcalendar.xml
```

After loading your URL into this gadget and confirming a few parameters (all drawn from the metadata previously discussed in this chapter), it will generate a link for installing your gadget onto Calendar. You can then test your gadget by clicking the link or use it to promote your gadget on Calendar from your own web site. Such a promotional link might look like this:

```
<a href="generated_link">
  <img width="104" height="17" alt="Add to Google Calendar" style="border:none"
      src="http://www.google.com/calendar/images/calendar_plus_en.gif" />
</a>
```

where generated_link should be replaced with the actual link created by the gcalendar.xml gadget shown earlier.

Difficulty of installation isn't the only issue with Calendar gadgets; the support for gadgets after they're installed is frankly one of the most limited in the Google ecosystem. Known limitations include the following:

- Fixed height and width. Both dimensions must be specified when the gadget is installed and can't be modified later. Specifically, crossPlatform.adjustHeight() doesn't work here.

- No persistent storage. The crossPlatform.Storage class doesn't work in Calendar, even with the workaround that is possible on other platforms (like Blogger and Toolbar). It appears that Google just hasn't implemented the UserPref infrastructure for Calendar.

- Correspondingly, there's also no Google-supplied user interface for setting preferences.

Even with these restrictions, some generic gadgets are still useful on Calendar, particularly those that provide fresh information on a daily basis. Your cross-platform gadget installed on Calendar will show its Icon on the current day and then display the gadget itself when the icon is clicked. On the other hand, making gadgets show on past or future days requires specialized server-side code for the Calendar Data API and is beyond the scope of this book. For more information, see http://code.google.com/apis/calendar.

OpenSocial

The final category of container based on iGoogle Gadgets is OpenSocial, Google's entry into the world of social networking. Like Mapplets, OpenSocial is an API in its own right, built as an extension to the Gadgets API; it includes everything in the gadgets.* namespace, plus much more. These extensions have to do with traversing the user's social graph, retrieving information from and posting updates to their friends and colleagues.

There is no single OpenSocial container, like iGoogle or Gmail. Instead, the API includes a container specification that is implemented by a host of web sites: Orkut, MySpace, LinkedIn, and others. Although each of these more or less adheres to the specification, there naturally are individual differences. In this chapter, I don't have room to cover these idiosyncrasies in detail, but they generally fall into two categories, with the split being dictated by the owner/user divide (see "Gadget Owners vs. Users" sidebar in Chapter 4 for background).

In the first class are web sites where the page owner and user are the same person, such as iGoogle and Gmail (two OpenSocial-enabled Google properties). Gadgets on these containers are generally structured like any web gadget; the OpenSocial extensions simply provide new channels for data and functionality. Your general-purpose web gadgets should function fine on sites like these as a rule.

The second class of container includes the true social-networking sites, where a site member owns a public-facing page that can be viewed by other users. This separation opens a new dimension in gadget programming, and toward that end the OpenSocial specification supports a range of different *views*, with different groups of functionality available in each (these correspond to the view attribute values from the Content XML element discussed earlier in the chapter). But because these views are specific to the Google APIs, cross-platform gadgets aren't going to be able to take full advantage of them—and might not even run especially well in certain views. The only way to be sure is to test your gadget on containers of interest.

As with the other containers in this section, taking full advantage of OpenSocial will require you to retreat from cross-platform development and customize your iGoogle gadget specifically for this platform. You can find plenty of information on this in the OpenSocial developer documentation at http://code.google.com/apis/opensocial.

Google-Specific Optimizations

Since Google's gadget ecosystem has so many users and so many different places where its gadgets will run, it may well be worth your while to create a Google-specific version. This is especially true if you have an external reason for focusing a specific container (such as company-specific Google Apps) or your proposed gadget requires one of the extended APIs (like OpenSocial). In any of these cases, building a gadget solely for Google opens the door to several platform-specific optimizations and extensions. In this section of the chapter, I'll introduce you to the most notable of these.

■ **Note** Because these optimizations are specific to Google, they make less use of the crossPlatform library and may require you to consider the Legacy/gadgets.* API split more closely than you have up until now.

Specifying Style and Script Inline

Any time you shift your focus away from cross-platform development and onto a single platform, you can usefully decrease your gadget's latency by moving CSS and JavaScript resources from external .css and .js files to inline style and script elements. As with Netvibes (covered in Chapter 4), this is the technique that Google recommends for gadgets, as evidenced by the Gadget Checker warnings discussed earlier. Because your gadget's XML is cached by Google, this technique also reduces the load on your own server (though an alternate technique for doing so will also be introduced in a couple of sections).

Using Additional Preference Types

In the UserPref section of Listing 5-2, all of the Preference elements needed for the gadget were included with a type attribute of hidden. This is appropriate if you've built your own cross-platform preference-setting user interface (as discussed in Chapter 3), but if you're only deploying to Google containers, additional types are available. If you select one of these other types, iGoogle (or other Google container) will generate its own user interface for setting the preference, removing the need for you to do so. Table 5-2 shows the available types.

Table 5-2. *Preference Types for Google Gadgets*

type	Description	HTML User Interface
string	An ordinary text value	`<input type="text" />`
bool	true or false	`<input type="checkbox" />`
enum	A string from a supplied list of values	`<select>`
list	A dynamic list of values	No equivalent
hidden	A string value used for storage behind the scenes	None

You can still use the `crossPlatform.Storage` class to retrieve the values from all of these preference types, as well as setting them programmatically if needed. For other information on these types, including additional attributes, the XML syntax of the enum type, and the data format of the list type, please see the official documentation at `http://code.google.com/apis/gadgets/docs/reference.html#Userprefs_Ref`.

■ **Tip** Several of these content types are similar to those found in Netvibes, so using them won't prevent you from deploying your gadget there (in addition to Google). See Chapter 4 for details.

Although Google will create its own user interface for setting these preference types (saving you the trouble), it's not very sophisticated, and you have little control over it. Figure 5-13 shows an example of this user interface. If you require a more sophisticated preference dialog box than this, you'll still need to create it yourself, like for a cross-platform gadget. There's also no presupplied user interface for settings on Gmail or Calendar, so keep that in mind if you're considering going this direction.

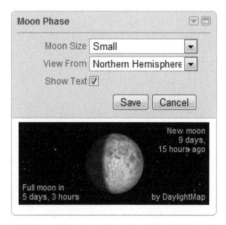

Figure 5-13. *An alternate version of Moon Phase using the default iGoogle preference interface*

GADGET OWNERS VS. USERS, REVISITED

In Chapter 4 I introduced the division between the gadget *owner* (the webmaster) and the *user* (the page visitor), noting that there's an open question of which should be in control of aspects such as preference settings. This issue arises again when deploying gadgets to Google containers such as Blogger, Google Apps, OpenSocial, and open syndication. In all of these cases, the cross-platform approach (saving preferences through a UI in the gadget itself) breaks down, either conceptually or through lack of support on the container. There are two ways to address this in Google gadgets; which one you choose depends on whether owner-centric or user-centric control makes more sense for your specific gadget and situation.

For owner-centric control, you'll need to code your gadget to use non-hidden preferences, as outlined in this section of the chapter. Google will then ask the page owner for their preferences when setting up the gadget for deployment to their page, and these settings will be applied every time the page is rendered. In this case, you can continue to use crossPlatform.Storage as normal to retrieve preference values.

For user-centric control, the best approach available is to use storage within the browser itself, and for widest compatibility, this means cookies. Fortunately, the crossPlatform.Storage class already contains code to save data in cookies (see Listing 3-7); we just need to apply it to this additional case. The following is a code snippet showing the required modifications:

```
if (/^(blogger|apps|open)/.test(crossPlatform.host)) {
  crossPlatform.emptyPref = '';
  crossPlatform.Storage = function (name, defaultValue) {
    var myName = name,
        myValue = crossPlatform.getCookie(name);

    this.get = function () {
      return myValue;
    };

    this.set = function (value) {
      crossPlatform.setCookie(myName, myValue);
    };
  };
} else {
  // Declare Storage class as normal
  crossPlatform.Storage = function (name, defaultValue) {
    ...
  };
}
```

Be aware that cookie-based storage moves away from the cloud model favored by Google and ties the user's preferences to a specific computer and browser. However, with current technology this is probably unavoidable; any storage online would require some means of authenticating the page visitor, and no such general mechanism is available.

Leveraging the Google Cache

More so than on any other platform, iGoogle gadgets are intended to scale. Google expects that any given gadget may potentially be installed by millions of users and recognizes that such a load is likely to be problematic for the gadget author's web host. So, in addition to always caching the XML source, the API includes a function that enables you to use Google's servers as a proxy for your own resources.

■ **Note** For forward compatibility, the code samples in this section use the `gadgets.*` API.

The Basic Cache Proxy

The fundamental cache-proxy function is `gadgets.io.getProxyUrl`, taking one URL as a parameter and routing it through the Google CDN. You can use it any time you are referring to external resources in JavaScript, calling `gadgets.io.getProxyUrl` on your resource's URL before you apply it.

For example, the Moon Phase gadget could use the Google cache to serve its moon images by changing a single line of Listing 2-4:

```
elements.moon.src =
  gadgets.io.getProxyUrl('http://daylightmap.com/moon/images/' + imgSrc);
```

■ **Note** The Google cache is already used by `crossPlatform`'s `fetchXML` and `fetchText` functions (see Listing 5-6), so there's no need for you to implement these yourself.

Caching External Code

One specific use of the cache proxy is common enough to warrant additional attention: you can use it to serve the external code resources, such as JavaScript and CSS, used by your gadget. Such an approach yields the increased maintainability of separate source files without incurring the server load of multiple retrievals per gadget.

The basic technique is to include your external code via DHTML generated from JavaScript, incorporating the cache proxy along the way. It's probably easiest to see how this works with a real example: the following code (from Listing 5-2) will serve as your starting point, showing the default elements for including the external CSS and JavaScript into Moon Phase.

```
<link type="text/css" rel="stylesheet"
      href="http://daylightmap.com/moon/phase.css" />
<script type="text/javascript"
        src="http://daylightmap.com/moon/phase.js"></script>
```

To deliver these resources through the Google cache, you need to generate them via JavaScript (rather than placing them directly in the HTML) and integrate the proxy call, as follows:

```
<script type="text/javascript">
  var url = 'http://daylightmap.com/moon/phase.css';
```

```
document.write('<link type="text/css" rel="stylesheet" href="' +
   gadgets.io.getProxyUrl(url) + '" />');

url = 'http://daylightmap.com/moon/phase.js';
document.write('<script type="text/javascript" src="' +
   gadgets.io.getProxyUrl(url) + '"><\/script>');
</script>
```

■ **Caution** Notice that the closing `script` tag in the second `document.write` call has its backslash escaped, as `<\/script>`. This is crucial to avoid prematurely ending the *containing* `script` element.

Although such a technique can significantly reduce your server load, it's not without its drawbacks. First, serving your code through the Google cache can make debugging difficult, because a stale version of your code may be served to your gadget. Mitigation techniques for this were outlined in Chapter 3 (in the sidebar "Cache Control for Developers"); be aware that Google's cache does not honor server-side cache controls sent in HTTP headers. And second, such dynamically generated includes can actually *increase* client-side latency for your gadget, because the containing JavaScript has to be run by the browser before the resource is fetched. This delay can also introduce hard-to-debug timing issues in the JavaScript itself. So although this technique is a valuable one to have at your disposal for extremely high-traffic gadgets, it's probably not one to be used every time.

■ **Note** External code resources are independently cached by myAOL, so this technique shouldn't be used on gadgets deployed there.

Internationalization

One area that's easy to overlook in web application development is internationalization; most of us tend to think of our own languages first and other languages a distant second. However, Google is a company with truly global reach, and it actively encourages development of gadgets for multiple languages. Toward this end, it provides a library of internationalization and localization tools for gadgets on its platform, and for Google-specific gadgets, it's definitely worth considering. Under the right circumstances, it can multiply the reach of your gadgets, delivering them to a far wider audience than just English speakers.

The iGoogle gadget internationalization API is necessarily somewhat complicated, but in a nutshell, it's based on the concept of moving user interface text out of your gadget source and into external XML files called *message bundles*. You then create a bundle for each language you want to support, containing equivalents for each text string in that language, and specify what bundles you have available back in your gadget XML. Finally, the platform replaces individual strings with text from the appropriate bundle when it renders your gadget for another language.

One major issue is that this is possible only if your gadget is fundamentally international at its core. A simple graphical gadget like Moon Phase would be well suited to internationalization; a gadget that delivers mostly text content or a text-based application would not, because the text itself would need to be localized. Unless your content already exists in several languages, it would do you no good to translate only the text within the gadget code.

And as with all topics in this part of the chapter, internationalization is only worth pursuing if your gadget is being deployed solely to Google properties. Not only is the internationalization library itself unavailable on other platforms, but its text replacements can be done only to code embedded within the gadget XML, not to external resources.

Consequently, I'm not going to cover internationalization further here. If it sounds promising for your gadget, however, I encourage you to read more at `http://code.google.com/apis/gadgets/docs/i18n.html`.

Learning More About iGoogle Gadgets

As indicated by the frequent links throughout the latter sections of this chapter, there is a lot more information about iGoogle gadgets than I can cover in this book. I've given you a good introduction and sufficient information to include Google properties in the deployment of most cross-platform gadgets, but it's likely you'll need to delve further at some point.

- Your first port of call should be the official API documentation at `http://code.google.com/apis/gadgets/docs`. Don't forget that iGoogle is two APIs in one—Legacy and `gadgets.*`—and the documentation is divided accordingly!

- Google maintains the iGoogle Developer Blog at `http://igoogledeveloper.blogspot.com`, where the latest news about the ecosystem is posted.

- There's also an official Gadgets API blog, `http://googlegadgetsapi.blogspot.com`, although it is updated much less frequently.

- A list of open issues, including known bugs and feature requests, is maintained at `http://code.google.com/p/igoogle-legacy/issues`.

- Last but not least, the iGoogle Developer Forum is the official discussion group for all things gadget-related. Monitored by both Google staff and experienced outside developers, it's the place to go with gadget programming questions. Find it at `http://groups.google.com/group/Google-Gadgets-API`.

Summary

Although Google gadgets will run on a large and diverse collection of web sites, they all share a single root API and so offer an excellent return on your development effort. A single adaptation of your core gadget can expose your web assets to millions of users across many different areas:

- The iGoogle home page

- Hosted third-party sites, from vendor portals through Blogger and Google Sites

- Client-side containers on the desktop and browser

- High-profile Google web apps, such as Gmail, Calendar, Maps, and Spreadsheets

- Popular social-networking sites (via OpenSocial)

In addition, many of these containers offer specialized capabilities not found on other platforms, such as geographic tools, social graphs, and data visualization. If your gadget concept can take advantage of these opportunities, the iGoogle API will serve as a foundation you can build from.

In the next chapter, we'll move off the traditional Web and onto the Windows desktop, learning how web gadget technology can be applied to what is traditionally the stronghold of native applications.

Desktop Platforms

■ ■ ■

CHAPTER 6

Windows

With the release of Microsoft Windows Vista in 2007, web gadgets on the desktop became available to all users of this market-dominant operating system, and support for the technology is further developed in Windows 7. If for no other reason than the size of its installed base, Windows is a major platform for gadget development and should feature strongly in your own deployment plans. In this chapter, I'll walk you through the straightforward process of porting a generic gadget to the Windows desktop and establishing a presence with this user base for your own web application.

Introducing Windows Gadgets

From a user's standpoint, gadgets on Windows don't look like web applications at all; they apparently run outside of a browser and thus lack the usual visual cues of web sites (like URLs and a Back button). On both Windows Vista and 7, gadgets can be installed directly on the user's desktop (flip back to Figure 1-4 for an example); on Vista, there's also the option of the Windows Sidebar, a dedicated gadget container that's ordinarily docked to one side of the desktop (visible in Figure 6-1).

Despite appearances, gadgets on Windows are indeed web-based and are fundamentally little different from those on more conventional web platforms: they're built of HTML, styled with CSS, and activated by JavaScript. As such, the generic web gadgets built in Part 1 of this book will readily deploy to Windows; you'll just need to be aware of a few special considerations.

Developing a Windows Gadget

The first departure from the web-gadget norm is a matter of packaging: rather than being distributed as discrete source files, a Windows gadget is deployed as a single file of type `.gadget`. Although this looks like a custom file type, and one you may not have seen before, it's actually just a renamed `.zip` archive. In other words, your gadget will be distributed by collecting all its component source files into a single zip file and then renaming that file so that its extension is `.gadget` rather than `.zip`. Accordingly, it's also easy to see the source of any Windows gadget you may download from the Web; simply rename it from `.gadget` back to `.zip`, and open it as you would any other zip file.

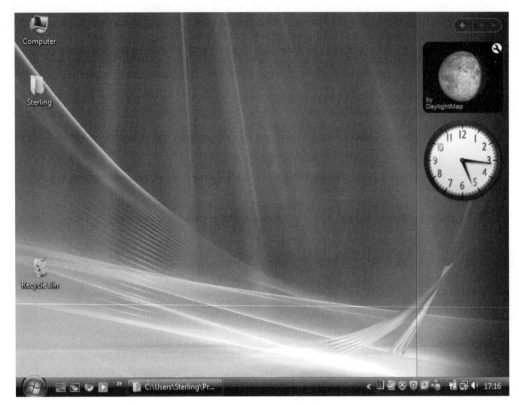

Figure 6-1. Gadgets in the Windows Vista Sidebar

■ **Tip** Windows gadgets can also be created from .cab files, Microsoft's own compressed-folder format. So if you rename a .gadget file to .zip and are unable to open it, try .cab instead.

Within the zip archive are all the usual suspects for a web gadget: HTML, CSS, JavaScript, and image files. They can be organized into subdirectories if you want, though this is not required. The only absolute requirements are that the root of the zip file contain a gadget *manifest*, an XML file containing the gadget's metadata, and that the manifest be named gadget.xml. I'll be covering the contents of the manifest in detail slightly later in the chapter in the "Creating the Gadget Manifest" section.

The second consideration is size on-screen. In their original home on Vista, Windows gadgets have two distinct size modes: a *docked* state within the Sidebar and an *undocked* or *floating* state when dragged off the Sidebar to elsewhere on the desktop. And this split continues on Windows 7, even though the Sidebar is no longer relevant; the two distinct sizes are still supported, though now with a simple button to toggle between them.

When docked to the Sidebar (simply called the *Smaller* size on Windows 7), gadgets are a maximum of 130 pixels wide. Effectively, they are contained in a browser window of this width, so content beyond this limit either may be cropped or may cause a horizontal scroll bar to appear, depending on your layout. Undocked (or *Larger*) gadgets are permitted to be somewhat larger; no hard limits are imposed, but it's recommended that you not exceed 400 pixels in width.

The height in either state is quite flexible; it's determined by the flow of your gadget content. This can be controlled by setting an explicit height to the body (or other container) and can also be changed dynamically from code. There are some limits, though: Microsoft recommends a maximum initial height for gadgets of 200 pixels and recommends that they never grow to more than 400 pixels tall. In the other direction, Vista enforces a minimum height of 57 pixels, while Windows 7 has no absolute minimum.

Adding a Border

Although Windows gadgets are displayed within an embedded instance of Internet Explorer, there is no manifestation of this to the user; the visual effect is that the gadget is running independently, with nothing outside its borders except the desktop. Consequently, to achieve a good visual appearance on Windows, you'll want to create a border of some nature for your gadget. Figure 6-2 shows the effect of a simple border (created as a background image) on a trivial Windows gadget.

Figure 6-2. *A simple web gadget, with and without a border*

Specifically how you create your border is up to you. Common techniques range from simple border rules in CSS to more complicated image-based solutions. For a fixed-size gadget, a single background image (as in Figure 6-2) may be sufficient, or for variable sizes, you may need to build up a border from multiple images. And ideally, your border imagery will incorporate the rounded corners and shadow effects commonly seen on Windows to seamlessly blend into the desktop environment.

In all cases, you'll construct the border from within your gadget using ordinary web presentation techniques, usually CSS and background images. However, any border that's not purely rectangular will have one additional requirement: it will need some transparency at the edges. You'll need to design this into your background images (like the second "Hello World" in Figure 6-2, which has rounded corners with transparency behind). In a few pages, I'll show you how to make this work on the Windows gadget platform.

Adapting the Core Gadget

With these basic architectural considerations in mind, you're ready to look at a real example, converting your core web gadget from Chapters 2 and 3 to run on the Windows desktop. At a high level, the modifications required are the following:

1. Create a gadget.xml manifest file.

2. Adapt the main HTML code for use on Windows.

3. Add some visual design elements—in this case, new background images.

Creating the Gadget Manifest

From the platform's perspective, the most important file in the gadget is its manifest, an XML file containing its metadata attributes and a pointer to its main HTML document. Most concepts in the manifest will look familiar to you by now, because they're similar to those found on other platforms. Listing 6-1 shows the manifest for my Moon Phase example gadget; as is always the case on Windows, it's named gadget.xml and will be placed in the root of the gadget's zip archive.

Listing 6-1. *The gadget.xml Manifest for Moon Phase*

```
<?xml version="1.0" encoding="utf-8" ?>
<gadget>
  <name>Moon Phase</name>
  <version>1.0.6</version>
  <description>Shows the phase of the moon on a field of stars.</description>
  <author name="Sterling Udell">
    <info url="http://sterlingudell.com" text="SterlingUdell.com" />
    <logo src="su_64.png" />
  </author>
  <copyright>&#169; 2009 Udell Enterprises, Inc</copyright>
  <icons>
    <icon height="64" width="64" src="moon_64.png" />
  </icons>
  <hosts>
    <host name="sidebar">
      <base type="HTML" apiVersion="1.0.0" src="phase_windows.html" />
      <permissions>Full</permissions>
      <platform minPlatformVersion="1.0" />
      <defaultImage src="moon_64.png" />
    </host>
  </hosts>
</gadget>
```

A Windows gadget manifest should always be encoded UTF-8, and the root XML element is always gadget; the remaining elements are described in the following sections. Apart from the hosts element, most of the metadata here is used to build your gadget's display in the *Picker*, Windows' on-screen list of the user's installed gadgets. Figure 6-3 shows a typical Picker (with Moon Phase installed).

■ **Note** The Picker is sometimes called the Gadget Gallery within Windows, but that term is also used for Microsoft's online gadget directory, so I'll refer to it here exclusively as the Picker.

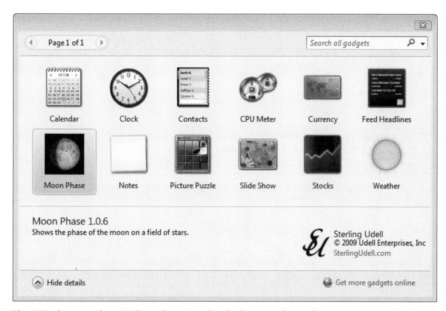

Figure 6-3. The Windows gadget Picker, showing the desktop gadgets the user has installed

name

This is your gadget's name, as it will appear with its entry in the Picker.

version

This is a free-form version string to accompany your gadget in its Picker detail view. If you change the version and reinstall your gadget, Windows will create a new Picker entry for it; otherwise, it will replace the existing one.

description

This is a short description of your gadget. This is optional.

author

This element contains several pieces of information about you, the gadget's creator. Although the `author` element is optional, if it's included, it must have an attribute of `name`, containing your (or your company's) name. It also has two optional subelements, both shown in Listing 6-1:

- The `info` element has two possible attributes; `text` is a string to use as a link (in the Picker) to `url`.

- The `logo` element is a path to a 64×64 graphic file (in the gadget's zip file) to display alongside the other author information. Not surprisingly, this will typically be your company's logo.

copyright

This is an optional intellectual-property string to display with the author data.

icons

This field's `icon` subelement should contain `height`, `width`, and `src` attributes for the main image to be used for your gadget's Picker listing. The `src` path should be to the image file in the gadget's zip archive; it may be any of `bmp`, `gif`, `jpg`, `png`, or `tif`. This image will be displayed at 64 pixels square, so ideally your source image will be that size as well.

Note that `icons` is optional; if you don't include it, Windows will display a generic gadget icon for you in the Picker.

hosts

This final manifest element is functional, rather than display-oriented; it tells the platform where to find your gadget's main HTML document. Apart from the attributes highlighted, your `hosts` element should contain exactly the same content as in Listing 6-1:

- A `host` subelement, with a `name="sidebar"` attribute.

- Attributes of `type="HTML"` and `apiVersion="1.0.0"` in the `base` element. The `src` attribute here contains the path to your base HTML document within the zip file.

- The `permissions` and `platform` elements, exactly as shown in Listing 6-1.

- The optional `defaultImage` element contains the path to an image Windows will use when dragging your gadget from the Picker to the desktop. This should optimally be a 64×64 graphic, so it's usually reasonable to simply reuse your `icon` image.

Again, the most important item within the manifest is here, the `base` attribute `src`. Without this link to your HTML file, your gadget will not display.

Changes to the HTML

It's appropriate, then, to look next at what changes are required to your HTML for a functioning Windows gadget. As usual, the changes are not extensive, but in order to keep the Windows branch separate from your main code base, I recommend making a copy of your main HTML file. I've called mine phase_windows.html, and you can find it in Listing 6-2 (with the body content omitted for brevity). I've highlighted the sections added for Windows in bold.

Listing 6-2. *The Main HTML Document for Moon Phase on Windows*

```
<?xml version="1.0" encoding="UTF-8"?>
<!DOCTYPE html PUBLIC "-//W3C//DTD XHTML 1.0 Transitional//EN"
                      "http://www.w3.org/TR/xhtml1/DTD/xhtml1-transitional.dtd">
<html xmlns="http://www.w3.org/1999/xhtml">
  <head>
    <meta http-equiv="Content-Type" content="text/html;charset=UTF-8" />
    <meta name="description"
          content="Shows the current phase of the moon on a field of stars." />
    <title>Moon Phase</title>
    <link href="moon_32.png" type="image/png" rel="icon" />
    <link href="phase.css"  type="text/css"  rel="stylesheet" />
    <style type="text/css">
      .moonPhase {
        background-color: transparent;
        background-image: none;
      }
      .moonPhase #main {
        font-size: 10px;
      }
    </style>
  </head>
  <body class="moonPhase">
    <g:background></g:background>

    <!-- body content goes here -->

    <script src="platform.js" type="text/javascript"></script>
    <script src="phase.js"    type="text/javascript"></script>
    <script type="text/javascript">
      crossPlatform.dockHandler = function () {
        if (System.Gadget.docked) {
          document.body.style.width = '130px';
          document.getElementById('main').style.backgroundImage =
            'url(stars_small.gif)';
        } else {
          document.body.style.width = '240px';
          document.getElementById('main').style.backgroundImage =
            'url(stars_medium.gif)';
        }
      };
      System.Gadget.onDock = System.Gadget.onUndock = crossPlatform.dockHandler;
      crossPlatform.addHandler(window, 'load', crossPlatform.dockHandler);
    </script>
  </body>
</html>
```

Style

The first addition to the gadget HTML is a block of inline `style` in the `head` section. This simply contains a couple of selectors for CSS specific to Windows, and I've chosen to include them in-line here (rather than in an external `.css`) to minimize the number of separate files I need to maintain for the Windows port.

First up are changes to the background of the `body` (which is using a CSS pseudo-namespace class of `moonPhase`, remember). I've decided my Windows gadget is going to have borders with rounded corners; this will require some transparency, and the first step in implementing that is to remove the gadget's existing background. If your gadgets require any transparency, you'll need to do something similar here; for Moon Phase, it's a matter of overriding the `background-image` and `background-color` styles inherited from `phase.css`. I'll be adding new background imagery a bit later.

And second, because the Windows platform's docked view is only 130 pixels wide, I've scaled down my gadget's text a bit—from the `11px` specified in `phase.css` down to `10px` here. It's a minor change, typical of the sort of appearance tweaking that's often required when porting to a new platform.

Background

You can see the next component required for transparent-background support on Windows just inside the `body` element of Listing 6-2. It's an empty XML element, `<g:background>`, that's specific to the Windows gadget platform—and it's a bit of an oddity here. The short explanation is that if you want your gadget to have any areas transparency to the desktop, this element needs to be in the body.

The slightly longer explanation is that the Windows gadget API supports a variety of operations that can be done on the gadget's background, both here in the HTML and dynamically in JavaScript, and this `<g:background>` element is the hook that it ties them to. But of course, all these operations are specific to Windows, so they are of little interest from a cross-platform standpoint. Nonetheless, in order to make transparency work, Windows needs at least this minimal stub of `<g:background>` to be in place.

On the other hand, if your gadget has no transparency, feel free to leave out `<g:background>`.

JavaScript

The largest addition to the gadget's HTML is the block of inline script that I've inserted at the very end of the body. Naturally, this is where you'll find any Windows-specific JavaScript—and a common use for it is handling Windows' specific size modes, as shown here.

My code starts with the declaration of a function, `dockHandler`. As its name implies, it's an event handler for when the dock (size) mode changes, in other words, when the gadget is transitioning from its docked (smaller) view to its undocked (larger) one. For my gadget, there are two basic actions that need to occur when this happens; I set the width of the gadget to match its new mode and then the background image accordingly.

Because Moon Phase on Windows has essentially two fixed-size modes (docked/smaller and undocked/larger) and is of a predictable height, I can simply toggle between two static background images to generate my border effect. I created these images by taking rounded-rectangle crops of my original starry-sky background image and then saving them with transparency (see Figure 6-4). This is the final piece of the Windows-specific background handling that I've been building throughout this part of the chapter.

Figure 6-4. The background images for Moon Phase use rounded corners to create a border effect

With my dockHandler function declared, all that remains is to attach it to the relevant events: the API's dock and undock (within its System.Gadget namespace) and the main gadget window's load (using my own crossPlatform.addHandler function). This latter is necessary so that the gadget is initialized properly no matter which view state it starts out in.

Your own gadgets will have varying needs for Windows-specific JavaScript, but you'll probably find that dock/undock handling is a common requirement, and you should be able to model your code after dockHandler.

Additions to crossPlatform

Before our newly ported gadget is ready to run on the Windows desktop, a few additions will also need to be made to the crossPlatform middleware layer, bridging the gap between our newly ported gadget and the Windows API.

Platform Sniffing

Detecting the Windows gadget platform is an easy task: it declares a namespace of System.* that's found on no other platform that we use. Therefore, testing for the Windows API (and setting crossPlatform.api to 'windows') is as simple as we could ask for:

```
if (!!window.System) {
  // Windows Desktop API
  crossPlatform.api = 'windows';
  crossPlatform.emptyPref = '';
}
```

Persistent Storage

As a full-featured API intended for creating all types of gadgets, Windows provides a storage subnamespace, Settings, that's nicely compatible with the needs of my crossPlatform.Storage class (from Listing 3-7). The access mechanism is a simple readString function under that namespace:

```
switch (crossPlatform.api) {
  case 'windows':
    myValue = System.Gadget.Settings.readString(name);
    break;
  ...
}
```

and the retrieval, using writeString, is equally easy:

```
switch (crossPlatform.api) {
  case 'windows':
    System.Gadget.Settings.writeString(myName, myValue);
    break;
  ...
}
```

The only potential issue here is that Settings value names have a maximum length of 1,024 characters, and the values themselves have a maximum of 2,048 characters. So, as usual, you can't use Storage for large quantities of data, but it's generally enough for most preferences and the like.

Resizing

When we get to dynamic-size support, the crossPlatform integration does get a bit more complicated. Although in theory Windows automatically resizes gadgets based on their content, in practice it often needs a bit of help. It turns out that we can force its hand in crossPlatform.adjustSize by manually setting the height of the body to the value of its scrollHeight property:

```
crossPlatform.adjustSize = function () {
  switch (crossPlatform.api) {
    case 'windows':
      setTimeout("document.body.style.height = document.body.scrollHeight + 'px'",
                 100);
      break;
    ...
  }
};
```

You'll notice that there's one other workaround here, in that the entire statement needs to be wrapped in a setTimeout call, delaying it for one-tenth of a second. It appears that the rendering engine in Internet Explorer (the implied browser for Windows gadgets, remember) doesn't update scrollHeight immediately when the content is changed—but this short delay gives that update sufficient time to happen, without introducing latency perceptible to the user.

Testing and Debugging

When you have a first pass at porting your code completed, the first prerequisite to trying it out will be an installed copy of Windows Vista or 7. Ideally, you should have both on hand to identify any differences in gadget behavior between them. However, the API is generally quite similar on the two versions, so this is not strictly required. It's also worth noting that the Windows gadget platforms work fine in a virtual session, such as Microsoft's own Virtual PC; this can ease the burden of testing on a different host operating system.

■ **Tip** When Sidebar is running on Vista, it automatically hides behind other windows when they have focus. You can bring it into view again by pressing Windows+spacebar.

With Windows installed, a preliminary step in testing your gadget is to open its base HTML file in Internet Explorer. Assuming any files with relative URLs in the gadget are in their correct locations on your filesystem, the basic gadget functionality should work. Settings won't save and dock/undock handlers won't fire, because the System.* namespace required for these functions doesn't exist outside the gadget platform, but otherwise this should be a reasonable test of how your gadget will perform on the desktop—and as we'll see, debugging is much easier in a full instance of Internet Explorer.

Packaging Gadgets

The next step in preparing a Windows gadget for installation is to package it into a .gadget file. As described earlier in the chapter, this is simply a zip file renamed with a different extension, so you'll first need to create a zip archive for your gadget, either with a third-party application or by selecting New → Compressed (zipped) Folder from the Windows shell context menu. Name the file as you intend your final gadget to be named, apart from the extension; for example, I'll start with a file named phase_windows.zip.

■ **Tip** To change file extensions in Windows, you need to be able to see them, but the operating system hides them by default. To show them on Vista and Windows 7, open the containing folder, select Organize → Folder And Search Options, and then on the View tab deselect "Hide extensions for known file types."

With your zip archive created, copy in all your gadget's referenced source files. Remember that the gadget.xml manifest file must be in the root of the zip file; other files may be located in subdirectories, so long as the relative URLs are correct wherever they are referenced. My Moon Phase gadget doesn't require many source files, so I haven't bothered with subdirectories; you can see the contents of its zip archive in Figure 6-5.

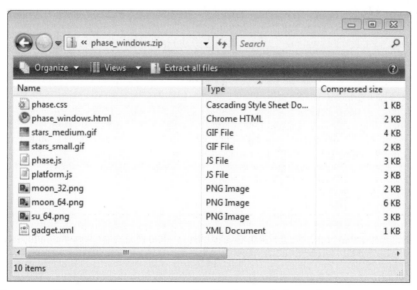

Figure 6-5. The source files for the Moon Phase gadget in phase_windows.zip

Once all the required source is copied into the zip file, rename it from a .zip extension to .gadget. Its icon should change accordingly; it's now ready for installation as a gadget.

NO HOSTING REQUIRED

Effectively, gadget source within the zip file is hosted locally; this includes both the main HTML file and any other files it references. If the URLs for any files used by your gadget are relative, Windows will attempt to resolve them from within the archive, including source files in subdirectories.

This local listing has several advantages:

- Local source files can be served much faster than those hosted remotely, significantly improving gadget performance.

- Your own server load will be reduced by not needing to serve these files every time a client gadget loads.

- If all your gadget's source files are local, it can run offline, when the client computer isn't connected to the Internet.

Of course, few web gadgets can run effectively in complete isolation; most require a network connection to download content or imagery, at least. So in the real world, the options for running offline are usually limited. And if your gadget does require a host connection, you may find the task of porting to Windows easier if most of its source files remain on your server; fewer changes will thus be needed from the code used on platforms where absolute URLs are required, like iGoogle.

Also, it's worth remembering that source files served on demand to the gadget will always be the latest version available on your server; as with most web applications, software updates are pushed implicitly to the client. On the other hand, any code contained within the .gadget file (and "hosted" locally on the user's computer) cannot be updated this way. Changes to local code will need to be packaged into a new version of the gadget, and this will need to be installed by the user manually; Microsoft supplies no mechanism for doing this.

At the end of the day, all that Windows requires to be in the zip itself are the manifest and those files referenced directly from it: the base HTML and the defaultImage and icon images. The location of other files is up to you, although my general recommendation is to place other static files (referenced directly from your base HTML) in the zip file as well and leave resources referenced from elsewhere on your server. This way, only your base HTML should need modification to run as a Windows gadget—and chances are, you'll be modifying it anyway.

Installing Your Gadget

After loading and renaming your zip file, copy it to the target version of Windows (if it's not there already); the initial installation is then as simple as double-clicking the .gadget file. You'll get an "Unknown Publisher" warning, as shown in Figure 6-6; I'll discuss this further later in the chapter, but for now, just click the Install button. On Vista, the Sidebar should open with your gadget installed; on Windows 7, it should simply appear on the desktop. In either case, you're ready to proceed with testing.

Figure 6-6. When your .gadget file is unsigned, Windows shows a security warning before installing it.

Unless everything works flawlessly the first time you run your gadget, you'll be needing to modify some source files and try again, usually several times. Unfortunately, you can't modify the source within a .gadget file: Windows doesn't know to open it as a zip archive, and you can't tell it to, or it will no longer install as a gadget. It's possible to rename it back and forth (between .zip and .gadget) every time you need to make a change, but fortunately there's an easier way. In Windows' Run dialog box, enter the following path:

%USERPROFILE%\AppData\Local\Microsoft\Windows Sidebar\Gadgets

This should open Windows internal gadget store—and in this location, the .gadget "files" are actually uncompressed folders, allowing you to see and manipulate their contents. You can therefore copy new source files here (or edit in place), with no renaming necessary.

When you change any of your gadget's source files, you'll need to reload the gadget for the changes to take effect. To do so, close the gadget (by clicking the *X* that Windows displays to its upper right), and then open the Picker:

- On Vista, right-click an empty space on the Sidebar, and select "Add gadgets."

- On Windows 7, right-click the desktop, and select Gadgets.

With the Picker open, double-clicking your gadget will reopen it on the Sidebar or desktop, with any source changes applied.

■ **Tip** Changes to your gadget.xml manifest may not take effect until you uninstall your gadget from the Picker. Occasionally, you may need to close the Picker as well to clear this cache.

Tracking Down Bugs

If you find that your gadget has bugs lurking in hard-to-find places, tracking them down in a Windows gadget can be a challenge. Naturally, there's no built-in debugger—and to prevent background gadgets from interrupting the user, Microsoft has disabled the JavaScript alert and confirm functions. So, debugging a gadget requires some extra effort; it can be difficult to ascertain what's happening at key points in your code.

First, I recommend that you attempt to reproduce the bug by running the gadget code stand-alone in Internet Explorer. Starting with version 8, it has a reasonable debugger built in, so if you can reproduce your bug here, you stand a good chance of tracking it down fairly easily.

If you can't reproduce a given bug outside the gadget framework, you'll have to find and fix it in place. Fortunately, Microsoft hasn't completely abandoned you; on Windows 7 it has added a special registry value that enables the display of any JavaScript errors from gadgets. In regedit (or an equivalent tool), import the following into the registry of your test environment:

```
[HKEY_CURRENT_USER\Software\Microsoft\Windows\CurrentVersion\Sidebar]
  "ShowScriptErrors"=dword:00000001
```

With this key in place, any JavaScript errors in your gadget will display the usual message.

If this isn't sufficient, one other useful technique is to use DHTML (such as document.write) in lieu of alert to output debugging information to the face of your gadget.

Finally, if you have Microsoft's Visual Studio or Visual Web Developer installed on your test environment, a JavaScript debugger statement in your code should invoke their built-in debuggers when execution reaches it. From here, you can examine variables and step through your gadget code line by line. As of this writing, a version of Visual Web Developer is available for free; download it from www.microsoft.com/express/vwd.

Deploying Windows Gadgets

Once you've squashed any recalcitrant bugs, you're ready to deploy your gadget to users' desktops. Before sending it out, one last step is recommended: removing the security warning of Figure 6-6. This isn't required—many gadgets are deployed without doing so and show this message to all their users—but for a finished appearance, it is a good idea.

It's accomplished by digitally *signing* the .gadget file with a code-signing certificate, but unfortunately, doing so isn't a simple process. It requires purchasing an appropriate certificate from a certification authority (CA) and then "imprinting" the certificate onto file via a signing tool. This imprint can then be examined by the recipient of the gadget to ensure that its code hasn't been tampered with en route—for example, by adding malware to the gadget source. Windows performs such an examination automatically before installing the gadget, and its failure is what invokes the security warning.

Acquiring and using a code-signing certificate is beyond the scope of this book; it's fairly involved, and the instructions depend upon your operating system. For Windows, you can find a guide to this process at http://msdn.microsoft.com/en-us/library/ms537361.aspx; for other systems, a bit of web searching should get you pointed in the right direction. And again, this step is not a requirement for gadget distribution but rather a best practice.

Submitting to the Gadget Gallery

The chief distribution channel for Windows gadgets is Microsoft's own Gallery, at http://vista.gallery.microsoft.com. Because it's linked to from the Picker (within Windows), this will be most users' first stop when looking for new gadgets. Like most gadget directories, the Gallery supports browsing by category and searching by keyword.

■ **Caution** The Gallery lists many types of Windows Live add-ons; make sure you're in the section for Sidebar Gadgets.

To list your gadget to the gallery, the address to start at is `http://gallery.live.com/submit.aspx`. Microsoft requires that gadget authors sign in with a Windows Live ID; if you don't already have one (from a Messenger account, for example), you'll find a Sign Up link at the same address.

Once you are signed in, the first part of the submission form is relatively straightforward and looks something like Figure 6-7. Note that all metadata here must be entered manually and is entirely separate from that contained in your gadget manifest. The details on this page apply only to your gadget's listing in the Gallery.

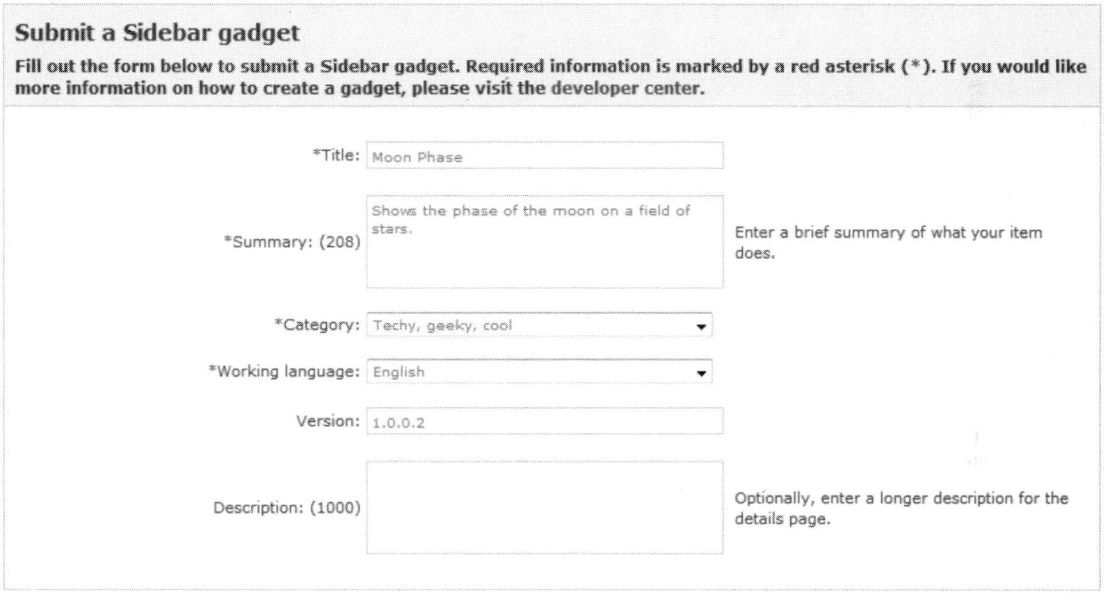

Submit a Sidebar gadget

Fill out the form below to submit a Sidebar gadget. Required information is marked by a red asterisk (*). If you would like more information on how to create a gadget, please visit the developer center.

*Title:	Moon Phase
*Summary: (208)	Shows the phase of the moon on a field of stars.
	Enter a brief summary of what your item does.
*Category:	Techy, geeky, cool
*Working language:	English
Version:	1.0.0.2
Description: (1000)	
	Optionally, enter a longer description for the details page.

Figure 6-7. Basic gadget information for the Sidebar Gadget Gallery

Further down the gadget submission page, you'll need to supply files for upload: an optional thumbnail image for use in the gallery and your `.gadget` file (see Figure 6-8). The thumbnail must be a `.jpg` file between 60 and 100 pixels square. One important note here is that, as of this writing, these file uploads work only from Internet Explorer; if this isn't practical for you, you'll need to upload the files to a web server separately and then link to them from this form instead.

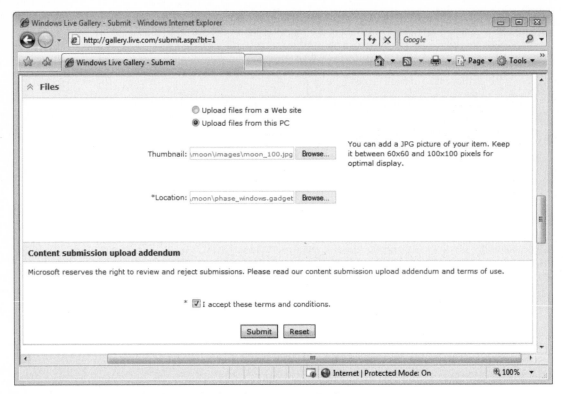

Figure 6-8. Gadget file uploads must be done from Internet Explorer.

Once your gadget is submitted, it'll need to be approved by Microsoft, which typically seems to take a couple of days. If your gadget is approved, you'll be notified via e-mail; if not, you should receive some feedback about the reasons why. You can find more information on rejection conditions at http://help.live.com/help.aspx?project=customize.

Assuming your submission is successful, Microsoft will also create a Profile page where you can manage your gadgets. Navigate to http://gallery.live.com/myProfile.aspx, and expand the Sidebar Gadgets section; you should see all your approved gadgets here, along with controls to edit, delete, and disable each. If you need to make a change to any aspect of a gadget's listing, you can do so from here.

■ **Note** Changes to your gadget's Gallery metadata or source files will need to be reapproved before they take effect.

Providing Direct Gadget Downloads

As usual, the official directory isn't the only channel for distributing your gadget. Because it's an installable Windows file, users can download (and use) a .gadget file from anywhere—including your own web site. From a hosting standpoint, this is no different from any other content: upload the .gadget file and link to it from a page on your site.

The only caveat is to ensure that your .gadget file is served with the correct content-type, application/x-windows-gadget. This should help make sure that the gadget is handled properly after downloading by a user. For the popular Apache web server, you can accomplish this by adding the following line to the relevant .htaccess or httpd.conf file:

```
AddType application/x-windows-gadget .gadget
```

Other web servers should be configured according to their own documentation.

Using Windows-Specific Extensions

If the Windows desktop is your primary (or only) deployment target, you'll be able to use some additional features of the API that aren't practical for cross-platform developers. In this section, I'll outline a few of these features and point you in the right direction for implementing them if you want.

Appearance

Because Windows gadgets are integrated directly into the desktop, Microsoft encourages developers to mimic the look and feel of its user interface as closely as possible. Toward this end, Microsoft has published very specific guidelines for user interface design, down to precise pixel dimensions for text and its spacing. You can find these specifics at http://msdn.microsoft.com/en-us/library/aa974179.aspx.

Although such a tailored integration isn't usually practical for cross-platform gadgets, it may be possible to implement some of these recommendations into Windows-specific CSS or background imagery.

Additional Content

In addition to the main HTML document that makes up the body of a gadget, the Windows API provides hooks for opening two other types of documents, *flyouts* and *settings dialogs*. These can be used to extend the user interface of a Windows gadget beyond the 130-pixel width limit of the sidebar.

For more information on both of these than I provide here, please see the official documentation referenced in the "Learning More About Windows Gadgets" section of this chapter.

■ **Tip** Because the flyout and settings dialog are in separate files, it's not necessary to refresh the entire gadget when developing these pages. Simply closing and reopening the flyout (or settings) is sufficient.

Flyouts

The first type of window, called a *flyout* by the API, is an extended view of the gadget offering additional detail on the content shown in the main view. For example, a feed reader gadget that shows news headlines might use a flyout to show a preview of the article associated with a particular headline.

To make a flyout, you'll need to create a second HTML page in your gadget (with associated CSS and JavaScript, of course) and then attach it to the API namespace during your gadget's initialization. So if you defined a flyout document of flyout.html, it would be instantiated by adding the following line to the inline <script> block shown in Listing 6-2:

```
System.Gadget.Flyout.file = 'flyout.html';
```

153

You'll always use the API namespace variable `System.Gadget.Flyout.file`; this is how Windows knows that the document in question is to be treated as a flyout. Note that a side effect of having only this single variable is that there can be only a single flyout at a time for any gadget.

With the flyout declared, you control its visibility by setting its Boolean `show` property. So, to display the flyout, simply set this property to `true`:

```
System.Gadget.Flyout.show = true;
```

and of course, set it to `false` again to hide the flyout.

Beyond these few API hooks, the control and appearance of the flyout are entirely up to you, using the same JavaScript and CSS techniques as you would for any HTML document. Because the flyout is still displayed within the Windows gadget platform, you're also free to use the transparent-background techniques discussed earlier in the chapter.

Settings Dialogs

The other type of visible extension for a Windows gadget is the *settings dialog*, an HTML document you specify as a user interface for setting configuration items. It works in tandem with the `System.Settings` persistent-storage class, discussed earlier in the chapter, completing the API's support for gadget setup. It's specified in a similar manner to a flyout, by setting a namespaced property to the name of your settings page:

```
System.Gadget.settingsUI = 'settings.html';
```

However, unlike the flyout, Windows provides the chrome to open the settings dialog: a small wrench icon that appears near the upper-right corner of the gadget when `System.Gadget.settingsUI` has been set. A user click on this icon opens the specified file; beyond this point, however, implementing the loading of the settings is up to you. You're welcome to use my `crossPlatform.storage` class; it works as well in a settings dialog as on your main page.

When laying out your settings dialog, there are a few concerns to be aware of. First, unlike the other gadget pages, Windows provides a full set of chrome here: a frame, background, title, and even OK and Cancel buttons (see Figure 6-9). As a result, all you need to provide are the data fields and labels. Second, Microsoft places a maximum width of 278 pixels on the settings dialog and recommends a maximum height of 400 pixels.

Figure 6-9. An API settings dialog for the Moon Phase gadget would look like this.

When the user clicks on the OK button, the dialog will close—but first, you need to save the settings. The API provides an event for this, System.Gadget.onSettingsClosing, so in your settings dialog you just need to create a handler for it. A template for this handler is as follows:

```
System.Gadget.onSettingsClosing = function (event) {
  if (event.closeAction == event.Action.commit) {
    // Save the new settings (from the UI to the Storage class) here
  }
  event.cancel = false;
};
```

There are two pieces here that you need to include in your own handler. First, although this event will fire whenever the settings dialog is closing, the (event.closeAction == event.Action.commit) test will be true only if the OK button was clicked—so place your configuration-saving code inside. And second, the event.cancel property needs to be set to false (as shown here), or the dialog won't be allowed to close. This enables you to validate the new settings and, if necessary, prevent the dialog from closing.

Finally, after the settings are saved and the dialog is closed, you'll need to refresh your main gadget display to reflect the changes. This is done with another event handler, as such:

```
System.Gadget.onSettingsClosed = function (event) {
  if (event.closeAction == event.Action.commit) {
    // Load and apply the new settings here
  }
};
```

This handler belongs back in your main gadget page and will be fired after the settings dialog is closed. Note the same event.closeAction test as in the previous listing, performing a similar function here—it ensures that we refresh settings only if the user clicked the OK button, not Cancel.

Localization

As a software package with a global reach, Windows is an excellent platform for internationalized gadgets. With relatively little additional effort, many gadgets can be translated into other languages and multiply their market accordingly. Of course, this won't work for every gadget—as usual, those that rely on text-based content would also require that content to be translated—but if your gadget has relatively little text, localization in Windows is worth considering.

Localization is based on organizing your content files into subdirectories within the gadget's zip archive, with each directory containing the content translated to a single language. When Windows loads any file in the gadget, it checks first in the subdirectory for the current display language and uses the file from there if it finds one. If not, it uses the main copy in the root of the gadget, effectively defaulting to your main language for any content/language pair you haven't localized.

■ **Caution** Translation to other languages also requires you to consider document encoding. Microsoft recommends UTF-8 for all localized documents; other encodings may give unpredictable results in the field.

Let's look at an example: I'm going to localize my Moon Phase gadget for Welsh. The first step, then, is to create a subdirectory in phase_windows.zip (of Figure 6-5) for the Welsh translations. For Windows to find the content, this directory needs to be named with the *locale name* for the target language; in the case of Welsh, this is cy-gb (case-insensitive).[1] You can find a complete list of locale names at http://msdn.microsoft.com/en-us/library/ms776260.aspx.

With my subdirectory created, I next need to translate the appropriate content files. The place to start is my gadget manifest, gadget.xml; you can find the Welsh translation in Listing 6-3. I've highlighted the two text strings that needed to be localized; the rest of the manifest is unchanged.

Listing 6-3. The Moon Phase Gadget Manifest Localized for Welsh

```xml
<?xml version="1.0" encoding="utf-8" ?>
<gadget>
  <name>Golwg Lleuad</name>
  <version>1.0.6</version>
  <description>Yn dangos gwedd y lleuad ar gefndir o sêr.</description>
  <author name="Sterling Udell">
    <info url="http://sterlingudell.com" text="SterlingUdell.com" />
    <logo src="su_64.png" />
  </author>
  <copyright>&#169; 2009 Udell Enterprises, Inc</copyright>
  <icons>
    <icon height="64" width="64" src="moon_64.png" />
  </icons>
  <hosts>
    <host name="sidebar">
      <base type="HTML" apiVersion="1.0.0" src="phase_windows.html" />
      <permissions>Full</permissions>
      <platform minPlatformVersion="1.0" />
      <defaultImage src="moon_64.png" />
    </host>
  </hosts>
</gadget>
```

In addition to the manifest, you can localize any file that's referred to in the gadget via a relative URL. Windows treats the localization subdirectory as the "root" of the localized gadget, so any URL paths will be relative to the subdirectory.

In my case, the other files with text that need translation are phase_windows.html (from Listing 6-2) and phase.js; they both contain text that displays on-screen. All my other gadget files—images, CSS, and other JavaScript—are unchanged, so there's no need to replicate them in the cy_gb subdirectory.

■ **Note** Files external to the gadget will need to be translated at source before downloading, of course. This may be facilitated by adding localized JavaScript to the gadget that downloads from a language-specific URL.

---

[1] All Windows locale names follow a similar pattern of [language]-[country], with a two or three letter abbreviation for each component. For Welsh, the components are cy (*Cymraeg* is the Welsh word for the language) and gb (because Welsh is spoken in Great Britain).

With my translation finished, I'm ready to rename from `.zip` to `.gadget` and reinstall. For a user with his display language set to Welsh, my gadget will now display in his native language, as shown in Figure 6-10.

Figure 6-10. The gadget Picker in Welsh, with localized Moon Phase

Localized gadgets need to be resubmitted to Microsoft's Gadget Gallery for each language they support. Simply repeat the instructions given earlier in the chapter in the "Submitting to the Gadget Gallery" section, selecting the target language and supplying translated text where appropriate. Note that not every locale has its own directory.

■ **Tip** An alternate approach to localization, by substituting strings in JavaScript rather than replacing whole files, is covered in the next chapter. Although the specific methods used there for Mac OS X are different, the general technique could easily be applied to Windows.

Non-Web Extensions

The last Windows-specific topic I'll cover moves beyond the world of pure web gadgets and into integration with the client operating system. The relevant code is well beyond the scope of this book, but because these integrations constitute a major aspect of Windows gadget development, they merit a brief mention here. They're also an inherently interesting direction in gadget development and one that we'll revisit for mobile platforms in Part 4 of the book.

First, the API includes numerous hooks to integrate directly with certain aspects of Windows from JavaScript. These functions (under the API's `System.*` namespace) access such services as contacts and messaging, CPU and power status, network connectivity, and the filesystem. With them, it's possible to create sidebar gadgets such as a laptop battery monitor, contact list, or the CPU and memory meter shown in Figure 6-11. With appropriate imagery and styling, gadgets like these are well removed from their web-application roots in both appearance and function. For details on these methods, see the official API reference in the next section.

Figure 6-11. *A Windows gadget that displays the system CPU and memory utilization*

Second, it's possible to extend this functionality even further and use native application code from within a gadget—opening the door to *any* functionality that's possible on Windows. This can be done simply using the API's System.shell.execute method to run any application specified in its parameters. Or, for a more advanced approach, it's possible to write ActiveX controls in a native language (such as C++) and embed their functionality directly in the gadget. It's far removed from web development, so I won't spend more ink on it here—but if you're interested, see http://tinyurl.com/gadgetx for more information.

Learning More About Windows Gadgets

This chapter provided an overview of Windows gadget development sufficient for cross-platform projects, but of course there is more to learn. The following links should point you to any information you may need for further exploration.

■ **Note** In much of the official documentation and online discussion, Windows gadgets are still referred to as *Sidebar Gadgets*, despite the Sidebar no longer being with us on Windows 7.

- You can find the main Microsoft documentation and API reference at http://msdn.microsoft.com/en-us/library/aa965850.aspx.

- A separate page documenting the differences between the Vista and Windows 7 implementations is at http://msdn.microsoft.com/en-us/library/dd370867.aspx.

- There's a good developer community, including participation by both Microsoft employees and experienced third parties, at http://tinyurl.com/mkdhda.

- Finally, if you're short on ideas, there's a gadget suggestion forum at http://tinyurl.com/lzquo8. Be aware that MSN forums are stringent about their browser support and, as of this writing, require either Internet Explorer or Firefox.

Summary

With 90 percent of the client operating system market, Windows offers an unparalleled opportunity to get your web gadget directly onto many users' desktops. The Windows gadget API is relatively straightforward to add to your cross-platform portfolio, requiring just a few simple steps:

1. Create a `gadget.xml` manifest, containing your gadget's metadata and a link to its main HTML file.

2. Extend that HTML slightly to support docked and undocked modes with desktop-oriented chrome.

3. Package all your static source and imagery into a zip file, and rename it to a `.gadget` extension.

4. Upload your finished package to the Gadget Gallery.

In addition, the Windows platform offers good opportunities for extensions beyond the core web gadget, including localization to multiple languages and even integration with native client applications. It definitely merits a place in your gadget development plan.

In the next chapter, we'll be porting our gadgets to the equivalent desktop API for the Mac, supporting those computer users who *aren't* running Windows.

■ ■ ■

CHAPTER 7

Mac OS X Dashboard

The natural complement to the Windows gadgets covered in the previous chapter are widgets for the Mac, so that's where you'll turn your attention next. Although Apple's OS X desktop operating system has a smaller market share, its users are unmatched in their dedication, and the very fact of its smaller size means that there's less competition for a good gadget. So, the Mac is another good choice for cross-platform development.

However, OS X is also not without its challenges for gadget developers. It's more particular in its requirements than any other platform, especially in terms of some very specific appearance guidelines. In this chapter, I'll guide you through these obstacles and out the other side.

■ **Caution** The code in this chapter will work *only* on a Mac running OS X 10.4.3 or newer. If you don't have access to a Mac for development, be aware that this chapter will unavoidably be academic for you.

Introducing Dashboard Widgets

Apple introduced widgets to the Mac desktop with OS X version 10.4 (Tiger) in 2005, and its support is continuing at least through 10.5 (Leopard) and onto 10.6 (Snow Leopard). Since the user interface design of OS X means that the desktop itself is seldom seen, Apple has instead grouped its gadgets into a container application called the Dashboard (see Figure 7-1). Consequently, mini-apps on this platform are often called Dashboard widgets, rather than Mac or OS X widgets. I'll use all three terms in this chapter, but I'll tend to use *widget* more than *gadget*, because that is Apple's preferred terminology.

Figure 7-1. The OS X Dashboard, with widgets

When the Dashboard is first opened from the Dock, it displays the user's active widgets in a translucent layer overlaid on other running applications. The user can click the + icon in the lower-left corner to reveal the Widget Bar (shown in Figure 7-2), which shows all widgets installed on the computer. And one of the standard widgets is Widget Manager; with it, the user can add new widgets or remove unwanted ones.

■ **Tip** You can open the Dashboard either by clicking its Dock icon or by pressing F12.

Figure 7-2. The Widget Bar

Developing a Dashboard Widget

As is the case with other desktop platforms, a Dashboard widget is deployed as a package—or, in Mac terminology, a *bundle*—which is a single file containing all the widget's component source code and other resources. And like other platforms, widget packages are identified by a particular file extension—in this case, .wdgt. However, unlike Windows, OS X supports extensions in directory names, and this means that an OS X widget bundle is simply a renamed directory, with no need for an intermediary format (such as a zip archive).

Within the bundle, there are four required files, three of which must have specific names:

- Info.plist, the widget's *information property list*, an XML metadata document.

- Default.png, your widget's default background image. This must be included even if your gadget handles its background internally, as with CSS.

- Icon.png, a 75-pixel square icon that will represent your app on the Dashboard's Widget Bar.

These files will all be discussed in greater depth in the next few pages.

■ **Caution** The names of these files are all case-sensitive, so make sure you capitalize the first letter of each.

The fourth required file is your core HTML document, but it can be named whatever you'd like; it will be specified in Info.plist. And within the bundle, you'll also include all local source and content files that your gadget requires. These can be placed in subdirectories, or not, as you prefer.

Conforming to the Mac User Interface

The distinctive Mac user interface is one of Apple's proudest possessions, and since this is where widgets reside, they are strongly encouraged to fit in visually. Unfortunately, though, the platform doesn't supply you with much chrome to ease this process, so it's up to you make the effort. In the following sections, I'll discuss modifications you'll want to make to your gadget's background imagery and other styles; a bit later in the chapter, I'll talk about appearance-related coding changes.

Backgrounds, Borders, and Shadows

Like other Mac application windows, the widgets supplied by Apple have rounded corners, and it's good practice that your Dashboard widgets do too. There are a couple of ways to go about this; the easiest is by simply applying some CSS to your existing background. A single rule (added to the selector that defines your gadget's background) is sufficient:

```
-webkit-border-radius: 10px;
```

Of course, it's only this easy because Mac widgets are always rendered with the Safari browser. Since Safari is based on the WebKit rendering engine, the `-webkit-border-radius` rule is safe to use, and we don't need to worry about cross-browser compatibility. However, remember that even if you create your background in CSS, you're still required to have a background image (named `Default.png`) in your widget bundle. Dashboard will show this image while your widget is initializing, before its CSS is invoked.

■ **Note** There's no official recommendation for *how* rounded your corners should be, and Apple's own widgets vary. A radius between 8 and 12 pixels should be fine.

The CSS option is probably your best choice if your content is of variable size, because it will be applied regardless of dimensions. If your gadget has only a few possible sizes, however, you can achieve better results by creating background images. This also enables you to create an Apple-standard drop shadow for your widget—another visual effect that is common on the Dashboard.

If you are going to add a shadow to your widget, these are the parameters recommended by Apple:

- 50 percent opacity
- 90-degree angle from horizontal
- 4-pixel offset
- 10-pixel Gaussian blur

■ **Note** This drop shadow will necessarily exist outside of the "body" of your background image and will require a corresponding adjustment to your content layout—but we'll deal with that later in the chapter in the "Dashboard-Specific CSS" section.

For my case-study Moon Phase gadget, I'm actually going to use both techniques: a background image (with shadow) for the main view, shown in Figure 7-3, and a CSS-based black background with rounded corners for the configuration pane. This gadget has only two possible sizes, so creating background images (and switching between them in code) is reasonable.

Figure 7-3. The `Default.png` *background image for Moon Phase, with drop shadow*

■ **Tip** Because your widget bundle is required to include a background image named `Default.png`, it makes sense to use this name in your own code for your most commonly used background image.

Configuration

This discussion of the configuration pane brings up another important design point for Dashboard widgets. If your gadget requires configuration, the standard approach on this platform is for a pane that's simply an alternate view of your gadget's ordinary appearance. In other words, you're encouraged to simply replace your gadget's main content with its settings user interface, without altering the gadget's size or shape. This can be problematic for some gadget designs, and it's not an absolute requirement, but it is the preferred approach.

One advantage to this is that you may be able to reuse visual elements between the two modes of your gadget, especially border and background imagery. Bear in mind, however, that it needs to be clear to the user that your configuration pane *isn't* your widget's main view—so you need to be careful not to reuse so much that they appear too similar. One common approach is to use a slightly different background color, preferably one that's darker or more muted than on your gadget's main view.

The reasoning behind this same-size approach is that Apple has adopted a paradigm that the settings are on the *back* of each widget. In support of this idea, the API supplies functions to animate the transition between main and settings views, visually appearing to flip the widget over on-screen to reveal its settings. However, this illusion works only if the two views are the same size.

For my Moon Phase gadget, making the configuration pane match the size of the main gadget view is both a blessing and a curse. The downside is that, in the gadget's smaller size mode, the settings won't physically fit within the default gadget bounds, so I've had to make the gadget slightly larger to accommodate them. But, the upside is that I am able to reuse background imagery. To keep the two sides visually distinct, I overlay the starry-sky backdrop with a black rectangle (with CSS rounded corners), but by carefully alignment, the drop shadow is still visible. You can see this effect in Figure 7-4, and I'll detail its implementation later in the chapter (in connection with Listings 7-2 and 7-3, where you'll also find code for integrating the flip animation).

Figure 7-4. *The settings pane on the "back" of Moon Phase*

Figure 7-4 also shows one other Dashboard user interface consideration: Apple discourages any promotional messages or links on the front of the gadget. Since I have such a link on my core Moon Phase gadget, as part of the Mac port I've moved it to the back of the widget. Such a move may or may not be practical (or even applicable) for your own gadget—and again, this is not an absolute requirement, but a recommendation.

Buttons

Because Apple expects most widgets to have a back, it supplies a standard button for accessing it. It's a small, italic *i*, and it's usually placed in the lower-right corner of the widget, as shown in Figure 7-5. Mac users have grown accustomed to this icon (and its placement) for flipping a widget over, so you're strongly encouraged to conform to this standard if at all possible. It's added with just a couple of lines of JavaScript, which I'll discuss when we get to Listing 7-4.

Figure 7-5. *This clock widget uses the standard widget info button.*

Finally, one last piece of chrome which Dashboard automatically supplies is a close button (visible on the Calculator in Figure 7-1). The platform creates this button for every widget and displays it at the upper-left corner, though you can exercise some control over its position from your widget's information property list.

■ **Tip** To show the close button for a widget on your screen, hold down the Option key and move your mouse pointer over the widget.

Widget Bar Icon

In addition to the visual appearance of the widget itself, you'll also need to create an icon for display on the Widget Bar (shown in Figure 7-2). Although I've generated icons for my gadgets on most platforms, Apple again has some specific recommendations to help your widget blend in seamlessly.

The base icon starts off 75 pixels square, with rounded corners; again, no specific rounding radius is given, but 10 pixels seems about right. This initial icon should also have a drop shadow applied according to the following parameters:

- 50 percent opacity

- 90-degree angle from horizontal

- 3-pixel offset

- 3-pixel size, using Gaussian blur

After applying the shadow, note that your icon will be larger than 75 pixels square, usually about 81. Save the image as Icon.png (case-sensitive); you'll be adding it to the widget's package a bit later. Figure 7-6 shows my Icon.png for Moon Phase.

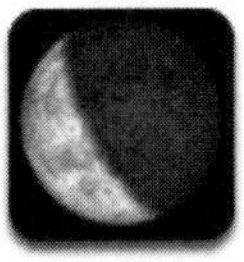

Figure 7-6. The Widget Bar icon for Moon Phase,with rounded corners and drop shadow

Although your widget is required to have an Icon.png in its package, it's not an absolute requirement that its appearance follow these guidelines. As shown earlier in Figure 7-2, even Apple's official Stickies widget deviates from this standard, with square corners and no overall shadow.

Adapting the Core Gadget

By now, you should have a reasonable idea of the visual changes that a successful Mac version of your gadget will require. In this part of the chapter, I'll walk you through the corresponding code modifications, using Moon Phase as a live example. These changes are grouped into metadata (here on the Mac, Info.plist), content (the main HTML document), presentation (CSS), functionality (JavaScript), and finally some crossPlatform middleware to tie it all together. The following sections discuss each of these areas in detail.

Creating the Information Property List

In addition to your actual content and code files, gadget platforms always require some extra information to tell them *about* your app, and the OS X Dashboard is no exception. As with other Mac applications, widgets store their metadata in a *property list* file named Info.plist.

A property list file is simply XML, and as such can be created and modified from any text editor, including the default Mac TextEdit application. However, I recommend that you install PListEdit Pro, a shareware utility that takes much of the drudgery out of this task. Download it from http://apple.com/downloads/macosx/development_tools/plisteditpro.html.

■ **Caution** Dashboard caches your Info.plist file at the moment you first install your widget and doesn't reload changes afterward, even if you uninstall. To apply Info.plist changes, you'll need to either modify the CFBundleIdentifier key (see the explanation following Listing 7-1) or reboot your Mac.

Listing 7-1 shows a typical widget Info.plist file, one that you can use as a template for your own Dashboard port. As you can see, it's made up of a number of key elements, each of which is followed by its corresponding value. In the following sections, I'll walk you through the individual keys and the significance of each to your widget.

Listing 7-1. The Moon Phase Widget's Information Property List

```
<?xml version="1.0" encoding="UTF-8"?>
<!DOCTYPE plist PUBLIC "-//Apple//DTD PLIST 1.0//EN"
  "http://www.apple.com/DTDs/PropertyList-1.0.dtd">
<plist version="1.0">
<dict>
    <key>CFBundleIdentifier</key>
    <string>com.daylightmap.moon.mac</string>
    <key>CFBundleName</key>
    <string>Moon Phase</string>
    <key>CFBundleDisplayName</key>
    <string>Moon Phase</string>
    <key>CFBundleVersion</key>
    <string>1.0</string>
    <key>CFBundleShortVersionString</key>
    <string>1.0.7</string>
    <key>CloseBoxInsetX</key>
    <integer>10</integer>
    <key>CloseBoxInsetY</key>
    <integer>8</integer>
    <key>AllowNetworkAccess</key>
    <true/>
    <key>MainHTML</key>
    <string>phase_mac.html</string>
</dict>
</plist>
```

CFBundleIdentifier

This required value specifies your widget uniquely on the Mac operating system. Traditionally, it's supplied as a Java-style (reverse-domain) namespace, as in `com.yourcompany.project[.subproject]`; this minimizes name collisions. Dashboard uses this value at install time to determine whether a widget is new or a reinstall; correspondingly, if you develop several different widgets, they *must* have different `CFBundleIdentifier` values.

CFBundleName and CFBundleDisplayName

These two required keys supply your widget's name to Dashboard. The `CFBundleName` value contains the name of your widget bundle on the Mac filesystem (without the `.wdgt` extension). `CFBundleDisplayName` is supposed to allow you to override this with another name to display in the Dashboard and Widget Bar—but in my experience, it's ignored, and the file name/`CFBundleName` is always shown. So, my advice is to simply set these both to the same value, matching your bundle file name.

In any case, endeavor to keep your widget name to 16 characters or less for display within its portion of the Widget Bar.

CFBundleVersion and CFBundleShortVersionString

You're required to include the full version number of your widget in `CFBundleVersion`, as a sequence of dot-separated integers. Optionally, you can also include a shorter, more user-friendly version number in `CFBundleShortVersionString`, although the same formatting rule applies.

MainHTML

This specifies the full name of your widget's core HTML document with the bundle. It's required.

CloseBoxInsetX and CloseBoxInsetY

These two values allow you to specify the position of the Dashboard-supplied close button (see the calculator widget in Figure 7-1). They contain the horizontal and vertical pixel offsets, relative to the widget's upper-left corner, where you want the *center* of the close button to display. And in practice, they usually require a bit of experimentation to get right. This is optional; if not supplied, it defaults to 0.

Permissions

A family of keys, rather than a single instance, these flags indicate any access to external resources that your widget requires. Although they're formally optional, they are required if your gadget needs such access. The following keys are available:

- `AllowNetworkAccess`: For access to any content over a network connection (either Internet or intranet)

- `AllowFileAccessOutsideOfWidget`: For access to filesystem resources, via the file: protocol

- `AllowInternetPlugins`: For use of standard browser plug-ins, such as Flash or QuickTime

- `AllowJava`: For use of Java applets within the widget

- `AllowSystem`: For command-line access using the `widget.system` interface (discussed later in the chapter)

- `Plugin`: For use of native plug-ins (also discussed later)

- `AllowFullAccess`: A shorthand key; if set, implies all previous permissions

Note that Moon Phase requires `AllowNetworkAccess`, as will most web gadgets that aren't completely self-contained.

Other Keys

The preceding `Info.plist` keys cover most common situations found in cross-platform gadget development. However, a few additional keys are available for special circumstances, detailed in the following sections.

Height and Width

If you want to specify initial dimensions for your widget, you may do so with these two `integer` values. However, if you're already using `crossPlatform.adjustSize` to register your gadget's dimensions with the API, you can continue to do so—and you shouldn't have need for `height` and `width` in your property list file.

BackwardsCompatibleClassLookup

In the JavaScript section a few pages hence, we'll be making use of some Apple-supplied classes to integrate Dashboard functionality into our widget—and the class names involved have only been in existence since OS X 10.4.3. If you have need to maintain backward compatibility with earlier versions of OS X, setting `BackwardsCompatibleClassLookup` to `true` will allow you to use the legacy class names.

In practice, however, few Mac users are still on 10.4.2 or earlier, so the vast majority of widgets have no need for this key.

Fonts

If you would like to use custom fonts in your widget, it's possible to include the font (`.dfont` or `.ttf`) files in your widget bundle and then add the font names to your `Info.plist` under the `Fonts` key. This is done as a string array, as follows:

```
<key>Fonts</key>
<array>
  <string>Courier.ttf</string>
  <string>Verdana.ttf</string>
</array>
```

Keep in mind that the preceding steps only make a font available; you'll also need to implement it in your code, with a CSS `font-family` rule. And although custom fonts are useful for good control of appearance, they're obviously limited to Dashboard widgets—there's no cross-platform equivalent to the `Fonts` key.

Plugin

Another Dashboard-only extension is the `Plugin` key, which is used to link native code into the widget. This will be covered more thoroughly later in the chapter in the "Non-Web Extensions" section.

Changes to the HTML

The source code changes required to port a generic web gadget to Dashboard are among the most extensive of any API covered in this book, largely because of the platform's very specific appearance recommendations. As a result, you're likely to need more new JavaScript and CSS for this platform than you have for most others. However, my advice is to still try not to modify your existing `.js` and `.css` source files; merging these changes into later versions of your gadget is sure to cause headaches. A better course is to create new source files for your Mac-specific code (perhaps appending _mac to their names) and link them all into your HTML. You'll still need to fork your main HTML document—no avoiding that—but with your other modifications in new files, the changes to it should be minimized.

In Listing 7-2, you'll find this Dashboard-modified HTML for my Moon Phase example widget. I'll discuss the changes here first and then move on to the new CSS and JavaScript. Throughout this part of the chapter, the changes I describe should be broadly applicable to any generic web gadget and so serve as a guide for your own conversions. You'll also find a few specific code snippets that you should be able to use verbatim.

Listing 7-2. phase_mac.html, the Core HTML Document of the Moon Phase Widget for Dashboard

```
<?xml version="1.0" encoding="UTF-8"?>
<!DOCTYPE html PUBLIC "-//W3C//DTD XHTML 1.0 Transitional//EN"
                      "http://www.w3.org/TR/xhtml1/DTD/xhtml1-transitional.dtd">
<html xmlns="http://www.w3.org/1999/xhtml">
  <head>
    <meta http-equiv="Content-Type" content="text/html;charset=UTF-8" />
    <meta name="description"
          content="Shows the current phase of the moon on a field of stars." />
    <title>Moon Phase</title>
    <link href="moon_32.png"    type="image/png" rel="icon" />
    <link href="phase.css"      type="text/css"  rel="stylesheet" />
    <link href="phase_mac.css" type="text/css"  rel="stylesheet" />
  </head>
  <body class="moonPhase">
    <div id="main">
      <div id="main_icons">
        <a id="config_icon" class="control_icon" title="Settings"
           onclick="moonPhase.showConfig()"></a>
      </div>
      <p id="last" class="text"></p>
      <p id="image_container">
        <img id="moon" alt="Current Moon Image" width="176" height="176"
             src="http://daylightmap.com/moon/images/luna_north_small.jpg" />
      </p>
      <p id="next" class="text"></p>
    </div>

    <div id="config" style="display: none">
<!--  <p><strong>Moon Phase Settings</strong></p> -->
      <p>
        <label for="size">Size:</label>
        <select id="size" name="size">
          <option value="small">Small</option>
          <option value="large">Large</option>
```

```
          <option value="auto">Auto</option>
        </select>
      </p>
      <p>
        <label for="text">Show Text:</label>
        <select id="text" name="text">
          <option value="yes">Yes</option>
          <option value="no">No</option>
          <option value="auto">Auto</option>
        </select>
      </p>
      <p>
        <label for="hemisphere">View From:</label>
        <select id="hemisphere" name="hemisphere">
          <option value="north">Northern Hemisphere</option>
          <option value="south">Southern Hemisphere</option>
        </select>
      </p>
      <p id="config_buttons">
        <input type="submit" value="Save" id="save_button"
               onclick=" moonPhase.saveConfig(); return false; " />
        <input type="button" value="Cancel" id="cancel_button"
               onclick="moonPhase.hideConfig();" />
      </p>
      <p id="credit" class="text">
        by <a onclick="widget.openURL('http://www.daylightmap.com')">DaylightMap</a>
      </p>
    </div>

    <script src="platform.js"  type="text/javascript"></script>
    <script src="phase.js"     type="text/javascript"></script>
    <script src="/System/Library/WidgetResources/AppleClasses/AppleInfoButton.js"
                               type="text/javascript"></script>
    <script src="/System/Library/WidgetResources/AppleClasses/AppleAnimator.js"
                               type="text/javascript"></script>
    <script src="phase_mac.js" type="text/javascript"></script>
  </body>
</html>
```

Apart from linking in the new external .css and .js files, there are only a couple of changes in this listing. First (and easiest), I've commented out the title of the configuration pane; the user already knows that the "back" of the widget is where she changes the settings, so no title is needed.

Second, I've moved my branding link from the "front" of the widget to the "back," on the configuration pane (as shown in Figure 7-4). But this raises one other issue: the Dashboard API doesn't allow links within the widget to natively open a browser window outside of it. Consequently, I've replaced the target and href attributes with an onclick handler that calls widget.openURL, an API function that accomplishes the same thing. If you have external links in your gadgets, they'll need similar treatment.

Dashboard-Specific CSS

Given the many Dashboard appearance requirements, it's slightly surprising that there aren't more modifications to the gadget's style than what you'll find in Listing 7-3. Your own equivalent of this file is where you'll place all Mac-specific style for your widget conversion.

Listing 7-3. The Dashboard-Specific Style Sheet for Moon Phase, phase_mac.css

```css
/* General widget appearance changes */
.moonPhase {
  font-weight: bold;
  background: transparent;
  padding: 4px 9px 14px 9px;
}

/* Modifications to the configuration pane */
.moonPhase #config {
  -webkit-border-radius: 12px;
  overflow: hidden;
}
.moonPhase #credit {
  position: relative;
  top: 40px;
}

/* Style related to the lower-right-corner Info Button */
.moonPhase #last {
  top: auto;
  bottom: 0;
}
.moonPhase #next {
  top: 0;
  bottom: auto;
}
.moonPhase #main_icons {
  top: auto;
  bottom: 1px;
  opacity: 1 !important;
}
```

The CSS in Listing 7-3 is grouped into three categories—general appearance, the configuration pane, and the Apple Info Button—so you'll find a section coming up that details each.

General Appearance

Listing 7-3 starts with a few general changes that are required to make the overall appearance acceptable on OS X. The first is to increase the font weight throughout the gadget; the Mac's smaller rendering standard means that the (already small) text in my gadget begins to suffer readability issues otherwise:

```css
font-weight: bold;
```

The other changes are needed to make the gadget work with its new background image. First, I needed to hide the default gadget background so that the Mac-only background is used instead:

```
background: transparent;
```

Note that the background image itself, `Default.png`, is displayed by the platform. You'll also be manipulating it in JavaScript a bit later.

Finally, the gadget's layout needs to remain within the extra border that the drop shadow adds around the body of the background image. This is fairly easy to accomplish by simply adding `padding` to the body element, equivalent to the space that the shadow occupies around all four sides:

```
padding: 4px 9px 14px 9px;
```

■ **Tip** If you've created a background-image shadow according to the standard guidelines, you may well be able to use this style rule exactly as shown earlier.

The Configuration Pane

As you'll recall from the "Conforming to the Mac User Interface" section earlier in the chapter, my configuration pane's background overlays the main starry-sky image with basic black. A rule of `background-color: black` already exists in `phase.css` (back in Listing 3-3), so here, all that remains is to put a 12-pixel rounding on its corners.

The other configuration-pane style rules are to do with moving the branding to here, the "back" of the widget. I've moved the `credit` element to the `config div` in the body of my HTML, and the `position` and `top` rules in Listing 7-3 place it where I want it. The only problem is that in the widget's smaller size mode, there's actually no room for the branding—but by setting `overflow: hidden` on its parent, I ensure that it's simply not visible off the bottom of the pane.

The Info Button

The largest block of Mac-specific style has to do with the Info Button, Apple's recommended replacement for my existing configuration icon. The actual inclusion of the Info Button will happen in JavaScript, where I'll be dynamically inserting it into my existing icon container, `<div id="main_icons">`. However, the integration will also require a number of appearance-related changes here in the CSS.

First, the Info Button interface supplies its own opacity handling, so I need to disable the icon `opacity` rules that I created for my default gadget (these were in Listing 3-4). This is accomplished with a single rule in Listing 7-2 of `opacity: 100%`, with an `!important` modifier to ensure that it takes precedence.

Second, I need to reposition the `main_icons` container from the upper-right to lower-right corner to conform to Apple's style guidelines. This is fairly easy, simply by setting `bottom: 0` and removing the existing top value.

This introduces a problem, though: I already had content in the lower-right corner, the display of the time until the next new (or full) moon. I can solve that by moving it to the upper-right corner—in effect, I've now swapped locations of the next and `main_icons` containers. But this creates one *more* issue: all of my text is now at the top of the gadget. To keep it aesthetically balanced, I'll also move the `prev` container to the lower-left corner. Space has been cleared here by moving my branding to the "back" of the widget, remember.

In the end, Apple's style recommendations sound simple, but it has caused me to rearrange nearly all my content. It's not an enormous amount of work (only 30 lines of CSS), but it does increase the effort required for the Mac version when compared to other platforms. You can see the result in Figure 7-7.

Figure 7-7. *The rearranged Moon Phase gadget*

CONTROL REGIONS

As with other desktop platforms, Dashboard allows the user to reposition gadgets by simply dragging them around the screen. This platform refines the concept a bit more with the introduction of *control regions*, areas on the widget that are excluded from the drag behavior. The idea is that a click on a button, text entry field, or other user-interface control should perform the default action for that control, rather than initiating a drag action. It's a subtle refinement but typical of Apple's attention to user interface details.

The creation of control regions is left to the widget developer, rather than the platform trying to guess which controls you want to exclude. Defining a control region is done in CSS with a widget-specific rule, `-apple-dashboard-region`. It's a functional rule, meaning that it takes parameters; in its most basic form, it can be used to simply define an entire HTML element as a control region:

```
button {
  -apple-dashboard-region: dashboard-region(control rectangle);
}
```

The first parameter is always `control`, and the second can be either `rectangle` or `circle` (for visually round buttons). In addition, the rule can take four additional parameters to specify padding from the edges of the element. These values are given in the usual order for CSS edges: `top right bottom left`. So to refine our example, if our button elements had 2 pixels of vertical padding (but none horizontally), the CSS would look like this:

```
button {
  -apple-dashboard-region: dashboard-region(control rectangle 2px 0 2px 0);
}
```

Control regions are a bit of extra effort, and it's your decision whether they're worth it for your widget, but they can lend an extra degree of polish to the finished product.

Dashboard-Specific JavaScript

With the visual changes complete, you can now turn your attention to making the widget function correctly on Dashboard. And again with the JavaScript, Apple's requirements will necessitate more code than you've needed for other platforms. Listing 7-4 shows my code for Moon Phase; your own will likely follow a similar pattern.

Listing 7-4. The JavaScript for Moon Phase on the Mac, phase_mac.js

```
// Ensure that the moonPhase namespace exists
var moonPhase = window.moonPhase || {};

// Override the default load method
moonPhase.defaultLoad = moonPhase.load;
moonPhase.load = function () {
  // Set the widget's visual style to match the preferred size
  if (moonPhase.prefs.size.get() === 'small') {
    document.body.style.width = '160px';
    document.body.style.backgroundImage = 'url(Default_small.png)';
    moonPhase.elements.config.style.height = '125px';
    moonPhase.elements.main.style.height = '132px';
    moonPhase.elements.moon.style.marginTop = '12px';
  } else {
    document.body.style.width = '240px';
    document.body.style.backgroundImage = 'url(Default.png)';
    moonPhase.elements.config.style.height = '185px';
    moonPhase.elements.main.style.height = '200px';
    moonPhase.elements.moon.style.marginTop = '';
  }

  // Call the default method
  moonPhase.defaultLoad();

  // Set up the Info Button
  moonPhase.elements.config_icon.style.backgroundImage = '';
  new AppleInfoButton(moonPhase.elements.config_icon,
    moonPhase.elements.main, 'white', 'black', moonPhase.showConfig);
};

// Also override the default methods for showing and hiding the config pane to
// include Apple's flipping animation

moonPhase.defaultShowConfig = moonPhase.showConfig;
moonPhase.showConfig = function () {
  if (window.widget) {
    widget.prepareForTransition('ToBack');
  }

  moonPhase.defaultShowConfig();

  if (window.widget) {
    setTimeout('widget.performTransition();', 0);
```

```
  }
};

moonPhase.defaultHideConfig = moonPhase.hideConfig;
moonPhase.hideConfig = function () {
  if (window.widget) {
    widget.prepareForTransition('ToFront');
  }

  moonPhase.defaultHideConfig();

  if (window.widget) {
    setTimeout('widget.performTransition();', 0);
  }
};
```

The first thing you're likely to notice about this listing is the use of *method overrides*; the three functions defined here don't stand alone, but rather they extend the functionality of the base moonPhase object. This is a fundamental concept of object-oriented programming but one that's not intrinsically part of JavaScript; as a result, it's up to the individual developer to implement method overrides. Here's an overview of my approach:

1. I *save* the default function (in a namespace variable named accordingly):

   ```
   moonPhase.defaultLoad = moonPhase.load;
   ```

2. I *define* a new method, replacing the default function in the namespace object.

3. At the appropriate point in the code of my new method, I *call* the default function, which I saved in step 1 (highlighted in bold here).

   ```
   moonPhase.load = function () {
     // Mac-specific code goes here
     ...

     // Call the default method
     moonPhase.defaultLoad();
   }
   ```

It's a fairly straightforward technique for extending the functionality in my core namespace and one that you might find useful if you need to extend some part of your own gadget's code to support a specific platform—not just Mac.

Overriding the Load Function

Within my load method override, the first priority is to handle the two different size modes of the widget. This is quite straightforward, as you can see; it simply requires setting style properties appropriate to the given size. The only slightly odd aspect is that the heights of the main and config panes are different; this is to compensate for a padding of 3 percent, which is applied to config in the default gadget style sheet.

■ **Note** Because Mac widgets are always rendered with Safari, there's no need to worry about the Internet Explorer box model bug when working with layout. And there was much rejoicing.

The other code you'll find in the new `moonPhase.load` of Listing 7-4 is the integration of the Info Button for opening the configuration pane. It's done by creating an instance of the API `AppleInfoButton` object, whose constructor takes no less than five parameters:

1. The HTML element that will contain the button. In my case, I have this predefined in my `moonPhase.elements` object, but a simple `getElementById` call would function just as well.

2. The HTML element that is your widget's main view (and on which the Info Button will be visible).

3. The color for the Info Button's *i*.

4. The color for the button's circular background. Note that this is never fully opaque, so the color specified here will appear as a wash on its background.

5. The function to call to show your widgets' configuration pane (its "back"). If you don't have a single function to do this, you'll need to define one for the Info Button, though you can do so with an inline function literal.

Note that my `AppleInfoButton` needs to be created after my ancestor `load` method call; this is because `moonPhase.load` sets the background image for the default configuration button. This is also why I clear `moonPhase.elements.config_icon.style.backgroundImage` manually here.

Flipping the Widget

Our Info Button is now in place—what happens when the user clicks it? The code described earlier would be perfectly functional as is; my existing `showConfig` function (back in Listing 3-5) would display the configuration pane, the same as it does on any other platform. For full compliance with the Mac platform, however, I go on to integrate the animation it supplies for the font-back transition, a simulated "flipping" of the widget.

This is accomplished with the API functions `prepareForTransition` and `showTransition` (both in the widget namespace), and it needs to be done in both directions, to and from the configuration pane. Since `moonPhase` already has functions in place for both of these actions (`showConfig` and `hideConfig`), my preferred course is to simply override them with versions that add the animation. The approach in each is the same:

1. Call `widget.prepareForTransition`, with a string parameter of either `'ToBack'` or `'ToFront'` indicating which direction we're going. This gets the animation ready and should be done before any operations which affect the visible DOM.

2. Call the ancestor function, which actually toggles the visibility of the HTML elements involved.

3. Call `showTransition` to invoke the animation that was prepared in step 1. Note that Apple recommends that this be wrapped in a `setTimeout` call to "ensure that both sides of the flip look correct." I've never seen a perceptible difference, but there's little harm in it.

■ **Tip** The API function calls in this section are preceded by a check for the existence of the widget namespace. By doing so, you enable your widget code to be run in an ordinary browser session—where widget doesn't exist, but other debugging may be easier.

Additions to crossPlatform

Dashboard's style recommendations are a somewhat time-consuming departure from the look and feel of a generic gadget—but fortunately, its internals are a good fit for the common infrastructure that makes such a gadget work. In the following sections, I'll go over the modifications required to the crossPlatform middleware layer I introduced in Part 1 of the book. Even if you're not using crossPlatform itself, these should serve as a guide for your own, equivalent integration layer.

Platform Sniffing

Listings 7-2 and 7-4 have already made use of the widget namespace, where Apple keeps much of its JavaScript API functionality. Accordingly, this is a good test for the existence of the Dashboard platform, as follows:

```
if (!!window.widget) {
  crossPlatform.api = 'mac';
  crossPlatform.emptyPref = undefined;
}
```

Persistent Storage

With the platform detected, its use is quite easy; Dashboard defines good methods for loading and saving preference data that dovetail nicely with my persistent Storage class. The former uses widget.preferenceForKey as such:

```
switch (crossPlatform.api) {
  case 'mac':
    myValue = myValue = widget.preferenceForKey(name);
    break;
  ...
}
```

and the latter, the corresponding setPreferenceForKey:

```
switch (crossPlatform.api) {
  case 'mac':
    widget.setPreferenceForKey(myValue, myName);
    break;
  ...
}
```

■ **Caution** If you're implementing your own API layer, note that setPreferenceForKey puts the data value *before* its name, the opposite order of most other APIs.

Resizing

The other crossPlatform area where you need to do a bit of work is in handling changes to gadget size. Dashboard gives your widget complete control over its size—but in order to correctly render the new dimensions, it does require to be notified when the size changes. Until you do so, your gadget will be visually cropped at its old dimensions.

Fortunately, it's an easy requirement to fulfill. My crossPlatform namespace already has an adjustSize method to handle similar functions on other platforms, and it's no problem to add another case for the Mac:

```
crossPlatform.adjustSize = function () {
  switch (crossPlatform.api) {
    case 'mac':
      window.resizeTo(crossPlatform.getWidth(window),
                      crossPlatform.getHeight(window));
      break;
    ...
  }
};
```

I simply retrieve the gadget dimensions from my existing getWidth and getHeight methods (visible near the end of Listing 2-5) and pass them to resizeTo, Dashboard's size notification function.

Testing and Debugging

It's now time to exercise your newly minted code as a Dashboard widget, and the first step is that you'll need a Mac to test on. Virtually any hardware will work, from the lowliest Mini to the mightiest multicore Pro; the only hard requirement is that it be running at least OS X 10.4.3 or newer.

In addition, I recommend that you sign up for the Apple Developer Connection at http://developer.apple.com. It's free, and without it you won't have access to the full range of documentation and tools that Apple makes available. This membership is also required for submitting widgets to the Dashboard directory.

Exploring the Dashcode Development Environment

Like all web gadgets, it's possible to develop widgets on a Mac with only the most rudimentary of tools: a text editor for source files and the built-in Dashboard for testing. However, there's an easier way: Apple produces a developer tool called Dashcode, a full-fledged IDE for web apps of all sorts, especially widgets.

Assuming you've registered with the Developer Connection, you can download Dashcode from http://developer.apple.com/mac. It comes as part of the larger Xcode Tools, which also includes an SDK for general Mac development. If widget development is your main interest, however, you only need the Essentials option when installing; that will include Dashcode.

■ **Tip** If you're planning to develop for the iPhone as well, install the iPhone SDK instead, from `http://developer.apple.com/iphone`. It includes both Xcode and Dashcode.

Once installed, Dashcode will become your default editor for `.html`, `.css`, and `.js` files, not to mention `.wdgt` files (discussed in the next section). It also includes Apple's Property List Editor, a reasonable alternative for working with your `Info.plist` file.

Packaging Your Widget

With your source files ready to test, the first step is to package them into a widget bundle. To do so, create a new directory and copy all your source files in, including any subdirectory structure that your gadget may employ. Then simply click the directory's name (in the Finder), and change it so that it has an extension of `.wdgt`. Its icon should change, and it will no longer be expandable as an ordinary folder. Congratulations! You've created a widget.

Just because your widget is packaged, however, doesn't mean that its contents are inaccessible. Still in the Finder, right-click your `.wdgt` bundle, and select Show Package Contents. A new window should open, displaying all your source files just as if they were in an ordinary directory. You can edit any of them in place here, copy in new versions, and so forth.

The other task that you'll find useful for `.wdgt` files is editing the widget as a whole in Dashcode. To do so, right-click the `.wdgt` bundle and select Open With → Dashcode. You'll be presented with a widget-oriented IDE that lets you quickly select and edit various source files, modify your HTML layout, and even make some changes to your Information Property List. But best of all, Dashcode includes support for running your widget internally, indispensable for real development work. To do so, simply click the Run icon, or press Cmd+R.

You can also debug any of your JavaScript here by placing breakpoints on the required lines; Dashcode will stop when it reaches them. It features a debugging console as well, which supports the standard `console.log` function common to many browser debuggers.

■ **Tip** When running in Dashcode, JavaScript `alert` calls also log to the console, rather than displaying a pop-up message.

Installing in Dashboard

When your widget is running satisfactorily in Dashcode, the next step is to install it into Dashboard, its home environment. Make sure you've closed your widget from Dashcode (or any other editor), then in Finder, simply double-click your `.wdgt` file. You'll be prompted for confirmation and then presented with a preview of your app; make sure you click Keep at this point, even if it's not working correctly. The other option, Delete, will move your widget bundle to the Trash!

After clicking Keep, Dashboard will remain running, with your widget front and center. Make sure you test all of its functionality here, even if it was working well in Dashcode. Small inconsistencies do occasionally appear.

Behind the scenes, installing a widget into Dashboard simply moves its `.wdgt` bundle to your user-level `/Library/Widgets` directory. If you do need to make additional changes to your widget, you'll want to move it out of your Library to do so; Dashcode won't save changes here. You'll also need to reinstall it to Dashboard to see the effect of any changes; uninstall it first, using the Manage Widgets button.

■ **Caution** Remember that changes to your `Info.plist` file aren't picked up by Dashboard unless you reboot your Mac or change your widget's `CFBundleIdentifier` key. If you're using a version control system, you can often make this happen automatically.

When working with Dashboard, there are a few keyboard shortcuts you might find useful:

- Pressing F12 toggles Dashboard.
- Pressing Cmd+R reloads a widget (make sure it has focus first).
- Holding down the Option key makes widgets' close buttons appear.

Deploying Dashboard Widgets

Once your widget is thoroughly tested and debugged, it's nearly ready for distribution to the wider world. Before it's ready to go, however, there's one last step to make your widget deployment-ready: zipping its bundle. This isn't just a good idea for decreasing download times and bandwidth usage, it's a requirement for submitting it to the Apple widget directory.

Conveniently, it's also true that the Mac makes handling zip files especially easy. To create one, simply right-click your `.wdgt` bundle and select Compress; a new copy (with a `.zip` extension) will be created for you. And when users download your zipped widget to their Mac, Safari will automatically uncompress it and install the widget inside. It almost couldn't be easier.

■ **Tip** If your widget name contains spaces, feel free to rename the zip file to something more download-friendly; it won't affect the widget inside.

Like most dedicated gadget platforms, Dashboard has a good directory to connect developers with users, and this will likely be the main distribution channel for your new Mac widget. You can find the directory at `http://apple.com/downloads/dashboard`; users will either follow links to it from elsewhere on Apple's site or arrive from the More Widgets button in Dashboard's Widget Manager.

To submit a widget for listing, it will need to be zipped (see the instructions at the beginning of this section), and you'll need to have joined the free Apple Developer Connection (at `http://developer.apple.com`). In addition, Apple imposes one other requirement: your widget needs to have a couple of web pages that the directory can link to. First, it needs a general page describing the widget, and second, it needs a download page hosting the widget. But there's no reason why these can't be the same page, and there's no restriction on what other content the page may have. For instance, it could be a page describing many widgets you offer or gadgets for multiple platforms. It simply needs to have both information about the Dashboard widget that you're submitting and a link to download it.

Once you've fulfilled the prerequisites, browse to http://adcweb.apple.com/downloads/index.php (or follow the Submit a Widget link from the directory), and log in to your Developer Connection account. You'll be greeted with a submission form for listing a widget; most of the fields are self-explanatory, but here are some tips for a few specific ones:

- *Product Type*: Use "Dashboard Widget".

- *Product Info URL*: This is a page describing the widget, as discussed earlier.

- *Product Summary*: This is a short description used in the main directory.

- *Product Description*: This is a longer write-up of your widget, which will appear on its detail page.

- *Version*: This should match your Info.plist's CFBundleShortVersionString value.

- *Mac OS X Version*: To avoid unseen problems, enter the lowest version you've actually tested on.

- *Universal Binary*: Use Yes (widgets run fine on any Mac CPU).

- *Download Page*: This is a page containing a link to your widget, as discussed earlier.

- *Mac OS X Download*: This is the URL of your .wdgt zip file itself.

- *Screenshot*: This is a full-size capture of your widget. I recommend you use the OS X Clip utility and capture it while running in Dashcode.

- *Product icon*: Use the 81×81 (75×75 plus shadow) Icon.png file from your widget bundle.

Once your widget is submitted, you'll receive a notification from Apple. After that, they'll review your widget; if approved, it'll appear in the directory, but if not, you won't be told why. The approval process usually takes a day or two.

■ **Tip** Apple does offer an RSS feed of the latest widget listings, so it's possible to watch for your submission that way. Subscribe to http://images.apple.com/downloads/dashboard/home/recent.rss.

When the time comes to resubmit your widget for any reason, note that you'll need to increment the version number entered into the submission form. Apple disallows multiple submissions of the same version of a single widget (identified by download URL).

Dashboard-Specific Extensions

In many ways, the Mac is a universe unto itself, and accordingly there are a lot of Mac-only API features available. If you have reason to make a specialized widget for Dashboard (rather than a cross-platform gadget), the following sections should get you started with some of these nonportable aspects. However, because they are not the main focus of this book, you won't find more than a taster here—just enough to determine whether each is a viable option for you.

For more information on any of these technologies, your best bet is the Safari Developer Center, at http://developer.apple.com/safari.

HTML 5 on Safari

In this chapter, we've already taken advantage of the fact that Dashboard widgets are always rendered in Safari by using CSS rules (and a few other tricks) specific to that browser. However, Safari is quite an advanced web client; at this writing, it's one of the few supporting next-generation HTML 5 technologies. If you're so inclined, you can leverage these technologies to significantly increase what's possible in a pure web gadget.

For example, Safari's WebKit engine fully supports the canvas tag. This next-generation HTML element allows you to draw sophisticated graphics directly in the browser window using only JavaScript. This is how the default Mac clock widget (back in Figure 7-5) is implemented; the hands are drawn on the face dynamically.

Beyond canvas, other important HTML 5 technologies supported by WebKit include the video tag (a plug-in-free technique for showing video in the browser) and client-side storage (a SQLite database accessible from JavaScript). Apple has also committed support to the W3C geolocation API, allowing widget code to deliver location-sensitive content and functionality.

This topic is explored further in Chapters 11 through 13, as we look at the leading edge of web gadgets. What we thought was impossible with pure web technology is now becoming possible—for advanced browsers like Safari, at least.

Mac User Interface Elements

Moving beyond pure web programming, Apple also provides widget API hooks for some Mac-specific user interface elements. One example is the Apple Slider, a variable range control with no native HTML equivalent (see Figure 7-8). Another is the Apple Button, allowing you to style buttons on your widget to exactly match the standard button found in OS X applications. Finally, the animation class that I used in Listing 7-4 to visually "flip" the widget has many other effects available for transitioning smoothly between states.

Figure 7-8. An Apple Slider

All of these controls can lend a very polished appearance to your widget and enable it to blend completely seamlessly with the OS X user interface.

Localization

As always, if your widget could make sense in other languages, you can multiply your audience by translating it. Dashboard is another platform with built-in localization support; it's relatively simple, so a quick overview should be enough to get you started.

First, within your widget bundle, you'll need subdirectories for any language you support. These must be named with the (usually) two-character code for the target language, plus an extension of .lproj (for "language project"). For example, if you were translating your widget into French, you'd create a subdirectory named fr.lproj.

Second, within those directories, place copies of any files that require localization. These can be .css and .js files, images, or any other bundled resource. When your widget loads such a resource, Dashboard will first look in the .lproj subdirectory for the current user language (if one exists) and load that file in preference to the default (in your main .wdgt root).

In practice, the easiest way to implement localization is usually with a JavaScript associative array that you then refer to elsewhere in your widget. For example, if your widget had buttons labeled Next and Previous, you'd start with an English JavaScript file—let's call it local_text.js—in your bundle's root directory:

```
localText = {
  'next': 'Next',
  'prev': 'Previous'
}
```

Then in your French localization directory (fr.proj) would be another copy of local_text.js, with the French translations:

```
localText = {
  'next': 'Suivante',
  'prev': 'Précédente'
}
```

When your widget loads local_text.js through a script tag, Dashboard will automatically choose the one best suited to the user's selected language. This means that localized text is available to you elsewhere in your code, and all you need to do is use it:

```
document.getElementById('next').value = localText.next;
document.getElementById('prev').value = localText.prev;
```

One advantage to this approach is that, once implemented for Dashboard, the same gadget could still be distributed to other platforms. You'd just need to distribute the appropriate local_text.js file for any language to which you deployed it.

Non-Web Extensions

The final area of Dashboard-specific optimizations I'll cover involves making calls to arbitrary program code from within your widget. These calls will invoke native OS X functionality, ranging from stand-alone applications to custom interface layers. Although such calls will be completely Mac-specific, they have the potential to open your widget's functionality to encompass anything that's possible with a client-side application, instead of being limited to web-based tools like HTML and JavaScript. It's outside the scope of this book to cover these in detail, but their power is such that they do merit a brief mention.

The easiest way to invoke native functionality is with an API method openApplication (in the widget namespace). It takes a single parameter, containing the bundle identifier for the target application, and runs it. For example, to open the standard Apple dictionary application, you'd include a line of JavaScript like this:

```
widget.openApplication('com.apple.Dictionary');
```

■ **Tip** All Mac applications are packaged in a similar manner to widgets. So, to find the bundle identifier for any app, right-click it, select Show Package Contents, and then copy the CFBundleIdentifier value from its Info.plist.

For slightly more advanced interactions, the system method provides an interface to the OS X command shell; any command that the user could execute in the Terminal can be run with system. Among other uses, this enables your widget to pass parameters to applications, be they standard Mac commands or custom executables bundled with your widget. An example of this might be using the Unix touch command to update a file's time stamp:

```
widget.system('/usr/bin/touch ' + filename, null);
```

Note the second parameter to system; this is a reference to a callback function. If it's null (as in this example), system will run synchronously, and JavaScript execution will simply continue after it completes. If a function is passed, however, the system call will be asynchronous, and the given function will be called when it completes. There are also a variety of other related API properties and methods for use with asynchronous system calls; see the Dashboard documentation in the next section for more details.

Finally, it's possible to actually extend the API by constructing plug-ins that your JavaScript code can richly interact with. These are written in Cocoa and Objective-C, Apple's native development frameworks for the Mac; the paradigm is that native application code is "pushed" into the widget, where it is exposed as a JavaScript interface. Using this approach, a dashboard widget can access any resources or functionality possible in a native Mac application, such as the filesystem, multimedia, and system APIs (to name a few). The sophistication of this interface is too much for me to cover here, but if it sounds useful for your application, please refer to Apple's Dashboard Programming topics for more information.

■ **Note** If you're going to use either widget.system calls or native plug-ins, you'll need to provide the corresponding AllowSystem or Plugin keys in your Info.plist file, as mentioned earlier in the chapter.

Learning More About Dashboard Widgets

The Dashboard widget API is quite rich, and although this chapter should be enough to get you started, there will undoubtedly be times that you require more detail than I've been able to provide here. When this need arises, the official Apple documentation is your best bet; it's both comprehensive and well organized.

■ **Tip** Although dashboard widgets run directly on OS X, you'll find most of their documentation with Apple's Safari Developer Center, http://developer.apple.com/safari. The following links are relative to this URL.

- The complete developer guide has good articles covering most widget topics:

  /library/documentation/AppleApplications/Conceptual/Dashboard_ProgTopics

- The API reference describes all Info.plist keys and widget namespace properties:

  /library/documentation/AppleApplications/Reference/Dashboard_Ref

- To help get you started, there are sample widgets available here:

  /samplecode/AppleApplications/idxDashboard-date.html

- You'll also find specialized widget debugging advice here:

  `/technotes/tn2005/tn2139.html`

Finally, if you get irretrievably stuck, there is paid developer support available directly from Apple. Log into your Developer Connection account (at `http://developer.apple.com`), and click the Support link at the top of the page.

Summary

Like the Mac itself, Dashboard widgets are a bit idiosyncratic. Generic web gadgets will run here only with a greater-than-usual amount of massaging to make them fit into the specific technical and visual requirements of OS X. Among the tasks you'll need to accomplish are the following:

1. Creating compliant imagery for your widget icon and background

2. Laying out your settings on the "back" of your widget

3. Providing an Info Button (and its associated animations) to access those settings

4. Packaging as a `.wdgt` file, including specific file location and naming conventions

Although these hurdles are many, none of them is especially high, and—once you've cleared them—the Mac will reward you with a widget that's exceptionally well integrated into its environment. Your Dashboard widget will also be granted access to the loyal user base that Apple has always enjoyed.

In the next chapter, we'll wrap up the desktop platforms with a look at the Opera widget API, which is closely related to Dashboard behind the scenes but with a quite different end product. It will also lay the foundation for the transition to mobile platforms coming in Part 4 of the book.

■ ■ ■

CHAPTER 8

Opera

In this chapter, I'll round out my coverage of desktop gadget platforms with one that's independent of the underlying operating system. Mini web applications built for the Opera Widgets API can be deployed anywhere the Opera browser will run: Windows, Mac, and several varieties of *nix. In addition, these gadgets will run natively on Opera Mobile, and several handset vendors have adopted the platform for themselves.

As a result, Opera is an excellent place to port your own widget. There is no other API that natively supports so many hardware and software platforms, so it's a natural fit with cross-platform development. Also, Opera's widget specification formed the original basis for the W3C's generic widget proposal (mentioned in Chapter 1). This standard is still under evaluation, but already other APIs are emerging that use some variation of the interface described in this chapter.

This chapter will focus on Opera widgets for desktops; the mobile incarnations are covered in Part 4 of the book.

Introducing Opera Widgets

As you've no doubt already guessed, Opera is another platform that refers to its mini web apps as *widgets* rather than gadgets. I'll be using the two terms interchangeably throughout the chapter, as I did for the Mac Dashboard. And overall, Opera's widgets are conceptually quite similar to the Mac's, so many of the ideas in this chapter should look a bit familiar to you.

As with other platforms in this part of the book, gadgets for Opera visually appear to run directly on the desktop (see Figure 8-1), although they are actually contained within individual browser instances. But because this browser is external to the operating system, this means that Opera must be running in order for gadgets to display. The browser also serves as the user's gadget management console. When Opera is started, it automatically reopens whatever gadgets the user last had running; the paradigm is that these gadgets are separate but parallel tasks.

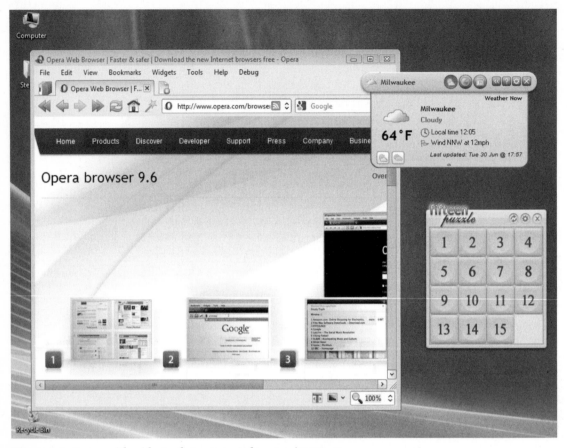

Figure 8-1. Opera with widgets: three separate browser instances

Developing for Opera

Opera's API is another that packages each gadget into a single zip-format archive, renamed from an extension of `.zip` to `.wgt`. In the root of this archive, the platform requires an XML *widget configuration file* (named `config.xml`) and your main HTML document (which must be named `index.html`). The `.wgt` file should generally also contain all your static source files and content, accessed via relative URLs; in effect, this archive becomes the web directory for serving your widget. And apart from `config.xml` and `index.html`, you're free to place files wherever you like in the archive; Opera recommends a single subdirectory for each of `images`, `script`, and `style`, but they're not compulsory.

You can also access remote content and source files from your widget, but here there are some additional restrictions:

- Your gadget is not allowed to access filesystem resources (with a `file:` protocol).

- You're encouraged to specify the domains, ports, and protocols you'll be using in your configuration file.

- You also need to specifically grant access to Java, Flash, or other plug-ins that your gadget may use.

■ **Note** For the latter two points, you can grant access using the `security` element of the configuration file; see the "Security" section (later in the chapter) for the specific techniques to use.

Defining the Appearance

One of the minor challenges in developing Opera widgets is that the platform doesn't supply any visual elements whatsoever to your application. In other words, it's up to you to generate all the chrome your gadget will require, from background to controls to the frame. This means that an Opera widget displays with a transparent background by default (unlike Windows desktop gadgets).

The advantage of this approach, of course, is that you have complete freedom over your gadget's visual design—with one exception: Opera strongly recommends that all widgets have a *close* button. Although this isn't expressed as an absolute requirement, it is nonetheless a good idea, and you may have difficulty getting your gadget listed in Opera's directory without one. Fortunately, a close button is quite easy to implement, and I'll walk you through it later in the chapter.

■ **Note** Opera's freedom of choice in appearance also extends to size: there are no size rules imposed on your gadget by the platform.

Generally, you'll create your gadget's visual appearance using standard web-design techniques, such as background colors and images in CSS. This is similar to other desktop platforms; you'll simply include these new rules in an Opera-specific `style` element in `index.html`. To relieve some of the burden of creating your own imagery and to encourage consistency between widgets, Opera has a set of standard icons available for download from `http://dev.opera.com/articles/view/opera-widgets-resources`.

GENERATING BACKGROUNDS WITH SVG

One upside to a platform like Opera is that knowing the client browser allows you to utilize techniques that aren't necessarily cross-browser compatible. One example is Scalable Vector Graphics (SVG), which is a flavor of XML that lets you draw images directly to the browser window from within your code, rather than simply displaying static images or single colors. This can be useful for any nontrivial background or border effect that needs to scale to different sizes (along with your gadget). Rather than creating multiple images at different sizes or employing a glyph-based approach, you can generate the images directly from your gadget.

For example, let's say you wanted a simple black background but with rounded corners. The first step is to create the SVG file to produce the effect, in a file named `rounded_corners.svg`:

```
<?xml version="1.0" encoding="UTF-8" ?>
<svg xmlns="http://www.w3.org/2000/svg">
  <rect fill="black" x="0" y="0" width="100%" height="100%" rx="10" />
</svg>
```

It's an easy example, and you can probably see what's going on: a single XML element, `rect`, defines a black rectangle the full size of its container, and `rx="10"` specifies corners rounded to a radius of 10 pixels. Now, all you need to do is use this SVG as the background image in CSS:

```
background: url(rounded_corners.svg);
```

I use this specific, simple technique for the configuration pane in my Moon Phase case study for Opera, but SVG supports a wide range of more advanced functionality, such as gradients, rotation, and patterns. You can find the official documentation at `www.w3.org/Graphics/SVG`, and you can find a good tutorial at `http://kevlindev.com/tutorials/basics/index.htm`. Higher-end graphics software (such as Adobe Illustrator) will often save files as SVG also.

Although a browser-specific technique like SVG is of little use in the wider, cross-gadget world, there's no reason not to use it when porting your gadget to Opera, given that you need to create chrome anyway.

Adapting the Core Gadget

Once you've made some decisions about gadget appearance and begun to create the necessary imagery, you're ready to begin coding your new Opera widget. The following sections will guide you through the modifications necessary to make a core HTML gadget (from Chapters 2 and 3) work on Opera. I'll discuss each change in the context of my Moon Phase sample gadget; the steps involved can serve as a guide for porting your own application.

To start, I recommend creating a new directory for files related to the Opera version. You can copy in all local source and content files for easy testing (discussed later in the chapter), and when the time comes for packaging it into a `.wgt` archive, you'll have everything you need in one place. For a cross-platform gadget, such an approach necessarily requires some replication of files. To minimize this problem, I recommend that you delete duplicate files from Opera-specific folders once your Opera widget is complete.

Creating the Widget Configuration File

The core file in your new widget will be its configuration XML, which must be named `config.xml` and placed in the root of your gadget package. Listing 8-1 shows a typical configuration file, and you'll find explanations for each element in the following sections.

Listing 8-1. *The Widget Configuration File for Moon Phase*

```xml
<?xml version="1.0" encoding="UTF-8"?>
<widget network="public">
  <widgetname>Moon Phase</widgetname>
  <description>Shows the phase of the moon on a field of stars.</description>
  <width>240</width>
  <height>200</height>
  <icon width="32" height="32">moon_32.png</icon>
  <icon width="128" height="128">moon_128.png</icon>
  <author>
    <name>Sterling Udell</name>
    <email>sterling.udell@gmail.com</email>
    <link>http://sterlingudell.com</link>
    <organization>Udell Enterprises, Inc.</organization>
  </author>
  <id>
    <host>daylightmap.com</host>
    <name>Moon Phase</name>
    <revised>2009-06-29</revised>
  </id>
  <security>
    <access>
      <host>daylightmap.com</host>
    </access>
  </security>
</widget>
```

widget

The root XML element, `widget`, needs an attribute of `network` if your widget accesses any content over a network (outside of its `.wgt` archive). If the resources you require are on an *intra*net, specify a value of private; if they're on the wider *Inter*net, specify `public` (as shown in Listing 8-1). If you need to access both intranet and Internet resources, specify both values, like this:

```xml
<widget network="private public">
```

■ **Note** As of this writing, the `network` attribute is not documented in the Widgets API specification on the Opera web site.

---

widgetname

This is simply your gadget's title as you want it to appear in any listings. It's required.

description

This is a short text description of your gadget for its listing in Opera's directory. This is optional, with a maximum length of 150 characters.

width and height

These are the initial pixel dimensions for your widget. Although these fields are required, you're free to alter both dimensions later in your widget's CSS or JavaScript code.

icon

Opera uses several icons to represent your gadget, in four sizes: 16, 32, 64, and 128 pixels (all square). Accordingly, you may have several icon elements in your configuration file, specifying different source files (of type `.png` or `.gif`) for each size. Opera will attempt to interpolate any icon size that is not included here, either by shrinking a larger size or by expanding a smaller one—although to avoid pixelation, it won't expand more than one size increment. Only the 16-pixel version is used at runtime on the desktop; the others are for mobile use and directory listings.

For Moon Phase, you can see that I've included 32- and 128-pixel versions; I'm happy for 16 and 64 to be interpolated from these.

author

The subelements here contain your contact details as you want them to appear in Opera's widget directory. The `name` field should contain your own name, with your company name in `organization`. Note that these are all optional (as is the `author` element itself), so feel free to leave out any that don't apply.

id

This element uniquely identifies your gadget in Opera's directory; once a widget with a given `host` and `name` combination is listed, later submissions with identical values are assumed to replace the existing one. The `revised` subelement functions as a version identifier; it contains the release date of this version of your gadget in either YYYY-MM or YYYY-MM-DD format. Opera recommends that you use the shorter format unless your widget specifically changes more than once per month.

Although the `id` element itself is optional, if it is included, all three subelements are required.

security

By default, Opera widgets can access any content from any domain on the Internet; this is different from the same-origin policy enforced on ordinary web sites and has the potential to create security problems if any cross-site scripting vulnerabilities exist in your code. To mitigate this issue, the API defines a `security` element for your configuration XML; it's used to restrict your gadget's network access by whitelisting only those addresses that you actually need to reach. This section is also where you can permit the execution of Java applets, Flash movies, or other plug-ins. If you don't do so, these external modules won't run in an Opera widget.

Although a security element is not strictly required, it is nonetheless a good practice. In addition to making your gadget more secure, Opera has intimated that this configuration item may become a requirement at some point, so if you include it now, you'll be ready—if and when that occurs.

Whitelisting Addresses

Beneath security are one or more access elements, which specify network addresses that you want your widget to be able to reach. Subelements of access (protocol, host, port, and path) that are supplied will restrict your gadget to only those values. So, for example, a fully specified access section for Moon Phase might look like this:

```
<access>
  <protocol>http</protocol>
  <host>daylightmap.com</host>
  <port>80</port>
  <path>/moon/next_last.xml.php</path>
</access>
```

■ **Tip** If the path element is included, it must specify individual resources completely (including both the path and resource name), as shown in this example.

The most important subelement is host; this specifies the domains that your gadget is authorized to connect to. Including a host element will ensure that your gadget is only able to request data from your domain. The other subelements of access (protocol, port, and path) are all optional, but any that are omitted default to *all*, allowing unrestricted access. Although this somewhat defeats the purpose of a whitelist in the first place, in reality the host is the important restriction for preventing cross-site scripting attacks. So, unless your application has specific requirements for accessing (or restricting) specific addresses, it's generally safe to leave these three off. Accordingly, Listing 8-1 shows an example of a simple security element for accessing resources from a single domain.

For more complex situations, you may include multiple locations with any combination of the following:

- You can have multiple access elements (although only one top-level security element), defining different locations in each.

- The port element may contain ranges, like <port>472-496</port>.

- Any subelement of access may be repeated, like this:

  ```
  <access>
    <host>daylightmap.com</host>
    <host>sterlingudell.com</host>
  </access>
  ```

- The subelements of access may also have comma-delimited lists of any valid values, like this:

  ```
  <access>
    <host>daylightmap.com,sterlingudell.com</host>
    <port>80,472-496</port>
  </access>
  ```

Finally, remember that the file: protocol is not permitted, even if specified in a protocol element here. Widgets may not explicitly access filesystem resources outside of their own .wgt archive.

Enabling Plug-ins and Java

In addition to whitelisting network locations, the security element is used for allowing widgets to include plug-ins (such as Flash) and Java applets. If your gadget requires either of these, you'll need to add a content subelement to security, with one of the following attributes:

```
<security>
  <content java="yes" plugin="yes" />
</security>
```

Note that content is in addition to any access elements that you may need.

Changes to the HTML

Your configuration XML should now be complete, specifying what Opera needs to run your new widget. The next step is modifying the source code from your existing gadget so that it will run on Opera. Apart from the chrome-related image files mentioned earlier, the changes should be restricted to your main HTML document, allowing you to deploy any other source files to Opera unchanged. Assuming that you're starting with a native web gadget (as outlined in Chapters 2 and 3), I recommend that you simply make a copy of your core HTML file for use on this platform.

■ **Caution** Remember that your gadget's main HTML file must be named index.html.

In this section, I'll walk through the required modifications to this file, illustrated with specific examples from my Moon Phase case-study gadget. Listing 8-2 shows my new HTML, with the Opera-specific code highlighted in bold.

Listing 8-2. The Core HTML Page for Moon Phase on Opera

```
<?xml version="1.0" encoding="UTF-8"?>
<!DOCTYPE html PUBLIC "-//W3C//DTD XHTML 1.0 Transitional//EN"
                      "http://www.w3.org/TR/XHTML1/DTD/XHTML1-transitional.dtd">
<html xmlns="http://www.w3.org/1999/XHTML">
  <head>
    <meta http-equiv="Content-Type" content="text/html;charset=UTF-8" />
    <meta name="description"
          content="Shows the current phase of the moon on a field of stars." />
    <title>Moon Phase</title>
    <link href="moon_32.png" type="image/png" rel="icon" />
    <link href="phase.css"   type="text/css"  rel="stylesheet" />
    <style type="text/css">
      .moonPhase {
        background: transparent;
      }
```

```
      .moonPhase #main {
        background: left top no-repeat;
      }
      .moonPhase #close_icon {
        top: 1px;
        background-image: url(x_16.png);
      }
      .moonPhase #config_icon {
        top: 20px;
      }
      .moonPhase #config {
        background: url(rounded_corners.svg);
      }
    </style>
  </head>
  <body class="moonPhase">
    <div id="main">
      <div id="main_icons">
        <a id="close_icon" class="control_icon" title="Close"
          onclick="window.close()"></a>
        <a id="config_icon" class="control_icon" title="Settings"
          onclick="moonPhase.showConfig()"></a>
      </div>
      <p id="last" class="text"></p>
      <p id="image_container">
        <img id="moon" alt="Current Moon Image" width="176" height="176"
            src="http://daylightmap.com/moon/images/luna_north_small.jpg" />
      </p>
      <p id="next" class="text"></p>
      <p id="credit" class="text">
        by <a target="_top" href="http://www.daylightmap.com">DaylightMap</a>
      </p>
    </div>

    <div id="config" style="display: none">
      <p><strong>Moon Phase Settings</strong></p>
      <p>
        <label for="size">Size:</label>
        <select id="size" name="size">
          <option value="small">Small</option>
          <option value="large">Large</option>
<!--      <option value="auto">Auto</option> -->
        </select>
      </p>
      <p>
        <label for="text">Show Text:</label>
        <select id="text" name="text">
          <option value="yes">Yes</option>
          <option value="no">No</option>
          <option value="auto">Auto</option>
        </select>
      </p>
```

```
    <p>
      <label for="hemisphere">View From:</label>
      <select id="hemisphere" name="hemisphere">
        <option value="north">Northern Hemisphere</option>
        <option value="south">Southern Hemisphere</option>
      </select>
    </p>
    <p id="config_buttons">
      <input type="submit" value="Save" id="save_button"
             onclick=" moonPhase.saveConfig(); return false;" />
      <input type="button" value="Cancel" id="cancel_button"
             onclick="moonPhase.hideConfig();" />
    </p>
  </div>

  <script src="platform.js" type="text/javascript"></script>
  <script src="phase.js"    type="text/javascript"></script>

  <script type="text/javascript">
    moonPhase.defaultLoadFunction = moonPhase.load;
    moonPhase.load = function () {
      // Set the gadget's visual style to match the preferred size
      if (moonPhase.prefs.size.get() === 'small') {
        document.body.style.width = '160px';
        moonPhase.elements.main.style.height = '120px';
        moonPhase.elements.main.style.backgroundImage =
          'url(stars_small.png)';
      } else {
        document.body.style.width = '240px';
        moonPhase.elements.main.style.height = '200px';
        moonPhase.elements.main.style.backgroundImage =
          'url(stars_medium.png)';
      }

      moonPhase.defaultLoadFunction();
    };
  </script>
  </body>
</html>
```

Style

The first major set of modifications is an inline style block in the document's head section; naturally, this controls Opera-specific changes to the gadget's appearance. In the case of Moon Phase, these changes all have to do with Opera's chrome requirements.

Backgrounds

The default Moon Phase gadget has a simple background of stars on black, simulating the night sky. Although this would function on Opera, the lack of a frame looks a bit odd for a stand-alone desktop widget. As with the other desktop platforms in this part of the book, the alternative I've chosen is to simply create rounded-rectangle crops of my starfield image as background images for the gadget. As shown in Figure 8-2, this gives a slightly more finished appearance.

Figure 8-2. Rounded-rectangle starfield background image for Moon Phase

Because my gadget comes in two distinct sizes, I'll actually need two such images, and I'll swap them dynamically in the JavaScript section a bit later. Here in the CSS I just need to override the default gadget background and set up the positioning for the background that I will be applying to the main content div:

```
.moonPhase {
  background: transparent;
}
.moonPhase #main {
  background: left top no-repeat;
}
```

There's one other background-related change to my gadget's style. As mentioned in the SVG sidebar earlier in the chapter, I can take advantage of Opera's support for in-browser drawing to create some chrome dynamically. The single CSS rule required should look familiar to you from the SVG sidebar:

```
.moonPhase #config {
  background: url(rounded_corners.svg);
}
```

As described there, this causes the background for my configuration panel to be generated using the SVG code in rounded_corners.svg. This is an easy way to continue my rounded-corners theme in the settings pane, no matter what size it may be, which is difficult to achieve with static background images.

Close Button

The other main chrome-related change is the addition of a button for closing the gadget. As mentioned earlier, it's a strong recommendation of the Opera platform that all widgets include such a button. I'll be introducing a bit of markup for the button itself in the next section, but once it exists, it will need some CSS to control its appearance. It'll inherit from my existing button-icon style (shown in Listing 3-4), so very little additional code is required:

```
.moonPhase #close_icon {
  top: 1px;
  background-image: url(x_16.png);
```

```
}
.moonPhase #config_icon {
  top: 20px;
}
```

The first rule positions the new button near the top edge of the widget and sets its background to a new icon image I've created for the purpose (see Figure 8-3). And because it's customary for the close button to be in the upper-right corner, I'll need to move my configuration button out of the way, which is the reason for the second style rule in the previous code.

Figure 8-3. Icon for my close button

Content

I usually try to avoid making changes to my gadget content for specific platforms, but sometimes there's no getting around it, and Opera is one such case. The changes are still quite limited, though, so any content modifications I may make to my core gadget at a later date should still be easy to integrate here.

The first change was mentioned in the previous section: I need to add a close button to my gadget. A single a element will suffice, modeled on (and adjacent to) my existing button to open the settings pane:

```
<a id="close_icon" class="control_icon" title="Close"
   onclick="window.close()"></a>
```

I've set its class to control_icon to inherit much of the CSS I already had in place for the settings button. Then it simply needs an onclick handler to implement its functionality, and all that happens in it is to close the gadget window. Your own widget close button shouldn't need to be much more complicated than this.

There's one other minor change in my content highlighted in Listing 8-2, one that may or may not apply to your gadgets. As you may recall, my core Moon Phase has a size option of auto, which allows my gadget to adjust smoothly to size constraints that are imposed upon it by the platform. But because Opera has no predetermined size limits, this option doesn't apply here. So, I simply comment it out of my HTML, and the user will never see it:

```
<!-- <option value="auto">Auto</option> -->
```

JavaScript

As usual, Opera requires a bit of platform-specific functionality, so I place it in my usual location: an inline script block at the end of my HTML. Keeping it in the HTML reduces the number of source files that I need to maintain for the platform, and placing it at the end means that the widget's visuals will load before the JavaScript is processed, reducing perceived latency a bit.

As alluded to earlier in the chapter, the coding I need to do here is to support the two different widget size modes. If you refer to the end of Listing 8-2, you'll see that the actual size-related code is quite simple: it checks my size preference and sets some style attributes accordingly.

> ■ **Note** The size-handling code here needs to happen whenever the gadget reloads, so it's wrapped in a method override for the default `moonPhase.load` function. For details on my override technique, please see Listing 7-4.

Additions to crossPlatform

Of course, our core gadget code relies upon the `crossPlatform` middleware layer (introduced in Chapter 3) to make the connection with the Opera API, so without extending this layer, that connection won't happen. Opera's is a well-behaved API, however, so these extensions are quite straightforward. This part of the chapter details the changes needed to make your cross-platform gadget work here.

Platform Sniffing

The first step is always to ascertain which platform a given gadget instance is running on; without knowing that, it's impossible to employ the right middleware connections. In Opera's case, this task is complicated slightly by its resemblance to the Mac Dashboard Widget API that I mentioned previously. Consequently, we need to extend the platform-sniffing code introduced in Chapter 7 to differentiate Opera from Mac (the highlighted code is new):

```
if (!!window.widget) {
  if (!!widget.getAttention) {
    crossPlatform.api = 'opera';
    crossPlatform.emptyPref = '';
  } else {
    crossPlatform.api = 'mac';
    crossPlatform.emptyPref = undefined;
  }
}
```

Both platforms declare a `widget` namespace in the global `window` scope; once we have detected that, we need to look a bit closer to determine which of the two it is. They're similar enough that they actually share many identically named methods—but one that Opera defines (and Mac doesn't) is getAttention, so I'm using that.

Other Functions

The close parallel between Opera and the Mac continues throughout the API internals, so much so that `crossPlatform` can actually use the same code for all its other interface tasks. In the following sections you'll find the actual code snippets; in each, you'll see that I've simply added a new `'opera'` case to the existing `'mac'` handler.

For more information on each of these integrations, please refer to Chapter 7.

Retrieving Preferences

```
switch (crossPlatform.api) {
  case 'mac':
  case 'opera':
    myValue = myValue = widget.preferenceForKey(name);
```

```
    break;
    ...
}
```

Storing Preferences

```
switch (crossPlatform.api) {
  case 'mac':
  case 'opera':
    widget.setPreferenceForKey(myValue, myName);
    break;
  ...
}
```

Resizing

```
crossPlatform.adjustSize = function () {
  switch (crossPlatform.api) {
    case 'mac':
    case 'opera':
      window.resizeTo(crossPlatform.getWidth(window),
                      crossPlatform.getHeight(window));
      break;
    ...
  }
};
```

Testing and Debugging

A first pass at your code modifications should now be complete, so it's time to begin testing your gadget on Opera. The first step is to install the Opera browser itself; without it, no widgets will function. You'll find the download for most major operating systems from http://opera.com/browser/download, and it will happily install alongside your existing browser (assuming you're not already using Opera).

Installing Your Widget

Although Opera widgets are packaged and distributed as renamed zip archives, there's no need to perform that step while you're still actively working on your code. As a developer-friendly product, Opera gives you an easier route: you can load your gadget's configuration XML directly, bypassing the zip and rename steps.

Before you do so, however, a bit of preparation is required. Recall that config.xml only contains widget metadata, not actual source code. The platform still needs to be able to find that code: index.html to start with, as well as any other local source and content (via their relative URLs).

To enable this, I recommend that you create an opera subdirectory for debugging your widget. You'll use this directory to simulate your widget's package during development; consequently, you'll need to replicate the file and directory structure of your live widget package herein. At a minimum, this means copying in all your local source files (including config.xml), though if you use any relative subdirectories, they'll need to be created and populated too. See Figure 8-4 for an example.

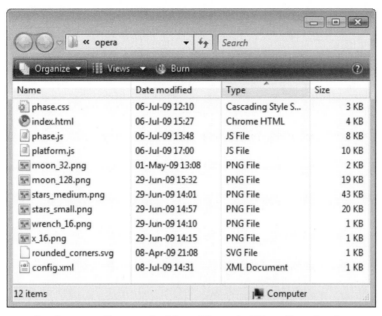

Figure 8-4. The opera development directory for Moon Phase, holding all my local source and content files

With your development directory in place, you're ready to run your widget; you do this by opening your `config.xml` file in Opera. There are a couple of different ways to do so:

- From within Opera, select File → Open, and browse to your `config.xml` file.

- In Windows, you can right-click your `config.xml` file and select Open With → Opera. You may need to find the Opera executable the first time you do this, typically at `C:\Program Files\Opera\Opera.exe`.

- You can drag `config.xml` from a shell window to a running instance of Opera.

By opening your configuration XML, you have effectively installed your new widget in Opera. In addition to running the widget itself, this will also add it to Opera's Widget Manager, a console within the main browser that lets the user start, stop, organize, and uninstall the widgets on his system. The Widget Manager is opened from within Opera by selecting Widgets → Manage; Figure 8-5 shows a typical view.

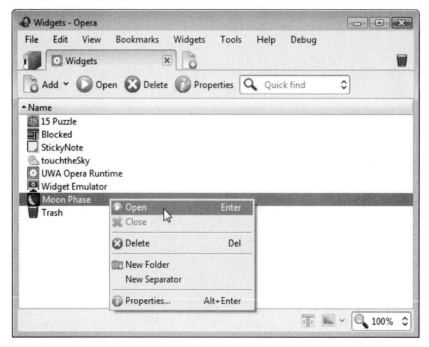

Figure 8-5. *The Opera Widget Manager*

It's probably safe to assume that everything *won't* go perfectly the first time you open your widget in Opera, so you'll need to make some changes to your source code and reload. Changing the code is easy enough: in your development directory, simply edit the required files in place. And if the file you changed was any except `config.xml`, you can also simply reload in place, either by pressing F5 in your widget or by right-clicking it and selecting Reload.

If you have changed your configuration XML, though, you'll need to reinstall your widget into Opera. Do this by deleting it from the Widget Manager (shown in Figure 8-5) and then reopening your `config.xml` file in Opera as you did before.

■ **Tip** Deleting a widget from the Widget Manager simply moves it to the Trash, also visible in Figure 8-5. You can find an Empty Trash command by right-clicking there.

Debugging in Opera

One advantage to widgets running within Opera is that you have the browser's development tools at your disposal. First and foremost, recent versions come with the Dragonfly debugger. Although it's still lighter on features than some of its equivalents (like Firebug), it is nonetheless a huge improvement over not having a debugger at all. With it, you can place breakpoints in (and step through) your widget's JavaScript, as well as examining CSS on the fly. Find more information at `http://opera.com/dragonfly`.

■ **Note** The JavaScript `alert()` function doesn't work in Opera widgets.

In addition, Opera also has a Debug menu that you can install. It gives direct access to many useful development features, such as source code validation, CSS controls, and reference materials. You can find the download link on the Dragonfly home page.

Deploying Widgets for Opera

Once you've worked the bugs out of your code, you're ready to deploy your Opera widget. The first step is to package it for distribution; assuming you've been working from a development directory, this should be a simple matter of replicating that directory in a `.zip` file and then renaming it to have a `.wgt` extension. In Windows, you can create a zip file by right-clicking in the Windows shell and selecting New → Compressed (zipped) Folder. Copy in your source and content files (and subdirectories, as appropriate), and then rename it from `.zip` to `.wgt`. Once you confirm that everything still works, your new widget is ready for distribution.

■ **Tip** Once you've packaged the release version of your Opera widget and are no longer actively debugging it, I recommend you delete your development directory (remembering to save copies of any Opera-specific files you created, such as graphics and your core HTML). This will reduce the number of duplicate files you have and, correspondingly, your chances for getting files out of sync.

Submitting to the Directory

The primary conduit for distributing widgets is a directory that Opera maintains. Users access it from within the browser (using various Add Widgets links) or from `http://widgets.opera.com`. To submit widgets to the directory, you'll need to register and log in, which you can also do at this URL.

Once you're logged in, the submission process begins at `http://widgets.opera.com/upload`, where the first page will ask you to upload your widget archive file from your local computer. After doing so (and agreeing to Opera's terms), you'll move on to the main directory submission page.

■ **Tip** The widget directory will take `.zip` files—they don't have to be renamed `.wgt`.

Here you'll find a variety of fields from which your widget's directory listing will be built. Many (such as author information and icons) are drawn from your configuration XML and were discussed earlier in the chapter, but there are some additional fields here as well.

- *Screenshot*: A "full-size" image of your widget in action. This will display alongside your directory listing in the browser (so the usual browser graphics file types are supported here), at a size of 300×225 pixels.

- *Long description*: Here you can create an extensive write-up about your gadget, including full HTML formatting. Be aware that this shows alongside your short description (from `config.xml`) in the directory, so don't just repeat that text here.

- *Category*: This can be something such as *science*, *news*, *fun & games*, and so on.

- *Language*: If your widget supports multiple languages, you'll need to submit it separately for each.

- *Country*: This is the country or other region, such as World or Americas.

- *Target Devices*: For now, select Desktop and TV.[1] I'll be converting the widget for handheld use in Chapter 9.

When you have completed the form, you'll be given a link to your widget's home page, where you can edit its details, see its statistics, and so forth (this page is also available from `http://widgets.opera.com/upload`). Meanwhile, your widget will go to Opera for approval, and they'll let you know one way or the other, usually within a day or two. Assuming your widget has no obvious bugs and doesn't contain blatantly objectionable content, it should have no trouble getting approved.

Once your widget is listed in the directory, you can make minor changes to its listing from its home page. For changes to its package, however, or changes to certain directory fields (such as Category and Language), you'll need to resubmit it. It will also need to be reapproved by Opera.

Providing Direct Widget Downloads

In addition to Opera's directory, you can also distribute your widget yourself by simply hosting it on your own web site and providing a link. Visitors with Opera installed who click it should be immediately prompted to install the widget, but those who don't have Opera will be unable to open it, so you'll probably want to provide instructions to that effect. For best compatibility, you should also configure your web server so that `.wgt` files are served with a MIME type of `application/x-opera-widgets`.

In addition to explicit downloads, the Opera browser also supports a built-in notification to the user when she is visiting a site with a widget available. The mechanism is similar to a favicon or RSS feed: if a particular tag is detected in a page's `head` section, Opera will display a widget icon (see Figure 8-6); clicking it will immediately install the widget.

---

[1] Opera widgets also run on set-top boxes that use their Opera 9 SDK for devices. You can find more information at `http://opera.com/devices`.

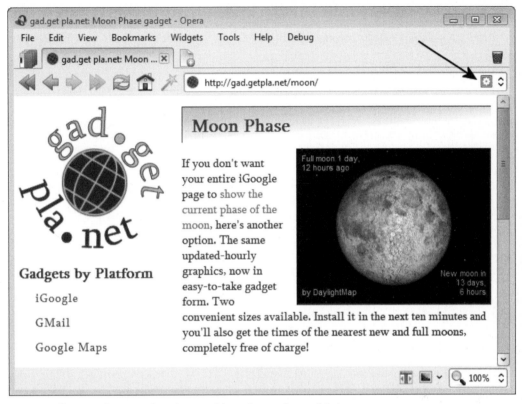

Figure 8-6. *When a web page advertises a widget, Opera shows this icon.*

To advertise your own widget in this fashion, simply add a link tag to the head of the appropriate page's HTML, as such:

```
<link rel="alternate" type="application/x-opera-widgets"
    title="widget_name" href="widget_url" />
```

You'll need to substitute your own widget's name (like Moon Phase) and the URL for its package (like phase_opera.wgt—note that this can be relative) into the title and href attributes, respectively.

Learning More About Opera Widgets

As usual, there's more to the Opera Widgets API than I can cover in one chapter, but you can find additional information at the Opera developer mini-site, http://dev.opera.com. The following are of particular interest:

- The widget documentation is organized into articles at http://dev.opera.com/articles/widgets.

- For specific details, consult the API reference, http://dev.opera.com/libraries/widgetobject.

- There's no widget-specific forum, so you can find a discussion of the platform in the general Opera Web Development group at http://dev.opera.com/forums/forum/3590.

Summary

Opera widgets are a good conclusion for our discussion of desktop platforms; they can be run on any operating system that the Opera browser supports, representing another good opportunity to get your mini-application in front of users. And porting a generic widget to Opera is quite straightforward, requiring little more than some additional chrome and the code to make it work, packaged into a .wgt archive. Additionally, a reasonable debugger and browser-based management make Opera a relatively painless widget development experience.

In Chapter 9, I'll move from the desktop to the handheld, beginning the coverage of gadgets on mobile devices with Windows Mobile. As you move into Part 4 of the book (Mobile Platforms), it'll be helpful that the Opera API is fresh in your mind, because the popular mobile version of this browser supports widgets as well.

PART 4

■■■

Mobile Platforms

CHAPTER 9

■ ■ ■

Windows Mobile

In this, the fourth and final part of the book, we'll move our widgets off the traditional Web—on the screen of a desktop or notebook computer—and out into the wider world. Our vehicle for doing so is the *smartphone*, a handheld computer that utilizes its wireless capabilities to access the Internet from virtually anywhere. In recent years, smartphones have been the fastest-growing segment of the mobile phone industry, and the possibilities that they offer to gadget developers are unprecedented.

In this chapter, we'll begin our smartphone tour with the venerable Windows Mobile platform. Although Microsoft doesn't enjoy nearly the dominance in smartphones that it does in deskbound computers, it's still a major player in the segment and one that you need to be aware of when considering a mobile web app strategy. It's also a natural place to start, because the foundation laid here will be built upon as we progress into the other platforms.

The chapters in this part of the book all follow a similar pattern. First, I'll introduce you to the mobile operating system in question and get you started using the appropriate emulator. Second, I'll discuss running web apps in their native environment—the browser—and what you can expect from that platform. Finally, I'll walk you through techniques for deploying web gadgets as stand-alone entities on the handset; in this chapter and the next, these will be true widgets, while later they'll actually become applications on the phone OS. As you'll see, you have plenty of options when it comes to deploying gadgets beyond the desktop.

Introducing Windows Mobile

Microsoft originally introduced Windows Mobile as an operating system for Pocket PCs around the turn of the millennium, before the category had merged with cellular phones to create the smartphone. Internet connectivity was unavailable on these early devices (as it still is on a fraction of handheld computers), and consequently, Windows Mobile is not inherently a connected operating system. This means that it can't be assumed that Windows Mobile devices will necessarily have Internet connectivity, and when they are connected, the user will often pay by the byte.

For the web gadget developer, this presents a basic constraint: on Windows Mobile, the usage of traditional web apps is naturally going to be somewhat limited. If your gadget is (or can be) designed to work entirely offline, it will have greater potential on this platform. This isn't to say that connected web gadgets have no place here, but—at least currently—Windows Mobile isn't their most natural home.

At this writing, two versions of Windows Mobile can be considered current. Version 6.1 was released in 2008 and accounts for the majority of Microsoft-powered smartphones in use. Its replacement, 6.5, was released while this book was being written and is found on most phones released since mid-2009. Although 6.5 is replacing 6.1, in reality there will be a significant number of legacy devices in the wild for some time, so both need to be considered.

■ **Note** On-device upgrade from one Windows Mobile version to another is not common; the reality is that these handhelds generally keep the version they were originally sold with.

From a web developer's perspective, the principal difference between the two versions is Internet Explorer Mobile, the built-in browser. In Windows Mobile 6.1 and earlier, Microsoft didn't use numbered versions of IE Mobile; instead, they were identified simply by the operating system version in which they lived (such as *Internet Explorer for Windows Mobile 5*). That changes in 6.5, however, which includes IE Mobile 6, a major upgrade from its predecessors. I'll go further into the details a bit later in the chapter, but for now, simply be aware that an important browser change happened between Windows Mobile 6.1 and 6.5.

In addition to numbered versions, Microsoft also maintains several distinct editions of Windows Mobile, paralleling the similar trend on Windows Vista and Windows 7. For gadget developers, the two editions of interest are Windows Mobile Standard and Professional. The important distinction is that Professional is meant for touchscreen devices, while Standard is not. The two editions have substantially different user interfaces, reflecting their different interaction models, but otherwise they are technologically very similar. You can generally treat them as a single operating system version, but you will occasionally need to know the difference on a practical level, such as when interacting with an emulator.

Windows Mobile Emulators

To enable mobile development without a large investment in hardware, most vendors have created *emulators*, and Microsoft is no exception. A smartphone emulator is a virtual handset running within a desktop operating system, and it allows you to do the vast majority of your mobile development without an actual device. Figure 9-1 shows a Windows Mobile emulator in action. Most emulators look something like this: they depict the case of a typical phone of the type, with mouse-clickable buttons and a display running at its native resolution, in a window on the host operating system. They enable you to interact with the virtual device on-screen as if it were a real one in your hand.

Figure 9-1. *Windows Mobile 6.5 displaying a web page*

However good an emulator is, though, it's never more than a simulation of a real handset. If at all possible, you should always test your code on an actual device before releasing it into production.

Setting Up the Emulator

Device emulators are an indispensible tool, but they can be some hassle to install and use—Microsoft's more than most. The difficulty is that connecting a Windows Mobile emulator to the Internet (a crucial aspect for web developers) requires several components, and the setup procedure is different depending on your host software configuration. In all cases, though, the following basic pieces are required:

- The *Device Emulator*, the core emulation software that runs the virtual machine.

- One or more *emulator images* to provide the user interface for the emulation. These typically come in packs, with each pack containing the different Windows Mobile editions, at several screen resolutions, for a single version (such as 6.5).

- Microsoft's *Mobile Device Center*, which provides file and network connectivity for the handset on the host.

- The *Emulator Manager*, a virtual "docking station" that makes the final link between the emulator and the Mobile Device Center.

■ **Note** A recent version of Microsoft Windows—XP at least, preferably Vista or 7—is also required as the host operating system for the emulator.

In the following sections, I'll detail the setup steps required for the most common configurations. Although you'll find specific download links for each component in the following sections, they're also all available at `http://msdn.microsoft.com/en-us/windowsmobile/bb264327.aspx`. Please make sure that you're getting the correct versions of each.

These instructions (and the URLs that they reference) were correct at the time of writing, but such things are quite fluid, and by the time you read this, the procedure may have changed somewhat. Use this part of the chapter as a guide to your own Windows Mobile environment setup.

■ **Tip** Much of Microsoft's web site, from download links to the MSDN reference, works better on Internet Explorer (desktop, not mobile) than on other browsers.

With Visual Studio

If you do other Windows development or use Microsoft's web development tool set, you're likely to have Visual Studio installed on your development machine—and you're well on your way to Windows Mobile emulation. Visual Studio comes with both the device emulator core and the Emulator Manager application; you'll just need to install the emulator images and possibly the Mobile Device Center (both discussed in a few pages).

Optionally, you can install the Windows Mobile 6 SDK; this will add mobile-specific documentation and sample code to your IDE. It can be downloaded from `http://tinyurl.com/32bycn`. It does include Windows Mobile 6.0 emulator images, but I recommend you also install images for 6.1 and 6.5 (the more current versions), as detailed in the "Emulator Images" section.

When the time comes to start the Device Emulator, select Device Emulator Manager under Visual Studio's Tools menu.

Without Visual Studio

If you don't have Visual Studio, you'll need to download and install the stand-alone Device Emulator. As of this writing, the current version is 3.0, available for download from `http://tinyurl.com/2ujem8`. However, a newer version may be available by the time you read this, so it's worth checking on MSDN to confirm that you're getting the latest.

The Device Emulator also includes the Emulator Manager, needed for file and network connections. After installing the emulator, you should have a Start menu item (under All Programs → Windows Mobile 6 SDK → Tools) for Device Emulator Manager; if not, look for the executable at `C:\Program Files\Microsoft Device Emulator\1.0\dvcemumanager.exe`. Note the `1.0`: this is unrelated to the Device Emulator version number shown.

Emulator Images

With or without Visual Studio, you'll need emulator images to provide the user interface with which you'll interact on-screen. For full compatibility with the current versions of Windows Mobile, I recommend you install emulator images for both version 6.1 and 6.5.

■ **Tip** Unless you need to troubleshoot an issue specifically related to the Standard edition, it's only necessary to install the Professional images. They're the touchscreen versions, making them much easier to work with.

First, download and install the Windows Mobile 6.1 Emulator Images from `http://tinyurl.com/lb3dbq`. I find that occasionally Start menu shortcuts are not created the first time that these images are installed, but a Repair installation usually resolves the matter.

■ **Caution** Version 6.1.4 is also available, which includes IE Mobile 6, the newer browser included in Windows Mobile 6.5. If you want to do compatibility testing with the older IE Mobile, make sure you install the 6.1 emulator images, not 6.1.4.

For 6.5, the package has been renamed the Windows Mobile 6.5 Developer Toolkit (DTK), but it's an equivalent set of emulator images. It's available at `http://tinyurl.com/onp8ry`, localized to a number of different languages.

With the emulator images installed, you should be able to run various simulated screen resolutions and hardware configurations from Start → All Programs → Windows Mobile 6 SDK → Standalone Emulator Images, with results similar to Figure 9-1. Unless you already have experience with Windows Mobile, I recommend you spend a few minutes becoming familiar with its operation and user interface.

The Windows Mobile Device Center

One last piece is required to connect your emulators to the Internet, and it's the same utility that Microsoft distributes for connecting real handsets, the Windows Mobile Device Center. If you happen to have a Windows Mobile smartphone, you may well have this program already installed; if not, download it from `http://microsoft.com/windowsmobile/devicecenter.mspx`.

■ **Note** Windows Mobile Device Center is for Vista (and later) only. On Windows XP, install ActiveSync instead, from `http://tinyurl.com/antohb`. The setup instructions are similar to those for Device Center covered next.

Once installed, the Device Center provides connectivity to Internet and file browsing on the device from the host computer. It doesn't care whether the device in question is a physical handset or an emulator image; its function is the same. The only difference is how that connection is made. Physical devices would use a USB or Bluetooth connection; emulators use direct memory access (DMA) instead.

To enable this connection, start Device Center (from the Start menu), and click Mobile Device Settings → Connection Settings. Select "Allow connections to one of the following," and select DMA from the drop-down (see Figure 9-2). Device Manager should now be ready to connect.

Figure 9-2. Enabling DMA in Windows Mobile Device Center

Using the Emulator

Having installed and configured all the various components, you're now ready to run an emulator image and connect it to the Internet. Whenever you need a Windows Mobile emulator for testing, you'll need to perform the following steps to start it:

1. Start the Windows Mobile Device Manager, described in the previous section. Assuming you've already enabled DMA connections (Figure 9-2), that setting should be remembered and not need to be performed each time.

2. Start the emulator image for the required Windows Mobile version, edition, and screen resolution. Shortcuts for these should all be found under Start → All Programs → Windows Mobile 6 SDK → Standalone Emulator Images. The emulator may take a minute or two to boot.

3. Start the Device Emulator Manager; the procedure for this depends on whether you're using Visual Studio (as discussed earlier). When it starts, you'll need to connect the emulator to the host operating system; this is done by clicking its entry in Emulator Manager, right-clicking, and selecting Cradle (see Figure 9-3). This simulates docking the handheld, and you should hear the standard Windows device-connection tones.

4. The emulated device should be recognized by Device Center. Click "Connect without setting up my device" to finalize the connection.

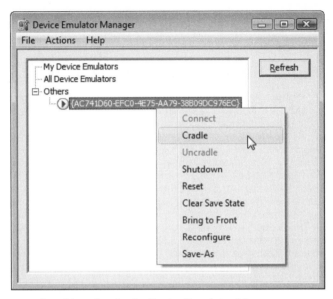

Figure 9-3. Cradling an emulated handset in the Device Emulator Manager

With the connection made, your emulator should now be online; confirm this by opening Internet Explorer Mobile (on the emulator) and browsing to a web site. You should also have access to the handset's filesystem through Windows: it should appear as an additional "disk drive" called Pocket_PC, the same as if it were a real device connected via USB.

■ **Note** If you're using a Windows Mobile Standard emulator, the handset's "disk drive" will be named Smartphone instead of Pocket_PC. Or for a real device, it will be whatever you've named your handset.

When you go to close the window containing an emulator, you'll be prompted for whether you want to save its state. If you do so, the next time you start the image, it will be exactly where you left it; no virtual "reboot" of the emulator will be required.

Each emulator image (combination of version, edition, and resolution) is a separate instance; no state is shared between them. This can be handy for testing different configurations. The state itself is saved on the host under C:\Users\[Username]\AppData\Roaming\Microsoft\Device Emulator as an ordinary file that can be copied, backed up, and so forth.

Running Web Applications

We're now ready to get back to the real topic of the chapter, running your gadget—your miniature web application—on Windows Mobile. Since the "miniature" part is implicit in the dimensions of the device's screen, the most obvious first approach is to simply open your gadget in a browser on the handset. The following sections will look at the issues associated with doing just that; they assume that you have your core gadget configured at a reachable URL, as described in the later sections of Chapter 2.

Web Apps in Internet Explorer Mobile 6

Prior to Windows Mobile 6.5, the built-in browser was quite rudimentary, lacking support for even such basics as CSS nested child selectors and the JavaScript `createTextNode` function. As a result, the fact is that only the simplest web apps will stand a chance of running here.

The situation improves considerably with Internet Explorer Mobile 6, the version that ships with version 6.5 of the operating system. This is a major browser upgrade, and it now supports the majority of the same style and functionality as the desktop Internet Explorer. Although this still lags behind some other, more leading-edge web clients, it's good enough that running web applications is at least a possibility here.

So, for the remainder of this chapter, I'm going to assume Windows Mobile 6.5 when discussing native browser support, on the basis that there effectively was none in previous versions.

Correspondingly, the first step in assessing your web gadget's compatibility with Internet Explorer Mobile is to open a version 6.5 emulator instance and browse to its URL.

The first issue you're likely to notice is that much of your content is off the side of the screen, but if you "swipe" sideways with your mouse (on the simulated touchscreen), it will scroll horizontally into view. This is because IE Mobile 6, like some other newer mobile browsers, misrepresents its screen size as something greater than it is. The idea is that pages will render at an "ordinary" screen width, which the user can then navigate within. This is beneficial on many web pages; they're not built for a 240-pixel width, but for a page that is (like a gadget), it's exactly the wrong thing to do.

Fortunately, there's an easy fix. A single line added to the head section of your gadget's HTML should do the trick:

```
<meta name="viewport" content="width=device-width" />
```

The `meta viewport` tag was introduced by Apple for the iPhone's Mobile Safari browser, one of the first to use this size-misrepresentation technique to display full-sized web pages on a small screen. Many web designers set the `width` attribute shown earlier to a specific pixel value optimized for their page—and you can do the same, if you like. But for gadgets, which will typically work well on any small screen width, a value of `device-width` will automatically scale them to the width of the screen, exactly the behavior we want.

If your gadget has a variable height, perhaps scrolling to bring more content into view, the `meta viewport` tag shown earlier is probably right. But for a gadget with a fixed height as well, you can use the same trick in the other dimension too:

```
<meta name="viewport" content="width=device-width, height=device-height " />
```

This will cause your gadget to occupy the entire device screen, and assuming that you've positioned your content appropriately, the appearance should be reasonable. Figure 9-4 shows my example Moon Phase gadget, rendered natively in IE Mobile 6, with just this single line of extra code.

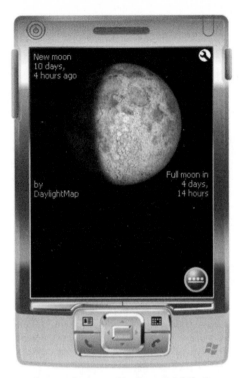

Figure 9-4. The Moon Phase core gadget on Internet Explorer Mobile 6

As you can see, the width of the page matches the width of the screen: support for meta viewport has now spread to IE Mobile, far beyond Mobile Safari. Accordingly, I unconditionally recommend placing the version of this tag most appropriate to your gadget in your head section; any browser that supports it will probably benefit, and any that don't support it will ignore it.

If your gadget requires additional tweaks for Internet Explorer Mobile, your best guide is probably Microsoft's own reference, at http://msdn.microsoft.com/en-us/library/bb415428.aspx. Here you'll find a complete list of which HTML elements and CSS selectors are supported, enabling you to modify your code accordingly.

We'll revisit IE Mobile 6 a bit later in the chapter—it serves as the basis for a built-in widget platform, also introduced with version 6.5 of the operating system—but for now, let's move on to the other widely used mobile browser.

Web Apps in Opera Mobile

Because Internet Explorer Mobile had been so weak for so long, a vibrant ecosystem of third-party browsers grew up in its place, and chief among these is Opera Mobile. What Opera lacks in desktop browser share, it makes up for on handhelds; its other mobile browser, Opera Mini, is described as "the world's most popular mobile web browser" (see the "Opera Mobile and Mini" sidebar).

On Windows Mobile smartphones, however, Opera Mobile has long been the browser of choice, and for good reason. Even compared with IE Mobile 6, it's still more standards-compliant and feature-rich. Most web pages render flawlessly on Opera Mobile—and similarly, most web apps run just fine. In particular, if you got your gadget working for the Opera Widgets platform in Chapter 8, the same base code should work here.

Moon Phase is no exception; Figure 9-5 shows my core gadget from Chapter 3 running in Opera Mobile. It doesn't require the meta viewport tag from the previous section (although it doesn't hurt).

Figure 9-5. *Moon Phase again, this time on Opera Mobile 9.7*

To test your own gadget's compatibility with Opera Mobile, you'll need to install it, whether onto an emulator image or a real handset. The easiest way to do so is to browse to http://opera.com/mobile/download from the device itself and follow the download and installation instructions you'll find there for the current version. It will generally install with minimal trouble (you can see it on the handset Start menu of Figure 9-6 in a couple of pages), and you can then test your core gadget directly.

■ **Tip** For a thorough guide to installing applications on Windows Mobile—including alternatives to the browse-and-download approach described earlier—see www.wmexperts.com/articles/howto/how_to_install_uninstall_and_t.html.

OPERA MOBILE AND MINI

Opera Mobile is the topic of this section, but it isn't the company's most popular mobile browser. That honor goes to Opera Mini, which claims more than 20 million users worldwide, and the reason is the difference in the browsers' respective platforms. Opera Mobile is used on smartphones, which (while growing) is still a minority of all handsets. Opera Mini, on the other hand, is the dominant browser on older, so-called "feature phones"—handsets that don't run an integrated general-purpose operating system and thus don't offer the same level of functionality to client applications.

Not surprisingly, the more limited environment on these devices is a challenging one for a web browser. To meet this challenge, Opera Mini is what's called a *thin client* browser: much of its functionality isn't actually implemented on the handset. Instead, web requests are routed through a server at Opera, which formats the page, compresses the output, and then sends it to the phone. This results in a better web-surfing experience than would be possible on such a resource-limited client, though it's still noticeably inferior to what's achievable with a good smartphone browser.

And from a web application perspective, the reality is that Opera Mini will still only support the most basic of functionality. Both its CSS and JavaScript are a small subset of what's available on any modern desktop or smartphone browser. For the purposes of this book, then, there's very little we can do with Opera Mini—we'll stick with Mobile.

Windows Mobile Web Widgets

With the release of Windows Mobile 6.5, Microsoft introduced support for web widgets built right into the operating system. This is good news for widget developers looking to deploy to the platform: it means that we can effectively create Windows Mobile applications from the gadget code we already have. When installed on a handset, Windows Mobile widgets appear on the device's Start menu just as any other application, and from the user's point of view, there's very little difference.

The Windows Mobile widget API is based on the W3C widget specification, as were the Opera widgets from Chapter 8 and (to a lesser extent) the Mac OS X widgets from Chapter 7. Since the W3C specification is still coalescing, you'll find that there are some variations between all the APIs that refer to it; nonetheless, the similarities are greater than the differences, and your experience from those chapters will serve you well here.

Built-in Widget Architecture

As with most off-the-Web platforms, Windows Mobile's widgets are packaged as a zip archive renamed with a different extension (than `.zip`). In this case, the extension can be either `.wgt` or `.widget`. Since Opera widgets already use `.wgt`, I recommend using `.widget` for your Windows Mobile port and leaving `.wgt` for Opera.

Within the archive, the structure is virtually identical to that found in an Opera widget: the root of the archive is effectively the web root for the gadget, from where the static source and content files are all served. The use of subdirectories is optional, so it's your decision whether your gadget warrants the additional complexity. The only major source difference from Opera is that your gadget's core HTML file needn't be named `index.html`. You can give it any name you like; you just need to specify it in the configuration XML (covered in the next section).

A Windows Mobile widget will also need an icon to represent it on the handset's Start menu. Ideally, your icon should be 48 pixels in both height and width, with a few pixels of padding on all sides. Other sizes will work but will appear pixelated on the phone. Also, the nature of the Start menu on Windows Mobile 6.5 means that icons with transparent backgrounds look much better, so I recommend using the PNG format and antialiasing your icon's edges.

Figure 9-6. *The Moon Phase widget icon, highlighted on Windows Mobile 6.5's Start menu*

Figure 9-6 shows the Start menu with a widget icon (for my Moon Phase example) installed. Note that the icon is shown against a light background when it's selected and a dark background when it's not, so make sure your icon works in both cases.

■ **Note** At this writing, custom widget icons only seem to work in Windows Mobile 6.5 Professional. On Standard, a generic widget icon will be used on the Start menu instead.

Adapting the Core Gadget

If your gadget was working fairly well on Internet Explorer Mobile 6 earlier in the chapter, it'll be well on its way to running as a Windows Mobile widget, because they use the same rendering and JavaScript engines. All you'll need to do is create the manifest and package it up. Or, if some additional platform-specific tweaks would be beneficial, now is your opportunity to make them. In either case, the following sections will point you in the right direction.

Creating the Manifest

Like most platforms, Windows Mobile requires a metadata file to tell it *about* your gadget before it can be displayed. Windows Mobile follows the W3C specification by using a manifest file named config.xml to do so, and the contents of that file adhere to the specification more closely than Opera does. In the next few sections, I'll detail the XML elements found in the manifest; you can see them *in situ* in Listing 9-1.

Listing 9-1. The Widget Manifest (Configuration File, config.xml) for Moon Phase

```
<?xml version="1.0" encoding="UTF-8"?>
<widget xmlns="http://www.w3.org/ns/widgets" version="1.0">
  <name>Moon Phase</name>
  <description>Shows the phase of the moon on a field of stars.</description>
  <icon src="moon_48.png" />
  <author href="http://sterlingudell.com"
          email="sterling.udell@gmail.com">
    Sterling Udell
  </author>
  <content src="phase_win_mob.html" type="text/html" />
  <access network="true" />
</widget>
```

widget

As the root XML element, widget mostly just contains the rest of the manifest. Like all well-formed XML roots, it also has an xmlns attribute for the namespace in use. The version of the W3C spec (here, 1.0) is also recommended.

name

This is the name of your gadget as it will appear on the system Start menu.

description

This is a short plain-text description, displayed while your widget is being installed.

author

This element should contain your name (or your company's); it can also take optional attributes of href, email, and img. Currently, it doesn't appear that any information from the author element is used by Windows Mobile.

content

This required element gives the name of your gadget's main HTML file in its src attribute. The type attribute, with a value of text/html, is good practice but not strictly required.

access

This element enables access to the Internet from your code. Unless your widget is entirely self-contained (with all its resources in its .widget archive), the access element is required, with the network attribute of true shown in Listing 9-1. Note that the user's permission will be required at runtime for this access to occur.

Changes to the HTML

If you were happy with the way that your core gadget appeared under Internet Explorer Mobile 6 earlier in the chapter, no changes to your HTML are required! When you install it a bit later in the chapter, it should run exactly as it did in the browser.

However, most gadgets will benefit from some modifications, so in this section you'll find a guide to integrating such changes—as well as one specific change that will probably do your gadget good. As usual, I recommend confining your changes to your core HTML as much as possible. For small changes, inline style and script blocks are probably easiest (as shown here); for larger modifications, create Windows Mobile–specific .js and .css files (as I did for Mac OS X in Chapter 7). Isolating your changes in this way will ease your maintenance burden down the road.

Listing 9-2 gets us started; I've highlighted the few changes to my standard Moon Phase example for Windows Mobile. The body content is unchanged from Chapter 3, so I've left it out of this listing for the sake of brevity.

Listing 9-2. The Moon Phase Example Gadget's HTML, Modified for a Windows Mobile Widget (phase_win_mob.html)

```
<?xml version="1.0" encoding="UTF-8"?>
<!DOCTYPE html PUBLIC "-//W3C//DTD XHTML 1.0 Transitional//EN"
                      "http://www.w3.org/TR/xhtml1/DTD/xhtml1-transitional.dtd">
<html xmlns="http://www.w3.org/1999/xhtml">
  <head>
    <meta http-equiv="Content-Type" content="text/html;charset=UTF-8" />
    <meta name="description"
          content="Shows the current phase of the moon on a field of stars." />
    <meta name="viewport" content="width=device-width, height=device-height" />
    <title>Moon Phase</title>
    <link href="moon_32.png" type="image/png" rel="icon" />
    <link href="phase.css"   type="text/css"  rel="stylesheet" />
    <style type="text/css">
      .moonPhase #main_icons {
        display: none;
      }
    </style>
  </head>
  <body class="moonPhase">
```

```
  <!-- body content goes here -->

  <script src="platform.js" type="text/javascript"></script>
  <script src="phase.js"    type="text/javascript"></script>
  <script type="text/javascript">
    // Ensure that the moonPhase namespace exists
    var moonPhase = window.moonPhase || {};

    // Add an additional load event handler to set up the softkey menu item
    crossPlatform.addHandler(window, 'load', function () {
      moonPhase.settingsMenuItem = widget.menu.createMenuItem(1);
      moonPhase.settingsMenuItem.text = 'Settings';
      moonPhase.settingsMenuItem.onSelect = moonPhase.showConfig;
      widget.menu.append(moonPhase.settingsMenuItem);
    });

    // Hide and show the menu item (as appropriate) along with the config pane
    moonPhase.defaultShowConfig = moonPhase.showConfig;
    moonPhase.showConfig = function () {
      widget.menu.remove(moonPhase.settingsMenuItem);
      moonPhase.defaultShowConfig();
    };
    moonPhase.defaultHideConfig = moonPhase.hideConfig;
    moonPhase.hideConfig = function () {
      widget.menu.append(moonPhase.settingsMenuItem);
      moonPhase.defaultHideConfig();
    };
  </script>
  </body>
</html>
```

Before I get into the new code, a bit of background is in order. Because Windows Mobile widgets run directly on the handset's operating system, they have access to some of that operating system's features. One such feature is the soft keys under the device's screen; for widgets, the left key is ordinarily Exit, and the right one is Menu. So, what I've decided to do for Moon Phase is to move its Settings button functionality onto the right-key menu, where the user will logically look for it. All the code changes in Listing 9-2 are centered around this modification; if your gadget has a Settings button, you might consider doing the same.

Style

The style changes in Listing 9-2 are extremely simple. Since I'm moving the Settings button's functionality elsewhere, there's no need to show it anymore—so I don't. A single CSS rule on the main_icons container div is sufficient:

```
display: none;
```

225

JavaScript

A bit more work is required here, but it's still not a great deal. The new code is split into two basic areas: a new `window.load` event handler and extensions to the functions that show and hide the configuration pane.

First, in the `window.load` event I need to create the new menu item. This happens in three steps:

1. In the API's `widget` namespace is a `menu` object; calling its `createMenuItem` method returns a new menu item object. Note that it takes an integer ID as a parameter; if you're creating multiple menu items, their IDs must be unique.

   ```
   moonPhase.settingsMenuItem = widget.menu.createMenuItem(1);
   ```

2. I set a couple of properties of the new menu item, its `text` and `onSelect` handler. The latter is a reference to my existing function to show the configuration pane.

   ```
   moonPhase.settingsMenuItem.text = "Settings";
   moonPhase.settingsMenuItem.onSelect = moonPhase.showConfig;
   ```

3. The menu item is now complete, so another API function call appends it to the menu.

   ```
   widget.menu.append(moonPhase.settingsMenuItem);
   ```

Second, there's no need for the Settings menu item to be visible when the configuration pane is active, so I extend the `moonPhase.showConfig` and `.hideConfig` functions to `remove` and re-append the menu item as appropriate. The method-override technique is the same as I employed in Chapter 7; please refer to that chapter (in the "Flipping the Widget" section) for additional details on how it works.

And I'm done. Figure 9-7 shows the result: the Moon Phase widget running directly on Windows Mobile 6.5, with the new Settings menu item visible.

Figure 9-7. *The Moon Phase example on Windows Mobile's built-in widget platform*

Additions to crossPlatform

Before we move on, one other small set of changes *is* required: to my `crossPlatform` middleware layer. But because Windows Mobile is following the same core widget specification as Opera and Mac OS X, the incremental changes will again be quite small. First, I need to detect the platform:

```
if (!!window.widget) {
  if (!!widget.getAttention) {
    crossPlatform.api = 'opera';
    crossPlatform.emptyPref = '';
  } else if (!!widget.menu) {
    crossPlatform.api = 'windows_mobile';
    crossPlatform.emptyPref = null;
  } else {
    crossPlatform.api = 'mac';
    crossPlatform.emptyPref = undefined;
  }
}
```

As did Mac and Opera, this platform relies on a `widget` namespace, so I only need to differentiate it from those two—which I do by detecting the `widget.menu` object. Interestingly, all three platforms return different values for preferences that haven't been defined; these are stored in my `emptyPref` variable for each.

With the platform detected, the only other changes I need to make are to the preference getter and setter code, and because the underlying API is so similar, I can again just extend the Mac/Opera case for each:

```
switch (crossPlatform.api) {
  case 'mac':
  case 'opera':
  case 'windows_mobile':
    myValue = widget.preferenceForKey(name);
    break;
  ...
}
```

```
switch (crossPlatform.api) {
  case 'mac':
  case 'opera':
  case 'windows_mobile':
    widget.setPreferenceForKey(myValue, myName);
    break;
  ...
}
```

With these small changes, your app should indeed run as well as a Windows Mobile widget as it did in the handset's browser.

Testing and Debugging

Of course, to find out how your new Windows Mobile widget works, you'll need to install and run it. This section will walk you through that process, as well as give you some guidance on how to proceed if trouble does arise.

The first step is to package your code into a `.widget` archive. As with Opera, I suggest creating a development directory for your Windows Mobile code and copying in the relevant source files from your master gadget. This serves as a convenient staging area for the archive and gives you an easy place for working on your manifest (and other files). When you have the source files ready, create a zip archive (by selecting New → Compressed (Zipped) Folder from the Windows shell context menu) and give it a descriptive name. Copy your source files into it (see Figure 9-8), preserving any subdirectory structure you're using, and then rename its extension from `.zip` to `.widget`.

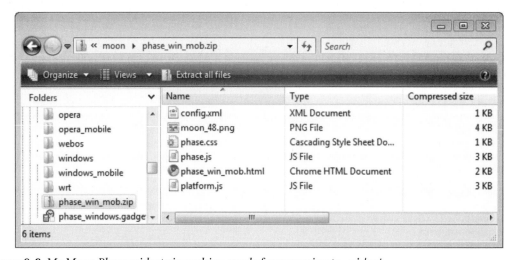

Figure 9-8. *My Moon Phase widget zip archive, ready for renaming to* `.widget`

■ **Tip** To reduce confusion, I like using a file name that succinctly combines both the gadget and the platform in question. For Moon Phase on Windows Mobile, for example, I'm using `phase_win_mob.widget`.

Installing Your Widget

Your widget is now ready to go, so you need a device to test it on. If you're using an emulator, start the desired image and connect it to your host operating system using the directions earlier in the chapter. If you're going to use an actual device, you'll still need the Windows Mobile Device Center to access its filesystem, but the process is otherwise the same.

■ **Caution** Remember that widgets are supported only on Windows Mobile 6.5 (and beyond), so make sure that your test device has the correct OS version.

In either case, once the connection is made, you should be able to browse to the device using Windows Explorer on the host system. Copy your `.widget` file into a location where you'll be able to find it easily on the device; I like using `Pocket_PC\\My Documents` (see Figure 9-9), because it's the default location for the handset's own File Explorer.

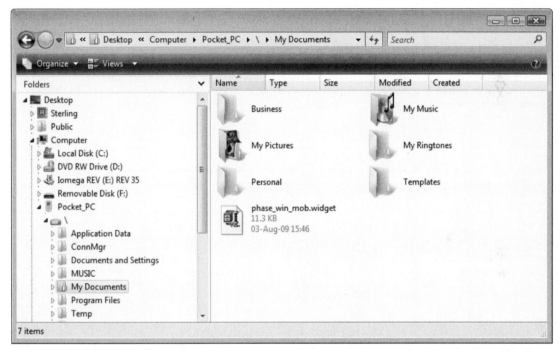

Figure 9-9. *My Documents on the handset, seen from the host operating system, with the* `.widget` *file copied into place and ready for installation*

Now on the handset (emulated or real), select Start → File Explorer, browse to the location where you copied your `.widget` archive, and click it. After a confirmation or two, it should open, and you can begin testing it. Your widget is now installed on the handset, so you should also be able to find it on the Start menu.

■ **Tip** New programs (including widgets) get added to the bottom of the handset's Start menu; make your life easier by long-pressing it (on the emulator, click and hold for a moment with your mouse) and selecting Move to Top.

Applying Changes

After your widget is installed, the handset doesn't run it directly from the `.widget` archive. Instead, the source files get unpacked to a subdirectory of `Pocket_PC\\Program Files\Widgets\User\`. These subdirectories are sequentially numbered as you install widgets, so your first installed widget will be in 1, and the highest-numbered directory will contain your latest installation. Within these subdirectories, you can edit any of your widget's source files in place, *except* `config.xml`. Your changes will take effect as soon as you exit and restart the widget.

■ **Caution** Make sure you use the Exit button at the bottom left of the widget, not the X at the top right, to apply changes to the source code (visible in Figure 9-7). The X button only suspends the widget, rather than fully exiting it.

If you make changes to your `config.xml` manifest, you'll need to reinstall your widget for them to take effect. First, uninstall the widget from the handset: from Start → Settings → System → Remove Programs, select your widget, and click Remove. Then install the new version from the host operating system as described in the previous section.

■ **Tip** As in Chapter 8, once you have your widget working correctly, I recommend that you delete your development directory to avoid unintentionally branching the source files within.

Deploying Windows Mobile Widgets

One of the most interesting aspects of Windows Mobile widgets is that they can be distributed through the Windows Marketplace for Mobile—including for pay. This is a recent development in the world of web gadgets; until very recently, there has been no venue for direct monetization of a gadget.

As of this writing, the marketplace has not yet gone live, though it's expected to very soon—well before this book is published. What is known is that there will be a fee (currently US $99) for developers to register and list an application. For the most up-to-date information, please visit `http://developer.windowsmobile.com/Marketplace.aspx`.

In addition to the marketplace, you can also host and distribute your widget yourself. You'd do this just as you would any other off-the-Web gadget file: host it on your web server, and provide a link labeled something like "Install our Windows Mobile 6.5 widget." With an extension of `.widget` (or `.wgt`), compatible handsets will automatically install the widget after download.

■ **Note** If hosting the widget yourself, make sure you make clear that Windows Mobile 6.5 is required for its use.

Windows Mobile–Specific Extensions

One of the great appeals to Windows Mobile widgets is that you can deploy your existing web gadget code to the platform with little modification, the ongoing rationale for cross-platform development. Like most platforms, however, there are nonstandard extensions that you can make use of if you are developing a widget that will only run on Windows Mobile. Or looking at it from the other direction, if you have a situation that can make exceptionally good use of one of these extensions, it may be worth your while to create a specific version just for it.

In the following few sections, I'll briefly discuss the major areas where Windows Mobile offers additional functionality.

Localization

Although Windows Mobile widgets use a completely different API than Windows desktop gadgets, their localization scheme is virtually identical. It's based on locale-specific files placed in directories named for the locale in question; for example, generic French-language files would be placed in directories under /fr from the widget archive root, while French-Canadian ones would go under /fr-ca. The platform then uses such files (rather than those off the archive root) when the corresponding locale is selected by the device user.[1]

For more detailed instructions, please see the "Localization" section of Chapter 6. Apart from the slight difference in naming described earlier—fr-ca for Windows Mobile vs. fr_ca on the desktop—the techniques and procedures are identical.

Menus and Soft Keys

In Listing 9-2, I made use of the Windows Mobile API's widget.menu object to add a new item to the menu attached to the right soft key. Obviously, this technique can be extended to add multiple menu items, but a few other tricks are available as well.

First, the menu item object (returned from the widget.menu.createMenuItem function) has append and remove methods of its own. With these, you can add (and remove) child menu items, allowing you to create complex multilevel menus. This can be a good technique for integrating a large amount of widget functionality into the native user interface.

Second, widget.menu has a setSoftKey method, which allows you to directly replace the root functionality for either of the device's soft keys. So for example, if I had used the following line of code (instead of widget.menu.append), I would have created a Settings soft key function instead of adding to its menu:

```
widget.menu.setSoftKey(moonPhase.settingsMenuItem, widget.menu.rightSoftKeyIndex);
```

The setSoftKey method takes two parameters: the menu item to attach to the key and a constant indicating which key to affect (there's also widget.menu.leftSoftKeyIndex). Figure 9-10 shows the result, where Settings are directly accessed from the right soft key.

---

[1] This localization technique is a slight departure from the W3C widget standard. Although the basic idea is the same, the W3C spec groups all locale-specific files under a top-level directory of /locales, rather than directly off the archive root. So in the W3C specification, Canadian French files would be in /locales/fr-ca, rather than just /fr-ca.

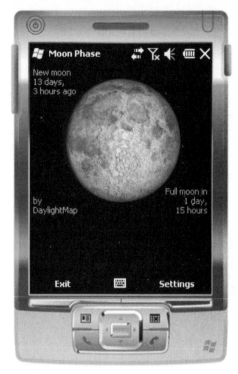

Figure 9-10. Replacing soft key functionality

Note that this wouldn't actually be a good solution for Moon Phase, because there's no way to hide the soft key when the configuration pane is open. It does demonstrate the use of setSoftKey, however, in case you do have a good use for it yourself.

The SystemState Object

In addition to the soft keys, the API also grants access to various device information via an object called SystemState. This is created through the widget.createObject method, as such:

```
moonPhase.systemState = widget.createObject('SystemState');
```

Once created, SystemState provides a variety of information about the device's network, connectivity, and battery status.

For an example of this in action, imagine that I wanted to make Moon Phase more responsive to the state of the handset and not retrieve my remote data if the device was in roaming coverage (to save the user from accruing data-roaming charges). After initializing the SystemState as done earlier, I could do so by adding a few lines to my existing load function:

```
moonPhase.load = function () {
  if (moonPhase.systemState.PhoneRoaming) {
    alert('Unable to load Moon Phase when not in home coverage');
```

```
    return;
  }
  ...
};
```

As you can see, if `PhoneRoaming` is `true`, the function will message the user and `return`, rather than loading the gadget. This is a fairly trivial example, but `SystemState` has other useful properties, and more are actively being added. For a current list, see Microsoft's documentation at `http://msdn.microsoft.com/en-us/library/dd721906.aspx`.

Opera Mobile Widgets

Windows Mobile's built-in widget platform is an excellent solution for newer handsets, but what about the large number of legacy, pre-6.5 units? It turns out that there's a solution nearly as good there as well: the Opera Widgets API, covered thoroughly for desk-bound computers in Chapter 8, has a smartphone counterpart. This allows you to run virtually the same widget on all recent versions of Windows Mobile—and, as you'll see in the next chapter, the Symbian S60 phone OS as well.

In fact, your phone widget may actually be simpler than on the desktop. Recall that in Chapter 8, much of your effort was expended in generating chrome for a good appearance as a desktop gadget. On a handheld device, widgets generally render full-screen—meaning that the "chrome" is generated by the operating system, or even supplied by the device itself.

■ **Note** The remainder of this chapter assumes that you have read Chapter 8.

Taking Your Opera Widget Mobile

The basic architecture of an Opera Mobile widget is identical to one for Opera on the desktop. It's a zip archive renamed to a `.wgt` extension, containing a `config.xml` manifest, a core HTML file named `index.html`, and all the other static content for the gadget. That's our starting point. Unless otherwise stated here, the structure and source of the mobile widget will be the same as in Chapter 8.

As mentioned in the previous section, the major difference is that on handheld devices, we want our widget to occupy the device's full screen. To ensure that this happens, we need to add an attribute to the root widget element of the `config.xml` file (from Listing 8-1):

```
<widget network="public" defaultmode="fullscreen">
```

Without `defaultmode="fullscreen"`, Opera Mobile will instead render the widget at whatever `width` and `height` are specified in the configuration file. Since this will usually be the majority of a handheld screen anyway, we're better off just taking the whole thing and acting like a native application.

That gets us started, allocating the full screen to the widget. To properly make use of it, however, we'll need to actually use that space—and the best way to do that is going to depend on the design of your gadget. Considerations include the following:

- You'll be working within a fixed size, so you'll be more likely to scroll long content blocks that expand your gadget to accommodate them.

- Conversely, small content blocks will want to be centered or distributed evenly within that fixed size.

- If you have a variable amount of content—say, a game field or image—your best choice is probably to scale it to fit the content area as best you can.

In other words, it's up to you to decide what approach is best for your gadget and how best to implement it. In the next couple of pages, I'll walk you through my solution, but the bad news is that yours will most likely be different. The good news is that Opera Mobile is quite a good, standards-compliant little browser, so it will probably handle whatever layout techniques you need to use.

■ **Tip** Although your code will differ from mine, one line of JavaScript you *will* probably want is `window.resizeTo(screen.availWidth, screen.availHeight)`, telling Opera to expand your widget to occupy the full screen that you've requested. You can find details in the upcoming "JavaScript" section.

My Moon Phase example gadget is mostly in the second, small-content case from the list shown earlier. The moon image is generated on the server side at a fixed size and would degrade in quality if I scaled it on the client, so I'll try to center it within the screen instead. Naturally, this will require a bit more CSS and JavaScript code than my basic gadget has; these are highlighted in Listing 9-3. As usual, the changes are confined to a few inline `style` and `script` blocks; note also that this code is based from the basic HTML gadget, *not* from Listing 8-2.

Listing 9-3. The Opera Mobile Widget HTML for Moon Phase

```
<?xml version="1.0" encoding="UTF-8"?>
<!DOCTYPE html PUBLIC "-//W3C//DTD XHTML 1.0 Transitional//EN"
                    "http://www.w3.org/TR/xhtml1/DTD/xhtml1-transitional.dtd">
<html xmlns="http://www.w3.org/1999/xhtml">
  <head>
    <meta http-equiv="Content-Type" content="text/html;charset=UTF-8" />
    <meta name="description"
          content="Shows the current phase of the moon on a field of stars." />
    <meta name="viewport" content="width=device-width, height=device-height" />
    <title>Moon Phase</title>
    <link href="moon_32.png" type="image/png" rel="icon" />
    <link href="phase.css"   type="text/css"  rel="stylesheet" />
    <script type="text/javascript">
      if (parent.emulator) parent.emulator.begin(window);
    </script>
    <style type="text/css">
      .moonPhase #image_container {
        margin: 0;
        padding: 0;
      }
      .moonPhase #moon {
        position: relative;
        z-index: -1;
```

```
      }
      .moonPhase .control_icon {
        right: 10px;
      }
      .moonPhase #config_icon {
        top: 10px;
      }
      .moonPhase #config {
        padding: 0;
      }
    </style>
  </head>
  <body class="moonPhase">

    <!-- body content goes here -->

    <script type="text/javascript" src="platform.js"></script>
    <script type="text/javascript" src="phase.js"></script>
    <script type="text/javascript" src="testMediaQuery.js"></script>
    <script type="text/javascript">
      // Ensure that the moonPhase namespace exists
      var moonPhase = window.moonPhase || {};

      // Override the default load method
      moonPhase.defaultLoadFunction = moonPhase.load;
      moonPhase.load = function () {
        // Set the widget's size to fill the viewport
        window.resizeTo(screen.availWidth, screen.availHeight);
        document.body.style.width = screen.availWidth + 'px';
        moonPhase.elements.main.style.height =
          moonPhase.elements.config.style.height = screen.availHeight + 'px';

        // Call the ancestor method
        moonPhase.defaultLoadFunction();

        // Center the moon image within the widget
        moonPhase.elements.moon.style.top =
          (screen.availHeight - moonPhase.elements.moon.height) / 2 + 'px';
      };
    </script>
  </body>
</html>
```

The new script block in the head of Listing 9-3 contains code that, although important, isn't really the main focus of this section—so I won't spend much ink on it here. The emulator.begin call will be discussed a bit later in the chapter, under the Opera Widget Emulator.

Style

The first set of CSS selectors in Listing 9-3 is preparing for centering the moon image. When not occupying the full screen, I usually have a bit of margin and padding on the moon image container—but this will throw off the centering, so I zero it out here. Then I prepare the moon image itself for centering, by giving it `position: relative` and a `z-index` to ensure it stays "underneath" my text. The actual centering will be done in JavaScript in the next section.

I also have a few style rules concerned with other elements. First up is my Settings button; ordinarily I have it hard up against the upper-right corner of the gadget, but such a hit zone can be awkward on a touchscreen device. So, I move it down and inward by 10 pixels. And finally, my configuration pane usually has a bit of `padding` too—but this will be too much on a full screen, so I zero that as well.

JavaScript

This is where I take control of the widget size, and the code is pretty straightforward. It's similar in structure to the JavaScript in both Listing 7-4 and 8-2; I override my default `load` function to set the widget's size, call the ancestor's `load`, and then do a bit of final processing. I've discussed the override and ancestor-call aspects in Chapter 7, so I'll focus on the other parts here.

Setting the widget's size is done in two parts. First is a call to the Opera API to expand the widget to occupy the full viewport, and it's done with the following line of code:

```
window.resizeTo(screen.availWidth, screen.availHeight);
```

This is pure API code, calling its `window` and `screen` extensions, and won't work anywhere except in an Opera widget. Here, though, it's exactly what is needed: the `defaultmode="fullscreen"` attribute in `config.xml` requested the full screen, but we don't actually *have* it until this line of JavaScript is run. Crucial.

With that out of the way, the other resizing code is much more ordinary; I simply set `style.width` and `.height` values of the appropriate HTML elements to occupy the full screen.

And then, after calling the ancestor's `load` function, I can finally complete my task of centering the moon image:

```
moonPhase.elements.moon.style.top =
  (screen.availHeight - moonPhase.elements.moon.height) / 2 + 'px';
```

I only need to center it vertically, because it was already centered horizontally (that's done in my standard CSS). And this needs to happen *after* the ancestor's `load` because it sets the size of the moon image based on user preferences.

My Opera Mobile widget is now functionally complete and ready to run. I'll discuss the specifics of doing so a few sections hence, but for now, Figure 9-11 shows a preview of what it looks like.

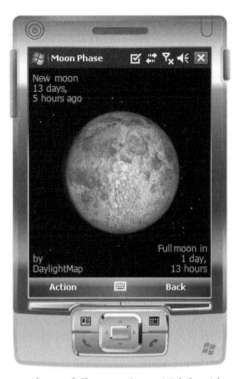

Figure 9-11. The Moon Phase example as a full-screen Opera Mobile widget

Widget Icon

Opera widgets on different devices require different icon sizes for best appearance. On Windows Mobile, it turns out that the optimal size is 64 pixels square, so an `icon` element like the following will need to be inserted into your Opera Mobile widget's `config.xml` file (this one is for Moon Phase):

```
<icon width="64" height="64">moon_64.png</icon>
```

■ **Caution** The version of Opera Mobile current as of this writing, 9.7 beta, doesn't handle multiple `icon` elements in `config.xml`. So for your mobile widget, you need to replace *all* `icon` elements from Listing 8-1 with a single line, like the previous one.

For optimal appearance on the Opera Mobile Widgets Manager, I also recommend that you give your new 64-pixel icon rounded corners—a 6-pixel radius looks about right (see Figure 9-12). Also, it seems to be required that the icon's PNG file be saved with alpha-channel transparency, although this may be another bug that's transient to the Opera Mobile 9.7 beta.

Figure 9-12. moon_64.png, the Opera Mobile widget icon for my Moon Phase example

Testing and Debugging

As you modify your existing Opera widget for mobile use, you'll naturally need to test it along the way. There are a couple of different avenues for doing so, described in the following sections; I suggest that you proceed with them in the order they're given here.

The Opera Widget Emulator

To facilitate testing mobile widgets, Opera has its own "emulator" that simulates widgets running on a handheld device, shown in Figure 9-13. It's nowhere near as realistic as a true Windows Mobile device emulator, but because it works from your desktop filesystem, it is significantly easier to work with. It's therefore a good place to begin your mobile widget testing, before moving up to a real mobile operating system. Also, the Opera emulator will run on any OS that the Opera browser supports (such as Mac and Linux), as opposed to the Windows-only emulators from Microsoft.

The Opera Widget Emulator is actually an Opera desktop widget itself, fundamentally no different from what we built ourselves in Chapter 8. Within the emulator is a client "screen" area where *other* widgets can be placed, however; it's this simulated device screen (really an iframe) that makes the emulator useful. This screen can be set to a variety of common handset resolutions or reconfigured to any custom resolution you choose. The Emulator also supports a variety of more advanced functions, such as bandwidth throttling and storage space monitoring, that are useful for comprehensive mobile widget debugging.

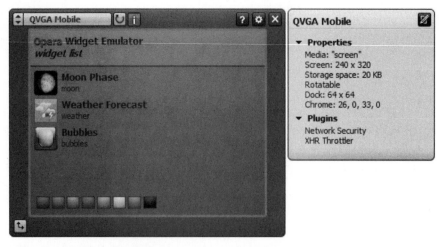

Figure 9-13. The Opera Widget Emulator

EMULATOR OR SIMULATOR?

Early in the chapter you learned about Windows Mobile emulators, and in subsequent chapters you'll be introduced to their equivalents for many other devices. And in this section you'll find the Opera Widget Emulator, which is really a different animal—although it's still being called an emulator. What's the difference?

A true emulator, like the Microsoft images installed earlier, *fully replicates* the software of one operating system inside of another, as a type of virtual machine. For example, Figure 9-10 was captured by running a virtual copy of Windows Mobile 6.1 inside Windows Vista. An emulator like this is capable of running any native code that has been compiled for the client operating system, in other words, code that would not run directly on the host OS. To programs running inside, a good emulator should be indistinguishable from an actual device.

A simulator, on the other hand, simply *looks* enough like the client system to be able to stand in for it in certain limited circumstances. Think of a flight simulator: nobody would mistake one for a real airplane, least of all the "program" running on the client system (the pilot). Nonetheless, a flight simulator can be very useful for the early stages of pilot training, before she's ready to actually leave the ground.

As you've probably guessed, Opera's so-called Widget Emulator is actually a simulator: it *simulates* a handheld device's widget environment, rather than actually *emulating* the device's operating system. Nonetheless, it is still a useful step in teaching your widget to fly.

To get started, you'll first need to install the emulator; it's available for download from http://dev.opera.com/articles/view/widget-emulator. Since the emulator is itself a widget, the download is a zip file containing its source (rather than an installer). And it would be possible to run the emulator as is, with the usual technique of renaming it from .zip to .wgt. However, you need to "install" your own widget into the emulator, so extract the contents of the zip file to a development directory. Inside, you'll find a directory named widgets; this is where widgets to be run in the emulator get installed, and you'll probably see a couple of samples there already.

■ **Note** You'll also need the Opera browser installed to run the emulator.

To install your own widget, the first step is to create a subdirectory under widgets for it—I'll name mine moon—and place your widget's source files in it. This directory will contain all your widget's code and resources, the same as its distribution package ordinarily would but in uncompressed (unzipped) form.

Second, you'll need to edit a file named dir.js, which you should find back in the main widgets directory. Essentially, this is a directory file that tells the emulator what widgets are installed and where to find them, and it consists of a single JSON string array:

```
var g_widgets = [
    'moon',
    'weather',
    'bubbles'
];
```

It should have a couple of entries already for the sample widgets that came with the emulator (here, 'weather' and 'bubbles'). All you need to do is add another string for your own widget, containing the directory name where you placed its source in the previous step. Since I named my directory moon, I've added 'moon' to dir.js. Save and close the file.

Third, you'll need to add a line of JavaScript to your own widget so that it runs smoothly within the emulator. The code is as follows:

```
<script type="text/javascript">
  if (parent.emulator) parent.emulator.begin(window);
</script>
```

Opera recommends that this occur early in the HTML, so accordingly I've added it to the head section of my source; you can see it there back in Listing 9-3.

■ **Note** This code runs only if the frame-parent emulator variable is set, so it's safe to leave in deployed code; it won't have any effect outside the Opera Emulator.

The emulator should now by ready to run. Recall from Chapter 8 that you can run an Opera widget by loading its config.xml into the Opera browser; that's the easiest way to run the emulator, so do this now (config.xml is back in the emulator's root directory). You should be presented with a view similar to Figure 9-13, a list of widgets—including yours. Click your widget to open it within the emulator (Figure 9-14).

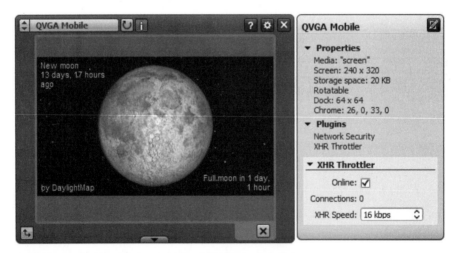

Figure 9-14. *My Moon Phase widget running in the Opera Emulator*

The debugging process now is just as it was in Chapter 8; edit your source files in their subdirectory under widget, and reload it in the emulator to see the effect (using the reload button visible at the top edge of the emulator). One nice aspect is that since your widget isn't running directly in Opera, changes to its config.xml will take effect immediately—there's no need to reinstall. But otherwise, it's very like working with any other Opera desktop widget.

Testing on Windows Mobile

Once your widget is working well on Opera's own emulator, the next step is to run it on Windows Mobile, either in an emulator image or on a real device. Doing so requires two components: Opera Mobile and the Opera Widgets Manager. Earlier in the chapter, you may have already installed the former for testing your core HTML gadget; if not, follow the instructions given there to do so now. You'll also need the Widgets Manager, and although this is a separate download, it is installed much the same as Opera Mobile itself: browse to http://opera.com/mobile/download, and select the download link for the Widgets Manager.

■ **Caution** Another issue with Opera Mobile 9.7 beta: the Widgets Manager isn't compatible with Windows Mobile 6.5. The solution is simply to install it on a Windows Mobile 6.1 emulator image.

With both components in place, you'll need to install your widget to begin testing. This means that you need to package it as a .wgt file, as described in Chapter 8. This package is then installed on the handset using a similar technique as for the built-in Windows Mobile widget platform, described earlier in the chapter. Connect to the handset's filesystem (with the Windows Mobile Device Center), and then copy your .wgt file onto the handset, into the following directory:

Pocket_PC\\\Program Files\Opera Mobile\profile\widgets

Your widget should now be installed and can be opened by running Opera Widgets (from Start → Programs on the handset). With a bit of luck, you'll be presented with a view like Figure 9-11.

But, it's probably a safe bet that your widget's Opera Mobile incarnation won't be perfect the first time out, and you'll need to tweak its code accordingly. Doing so involves several steps:

1. Modify the source as needed.

2. Repackage it as a .wgt archive.

3. Replace the old .wgt file in the Program Files\Opera Mobile\profile\widgets directory on the handset.

4. Close the widget and reopen in the Widgets Manager. If you changed your config.xml, you'll need to exit and reopen Widgets Manager instead.

This process is certainly a bit onerous—which is why it's best to work out as many bugs as possible on the Opera Widgets Emulator first.

Deploying Opera Mobile Widgets

The options for deploying an Opera Mobile widget are very similar to those for the Opera desktop widgets in Chapter 8: you can host it yourself, and you can list it on Opera's widget directory. The former option is as easy as linking to the .wgt file from your web site, though it is a good idea to differentiate between desktop and mobile Opera widgets, either by different download links (that the user can select) or by browser sniffing.

■ **Note** The `link` attribute used by desktop Opera to notify the user of an available widget, described in the "Direct Widget Downloads" section of Chapter 8, isn't supported by Opera Mobile.

You should also submit your widget to the Opera directory, however. Since the Add button in the Widgets Manager links to this directory, it's where most users will get their widgets. The submission procedure is basically the same as outlined in Chapter 8, with the following notes:

- You'll submit it as a new widget (not an update), because it uses a different `.wgt` file.

- During submission, select a device type of Handheld.

Once submitted, it will be subject to the same approval process as before and will then be available for download directly from Windows Mobile handhelds.

T-Mobile Web'n'Walk Widgets

Before we leave Windows Mobile, there's one last platform to discuss, the T-Mobile Web 'n' Walk SDK. This isn't an API in itself but rather a set of extensions to the Opera Mobile Widgets API that significantly increases the functionality available to widget developers. And as its name implies, it's a very narrow platform, available only on certain European T-Mobile handsets running Windows Mobile. It's also very new: it was announced during the writing of this book, and right now developer access to it is only by request, rather than being open to one and all. But it's worth discussing here because it may well expand to other markets and handsets, and in any case, it seems to foreshadow the direction in which the mobile widget ecosystem is headed.

In addition to the technical aspects of the platform, T-Mobile also maintains a directory of widgets for direct download by users, and this is potentially of interest to all widget developers—even those not using the API extensions.

Additional information on this platform is still quite skimpy; the main portal is a page at Opera's developer site, `http://dev.opera.com/articles/view/creating-t-mobile-widgets`. There you'll find a platform overview, downloads for the SDK itself, and a link for applying to T-Mobile's developer program.

T-Mobile-Specific Extensions

In technical terms, the Web'n'Walk SDK is a superset of the Opera Mobile Widgets API, building on its generic foundation to give significantly greater access to device functionality. These extensions include the following:

- Contact list, to-do, and calendar access

- Geolocation

- Messaging (SMS, MMS, and e-mail)

- Power management

- Network connectivity

- Native code integration

- Device soft keys

To support these API extensions, the SDK also includes a custom version of the Opera Widget Emulator, which provides JavaScript interface stubs. This emulator also comes preconfigured with screen layouts for the T-Mobile devices in the pilot program.

You'll notice that several of the previous items were also included in the extensions to the widget API built into Windows Mobile, discussed earlier in the chapter. You'll also see them recurring with greater frequency as we get into newer smartphone platforms later in the book. Through APIs like these, mobile widgets are breaking free from the limitations of web-only functionality, taking on roles traditionally available only to native applications.

Listing in the T-Mobile Gallery

From a developer standpoint, the T-Mobile Gallery is more sophisticated than most other widget directories. It supports different directory metadata for each country where T-Mobile has deployed the platform (currently Germany, Austria, the Netherlands, and the UK). The widget submission and management process is also more advanced: each widget uploaded is managed individually, and its status (in terms of metadata completeness and approval state) is clearly indicated (see Figure 9-15).

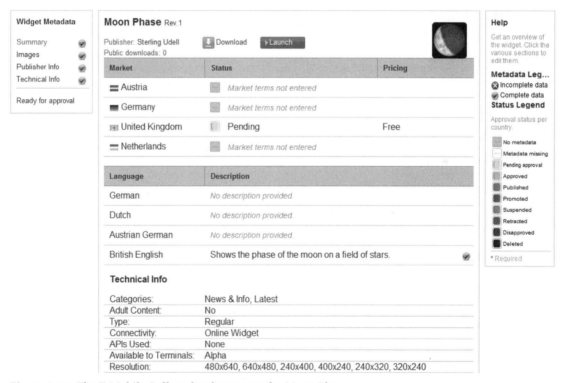

Figure 9-15. The T-Mobile Gallery developer page for Moon Phase

Like the Windows Marketplace for Mobile, the T-Mobile Gallery also gives developers the opportunity to charge for their widgets, something that's historically only been available to native applications. The possibility of a direct revenue stream presents yet another reason for building web gadgets and deploying them across multiple platforms. On the downside, because the T-Mobile

Web'n'Walk SDK is so specialized—supporting only a handful of phones from a single carrier—testing your code on an actual device can be problematic.

In any case, it's a platform to watch.

Learning More About Windows Mobile

As usual, there's far more information about Windows Mobile web development than I can fit into a single chapter. For current news, additional details on topics I've covered here, and leads to aspects I haven't, please consult the following links:

- You can find general developer information at http://developer.windowsmobile.com, including articles, blog posts, and more.

- For a technical reference, turn to http://msdn.microsoft.com/en-us/windowsmobile. Although it's more geared toward native Windows Mobile applications, it contains web development topics.

- You can find ongoing developer discussion of Windows Mobile (and ask your own questions) at http://social.msdn.microsoft.com/Forums/en/category/smartdevicedevelopment.

- Finally, Opera's documentation is available at http://dev.opera.com/articles, in both the Mobile and Widgets sections.

Summary

Although Windows Mobile doesn't have the appeal of newer, sexier platforms that have hit the market in more recent years, it has a substantial installed base—especially in Microsoft-centric enterprises—and so should not be excluded from your mobile web gadget plans.

It's also a good introduction to smartphone gadget development; the basic milestones found in this chapter establish the pattern that we'll follow for every platform covered in this book:

1. Set up your development environment for the platform by installing emulators, their associated tools, and learning how they work.

2. Test your core web gadget on the platform's major browsers—here, IE Mobile 6 and Opera Mobile—establishing a functionality baseline and informing the deployment of your mobile web app.

3. Port your code to whatever gadget APIs are supported on the platform, be they built in, third party, or both (as is the case for Windows Mobile).

4. Deploy these new gadgets to their APIs' respective directories.

In the next chapter, we'll apply these same steps to another "legacy" smartphone operating system, Symbian S60, including yet another incarnation of Opera widgets.

CHAPTER 10

■■■

Symbian S60

Together with Windows Mobile and BlackBerry, the other legacy smartphone operating system with significant market share is Symbian. I use the term *legacy* because these three platforms predate the shift (beginning around 2007) of smartphones into the mainstream. However, don't be fooled by its age; Symbian is still a dominant player in the smartphone market, especially outside the United States. As of mid-2009, Symbian still accounts for roughly 50 percent of smartphone use worldwide[1] and well over 90 percent in many developing countries.[2] As such, it shouldn't be left out of your web gadget plans.

In this chapter, I'll walk you through the process of setting up a Symbian S60 emulator and then discuss the support for web applications on Symbian's internal browser. You'll then look at S60's built-in web widget environment, called the Web Runtime; the steps involved in migrating your core web gadget to it; and what you can do with it afterward.

Introducing Symbian S60

In the world of smartphones, Symbian borders on the ancient, having started life in the 1980s as the EPOC operating system for the Psion family of PDAs. As the PDA gradually expanded into what we now know as the smartphone, Symbian grew along with it, supporting each successive generation of device. It's primarily Symbian's age that accounts for its market share, though development and innovation do continue today. On the downside, this longevity means that Symbian has far more versions in the marketplace than most other smartphone platforms, and trying to ensure compatibility with them all can be a daunting prospect. There are also a large number of different physical devices.

From a commercial standpoint, Symbian is nearly synonymous with Nokia, which has long used the Symbian OS for the majority of its smartphones and eventually acquired its parent company, Symbian Limited. Nokia has since begun the process of releasing it as open source, under the auspices of the Symbian Foundation. Throughout this chapter, however, you'll still find Nokia to be the source of much Symbian-related information.

Technically, *Symbian* is the operating system, and *S60* is the user interface, which is a distinction that doesn't exist on most other platforms. Symbian does support other UIs, but S60 is dominant in its modern smartphone line-up, so it's the one I'll cover here. From the standpoint of the gadget developer, S60 has a couple of attributes to recommend it, including a reasonably modern browser and a built-in web gadget platform. Nonetheless, it's undeniable that Symbian doesn't generally evoke the same

---

[1] www.gartner.com/it/page.jsp?id=1126812

[2] http://metrics.admob.com/wp-content/uploads/2009/07/admob-mobile-metrics-june-09.pdf

excitement (or capture the public interest) that newer smartphone platforms do. It's more hardworking than glamorous.

Emulating Symbian Devices

Working with Symbian will require an emulator, and several are dutifully supplied by Nokia. S60 emulators are generally a bit of a departure from the other emulators you'll find in this part of the book, however. First, as generic emulators—tied to OS versions rather than specific devices—they don't *look* as much like a handset as others do (see Figure 10-1). They're more an abstraction of mobile phone components than a simulation of an actual phone.

Figure 10-1. A Symbian S60 emulator

■ **Note** In later figures, I'll usually show only the device screen, not all the peripheral buttons.

Second, Symbian doesn't provide the same level of abstraction from the underlying machine architecture, meaning that its emulator doesn't do as complete a job of creating a virtual handset within your PC. Where most other emulators are capable of running any software made for a real device, the S60 emulator requires its applications to be compiled for the host PC's Intel x86 processor, rather than the ARM processor found in most handsets. As a result, you won't generally be able to install third-party software (such as another browser) onto the emulator. In other words, it's technically a simulator rather than a true emulator, as discussed in the previous chapter.

■ **Note** The S60 emulators require a Windows host computer, XP or later.

Installing an S60 Emulator

The process of installing an emulator for S60 is much simpler than it was for Windows Mobile in the previous chapter. This emulator is contained within a single package, the *S60 Platform and Device SDK*, and can be installed simply from one download.

The first step, then, is downloading that SDK, and you'll do so from http://forum.nokia.com, Nokia's developer portal. A free registration is required; once completed, you can find the current SDK in the Tools → Platforms → All-In-One section of the site. For full compatibility with this chapter, I recommend at least "3rd Edition Feature Pack 2" or "5th Edition."

During the installation itself, take note of the following tips:

- The Compact installation option is sufficient for web development. Or, if you use an Eclipse or Aptana IDE, plug-ins for these can be included by selecting a Complete installation.

- I've run into trouble if I try to install the SDK anywhere except the default directory, so I recommend that you not change this option.

- You can safely ignore any warnings regarding Perl, GCCE, or JRE during the installation; these are not relevant to mobile web development. You can also skip the ARM toolchain and MIDP installations, if so prompted.

Using the Emulator

■ **Note** Not all S60 emulator versions and modes simulate a touchscreen. If clicking the screen has no effect, navigate using the D-pad under the display, and select with the button in its center.

When the emulator installation completes, you should be able to find the appropriate version (such as "3rd Edition FP2 v1.1") under Start → All Programs → S60 Developer Tools. Ensure that the emulator runs, and acquaint yourself with its operation before proceeding to the next section. It should automatically use its host computer's network connection, although you may be prompted to confirm an "access point" to use.

■ **Tip** To disable the access point prompt, open the emulator's browser, and under Options → Settings → General, select Uncategorised and then Winsock.

The installation will also create a virtual filesystem for the emulator on your host PC; this will be useful to know about later in the chapter. In general, you can find the emulated handset's directory tree under C:\[install root]\epoc32\winscw\c\Data; the actual directory used depends on where you installed the SDK and what version you have. For the default location, a typical name for [install root] is S60\devices\S60_3rd_FP2_SDK_v1.1. Yours may differ slightly, of course.

Running Web Applications

The built-in browser on S60 is generally considered to be "second-tier"; it's better than most mobile browsers have been historically but not as good as you'll find on most newer smartphone platforms. Like many of the better mobile browsers, it's based on Apple's open source WebKit rendering engine; however, Symbian apparently branched its code from the WebKit trunk some time ago, and it has diverged somewhat in the interim.

You'll find, however, that it generally does a fairly good job with the simple web applications found in gadgets. It's entirely possible that your core web gadget (from Chapters 2 and 3) will run on S60 with no modification simply by opening it in the browser, as shown in Figure 10-2. At the least, most of your layout and some portion of your functionality should work, giving you a good base to start from.

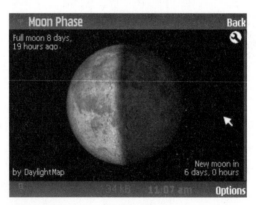

Figure 10-2. The Moon Phase core gadget on the S60 browser

For the rest, I have a couple of suggestions. First, you can find some excellent mobile browser compatibility tables and tests at http://quirksmode.org/m; these include a number of S60 examples and should give you a start in working around problems.

Second, for debugging JavaScript issues, the S60's browser supports a couple levels of error logging that will make your life easier. Enable them (in the browser) under Options → Settings → General → JavaScript Error Notifications, where you'll find two options:

- Log to File will write any JavaScript errors to a plain-text log on the emulator's filesystem, at `C:\[install root]\epoc32\winscw\c\Data\jslog_web.log`.

- Log to Console will display a pop-up message on-screen for every JavaScript error.

Putting this option to additional use, S60 supports the JavaScript `console.log` function, one of a growing number of mobile browsers to do so. Any string expression supplied to `console.log` will appear in whichever location (File or Console) you've enabled.

Finally, Nokia itself maintains a library of S60 browser compatibility guidance. Find it at `http://tinyurl.com/rxzjef`.

Creating Web Runtime Widgets

Getting your web gadget up and running on the S60 browser is an important step, because that browser serves as the basis for the platform's built-in widget platform, called the *Web Runtime* (usually abbreviated to WRT). WRT is yet another variation on the emerging W3C widget standard and, as such, bears a passing resemblance to the Opera and Windows Mobile APIs. Its nearest relation, however, is the Mac OS X Dashboard widget system; these similarities will be evident throughout this part of the chapter. The upshot is that, with all of these related platforms, you should already have a good head start on porting your core gadget to S60.

In addition to the basic widget architecture found in all the W3C-derived APIs, WRT also includes a variety of direct interfaces to phone features, such as geolocation and contact management. Access to these Platform Services (in Nokia's terminology) is provided through a JavaScript library. This is similar to functionality available on Windows Mobile, both natively to its built-in widgets and to Opera widgets by the T-Mobile Web'n'Walk extensions. It's becoming a more common occurrence on mobile widget platforms and opens up additional opportunities to the gadget developer. I'll be discussing this in more depth later in the chapter.

The Web Runtime is a fairly recent addition to the Symbian platform, having only been introduced at the end of 2007 and still (as of this writing) only being supported on a relatively small proportion of Nokia devices. Nokia appears committed to its future, though, and all new S60 smartphones carry the technology, so the number is increasing.

WIDSETS

Spend any time in the widget documentation at `http://forum.nokia.com` and you're likely to come across reference to *widsets*, another widget-like technology promoted by Nokia. When you do, I expect two questions to occur to you: what are widsets? And, why aren't they covered in this chapter?

To answer the first question, the widset concept is indeed gadget-like. It's a technology for delivering web-based content outside the traditional Web, essentially a mobile front end for RSS feeds, allowing them to be packaged into discrete entities that the user can install on his handset to keep up with news entries from wherever he has his phone. They're built with a combination of Java and Helium; the latter is a widset-specific scripting language.

The preceding should also answer the second question: I don't cover widsets here because they're not true web gadgets. They're not HTML-based and are in no way compatible with the generic web technologies on which this book is based. Superficially—to the Symbian user—they bear some resemblance to WRT widgets, but technology-wise they're almost unrelated.

In addition, widsets are now obsolete. They were created by Nokia as a vehicle for packaging and delivering web content to users but have now been deprecated in favor of the Ovi Store, which I'll be discussing later in the chapter.

Exploring the Web Runtime Architecture

If you've read any of Chapters 6 through 9, the basic architecture of WRT will look very familiar to you: widget assets are packaged in a zip archive, which is then renamed to have a different filename extension, in this case `.wgz`. Inside the archive you'll find the widget's core HTML document; any static JavaScript, CSS, and images that make the app function; and an XML metadata file. This latter is named `info.plist`, an *information property list*, and will be discussed in detail in the next section. You'll note that `info.plist` is a convention shared with the Mac OS X Dashboard, although the contents of the file are different.

Within the widget package, you'll also need an icon for your app; as with OS X, this file must be named `icon.png`. The size recommended by Nokia is 88 pixels square, although it may be scaled on different versions of S60. Installed WRT widgets appear on the phone's main application menu, which is where this icon will be shown. I recommend that your icon be placed on a transparent background, if possible, rather than having a visible square border; this should help it blend more naturally into S60 application menus (see Figure 10-3).

Figure 10-3. The Moon Phase WRT widget's `icon.png`, on the phone's application menu

---

■ **Note** For both `info.plist` and `icon.png`, the file names are case-insensitive. This is a point of difference from Mac OS X.

One important point about the `.wgz` archive, different from other widget packages I've covered, is that its virtual "web root" *isn't* the root of the archive. Instead, all the gadget source files must be placed in a directory with the same name as the gadget itself; this includes `info.plist` and `icon.png`. Within this "pseudo-root," you're free to use any subdirectories (or not) that you prefer; relative pathnames will find them.

To prepare for porting your gadget to WRT, I recommend that you create this structure in an uncompressed directory for development and copy in your core gadget source files (from Chapters 2 and 3). This will give you a single location from which to work and, later, to stage your WRT testing and deployment. Within this directory, it's best to rename your core HTML file to something WRT-specific to reduce the possibility of confusion with copies you already have for other platforms. We'll be modifying this file in a couple of pages. Figure 10-4 shows my WRT files for Moon Phase, ready for packaging.

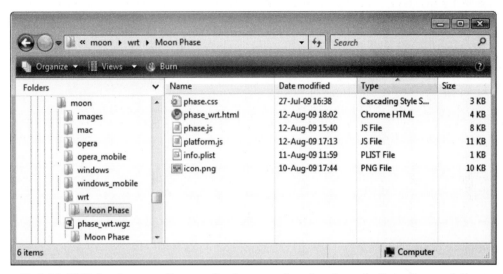

Figure 10-4. *My WRT development directory for the example gadget (note the* Moon Phase *subdirectory and renamed* phase_wrt.html *core HTML file)*

Adapting the Core Gadget

With your development directory created and a copy of all your source and image files in place, you're ready to begin porting your generic web gadget to Web Runtime. Apart from your icon graphic, these changes should generally be confined to two files, info.plist and your core HTML document.

Creating the Information Property List

As with all gadget APIs, WRT requires some metadata about your gadget and takes the typical approach of placing it in an external XML file (although without an .xml extension). Nokia takes its lead from Apple here, both in the name and the structure of its metadata file; it's called info.plist and uses the standard Mac property-list format. However, the actual keys and values used are quite different from on OS X.

In Listing 10-1, you'll find the information property list for my Moon Phase example gadget. You should be able to pattern your own info.plist file directly from this; the following sections will describe the specifics for each key.

Listing 10-1. The WRT info.plist *File for Moon Phase*

```
<?xml version="1.0" encoding="UTF-8"?>
<!DOCTYPE plist PUBLIC "-//Nokia//DTD PLIST 1.0//EN"
                "http://www.nokia.com/NOKIA_COM_1/DTDs/plist-1.0.dtd">
```

251

```
<plist version="1.0">
  <dict>
    <key>DisplayName</key>
    <string>Moon Phase</string>
    <key>Identifier</key>
    <string>com.daylightmap.moon.wrt</string>
    <key>Version</key>
    <string>1.0.10</string>
    <key>MainHTML</key>
    <string>phase_wrt.html</string>
    <key>AllowNetworkAccess</key>
    <true />
  </dict>
</plist>
```

DisplayName

This required value gives the short name of your gadget as you want it to appear on application lists within S60 (such as Figure 10-3).

■ **Caution** DisplayName must be the same as the pseudo-root directory name within your .wgz file containing all your widget resources (see Figures 10-4 and 10-6).

Identifier

This is a unique identifier string for your widget, typically in Java-style (reverse-domain) format, like com.yourcompany.project[.subproject]. This is required, and it's analogous to OS X's CFBundleIdentifier.

Version

An optional key, Version simply gives a unique identifier for each release of your widget. This is only used internally (it's not visible to the S60 user).

MainHTML

This is the name of your widget's core HTML file, found in its pseudo-root directory. It's required.

AllowNetworkAccess

If your widget uses any resources from the wider Internet, rather than purely operating from within its .wgz package, you must supply the key AllowNetworkAccess with a value of <true />, as shown in Listing 10-1.

■ **Note** At least under current S60 releases, supplying `AllowNetworkAccess` will ask the user for network permission every time your widget runs.

Making Changes to the HTML

Your WRT metadata is now complete, so it's time to move on to your actual widget code. For the usual reason of maintainability, I'll keep my code changes confined to my main gadget HTML file and recommend that you try to do the same. If significant CSS or JavaScript modifications are required, it's fine to place them in separate files (as I did in Chapter 7); otherwise, my advice is to inline them in your HTML.

In Listing 10-2, you'll find my Moon Phase widget's HTML, with the changes for WRT highlighted in bold. As usual, your own conversion won't follow this model exactly; your code changes will depend on how your own gadget behaves under S60. However, you should still find some useful tips in the following sections.

Listing 10-2. phase_wrt.html, the Web Runtime Port of the Moon Phase Example

```
<?xml version="1.0" encoding="UTF-8"?>
<!DOCTYPE html PUBLIC "-//W3C//DTD XHTML 1.0 Transitional//EN"
                "http://www.w3.org/TR/xhtml1/DTD/xhtml1-transitional.dtd">
<html xmlns="http://www.w3.org/1999/xhtml">
  <head>
    <meta http-equiv="Content-Type" content="text/html;charset=UTF-8" />
    <meta name="description"
          content="Shows the current phase of the moon on a field of stars." />
    <meta name="viewport" content="width=device-width, height=device-height" />
    <title>Moon Phase</title>
    <link href="moon_32.png" type="image/png" rel="icon" />
    <link href="phase.css"  type="text/css"  rel="stylesheet" />
    <style type="text/css">
      .moonPhase #main_icons {
        display: none;
      }
    </style>
  </head>
  <body class="moonPhase">
    <div id="main">
      <div id="main_icons">
        <a id="config_icon" class="control_icon" title="Settings"
           onclick="moonPhase.showConfig();"></a>
      </div>
      <p id="last" class="text"></p>
      <p id="image_container">
        <img id="moon" alt="Current Moon Image" width="176" height="176"
             src="http://daylightmap.com/moon/images/luna_north_small.jpg" />
      </p>
      <p id="next" class="text"></p>
      <p id="credit" class="text">
```

```
      by <a onclick="widget.openURL('http://www.daylightmap.com'); return false;"
          href="#">DaylightMap</a>
    </p>
</div>

<div id="config" style="display: none">
  <p><strong>Moon Phase Settings</strong></p>
  <p>
    <label for="size">Size:</label>
    <select id="size" name="size">
      <option value="small">Small</option>
      <option value="large">Large</option>
      <option value="auto">Auto</option>
    </select>
  </p>
  <p>
    <label for="text">Show Text:</label>
    <select id="text" name="text">
      <option value="yes">Yes</option>
      <option value="no">No</option>
      <option value="auto">Auto</option>
    </select>
  </p>
  <p>
    <label for="hemisphere">View From:</label>
    <select id="hemisphere" name="hemisphere">
      <option value="north">Northern Hemisphere</option>
      <option value="south">Southern Hemisphere</option>
    </select>
  </p>
  <p id="config_buttons">
    <input type="submit" value="Save" id="save_button"
           onclick="moonPhase.saveConfig(); return false;" />
    <input type="button" value="Cancel" id="cancel_button"
           onclick="moonPhase.hideConfig();" />
  </p>
</div>

<script src="platform.js" type="text/javascript"></script>
<script src="phase.js"    type="text/javascript"></script>
<script type="text/javascript">
  // Ensure that the moonPhase namespace exists
  var moonPhase = window.moonPhase || {};

  // Use tabbed navigation for this widget
  widget.setNavigationEnabled(false);

  // Add an additional load event handler to set up the softkey menu
  crossPlatform.addHandler(window, 'load', function () {
    moonPhase.settingsMenuItem = new MenuItem('Settings', 1);
    moonPhase.settingsMenuItem.onSelect = moonPhase.showConfig;
    menu.append(moonPhase.settingsMenuItem);
```

```
      menu.showSoftkeys();
    });

    // Hide and show the menu item (as appropriate) along with the config pane
    moonPhase.defaultShowConfig = moonPhase.showConfig;
    moonPhase.showConfig = function (menuID) {
      moonPhase.settingsMenuItem.setDimmed(true);
      moonPhase.defaultShowConfig();
      moonPhase.elements.size.focus();
    };
    moonPhase.defaultHideConfig = moonPhase.hideConfig;
    moonPhase.hideConfig = function (menuID) {
      moonPhase.settingsMenuItem.setDimmed(false);
      moonPhase.defaultHideConfig();
    };
  </script>
 </body>
</html>
```

Overall, you'll find that Listing 10-2 bears a strong resemblance to the Windows Mobile port of Moon Phase from Listing 9-2. As an implementation specific to a mobile gadget platform, the changes for WRT follow many of the same patterns.

WRT-Specific CSS

The similarity to Windows Mobile begins in the CSS; I'm going to be moving the Settings menu functionality into a softkey menu in the same way as I did in Chapter 9, so I have the same need to hide the default gadget's Setting button. This is done with a simple CSS rule of display: none—identical to that in Listing 9-2.

If your WRT port requires more style changes, this inline style block will be the place to implement them.

WRT-Specific HTML

There's one change to the markup from my core gadget, and it echoes a similar change needed for OS X, visible back in Listing 7-2. As on the Mac, WRT doesn't allow opening of external browser windows directly from a links in widget HTML; instead, the same API function of widget.openURL must be used. So, instead of the href attribute, I supply an onclick handler instead, as follows:

```
onclick="widget.openURL('http://www.daylightmap.com'); return false;"
```

■ **Note** As of this writing, the S60 emulators have a bug that prevents openURL calls from completing and may even crash the browser. With luck, this bug will be fixed by the time you read this—but if not, now you know.

WRT-Specific JavaScript

The largest change to my HTML comes in the form of inline JavaScript, and although it may look a bit daunting, it's mostly to accomplish a single task. As with Windows Mobile, I've chosen to move my Settings button functionality into the device's softkey menu for tighter integration with the underlying OS. So, the JavaScript code here follows a similar pattern as in the previous chapter.

Before that, however, there's one line to accomplish something truly WRT-specific. The code in question is this:

```
widget.setNavigationEnabled(false);
```

What it does is to override the S60 browser's default pointer-based navigation mode, which uses the device's D-pad to move a pointer around the screen (visible toward the right side of Figure 10-2). When this mode is turned off, by calling setNavigationEnabled(false), the alternative is tab-based navigation, where the focus simply moves from one editable field to the next (although the D-pad is still used to do so). The navigation mode doesn't matter much to Moon Phase's main view, but tab-based navigation works much better for its configuration pane. Consider which makes more sense for your own gadget—and be aware that you can switch modes dynamically, if that's your best option.

With the navigation mode out of the way, the remaining JavaScript in Listing 10-2 is concerned with moving the Settings button's functionality onto a softkey menu. As mentioned, these changes largely parallel those found in Listing 9-2; refer there for more information on the underlying theory. It works as follows:

- A new window.load event handler creates a MenuItem object for Settings, attaches its onSelect listener to my showConfig method, and adds it to the API's menu object. One addition is that I'm also calling menu.showSoftkeys to display the softkey labels (they're hidden by default).

- An extended showConfig method hides the Settings MenuItem (by calling its setDimmed method) when the configuration pane is open. Note that I also need to set focus to an element of my configuration pane; this workaround was necessary to make the configuration pane appear.

- An extended hideConfig method makes the MenuItem visible again by calling setDimmed with a parameter of false.

Figure 10-5 shows the result, my completed Moon Phase WRT widget (with the Settings softkey menu item).

Figure 10-5. The final Moon Phase example widget on WRT, with softkey menu visible

Additions to crossPlatform

The core gadget relies on the `crossPlatform` middleware layer to function, of course, so before the S60 port is complete, this code must also be visited to ensure WRT compatibility. Fortunately, this API is so similar to that on OS X that you can reuse virtually the entire `crossPlatform` Mac interface.

The first step is platform detection, and not surprisingly, the WRT code will be an extension to the case that detects the Mac. It works as follows (new code highlighted in bold):

```
if (!!window.widget) {
  if (!!widget.getAttention) {
    crossPlatform.api = 'opera';
    crossPlatform.emptyPref = '';
  } else if (!!widget.menu) {
    crossPlatform.api = 'windows_mobile';
    crossPlatform.emptyPref = null;
  } else {
    if (!!window.menu) {
      crossPlatform.api = 'wrt';
    } else {
      crossPlatform.api = 'mac';
    }
    crossPlatform.emptyPref = undefined;
  }
}
```

The differentiating feature between `mac` and `wrt` is the existence of the `widget.menu` object; WRT has an interface to the phone's softkey menus, not applicable on the Mac.

But in reality, that's the only change to `crossPlatform` required. It uses the same `emptyPref` value as did OS X, and so even without the previous code, the interface would function perfectly—the api would just be misidentified as 'mac', rather than 'wrt'. The previous code is purely a convenience for you, the gadget developer, in case *you* need to differentiate between the two platforms in your own code.

Testing and Debugging

Of course, to finalize your own WRT code, you'll need to run your ported widget on S60. In this part of the chapter, you'll find instructions and tips for doing so.

The process begins with packaging your widget resources into a .wgz file; this is as simple as creating a zip archive (in the Windows shell context menu, that's "Create new compressed folder"), copying your source directory in (see Figure 10-6), and then renaming its extension from .zip to .wgz. Don't forget that your "pseudo-root" top-level directory inside the archive must be named the same as the DisplayName value in your info.plist.

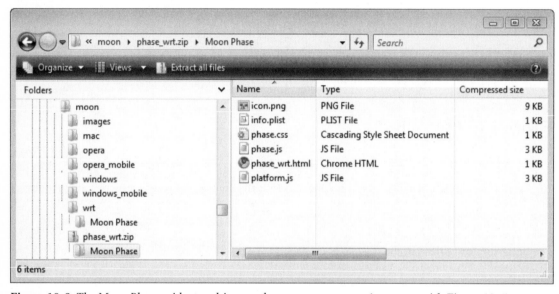

Figure 10-6. The Moon Phase widget archive, ready to rename to .wgz (compare with Figure 10-4)

Installing Your Widget

When you have your widget packaged, installing it on the S60 emulator is exceptionally easy. From the emulator's *parent window* (see Figure 10-7), select File → Open, and then find and open your .wgz file. Inside the emulator, you'll be prompted to install your widget. If asked where to install, select Phone Memory, not Memory Card.

■ **Note** The S60 third edition FP2 emulator gives an ALLOC error message after installing a widget. It doesn't impede the installation, though, and can safely be ignored.

Figure 10-7. *To install a widget, select File → Open from the emulator's parent window.*

■ **Tip** If you get a message saying "Unable to install – feature not supported" during widget installation, this typically means that the pseudo-root directory in your archive is incorrect (see the previous section).

If you're installing to a physical device, it obviously won't have a parent window, so the approach is slightly different. Your best option is to transfer your `.wgz` file to the handset using a Bluetooth or USB connection and then open it using the File Manager application (sometimes called Organizer) on the phone.

With either the emulator or a real handset, the procedure for running an installed widget is the same. From the home screen, open Menu (visible at the lower left of Figure 10-7's screen); then (depending on your S60 edition) select either Installations, Applications, or Applications → My Own. You should see a view similar to Figure 10-3, with your widget icon included; select it and begin your testing.

■ **Tip** If you turned on the emulator's JavaScript log earlier in the chapter, WRT widget errors will also be logged; you can find them in C:\[install root]\epoc32\winscw\c\Data\jslog_widget.log.

Applying Changes

As issues are uncovered during your testing, you'll need to load code changes into your installed widget. On a physical device, this typically means re-creating and reinstalling the .wgz package, which is unfortunately a fairly laborious process. On the emulator, though, there's an easier way; you can access your installed widget's source files directly and modify them in place. From the host (Windows) system, the place to look is as follows:

C:\[install root]\epoc32\winscw\c\private\10282822\[widget identifier]

where [install root] is the location you installed your emulator to, and [widget identifier] is the reverse-domain value you supplied for Identifier in your info.plist file (like com.daylightmap.moon.wrt). In this directory, you can either edit your widget source directly or copy new versions in. You'll simply need to restart your widget in the emulator for the changes to take effect.

Using Remote Device Access

In addition to testing on the emulator and any actual S60 phone you may have access to, Nokia also offers an innovative service called Remote Device Access. Free of charge to members of Forum Nokia (which is itself free), this tool allows developers to see and control real Nokia handsets remotely over the Web. Users may install applications from their local computer—including WRT widgets—and put them through their paces, with no expense and very little hassle. As shown in Figure 10-8, the experience is similar to using the local emulator but gives a much more accurate experience of testing on specific hardware.

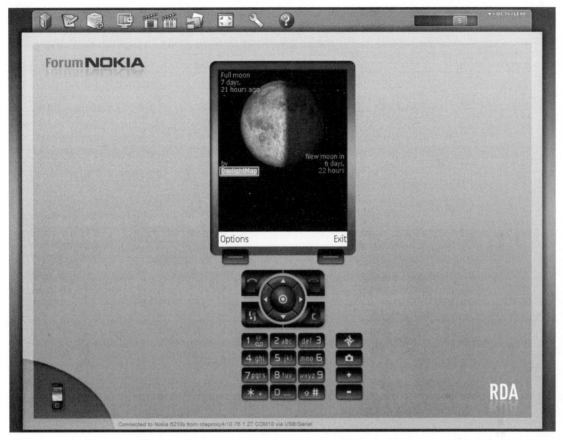

Figure 10-8. The Moon Phase WRT widget running on a Nokia 6210s via Remote Device Access

To get started, you'll need to register at `http://forum.nokia.com` and then log in at `http://apu.ndhub.net` (the RDA server site). From here, you'll select an available device and can start an RDA session.

- Not all host browsers are supported, though the list does include Firefox 2+, Internet Explorer 7+, Opera 9.6+, and Safari 3+.

- Java must also be installed on your host computer.

- Not every device supports WRT; you'll need at least "3rd Edition Feature Pack 2" or "5th Edition." For a guide to the S60 versions on various Nokia handsets, see `http://forum.nokia.com/devices`.

- If a compatible device isn't available when you log in, you may reserve one for later use.

- You can reserve a device in 15-minute increments, with a maximum usage of eight hours per day.

Once you are connected to an RDA device, you'll need to install your widget. To do so, either select Tools → Install Software from the containing window or click the "folder plus" toolbar icon in the RDA window (visible at the top of Figure 10-8). Select your .wgz package from your local filesystem, from which point the installation process is the same as on the ordinary emulator.

■ **Caution** Devices on RDA are real handsets and retain data between sessions. Be sure to delete any sensitive data before your session ends—this includes uninstalling any confidential, prerelease widgets!

Deploying Web Runtime Widgets

As with most web gadgets, the most basic technique for deploying a completed WRT widget is to host it on your own website. Start by uploading the .wgz package to your server and adding a link from one or more public-facing web pages. To automate installation, you'll also need to serve it with the correct MIME type; for WRT widgets, this is application/x-nokia-widget. To implement this on an Apache server, add the following line to your appropriate .htaccess or httpd.conf file:

```
AddType application/x-nokia-widget .wgz
```

Of course, you'll also need to integrate the link into your own site and make clear to visitors that the widget download is for specific Nokia smartphones—but I'll assume that's within your grasp.

In addition to self-hosting, Nokia has recently opened its own commercial widget directory, accessible directly from compatible handsets. It's called the Ovi Store, and in addition to WRT widgets, it also stocks content (such as ringtones and wallpapers), Flash apps, and native Symbian applications. However, widgets have some advantages: unlike native apps, they don't need to be digitally signed, and their approval process is somewhat less rigorous.

For more information on the Ovi Store, you'll need to sign up as a publisher at http://publish.ovi.com. Be aware that as of August 2009 this registration costs €50, whether or not you go on to publish any applications.

Using WRT-Specific Extensions

As with every platform in this book, there are a variety of platform-specific extensions that you can take advantage of if you are developing solely for S60 or if you have reason to optimize your widget specifically for Web Runtime. In the following sections, I'll outline some of the more important extensions that are available and tell you where to find complete information on each.

Localization

The ongoing similarity between WRT and Mac OS X widgets recurs in the process of creating local-language versions of a widget. The WRT approach is essentially identical to that for the Mac; create *.lproj subdirectories for each language you want to support, and place localized resources into those directories. The only difference is that, with WRT, these subdirectories will go under the "pseudo-root" in the widget package, rather than the actual root directory (as they did for OS X).

For further instructions, therefore, I refer you to the "Localization" section in Chapter 7. You can also find the official WRT localization reference at http://tinyurl.com/djpxg4.

■ **Tip** If you have localized a widget for OS X, the similarity with this platform means that you can easily deploy the same localization to WRT.

Menus and Softkeys

Similarly, the support for softkeys (and their associated menus) in S60 is a close analog to that covered in Chapter 9 for Windows Mobile. You were introduced to the WRT version in Listing 10-2; beyond that, it can be extended in the same ways as were discussed in the previous chapter.

- Each MenuItem object can contain subitems, managed with equivalent MenuItem.append and .remove methods, to support multilevel menus.

- The menu object itself has methods for setLeftSoftkeyLabel and setRightSoftkeyLabel, enabling functionality to be attached directly to the softkeys (rather than menus), as was detailed for Windows Mobile.

For more information on these (and related) functions, please see the menu and MenuItem sections at http://tinyurl.com/ou7z4a.

Nokia Platform Services

Continuing the parallel with Windows Mobile, softkey integration is just the beginning of the device-level interface that WRT provides to widgets. In this case, Nokia has gone further than Microsoft; its Platform Services API allows JavaScript access to many different device features:

- Calendar

- Contacts

- Call log

- Messaging (SMS and MMS)

- Application management

- Media management

- Geolocation

- Sensors (such as accelerometer)

- System information

Obviously, the specifics of each service will differ, but they generally follow a similar pattern. In the rest of this section, I'll walk you through a simple example of using a single Platform Service. Complete coverage would be beyond the scope of this book, but you can find a full reference in the Forum Nokia Library at http://tinyurl.com/ork2yp.

For my example, recall that the Moon Phase image displayed by my sample gadget differs by hemisphere (Northern or Southern) and that the user is allowed to select which they want to see. The basic gadget defaults this selection to Northern, because that's where most of the earth's population lives, but with access to the phone's location, I can do better.

The process starts by requesting access to the Location service, and (like all Platform Services) this is done with a call to an API object named device, as follows:

```
var locationService = device.getServiceObject('Service.Location', 'ILocation');
```

Obviously, the parameters to getServiceObject will depend on what sort of service you require, but such a call will always be your first step. When such access is requested, the user will be asked to confirm the request, ensuring control over her personal data.

■ **Caution** If access is denied by the user, getServiceObject will raise a JavaScript exception, so it should generally be placed within a try/catch block to handle this situation gracefully.

Assuming access is granted, the locationService variable will then be initialized to a special API class, called a *service object*, which implements an interface for the requested service (in this case, ILocation). This interface is what will provide access to the actual location service we're after. Calls to the service object will take the following form; note the interface, ILocation, in the call:

```
var locationResult = locationService.ILocation.GetLocation();
```

After this call completes, it's a simple matter to use the result to check the user's location (Latitude values are positive in the northern hemisphere and negative in the southern):

```
if (locationResult.ErrorCode === 0) {
  if (locationResult.ReturnValue.Latitude > 0) {
    moonPhase.prefs.hemisphere = 'north';
  } else {
    moonPhase.prefs.hemisphere = 'south';
  }
}
```

An important aspect to Platform Services is this interface-based architecture. Different service interfaces support different methods appropriate to their functional roles, but they all return the same basic result object. There will always be an ErrorCode (with 0 equating to success) and a ReturnValue, but the properties of that ReturnValue (like Latitude here) will depend on the service in use.

This simple overview barely scratches the surface, but if Platform Services sounds like it'd be of use to your widget, I encourage you to read further at the Forum Nokia Library. A few caveats to its use, however. First, the full range of Platform Services is available only on the S60 5th edition and newer. Second, all services may not be available on all phones; full geolocation, for example, is supported only by GPS-equipped devices. And third, some services are not available on the emulator or through RDA, necessitating a physical device for testing.

Learning More About Symbian S60

The material in this chapter is enough to get you started and should be sufficient to port many web gadgets to S60, but there's naturally a wealth of information that I haven't been able to cover here. For further reading, I recommend the following locations:

- The definitive reference to S60 development is the Forum Nokia Library at `http://library.forum.nokia.com`; it's also available for offline viewing by downloading from `http://tinyurl.com/pkctpk`. Most of the information of interest to you is in the section entitled Web Developer's Library.

- There's a good discussion group for WRT developers at `http://discussion.forum.nokia.com/forum/forumdisplay.php?f=160`.

- More general information on the Symbian operating system as a whole is available from the Symbian Foundation at `http://symbian.org`.

Summary

Symbian has a long and solid history in handheld devices, but it's not generally the first name that's thought of for smartphones, especially in North America. Nonetheless, its worldwide market share makes it a valuable platform to target.

It's also a quite straightforward one. Its built-in browser is fairly competent at executing web gadgets, and it includes better debugging tools than you often find on handhelds. In addition, the existence of a standards-compliant widget API like the Web Runtime gives gadget developers a head start in porting to the platform, and the Ovi Store means that a distribution channel for your S60 widget is ready and waiting. Finally, the existence of good localization support and device integration allows you to leverage this platform far beyond what pure web widgets can do—while still sharing some basic underpinnings with other APIs.

In the next chapter, I'll complete my coverage of smartphone operating systems that have been around for a while by discussing the BlackBerry.

CHAPTER 11

■ ■ ■

iPhone

Beginning in this chapter, you'll move into the realm of "modern" smartphones, which are platforms that have emerged since about 2007 and that represent a generational leap from the likes of Windows Mobile and Symbian S60. Leading the charge is Apple's iPhone, the first of this new wave and hands down the most popular. This single device took the dull, stodgy smartphone segment—previously the realm of enterprise IT and a few technophile enthusiasts—and brought it into the mainstream. It's no exaggeration to say that Apple singlehandedly changed the rules of the smartphone game.

For developers of web gadgets, iPhone is of particular interest because it was the first handheld device delivering "the real Web," rather than a cut-down, poorly rendered facsimile. Even though iPhone has no intrinsic support for web gadgets *per se* (in the form of a true gadget API), its basic friendliness to all things Web makes it a fundamentally hospitable environment for web developers.

In this chapter, you'll learn how to install the iPhone development environment, to test and develop your web applications on its simulator, to deploy your gadget as an iPhone web app, and, finally, to package your gadget as a "native" iPhone application.

■ **Note** All iPhone development requires an Intel-based Mac; there is fundamentally no support for Windows or Linux (for good reasons that I'll get into later). You absolutely need a Mac to make use of this chapter.

Introducing iPhone

When the original iPhone was released in mid-2007, it was clear almost immediately that the world of smartphones would never be the same. Apple had fundamentally rethought what was possible with a handset and, in the process, changed the course of an industry that it previously hadn't even been part of.

First, as already mentioned, iPhone was the pioneering web-connected handset. Prior smartphones had mediocre browsers tucked away somewhere in their application menus; in contrast, the iPhone included a first-rate browser, with an icon prominently featured on the device's home screen. Even though first-generation iPhones lacked high-speed cellular data connectivity (and a few early users got hit with large data bills), the web-centric way in which the platform was marketed fundamentally changed how the public thought about the Internet on their phones.

Second, Apple has made third-party applications a central part of the iPhone experience. Every user has the App Store in front of them, via another icon on the default home screen; as a result, iPhone users install third-party apps to a degree that phone users had never done before. To meet this demand, developers have flocked to the platform—and unlike previous smartphone platforms, anyone can write for the iTunes App Store. The result is an incredibly rich ecosystem of handset functionality. There are possibly more apps in existence for Symbian than iPhone, but in terms of real-world usage—the number of apps installed by the average user—there's just no comparison.

Finally, the iPhone handset itself was created with Apple's undeniable skill for hardware and user interface design. This has been a crucial part of its success: although the original iPhone didn't offer much more in the way of basic functionality than other smartphones of the day, what it did was make that functionality intuitive and approachable to the casual user. For example, its touchscreen-centric design was far more intuitive and engaging to interact with than the keypads, trackballs, and such that were the previous industry norm. All of this has served to bring iPhones into the hands of the general public, most of whom had never considered owning a smartphone before.

At this writing, there are four devices running the iPhone operating system: three generations of true iPhones, plus the iPod touch (effectively an iPhone without cellular radios, a microphone, or a camera). From a web development standpoint, there's effectively no difference; all four devices support the same interfaces and will run virtually all applications identically.

Installing the iPhone Simulator

The iPhone may be a paradigm shift from other smartphones, but developing for it begins the same way: you'll need a simulated handset on which to test your applications. In the case of iPhone, it's a simulator rather than a true emulator; it won't run code compiled for the ARM processor of an iPhone handset. Instead, Apple has taken advantage of the deep commonality between the iPhone OS and Mac OS X to produce a lightweight application that accurately simulates *most* iPhone functionality. This operating system overlap also explains the need for a Mac as a development platform; an iPhone emulator for Windows or Linux would be a fundamentally different beast.

■ **Note** iPhone apps can also be tested on a physical handset, but this requires *provisioning*, a complicated process. You can find more information on provisioning later in the chapter in the "Testing on a Real iPhone" section.

The simulator comes packaged as part of the iPhone SDK, which is available for download from the iPhone Dev Center at `http://developer.apple.com/iphone`. You'll need to sign up as a Registered iPhone Developer; this is free and allows you access to most of Apple's online resources, in addition to the SDK. Note that it's possible you have already downloaded and installed the iPhone SDK; it was mentioned in Chapter 7.

Once downloaded, open the package and begin the installation. For this chapter, you'll need to select at least the Developer Tools Essentials and iPhone SDK; other SDK components are optional but not required for the material I'll be covering here. And in contrast to some other mobile development platforms, it's usually a pretty painless install. When it completes, you should be able to simply open the iPhone Simulator application and see a pseudo-handset on your desktop, as in Figure 11-1.

Figure 11-1. *The basic iPhone Simulator*

■ **Tip** You can simulate the iPhone's multitouch user interface by holding down the Option key while dragging your mouse on the simulator's screen.

Running Web Apps

One of the first things you can do with your new iPhone Simulator is to open web pages with the Safari browser linked from the home screen. It's actually Mobile Safari, and it's quite a close kin to the desktop browser of the same name, with both based on Apple's own open source WebKit engine. As such, it's at the leading edge of mobile browsers and is generally capable of rendering most sites with very few problems.

Indeed, one of the few common problems gadgets have with Mobile Safari is that it sometimes tries too hard to emulate a full-size browser. For content that is already prepared for a small screen, this can lead to such awkward displays as a small gadget in a large field of whitespace or a small amount of content spread thinly across a page. Fortunately, Apple has provided a solution, the meta viewport tag:

```
<meta name="viewport" content="width=device-width, height=device-height" />
```

As discussed in Chapter 9, this element directs the handset's browser to display your page as exactly the size of its screen—usually a good choice for a stand-alone gadget on a phone. If your gadget would prefer to scroll its content vertically, simply leave out height=device-height.

If you do run into trouble with your gadget on Mobile Safari, you can enable an error console to display JavaScript, CSS, and markup problems, as well as calls to the console.log function in your code (see Figure 11-2). To do so, select Settings from the iPhone's home screen, and then open the page for Safari. At the bottom of the page will be a Developer item; open it, and enable the debug console.

Figure 11-2. *Mobile Safari's debug console*

■ **Tip** Mobile Safari also implements the JavaScript alert function.

As a last resort, keep in mind that much of Mobile Safari's behavior does mimic that of the desktop version—especially on the Mac—so it's often useful to track down bugs there instead. This is made easier on the more recent versions of Safari, which include a credible debugger.

Optimizing for iPhone

When the iPhone was first introduced, no native API was available; Apple instead encouraged external developers to create web applications optimized for the handset. To facilitate this, it produced a handful of HTML extensions to help web developers integrate their apps into the iPhone user interface.

The first of these was introduced in Chapter 9 and again in the previous section: the meta viewport tag. In addition to the viewport dimensions given in the previous example, viewport can also include directives that control zooming. These are supplied in the content attribute of the meta tag, like this:

```
content="initial-scale=1.0; maximum-scale=1.0; user-scalable=0;"
```

- initial-scale supplies instruction to Mobile Safari as to what zoom level should be used when your page first renders.

- maximum-scale provides a limit on what zooming may occur after page load.

- user-scalable, if set to 0, prevents user zooming via multitouch pinch gestures.

■ **Note** If width or height is also required (as in the previous section), all viewport directives should be supplied in the content attribute of a single meta tag.

Apple has also made it easy for users to place web bookmarks on the home screen; the vision was that these could be used to create shortcuts to web apps, allowing them to be accessed in the same way as native apps. If a user launches your gadget from such a shortcut, a couple of other meta tags become applicable:

```
<meta name="apple-mobile-web-app-capable" content="yes" />
<meta name="apple-mobile-web-app-status-bar-style" content="black />
```

The first of these, apple-mobile-web-app-capable, indicates to Mobile Safari that your web app is optimized for iPhone and should be displayed as an application rather than an ordinary web page. In practice, this means that it will be shown full-screen, without the browser's usual address and button bars.

In this mode, the apple-mobile-web-app-status-bar-style tag also comes into play. When present, this controls the color and appearance of the phone's status display. The valid values for it are default (no effect), black (opaque), and black-translucent. By using various combinations of these meta tags, a web app on iPhone can be well on its way to visually equaling a native application.

To complete the transformation, Apple provides a wealth of guidelines and metrics for specific visual effects; if you're interested in tailoring your gadget specifically for this platform, please visit http://developer.apple.com/safari for details.

■ **Tip** A third-party library called the Magic Framework is available for implementing a web user interface precisely in the iPhone style. Download it from http://jeffmcfadden.com/projects/Magic+Framework.

The final step in preparing your gadget for life as an iPhone web app is to create an icon for its home screen shortcut; if you don't supply one, the platform will just use a thumbnail image of the page. First, you'll need a 57-pixel-square PNG image (other sizes will work but will be scaled by the handset). Upload it to your site, and then add a link to it in your HTML's head section, like this one for my Moon Phase gadget:

```
<link rel="apple-touch-icon" href="moon_57.png"/>
```

When a user creates a shortcut to your gadget, their iPhone will generate an icon for it by adding rounded corners, a shadow, and a gloss effect to the image you've supplied (see Figure 11-3).

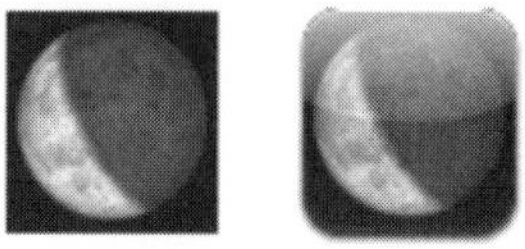

Figure 11-3. The shortcut icon for Moon Phase, before and after enhancement by the user's iPhone

It's worthwhile to take a copy of your gadget HTML and optimize it specifically for iPhone web access, rather than relying on your usual core gadget URL. This specialized version can be listed in the iPhone web apps directory, http://apple.com/webapps, which comes preprogrammed into every iPhone's browser. Unlike most of the catalogs covered in this book, the iPhone web apps directory doesn't actually host gadgets; it simply lists the URLs of iPhone-compatible web apps—and in your case, this can be the iPhone-specific version of your gadget.

Changes to the HTML

Toward this end, I've taken the previous steps (and more) for my example Moon Phase gadget. Listing 11-1 shows the iPhone-optimized HTML (without the main body content—it's unchanged from my original, generic gadget).

Listing 11-1. The index.html File for Moon Phase as iPhone Web App

```
<?xml version="1.0" encoding="UTF-8"?>
<!DOCTYPE html PUBLIC "-//W3C//DTD XHTML 1.0 Transitional//EN"
                     "http://www.w3.org/TR/xhtml1/DTD/xhtml1-transitional.dtd">
<html xmlns="http://www.w3.org/1999/xhtml">
  <head>
    <meta http-equiv="Content-Type" content="text/html;charset=UTF-8" />
    <meta name="description"
          content="Shows the current phase of the moon on a field of stars." />
    <meta name="viewport" content="width=device-width, height=device-height;
                          initial-scale=1.0; maximum-scale=1.0; user-scalable=0;" />
    <meta name="apple-mobile-web-app-capable" content="yes" />
    <meta name="apple-mobile-web-app-status-bar-style" content="black/>
    <title>Moon Phase</title>
    <link rel="apple-touch-icon" href="images/moon_57.png"/>
    <link href="moon_32.png" type="image/png" rel="icon" />
    <link href="phase.css"   type="text/css"  rel="stylesheet" />
    <style type="text/css">
      .moonPhase #main,
      .moonPhase #config {
        font-size: 17px;
      }
      .moonPhase .text {
        width: 40%;
      }
```

```
    .moonPhase #last {
      width: 50%;
    }
    .moonPhase #moon {
      position: relative;
    }
    .moonPhase #main_icons {
      opacity: 0.5 !important;
      top: 10px;
      right: 10px;
    }
  </style>
</head>
<body class="moonPhase">

  <!-- body content goes here -->

  <script type="text/javascript" src="platform.js"></script>
  <script type="text/javascript" src="phase.js"></script>
  <script type="text/javascript">
    moonPhase.defaultLoad = moonPhase.load;
    moonPhase.load = function () {
      // Set the gadget's size to fill the viewport
      moonPhase.elements.main.style.height = window.innerHeight + 'px';

      // Call the ancestor method
      moonPhase.defaultLoad();

      // Center the moon image within the gadget
      moonPhase.elements.moon.style.top =
        (window.innerHeight - moonPhase.elements.moon.height) / 2 + 'px';
    };
  </script>
</body>
</html>
```

As you can see, I've added the iPhone-specific meta tag attributes and `link rel="apple-touch-icon"` element in the head, as discussed in the previous section. The remaining changes are described in the following sections.

Inline CSS

Perhaps not surprisingly, the inline `style` block in Listing 11-1 reads like a combination of what I needed for my Mac OS X widget and what was required on the handheld widget platforms covered in the previous two chapters. Here's a summary:

- Apple encourages big, friendly fonts for iPhone, so I've ratcheted mine up to 17px.

- To accommodate these larger fonts, I've expanded the `width` of various text fields somewhat.

- I've decided to center the moon image vertically on the screen, so setting the #moon container to `position: relative` gets it ready. The actual centering will be done in JavaScript.

- Finally, I've moved the settings-pane icon 10px in from the corner of the screen for easier access on an iPhone touch screen.

Most gadgets have a more complicated user interface than Moon Phase and accordingly will require more style changes to conform with the iPhone look and feel, but this should give you a start.

Inline JavaScript

Compared with many platforms, iPhone usually requires little new JavaScript in the gadget. Mobile Safari is a good enough browser that most code simply works; what you'll find in Listing 11-1 is only to tweak the user interface.

Within an override of the `moonPhase.load` method, I manually set the gadget height to `window.innerHeight`—a viewport-height DOM property that works fine on Mobile Safari—and then center the moon image within that space vertically (see Figure 11-4).

Figure 11-4. The Moon Phase gadget running on an iPhone as a web app

Submitting to the iPhone Web App Directory

I'm now ready to submit my iPhone-optimized gadget to Apple's web app directory. Although it has largely been eclipsed in the public eye by the iTunes App Store, it is still very much active and in use, and it's an excellent place to get your gadget in front of iPhone users.

To list your app, browse to `https://adcweb.apple.com/iphone`, and log in with your (free) Registered iPhone Developer ID. After agreeing to the usual terms, you'll be asked to supply various basic information about your gadget, including the URL where it's hosted. You'll also need to upload a couple of graphics, namely, a 320×256-pixel screenshot and a 128-pixel-square icon.

After submission, your gadget will be reviewed by Apple, and you should be notified within a few days whether it has been accepted. Be aware that listed apps must generally conform to the iPhone user interface guidelines given by Apple at `http://tinyurl.com/mk57tw`.

Creating Native iPhone Applications

Of course, the web app directory *isn't* where most developers really want to have their iPhone applications listed. That honor goes to the iTunes App Store, the official Apple repository for native iPhone software. In the remainder of this chapter, you'll learn how to repackage your web gadget as just such a native application, ready for listing on the App Store. But before we start down that road, you need to ask yourself, should I do so?

The advantages to App Store listings are strong. First, it's the only place where most users can install applications from; Apple has coded this limitation into every iPhone it sells. The only way for the average user to install applications from elsewhere is to "jailbreak" the handset: a process of exploiting security flaws in the operating system to grant elevated privileges, such as granting the ability to bypass the App Store restriction (among other things). Although a substantial number of iPhone users have jailbroken their devices, most have not. So, to sell applications to this majority, the App Store is the only option.

■ **Note** The Enterprise-level iPhone Developer Program gives the ability to distribute native apps within your organization. For proprietary applications in a large company with many internal iPhone users, this may be a viable alternative to the App Store.

This brings us to the second advantage to App Store listings: selling your application. Because of the iPhone's tremendous success in the market, the App Store has many millions of customers, most of whom install scores of apps. In early 2009, the App Store logged its *billionth* download, and the frenzy continues at this writing. With this volume of traffic, there is the potential to make real money selling iPhone applications, and a number of high-profile instances of this have been well publicized. Apple keeps a 30 percent cut of every sale, but even with this overhead, a reasonable profit is possible.

Gaining access to the App Store is not a given, however. To submit an app, you'll first need to upgrade your free Registered iPhone Developer status to a full iPhone Developer Program membership; as of August 2009, this costs US$99 for the Standard level and US$299 for Enterprise. And second, your application will need to be approved; Apple is the sole gatekeeper to the App Store, and its approval process is notoriously inconsistent and opaque. Many developers have experienced delays of weeks or months before approval or, worse yet, had their apps summarily rejected for unclear reasons. Although there are some guidelines, nobody knows which apps will be approved and which will not.

■ **Tip** A list of unpublished Apple guidelines, compiled from real-world App Store rejections, is available at http://appreview.tumblr.com.

One thing that is known is that Apple isn't well-disposed toward pure web apps in the iTunes store; although iPhones are inherently connected devices, apps should also work when the device isn't online. We also know that they don't like apps that don't adhere to the iPhone user interface guidelines; this isn't good news for the cross-platform gadget developer, because you will likely have already developed your own user interface for your own needs.

■ **Caution** Apple is particularly suspect of any application whose functionality may change after approval. For this reason, gadgets that download JavaScript (or other executable code), rather than packaging it internally, are best avoided.

The upshot is that planning to sell a repackaged web gadget on the App Store is a risk and isn't the right course for many. If your gadget is fairly self-contained—meaning most of its resources can be packaged with it and, ideally, it can run in some manner without a network connection—you're off to a good start. Additionally, you'll need to be able and willing to make its user interface conform to the iPhone's standards, which can be a considerable task. If you can't honestly answer "yes" to both of these criteria, your gadget is probably not a good candidate for the App Store—and therefore there's probably no great need for it to become a native iPhone app.

Adapting the Core Gadget

If you think your gadget could make the cut, however, the following sections will walk you through the process of native-app repackaging. The approach you'll take is to create an extremely simple iPhone application, essentially consisting only of a single UIWebView, a native class that uses an embedded instance of Mobile Safari to display web content. In addition to this framework, you'll package your gadget's static resources (web documents and images) within the app. Although your code will still be able to access the Internet, these packaged resources will also be available when the handset is offline.

As your starting point, then, you'll want to have your gadget well tested on Mobile Safari in the iPhone Simulator and, if possible, on a real handset. You'll also need to have created a 57-pixel-square icon for your gadget, as described earlier; this is the same icon that will be used by the native application for its own shortcut. And you'll want to have assembled all your gadget's resources in a single directory, ready for packaging.

THIRD-PARTY FRAMEWORKS

In this chapter, I walk you through the process of building a native iPhone framework for your web app. This is a reasonable process for a basic, cross-platform gadget but one drawback is that the packaged code will still be limited to the functionality of a web application. This is in contrast with fully native iPhone apps, which can access most of the device's software and hardware resources (such as the address book, camera, or audio). Of course, these applications are not based on the web technologies you already know: they're written in the iPhone's native language, Objective-C, and they use its own proprietary layout and presentation APIs.

However, a best-of-both-worlds approach is also possible by building a framework that delivers the device services to the web code within a `UIWebView` component. This enables full-power iPhone apps to be built using standard web technologies, an attractive prospect to many. One additional benefit is that such frameworks can also be platform-agnostic, potentially deploying the same device-enabled web code to any modern smartphone.

Constructing such a framework is far beyond the scope of this chapter, but the demand is such that a number of independent organizations have done so. The following is a partial list of those available as of this writing:

- The open source PhoneGap initiative (`http://phonegap.com`) was one of the first independent frameworks. Although its strongest focus is on iPhone, support is also being developed for Android and BlackBerry, with plans for Symbian S60, Windows Mobile, and Palm webOS in the works.

- A similar project is QuickConnect (`http://quickconnect.pbworks.com`), also open source and cross-platform. Again, iPhone is the flagship interface, with other smartphones following behind; one difference is that QuickConnect is also targeting desktop operating systems, including Mac OS X, Windows, and Linux.

- Appcelerator's Titanium Mobile (`http://appcelerator.com/products/titanium-mobile`) is an open source but commercial product; as of August 2009, it's still in a free beta, and pricing has not been announced. It offers full support for both iPhone and Android.

- Rhomobile's Rhodes framework (`http://rhomobile.com/products/rhodes`) takes a slightly different approach: although it does compile web apps for handsets, the underlying technology is Ruby rather than pure JavaScript. It supports a wide range of devices (currently iPhone, BlackBerry, Windows Mobile, Symbian, and Android) and is free for open source projects or US$500 for a commercial license.

Of course, applications built with these frameworks are subject to the same iTunes App Store submission hurdles as any repackaged web app, and sometimes more: PhoneGap seemed to be specifically targeted by Apple for a time. So, be aware that, although a framework does lower the bar for iPhone app development, the opposite may be true for App Store approval.

Before you can get started building any native iPhone application, you'll need the full iPhone SDK from Apple. If you installed the simulator earlier in the chapter, the SDK will have come along, but if not, please do so now. Also, don't forget that you need an Intel-based Mac on the current level of OS X release.

Building the Framework

The primary environment for iPhone development is the Xcode IDE; after installing the SDK, you can find it in your Developer/Applications folder. The following instructions will guide you through the creation of the basic web framework application, with examples based on my Moon Phase gadget along the way.

1. In Xcode, select File → New Project → iPhone OS → Window-Based Application, and save it to a suitable directory and name for your gadget. iPhone apps are traditionally named to a camel-case standard, so I've called mine MoonPhase. In any case, you'll need to substitute your own app name wherever you see [your app] in these instructions.

2. Your new project should now be open in Xcode, with a few autogenerated files visible. In the Classes folder, edit the [your app]AppDelegate.h header file to look like Listing 11-2; you'll need to add two highlighted references to UIWebView (the rest of the file is autogenerated). Save the file when you're done.

Listing 11-2. My MoonPhaseAppDelegate.h Header File

```
#import <UIKit/UIKit.h>

@interface MoonPhaseAppDelegate :
        NSObject <UIApplicationDelegate, UIWebViewDelegate> {
    UIWindow *window;
    IBOutlet UIWebView *webView;
}

@property (nonatomic, retain) IBOutlet UIWindow *window;

@end
```

■ **Tip** Don't forget that this code is available for download at http://sterlingudell.com/pwg/chapter_11.

---

3. Next, edit the Objective-C file [your app]AppDelegate.m to match Listing 11-3; again, this is simply a matter of adding the few highlighted lines, all to do with the webView object. Save this one as well, finishing the required source code modifications.

Listing 11-3. My MoonPhaseAppDelegate.m Objective-C File

```objc
#import "MoonPhaseAppDelegate.h"

@implementation MoonPhaseAppDelegate

@synthesize window;

- (void)applicationDidFinishLaunching:(UIApplication *)application {
    webView.delegate = self;

    [webView stringByEvaluatingJavaScriptFromString:@"window.isIPhone = true;"];
    NSURL *appURL      = [NSURL fileURLWithPath:[[NSBundle mainBundle]
        pathForResource:@"index" ofType:@"html" inDirectory:@"content"]];
    NSURLRequest *appReq = [NSURLRequest requestWithURL:appURL
        cachePolicy:NSURLRequestUseProtocolCachePolicy timeoutInterval:20.0];
    [webView loadRequest:appReq];

    [window makeKeyAndVisible];
}

- (void)dealloc {
    [webView release];
    [window release];
    [super dealloc];
}

@end
```

4. Double-click MainWindow.xib (in the Resources folder) to open it in Interface Builder.

   a. Drag a Web View control from the Objects tab of the Library window to your xib file's main window. Make sure it covers the entire surface (see Figure 11-5); to confirm this, open Tools → Size Inspector, and check that your Web View control is 320×460 pixels (without the status bar).

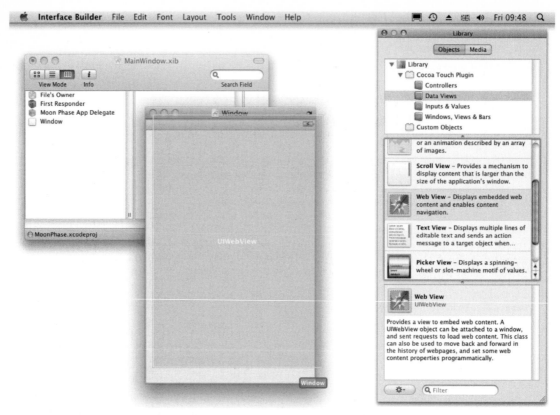

Figure 11-5. Dragging a Web View control onto your application's window

b. In MainWindow.xib, right-click your App Delegate object.

c. From the pop-up that appears, drag from the circle to the right of Outlets →
webView to connect it to the UIWebView in the main window (see Figure
11-6). This connects the UIWebView control to your Objective-C code from
Listing 11-2.

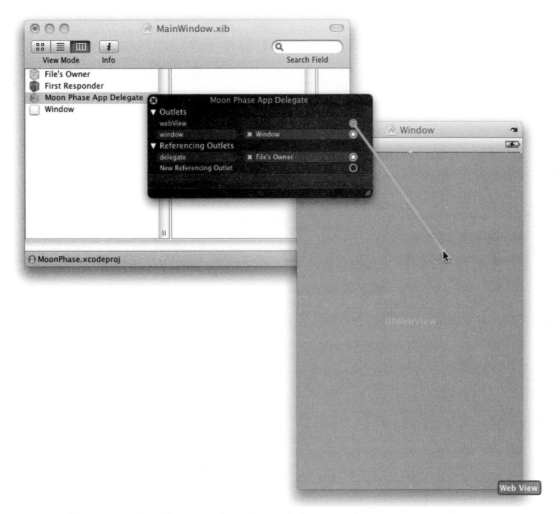

Figure 11-6. Connecting the webView *outlet to the* UIWebView *control*

> **d.** Save and close MainWindow.xib.

5. In Finder, create a folder named content under your application's project folder (created in step 1), and place in it all of the packageable resources your gadget uses. This will include its core HTML document, all CSS and JavaScript files, and any static images.

> **a.** *Important*: For compatibility with the code you created in the AppDelegate, your main HTML file *must* be named index.html and be located in the root of content.

> **b.** Other files can be located and named as you'd like; subdirectories (referenced via relative URLs) are fine.

6. Place your 57-pixel-square application icon in your project's root folder (*not* content).

7. Back in Xcode, open Project → Add to Project, select your content folder, and click Add. Make sure that "Copy items into destination group's folder" is not selected but that Create Folder References is, as shown in Figure 11-7.

Figure 11-7. Adding your web resources content folder to the application project

8. Also add your icon PNG file to the project, using the same procedure as in step 7.

9. Open your application's info.plist file (in the Resources folder), and make the following changes:

    a. For "Icon file," enter your icon file's name (for example, mine is moon_57.png).

    b. For "Bundle name" and "Bundle display name," enter the title of your app as you want it to appear on the iPhone's home screen (such as Moon Phase).

    c. For "Bundle identifier," enter a reverse-domain format string describing your iPhone project. Mine is com.daylightmap.moon.iphone; you can find more information in the "CFBundleIdentifier" section of Chapter 7.

Your native application framework is now complete, and if you had your gadget well-optimized for iPhone as a web app, the chances are good that you won't need to make many changes to the HTML now.

■ **Tip** You can make changes to your web source files right in Xcode by simply opening the files from within the content folder of your project.

Adding to crossPlatform

Despite its advanced nature, iPhone requires quite significant modifications to the `crossPlatform` middleware layer, with the majority needed to enable persistent storage here in the native-app framework. Since it's not a true gadget API, it doesn't inherently supply a storage interface, and as an embedded browser instance, neither does it support cookies.

As an alternative, I've turned to Mobile Safari's support of SQLite, part of the emerging W3C HTML 5 standard. This allows access to a true SQL database from within JavaScript, more than sufficient for `crossPlatform.Storage`'s needs. As you'll see, though, it's not without its complications.

Detecting the Platform

Before we can do that, however, `crossPlatform` needs to know that it's running on an iPhone. Without an actual gadget API to detect, I've had to take a more novel approach: I create a JavaScript variable *within* the native Objective-C, with the following line (from Listing 11-3):

```
[webView stringByEvaluatingJavaScriptFromString:@"window.isIPhone = true;"];
```

The effect is to "push" the `isIphone` value into the JavaScript, where I can then detect it with a conventional `if` test:

```
if (!!window.isIPhone) {
    crossPlatform.api = 'iphone';
    crossPlatform.emptyPref = undefined;
}
```

Creating and Reading the Database Table

Before a SQL table can be used to store data, it needs to be created. In `crossPlatform`, I do this during the module's initialization code so that the table is immediately ready for use (see Listing 11-4).

Listing 11-4. Creating and Reading a SQLite Table in `crossPlatform`

```
crossPlatform.data = {};
crossPlatform.db = openDatabase('crossPlatform', '1.0', '', 65535);
crossPlatform.db.transaction(
  function(transaction) {
    transaction.executeSql('create table if not exists cpStorage ' +
        '(name varchar(255) not null primary key, value text null);', []);
    transaction.executeSql('select name, value from cpStorage', [],
      function (transaction, results) {
        for (crossPlatform.i = 0; crossPlatform.i < results.rows.length;
            crossPlatform.i += 1) {
          crossPlatform.data[results.rows.item(crossPlatform.i).name] =
```

```
              results.rows.item(crossPlatform.i).value;
        }
    });
  });
```

First, the openDatabase function opens the database for business, creating it if necessary; note that I've specified a size of 64KB. It will stay open for the life of the page. The actual database operations are then enclosed in a transaction function: I start by creating my table (cpStorage) with two columns (name and value), which is simple but adequate for my standard Storage interface.

After the database table is initialized, though, notice that I proceed to read its data immediately, with the SQL statement select name, value from cpStorage. The first time that the gadget runs, this won't do anything (because the table has just been created), but in subsequent sessions it will immediately iterate over the returned rows and store them in an object named crossPlatorm.data.

This is a significant departure from my usual technique in crossPlatform of reading Storage data only when it's requested, and you might well wonder why I'm doing so. The answer lies in the fact that the SQLite database access is *asynchronous*; as a result, if I waited to retrieve the data on demand, I wouldn't be able to return it to the calling process immediately. This way, I load all the data at gadget startup, and it's ready and waiting in the data object.

Accessing data from the actual crossPlatform.Storage object, then, is very simple:

```
switch (crossPlatform.api) {
  case 'iphone': myValue = crossPlatform.data[name]; break;
  ...
}
```

Writing to the Database Table

At the other end of the process, saving data back to the cpStorage table requires a similar construct, as shown in Listing 11-5.

Listing 11-5. Writing to a SQLite Table in crossPlatform

```
switch (crossPlatform.api) {
  case 'iphone':
    crossPlatform.db.transaction(
      function(transaction) {
        transaction.executeSql(
          'insert into cpStorage (name, value) values (?, ?)',
          [name, value],
          null,
          function (transaction) {
            transaction.executeSql(
              'update cpStorage set value = ? where (name = ?)',
              [value, name]);
          });
      });
    break;
  ...
}
```

Again, I have a transaction function containing two SQL statements, an insert and an update. But you've no doubt noticed the unusual structure of the code: the update is passed (as an inline function) to the executeSql, which performs the insert. This fourth parameter to executeSql is actually a callback function, executed if the SQL in the first parameter fails. My assumption here is that the most likely reason for a problem on insert is a key collision, so I then update instead.

■ **Note** For a more thorough guide to SQLite on Safari, see Apple's own reference at http://tinyurl.com/n4ye9x.

With this addition, the modifications to crossPlatform are complete, and the code is ready to run. When I click the Build and Go button in Xcode, it automatically starts the iPhone Simulator (if necessary), installs my app, and runs it.

Testing and Debugging

The Xcode Build and Go command described at the end of the previous section launches the currently active project in the simulator, so whenever you need to test a change to your code, it's the button to use. One important note is that Xcode doesn't view your content folder as part of the project source and thus won't automatically rebuild the project if all you've changed is your web source—meaning that you won't automatically see your latest changes in the simulator. To force a rebuild, select Build → Clean, after which the Build and Go command will rebuild your entire app.

Debugging Packaged JavaScript

Generally, one drawback to packaging as a native app is that your web code will be harder to debug. The JavaScript and CSS are a level removed from the Objective-C that Xcode and the simulator are natively working with, so it's harder to get a look at any problems that arise. However, the good news is that the UIWebView control implements the same browser as Mobile Safari itself, so the vast majority of the time, your repackaged gadget should behave the same as it did when accessed on the web from the iPhone.

■ **Tip** If you've changed your gadget source code (HTML, JavaScript, CSS) from when it was running as a web app, make sure you test the new version back in Mobile Safari.

If you do run into a difference, such as a JavaScript problem that appears only in your native app, your best bet for debugging it is usually to inspect variables by placing their values in the innerHTML of a visible element in your gadget. This should allow you to see what's going on inside.

An alternative is to implement an Objective-C wrapper for JavaScript's alert function. It turns out that this isn't difficult, so it's a useful extension to the basic native-app framework presented in this chapter. All that's required is a single Objective-C function, shown in Listing 11-6; insert this near the end of the [your app]AppDelegate.m file (Listing 11-2), right before the @end statement.

Listing 11-6. Objective-C Wrapper for a JavaScript alert[1]

```
- (void) javascriptAlert:(NSString*)text {
    NSString* jsString = [[NSString alloc] initWithFormat:@"alert('%@');", text];
    [webView stringByEvaluatingJavaScriptFromString:jsString];
    NSLog(jsString);
    [jsString release];
}
```

In addition, you'll also need to add a forward declaration in [your app]AppDelegate.h (Listing 11-1). Insert the following line, again right before the @end:

```
- (void) javascriptAlert:(NSString*)text
```

With these two code changes in place, you should now be able to call alert from your JavaScript, the same as in an ordinary browser session.

■ **Tip** The content of an alert implemented as in Listing 11-6 will also be written to Xcode's console.

Testing on a Real iPhone

Up until this point, everything we've done has happened on the iPhone Simulator, installed on a Mac. If you want to take the next step and install your application on a physical handset, the process quickly gets quite a bit more complicated.

The basic issue goes back to Apple's strict control over what applications can be installed on iPhones. If every handset had the ability to easily install applications "under development," it would obviously represent a gaping hole in that policy. Consequently, before your can install your new app on a real phone, Apple needs various strong assurances that it will remain under tight control. Generally, iPhones will only run *signed* applications, and this signing is done by the App Store; for development, however, it's possible to self-sign your application so that it will run on specific, individual devices. Doing so is beyond the scope of this chapter to cover in detail (not to mention being dependent on current Apple policy), but in this section, you'll find a general overview.

Before you can begin, you'll need to have upgraded your free iPhone Developer registration to one of the paid account levels described earlier in the chapter; this can be done at http://developer.apple.com/iphone/program/apply.html. This is necessary for running your app on any physical handset; it will give you access to the iPhone Developer Program Portal, which contains the web-based tools necessary to prepare your app and iPhone for deployment.

■ **Caution** Some developers report that approval for the iPhone Developer Program can take weeks, or even months, so you'll want to start this process as early as possible.

---

[1] The javascriptAlert function of Listing 11-6 is taken directly from the open source of the PhoneGap project, with my thanks.

After joining the program, the high-level process is as follows:

1. *Register* the specific iPhone that you'll be using as a development device.

2. Create, download, and install development *certificates* in Xcode.

3. Create an *App ID* for your new application.

4. *Provision* the device, certificate, and App ID together as a single profile.

5. Install the provisioning profile in Xcode.

Be aware that, for inclusion in this chapter, the previous instructions are extremely simplified, and the full process can be confusing and frustrating for many beginners. You can find the official instructions under Managing Devices in the iPhone Reference Library at `http://tinyurl.com/nz7tsc`. For additional clarity, I also recommend the screencast at `http://mobileorchard.com/iphone-development-provisioning`; it costs US$5 to download but is well worth it in time and anguish. Or, consider seeking assistance from an experienced iPhone developer.

Deploying iPhone Applications

By this point in the chapter, you'll have realized that your options for deploying native iPhone applications are rather limited. Overwhelmingly, your main course is the iTunes App Store, but (as discussed earlier) getting your app listed there is not a simple process. It's also one that Apple reserves solely for paid members of their iPhone Developer program—so your first step will be to join the program, as outlined in the previous section. But beyond that, this is again a process outside the scope of this chapter to cover in detail. Sign into your Developer Program Portal, open the Distribution page, and follow the current instructions there.

Outside of the official Apple channels, applications can be installed only on "jailbroken" iPhones. Although most emphatically *not* sanctioned by Apple, this unlocked-iPhone subculture has nonetheless gained some significant traction, and a fair number of iPhone owners have gone down this route. Not only does this allow any app to be installed on the handset (beyond those approved by Apple), its "root" access to the operating system enables applications that aren't possible using the official iPhone APIs.

The relative popularity of jailbreaking has given rise to a few alternatives to the iTunes App Store, independent online marketplaces where apps for unlocked iPhones are distributed. As of this writing, two of the more popular are `http://cydia.saurik.com` and `http://rockyourphone.com`. If you choose not to deploy your repackaged gadget through the App Store, I encourage you to look into the possibilities here; they include the option of building an unsigned application, one that doesn't require the purchase of a Developer Program membership.

Learning More About iPhone

With its tight control of the platform, it's no surprise that Apple is far and away the dominant source of information for iPhone development. This can mostly be found under their main iPhone developer portal at `http://developer.apple.com/iphone`. For help on specific API calls, I recommend bookmarking the iPhone Reference Library, `http://developer.apple.com/iphone/library`.

Beyond static documentation, additional help is available to paid Developer Program members, including the Apple Developer Forums (`http://devforums.apple.com`) and two technician-level support tickets per year. If you're registered at the free level, you'll need to seek assistance outside of Apple; I recommend `http://iphonedevforums.com`.

Summary

Apple's iPhone is the golden boy of the smartphone world; both its popularity and its intrinsic web-enabled nature make it an extremely attractive target for web gadget developers. In this chapter, you've learned to install the iPhone Simulator on a Mac and to use it to develop your gadget into a full-fledged iPhone web app. In addition, you've seen how a few simple lines of Objective-C are sufficient to repackage your gadget as a native iPhone application. This has the potential to expose it for sale to the millions of iTunes App Store users worldwide—an opportunity that's hard to beat.

In the next chapter, you'll look at iPhone's most credible competition to date, Google's Android operating system. Despite its significant philosophical differences, it's a technically similar platform to iPhone and will present you with similar opportunities for your web gadgets.

CHAPTER 12

■ ■ ■

Android

After the iPhone changed the smartphone landscape in 2007, the first platform vendor to respond was Google, announcing that Android—its own mobile operating system—would be released the following year. In many ways, it's a very different take on the entire smartphone concept than the iPhone: the operating system and tools are open source, and the environment as a whole is much less tightly regulated. But in other ways—those that matter to a web developer—it's far more similar than different: as a platform, Android is web-enabled every bit as much as iPhone.

So, this chapter will largely mirror the previous one. You'll learn how to install the Android tool set (including the emulator), test and optimize your gadget as a pure web app, repackage it as a native application, and then deploy it to the wider world. Let's get started!

■ **Note** Android uses the term *widget* both for internal user interface elements and, more frequently, for home-screen applications (like the Google Search bar in Figure 12-1). Consequently, I'll stay well clear of the word when referring to web gadgets in this chapter.

Introducing Android

Android started life as an independent mobile software company and was acquired by Google in 2005, and the eponymous operating system was announced in late 2007. In contrast to iPhone's near-complete control by a single company (from hardware through OS to applications), Android is backed by the Open Handset Alliance (OHA), a loose affiliation of mobile phone handset manufacturers, software vendors, and carriers. Although Google still maintains a central role in Android development, the source code is open and is used on hardware from a variety of companies both within and without the OHA. This range of devices is beginning to branch out beyond pure mobile phones, presenting a diverse set of opportunities for your web gadget.

Although the overall merits of Android and iPhone are a subject of great debate, when you get into web development on the platform, you'll find that they are essentially equal. Android's browser is again based on the WebKit rendering engine and, apart from a slightly different user interface, is functionally a near twin to Mobile Safari. It's every bit as good at displaying web sites and running web applications in their full glory. The Android browser is also well integrated into the native programming environment—again, just as on the iPhone—and later in the chapter, you'll be exploiting this integration in much the same way to repackage your web gadgets as a full citizen of the Android community.

Installing the Android Emulator

As a platform, Android relies heavily on the Java language. Not only is it the primary means for developing native Android apps, but the software development tools all use Java themselves. Consequently, the first step toward developing for Android is to ensure you have a current version of the Java Development Kit (JDK) on your computer. At least version 5 is required for the examples in this chapter, though later versions should work as well. You can obtain the JDK from `http://java.sun.com/javase/downloads`; follow the instructions appropriate for your host operating system.

Being Java-based, the Android software development kit (SDK) is itself quite cross-platform. It'll happily run on Microsoft Windows (XP or later), Mac OS X 10.2.4+ (although only Intel-based), and most distributions of Linux. The instructions for this chapter tend to favor a Windows installation, but other systems are quite similar.

With the JDK installed, your next step is to download the Android SDK from `http://developer.android.com/sdk`. You'll want to select the current SDK version from that URL; at this writing, it's API Level 3, which equates to the v1.5 of the Android OS (aka Cupcake). The platform is new enough that significant changes are still occurring between versions, and new versions are coming quite quickly, so be aware that these instructions may have changed slightly by the time you read this.

The download itself is a zip file, rather than an executable installation; within this archive, you'll find a single directory containing the entire SDK, with a name like `android-sdk-windows-1.5_r3`. Unzip this directory to a location where you'll be able to find it easily, because I'll be referring to it throughout the chapter. In addition to the emulator, the SDK contains a variety of other tools, examples, and documentation. For the rest of the chapter, I'll be using `[SDK]` to refer to this extracted directory; substitute your local Android SDK path wherever you see `[SDK]`.

With the SDK extracted, the Android emulator is actually installed, but before you can use it, you need to create a *virtual device*. This is essentially a configuration package for an emulator instance; most other platforms (like Symbian S60) prepackage such instances independently, but with Android, you create your own. To do so, open a command prompt (in Windows, select Start → Run, and enter `cmd`), navigate to your `[SDK]/tools` directory, and run the following command:

```
android create avd --target 3 --name my_avd
```

This will create an instance of the default Android virtual device (AVD), named `my_avd`, for the given API release level. If you've installed a different API level than 3, please enter its number here instead.

You're now ready to run the Android emulator. Back in the command shell (and still in the `[SDK]/tools` directory), enter the following:

```
emulator.exe -avd my_avd
```

The emulator should now start, and when ready, it will look something like Figure 12-1. I recommend creating a shortcut for the emulator command in your host operating system, rather than typing the previous command every time you want to start it.

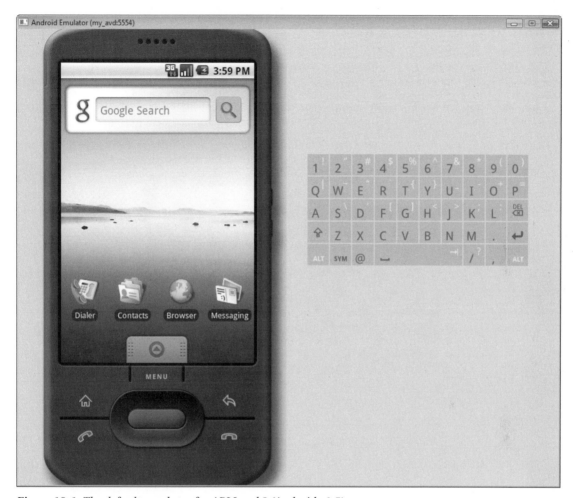

Figure 12-1. The default emulator for API Level 3 (Android v1.5)

Android's is a true emulator (rather than a simulator), meaning that it closely mirrors the environment of a physical device and is capable of running the same executable code. On the downside, this level of abstraction can take a minute or two to boot; contrast this with the iPhone Simulator, which leverages the architecture it shares with the underlying OS to start almost instantly.

As usual, I recommend you take a few minutes now to become familiar with the emulated Android environment.

■ **Tip** Save yourself some annoyance, by disabling the emulator screen's autodim functionality. From the home screen, select Menu → Settings → Sound & display → Screen timeout → Never timeout.

Running Web Applications

By this point in the book, you've probably opened your core HTML gadget on a number of simulated handsets and generally have it working fairly well with them. If so, Android's browser will likely be a bit anticlimactic; the strong odds are that your gadget will work fine the first time out—especially if you've already been through this process with iPhone's Mobile Safari.

Nonetheless, you'll need to confirm this and work through any problems that might arise. Prominently displayed on the emulator's home screen is a Browser shortcut, and not surprisingly, this is the place to start. Open it now, and enter the URL for your core web gadget to see how things look (as shown in Figure 12-2).

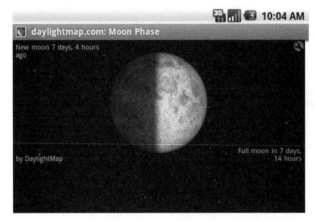

Figure 12-2. The Moon Phase core gadget in the Android browser

---

■ **Tip** To try your gadget on different screen orientations, rotate the emulator between portrait and landscape by pressing Ctrl+F11 on your host computer.

In the event that you do run into trouble, another tool in the SDK can help you. It's called the DDMS, for Dalvik Debug Monitor Service (Dalvik being the Java virtual machine inside Android), and you'll find it at [SDK]/tools/ddms. When you run it, you'll see a window similar to Figure 12-3; select your emulator instance in the upper-left pane, and the lower Log pane will show a stream of debug information (Figure 12-3).

Figure 12-3. *The Dalvik Debug Monitor Service, with JavaScript* `console.log` *output*

Within this log will be any JavaScript errors generated by the browser, and any calls to `console.log` that you place in your own script will appear here as well. In Figure 12-3, for example, I've highlighted the output from a JavaScript statement of `console.log('Debugging message')`. Be aware that DDMS requires `console.log` to be called with a printable string; it doesn't support object logging, like many built-in browser consoles do.

In addition to confirming that your core gadget is ready to serve the growing number of Android users in the wild, I recommend forking your HTML and optimizing a version specifically for Android. This copy will serve as your foundation for the remainder of the chapter, so take the time to ensure that it is working and looking its best, even if that means adding code that isn't appropriate in the core, cross-browser version.

■ **Tip** If you ported your gadget to iPhone in the previous chapter, use that as your starting point for Android. The two browsers' similarity will give you a head start.

Creating Native Android Applications

As another web-enabled smartphone platform, Android is well positioned to implement the same sort of technique that was used in the previous chapter: wrapping a pure web gadget as a "native" application, with all the privileges that will entail. In the rest of this chapter, I'll walk you through the process of creating such a wrapper for your own gadget and then explore what can be done with it after you do.

The architecture of the app, and the process to construct it, will be very similar to the native iPhone wrapper in the previous chapter. You'll generate a simple Android application with a single WebView control as its sole user interface element (notice even the control name closely parallels iPhone). You'll then package your gadget resources with the app, loading the core HTML into the WebView when it starts up, and you'll be on your way.

So, just as in the previous chapter, you'll need to get your gadget resources—all the static source files and images referred to in your web code—consolidated under a single directory. Obviously, this should be the Android-specific port you developed at the end of the previous section.

You'll also need an application icon for the Android launcher. On this platform, the standard is for 48-pixel-square PNGs, and your integration work will be easier if it's named icon.png. Also, I recommend that you create one on an alpha-channel transparent background if possible (such as Figure 12-4). Not only will this look best in the Android app tray, but users can place shortcuts to applications on their home screens, and a good antialiased PNG is definitely your best option here.

Figure 12-4. My Android application icon.png for Moon Phase

"NATIVE" ANDROID APPLICATIONS?

The phrase *native application* is a bit slippery on Android. Traditionally, the term refers to applications that are compiled directly for the target operating system and that run as full-fledged members of it. In this chapter, you'll certainly learn how to repackage your web app as a full-fledged Android app, but there's some question about how native it will truly be.

The issue is that you are repackaging in Java, and as you may know, very rarely is Java truly native. It was conceived as a portable language that would run in a virtual machine (VM) on many different host operating systems. By and large, that's still how things stand, and Android is no exception: Java bytecode executes in a VM called Dalvik, running on top of an underlying Linux kernel.

So, Java isn't fully native on Android either, despite being virtually the only language that real-world apps are written in. There actually is a native programming level available, compiling C and C++ code directly for the OS, and it's appropriate for performance-critical areas of functionality. When Android developers use the term *native*, this is usually what they're referring to. But an important point is that this NDK has no access to the user interface; the C/C++ routines must be called from within a larger Java app. So, in a real sense, there are *no* truly native applications on Android.

Of course, this is all a bit academic for a repackaged web app, where the core functionality is written in JavaScript. Nonetheless, knowing about the different definitions of *native* on Android might save you from some confusion at a later date.

Unlike iPhone, there are very few downsides to following the native-app repackaging process through on Android. This is primarily because of the openness of the platform: there is no Apple-like gatekeeper deciding which applications users can install on their phones. By a simple process (which I'll cover in the "Deploying Android Applications" section later in the chapter), any Android user can install any application, from anywhere. This means that the native application that you'll build from your gadget in the next few sections can be widely distributed via channels ranging from Google's official market to your own web site. There's no good reason not to do it.

Setting Up the Environment

It's possible to build Android applications with only the SDK you installed earlier in the chapter, using command-line tools to compile the code and load it onto the simulator. But that's definitely the hard way. Continuing with the cross-platform theme, Google has produced a good Android plug-in for the popular Eclipse IDE, and using it is the course I firmly recommend. It's also the assumption I'll make for the instructions throughout this part of the chapter.

■ **Note** If you are determined not to use Eclipse, you can find a guide to the equivalent command-line utilities at

`http://developer.android.com/guide/developing/other-ide.html`.

Installing Eclipse

If you've been doing web development for long, you may have Eclipse already installed, but if not, now is the time. As another open source tool, it's a free download from the Eclipse Foundation (`http://eclipse.org/downloads`). You'll need at least version 3.3 (Europa), though later versions generally work as well, and I recommend at least 3.4. The instructions in this section are specifically for 3.5 (Galileo); other versions are similar, and you can find guidance at `http://developer.android.com/sdk` if you need it.

■ **Tip** If you're installing Eclipse for the first time, choose the package named Eclipse IDE for Java EE (Enterprise Edition). It includes the Java support that Android needs, plus good code editors for HTML, JavaScript, and CSS, which will come in handy sooner or later.

Like the SDK itself, Eclipse comes packaged as a zip file; extract it when the download completes (on Windows, I recommend just placing the `eclipse` folder directly in your `C:\Program Files`). The app itself is `eclipse.exe` in the root directory; again, creating a shortcut somewhere convenient is a good idea.

The first time you run Eclipse, it'll ask you to select a *workspace* folder. This is simply a directory where all your Eclipse projects will reside. If you already have a main directory you use for your programming work, go ahead and use that for your workspace; Eclipse won't harm whatever is already there. Otherwise, Eclipse will create a new folder with the path you specify.

Installing the Android SDK Plug-In

The Eclipse installation in the previous section doesn't yet include the Android tools, so your next task is to install the plug-in:

1. In Eclipse, select Help → Install New Software (see Figure 12-5).

2. In the Install dialog box, enter the following URL in Work With, and click Add:

   `https://dl-ssl.google.com/android/eclipse/`

3. When prompted, give it a name like `Android SDK`.

4. Eclipse will display the plug-ins available at this site. Select Developer Tools, and proceed with the rest of the Install Wizard.

Figure 12-5. *Installing the Android plug-in into Eclipse 3.5*

Eclipse will most likely restart after installing the plug-in. When it has, you have one last task; it needs to know the location where you unzipped your Android SDK. In Eclipse, select Window → Preferences → Android, and then browse to your [SDK] directory.

Adapting the Core Gadget

With Eclipse and the Android plug-in installed, you should now be ready to create an Android application. As outlined earlier, your approach will be to create a `WebView` framework, with the gadget resources packaged inside.

Building the Framework

The Android plug-in for Eclipse includes good tools for generating the starting code for a project; the following instructions will walk you through the process of creating an Android app for your gadget:

1.   In Eclipse, select File → New → Project. In the dialog box that opens, select Android Project, and click Next.

2.   Complete the New Android Project dialog box (Figure 12-6) with the following values, and click Finish. This will create a project folder in your workspace directory.

   a.   The project name is an internal name for the project within Eclipse. This will also be the name of the project folder, so you may want to include *Android* in the name, like MoonPhase Android.

   b.   The application name is the name you want visible to users who install your app, such as Moon Phase.

   c.   The package name is effectively a namespace for your project, and since this is Java, it should be in reverse-domain format. It also needs to be unique for each Android app you release. Mine is com.daylightmap.moon.android.

   d.   Select the box for Create Activity, and give it a good short camel-case name for your project, like MoonPhase (without spaces). I'll be referring to this string as [your name] for the rest of these instructions.

   e.   For Min SDK Version, use whatever version you created your AVD for earlier in the chapter (in my previous example, it's 3).

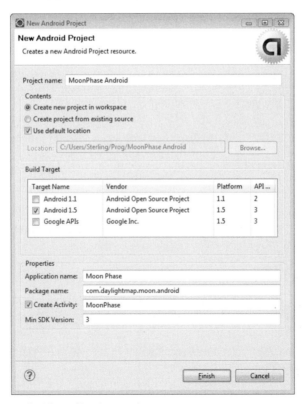

Figure 12-6. Creating an Android application project

3. When your project has been created, Eclipse's Package Explorer (usually open on the left side of the IDE) is what you'll use to navigate within it. Double-click AndroidManifest.xml to open it, and add the uses-permission tag highlighted in Listing 12-1. This element is required if your gadget uses any resources from the Internet; if it's entirely self-contained, you can skip this step.

Listing 12-1. *The Android Framework Application's Manifest,* AndroidManifest.xml

```
<?xml version="1.0" encoding="utf-8"?>
<manifest xmlns:android="http://schemas.android.com/apk/res/android"
      package="com.daylightmap.moon.android"
      android:versionCode="1"
      android:versionName="1.0.12">
    <uses-permission android:name="android.permission.INTERNET" />
    <application android:icon="@drawable/icon" android:label="@string/app_name">
        <activity android:name=".MoonPhase"
                  android:label="@string/app_name">
            <intent-filter>
                <action android:name="android.intent.action.MAIN" />
                <category android:name="android.intent.category.LAUNCHER" />
            </intent-filter>
        </activity>
    </application>
    <uses-sdk android:minSdkVersion="3" />
</manifest>
```

4. Open res/layout/main.xml, and make the changes highlighted in Listing 12-2 (note that the WebView element is created as a TextView by the project wizard, and you need to change it manually in the XML).

Listing 12-2. *The Layout XML(*main.xml*)* *Defines the Appearance of the Framework App*

```
<?xml version="1.0" encoding="utf-8"?>
<LinearLayout xmlns:android="http://schemas.android.com/apk/res/android"
    android:orientation="vertical"
    android:layout_width="fill_parent"
    android:layout_height="fill_parent">
  <WebView
      android:layout_width="fill_parent"
      android:layout_height="fill_parent"
      android:scrollbars="none"
      android:id="@+id/main_view" />
</LinearLayout>
```

■ **Note** In Listing 12-2, I'm assuming your gadget will fit within an average HVGA Android screen. If you need to scroll, substitute android:scrollbars="vertical" (or horizontal) for none.

---

5. Edit [your name].java (under the src directory) to match Listing 12-3; again, the additions you need to make are highlighted in bold. *Important*: use the name of your own gadget's core HTML file instead of phase_android.html.

Listing 12-3. The Main Java Source File to Make the Framework Application Run

```
package com.daylightmap.moon.android;

import android.app.Activity;
import android.os.Bundle;
import android.webkit.WebView;

public class MoonPhase extends Activity {
    /** Called when the activity is first created. */
    @Override
    public void onCreate(Bundle savedInstanceState) {
        super.onCreate(savedInstanceState);

        setContentView(R.layout.main);
        WebView mainView = (WebView) findViewById(R.id.main_view);

        mainView.getSettings().setJavaScriptEnabled(true);
        mainView.addJavascriptInterface(new Boolean(true), "isAndroid");
        mainView.loadUrl("file:///android_asset/phase_android.html");
    }
}
```

■ **Tip** Remember that you don't need to type all of this code yourself—it is available for download at http://sterlingudell.com/pwg/chapter_12.

6. Copy your web content into [your name]/assets, including any subdirectories you may be using; see Figure 12-7 for an example. Make sure that your core HTML file name matches the name in the loadUrl call near the end of Listing 12-3 (like phase_android.html).

■ **Note** In Listing 11-3, the URL base for the /assets directory was android_asset (without an "s"). This is correct; android_asset is an SDK constant for the /assets folder of a packaged app.

7. Copy your icon.png file into [your name]/res/drawable, replacing any icon.png that may have been automatically placed there by the project wizard.

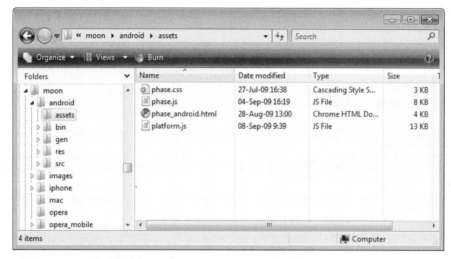

Figure 12-7. *The assets needed for Moon Phase as a native Android app*

Your Android application wrapper should now be ready to run. To run it from Eclipse, select your project folder in the Package Explorer, and then select Run → Run → Android Application or click the green-arrow button on Eclipse's toolbar.

Changes to the HTML

If you optimized a version of your gadget for Android earlier in the chapter, it's extremely likely that it will work just as well in the native-app framework—it is the same browser, after all. If there are some differences, now is the time to work them out.

As suggested earlier, for Moon Phase I've based my Android code from my existing iPhone port, and it turns out that the changes needed are few indeed. Listing 12-4 shows my HTML (with the body content omitted for brevity, as usual). The two changes from Listing 11-3 have been highlighted in bold, and I detail them after the listing.

Listing 12-4. *The HTML for Moon Phase on Android*

```
<?xml version="1.0" encoding="UTF-8"?>
<!DOCTYPE html PUBLIC "-//W3C//DTD XHTML 1.0 Transitional//EN"
                      "http://www.w3.org/TR/xhtml1/DTD/xhtml1-transitional.dtd">
<html xmlns="http://www.w3.org/1999/xhtml">
  <head>
    <meta http-equiv="Content-Type" content="text/html;charset=UTF-8" />
    <meta name="description"
          content="Shows the current phase of the moon on a field of stars." />
    <meta name="viewport" content="width=device-width, height=device-height" />
    <title>Moon Phase</title>
    <link href="moon_32.png" type="image/png" rel="icon" />
    <link href="phase.css"  type="text/css"  rel="stylesheet" />
    <style type="text/css">
```

```
      .moonPhase #main,
      .moonPhase #config {
        font-size: 15px;
      }
      .moonPhase .text {
        width: 40%;
      }
      .moonPhase #last {
        width: 50%;
      }
      .moonPhase #moon {
        position: relative;
      }
      .moonPhase #main_icons {
        opacity: 0.5 !important;
        top: 10px;
        right: 10px;
      }
    </style>
  </head>
  <body class="moonPhase">

    <!-- body content goes here -->

    <script type="text/javascript" src="platform.js"></script>
    <script type="text/javascript" src="phase.js"></script>
    <script type="text/javascript">
      moonPhase.defaultLoad = moonPhase.load;
      moonPhase.load = function () {
        // Set the gadget's size to fill the viewport
        moonPhase.elements.main.style.height = window.innerHeight + 'px';

        // Call the ancestor method
        moonPhase.defaultLoad();

        // Center the moon image within the gadget
        moonPhase.elements.moon.style.top =
          (window.innerHeight - moonPhase.elements.moon.height) / 2 + 'px';
      };
    </script>
  </body>
</html>
```

First, Android doesn't support the additional parameters to the meta viewport tag that iPhone does, so I've omitted them (along with the other Apple-specific head elements). And second, my preference is for a slightly smaller font size on this platform, so I've dropped it from 17px to 15px.

That's it! With these very minor changes, Moon Phase is running well as a native Android app (see Figure 12-8), and I trust your gadget will also.

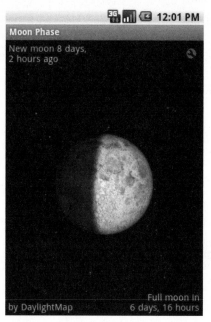

Figure 12-8. My Moon Phase example gadget running in the Android native-app framework

Additions to crossPlatform

You may have noticed that I ran my Android app before modifying the crossPlatform middleware layer to support it. That's because there are actually *no modifications required*: the Android browser will happily use the default plain-HTML handling already built into crossPlatform since Chapter 3. It just works.

However, in case you run into a situation where you do need (or want) to do some Android-specific handling, I have built detection of the framework into crossPlatform for your convenience. The JavaScript code is extremely simple:

```
if (!!window.isAndroid) {
  crossPlatform.api = 'android';
  crossPlatform.emptyPref = null;
}
```

It's powered by a technique analogous to what I used for iPhone in the previous chapter. Because the native-app framework isn't a true API, it has no namespaces that my code could detect. Instead, I "push" the isAndroid value through to JavaScript with the following line of Java code (also visible in Listing 12-3):

```
mainView.addJavascriptInterface(new Boolean(true), "isAndroid");
```

So if you need to do some special processing for Android in your JavaScript, simply test for crossPlatform.api === 'android', the same as you would for any other API in this book.

Testing and Debugging

The testing situation for the native-application wrapper is really quite similar to what it was when running your gadget directly within the Android browser. JavaScript errors and `console.log` calls will appear in DDMS, as will any native-framework errors if your Java code has gone awry. If your gadget was working well in the browser, the DDMS log should be sufficient to maintain that functionality as a native app.

Deploying Android Applications

The primary reason for repackaging your gadget as a native application is to be able to use the conventional Android distribution channels for it, and in the following sections, I'll talk you through several of these. As mentioned earlier, the openness of the platform means that the deployment opportunities are greater than for any other mobile platform in this book.

The Android Market

Google maintains the official Android Market for the distribution of apps but manages it with a much lighter touch than Apple exerts on the iTunes App Store. There's no prequalification or approval process for applications; Google does occasionally remove apps after they have been listed, but only when they're in violation of the content guidelines (available at `http://android.com/market/terms/developer-content-policy.html`) or are repeatedly flagged as objectionable by the Android Market users themselves. Otherwise, it relies on a crowd-sourced system of ratings and comments to rank applications against each other.

On a practical level, it currently costs US$25 to create a publisher account on the Android Market; once you do so, you can list as many applications as you like. Apps may be free for users, or a purchase price may be set, with transactions processed through Google Checkout. Like Apple, Google takes 30 percent of every sale, though in this case the holdback is distributed to the cellular carriers.

This tie-in to Google Checkout is also one of the disadvantages of the market. Not every Android phone owner has a Google Checkout account, and this hurdle is enough to prevent some from buying any applications at all. Also, Google Checkout does not accept certain payment cards from non-U.S. customers, further limiting its reach.

Publishing Your App

The official guide to publishing on the Android Market is available at `http://developer.android.com/guide/publishing`, and naturally, it will have more complete and up-to-date information than I can provide here. In this section, you'll find a general overview of the publishing process, but please refer to the previous URL as well.

Before you can actually distribute your new app, you'll need to build a signed version from Eclipse. This is a security mechanism; the Android operating system won't replace apps with the same package name but different signatures, thus ensuring that your app can't be supplanted by a (possibly malicious) impostor.

■ **Note** This package/signature security matching also means that you can't directly replace the unsigned app (that you've been using until now) with a signed version. One will need to be uninstalled from your phone or emulator before the other is installed.

As on the iPhone, signing an app will require a cryptographic key, but for Android it's fine to generate one yourself—the keys are neither issued nor controlled by Google or anyone else. Instead, they're generated by the Eclipse plug-in:

1. In Eclipse, right-click the project in the Package Explorer, and select Android Tools → Export Signed Application Package.

2. Confirm that your gadget project is selected, and click Next.

3. Select "Create new keystore," and enter a suitable directory on your disk where your private key will be stored. Important: you can name the keystore whatever you like; make sure you know where to find it later!

4. Enter and confirm a password for your keystore.

5. On the Key Creation page, you'll need to make up an alias name and supply another password, as well as contact information for yourself or your organization. For the validity period, Google recommends a period of 25 years.

■ **Tip** The contact fields on the Key Creation page cannot contain punctuation, such as commas or periods.

---

6. Finally, enter a pathname for your Android package (APK), the file that you will actually distribute. I recommend putting it in your Android project directory and giving it a short but descriptive name, such as `MoonPhase.apk`.

■ **Caution** If you lose your keystore or forget your password, you'll be unable to issue updates to your application.

> *Keep it secret—keep it safe!*

> —Gandalf the Grey

Your signed APK is now ready for distribution through the Android Market (or elsewhere); the next step is to create a market account at `http://market.android.com/publish`. A Google Checkout account will be required, both to pay the registration fee and to receive payment for any application sales. Once you've done this, a Developer Console page will be created for you, from which you can upload your APK and make it available for download through the market.

■ **Tip** Your Android market listing will allow you to include screenshots of your app. These can easily be captured from the emulator or a real device with DDMS; select Device → Screen capture.

Maintaining Your Listing

When you have published one or more applications through the Android Market, you'll use the same Developer Console (at `http://market.android.com/publish`) to maintain your account. Basic download statistics will be shown, and modifications to your listings can be made; they'll take effect almost immediately.

One category of information that is not currently available on the Developer Console is user comments. These are free-form text messages that can be created by Android phone owners who download your app; they appear on your market listing page and can be a valuable source of user feedback. To view these comments, you'll either need to browse the market from an actual Android device—it's not available on the simulator—or use a third-party web site that aggregates market listings. One example of the latter is `http://androlib.com`.

When the time comes to publish an update to your application, the process is much the same as the initial release described in the previous section, with one notable exception. Each release of an app through the market must have a unique `versionCode` and `versionName` in its manifest XML (see Listing 12-1). The meaning of these two fields is as follows:

- `versionCode` is an internal number indicating the direct version progression. Usually, you'll use 1 for your first public release, 2 for your second, and so on. It will need to be unique for each update you publish to the Android Market.

- `versionName` is a more conventional version string, such as `1.0` or `2.04.17`. This will be visible to users and appended to your APK name when it's downloaded from the market; use it as you would the version number for any software. Note that `versionName` doesn't need to be numeric; a string such as `1.3 BETA` will also work fine.

Other Deployment Options

Because Android app distribution is not limited to Google's own market, a number of independent marketplaces have sprung up as well. These offer different features than the official Android Market, such as alternative versioning schemes (alpha, beta, release, and so on) and more flexible purchase terms. Also, the main market is available only on so-called Google Experience phones, which are handsets that meet certain criteria required to carry the Google logo. Devices that operate outside this program frequently replace the market with an independent app directory instead.

This third-party distribution system is still relatively new as of this writing and is certain to evolve rapidly as more non-Google handsets are released. Currently, two emerging leaders in this segment are `http://andappstore.com` and `http://mobentoo.com`. I encourage you to investigate the possibilities of distributing your repackaged gadget through these channels as well.

Android applications can also be distributed from your own web site, though this isn't quite as straightforward as with some true gadget platforms. Although all Android devices are technically able to install apps from anywhere, Google Experience handsets come with this capability disabled by default; it needs to be enabled by the user before third-party installations are allowed. From the Android home screen, select Menu → Settings → Applications, and enable Unknown Sources. If you're distributing your own Android app, you'll want to include instructions like this alongside the download link to your signed APK file.

It's also true that the APK will only be useful to visitors browsing your site directly on their Android phone; there's no good route for users to install an APK downloaded to their desk-bound computer. An alternative that has emerged is to include a link to your market listing on your page instead as a QR code (two-dimensional barcode), shown in Figure 12-9. Users who have reader software on their handset can then scan this code from their computer screen and download the app directly—even if they haven't enabled Unknown Sources.

Figure 12-9. QR code for market://search?q=pname:com.daylightmap.moon.android

To generate a code like this for yourself, the URL you'll need is market://search?q=pname:[your package name], where [your package name] is the reverse-domain string you entered in Figure 12-6. With this URL in hand, a number of web sites or software packages will generate a QR code from it; one example is http://qrcode.kaywa.com. Simply save the image produced, and place it on your web page.

■ **Note** Because it allows you to leverage the Android Market's payment infrastructure, the QR code is an especially good alternative for nonfree applications.

Learning More About Android

Although Android is an open source project, its community involvement isn't as great as some. At this writing, most of the platform development is still done by Google and then released to public availability at certain milestones. As a result, most of the Android resources online are also still concentrated in Google's hands.

- The main developer portal is http://developer.android.com, where you'll find news, download links, programming guides, and a full API reference.

- A family of Google groups contains the majority of Android discussion online. Of most interest to gadget developers are http://groups.google.com/group/android-discuss and http://groups.google.com/group/android-developers.

- A variety of blogs cover general Android news and information, including http://androidguys.com and http://androidcommunity.com.

Summary

Google's Android platform is an up-and-coming contender in the modern smartphone segment. It's flexible, web-capable, and supported by the Open Handset Alliance, a consortium whose membership reads like a Who's Who of the mobile phone industry. For the web gadget developer, it is probably the best opportunity in the current smartphone climate, pairing excellent web standards support with a large, accessible distribution ecosystem. In this chapter, you've learned to take full advantage of that opportunity by optimizing your gadget for the Android browser and then repackaging and deploying it as a native Android application.

In the next and final chapter of the book, I'll cover even newer opportunities, with a survey of some emerging standards and technologies important to web gadgets.

CHAPTER 13

■ ■ ■

The Future of Web Gadgets

In the first 12 chapters of this book, you learned to deploy a single set of source code to every major web gadget platform on the market today. Like all web technologies, however, the gadget landscape is always on the move—and this is especially true where it intersects with the fast-paced world of smartphones. In this final chapter, I'll switch gears slightly and take you on a brief tour of where gadgets appear to be going.

At a high level, I see the important developments as being grouped into two areas. First, several emerging standards will impact gadget development to a greater or lesser extent, improving their cross-platform portability and extending what gadgets can do. Second, new operating systems will integrate web technologies deeper than they have ever been before, creating new opportunities for all web applications—including gadgets, of course.

As I write this, the technologies found here are generally not yet mature enough to be viable targets for porting your gadgets. But by the time you read this, that situation may well have changed, and in any case, these are topics to watch.

Better Standards

In the early days of web gadgets, each platform vendor created its own specification from scratch, and most of the older APIs in this book reflect that diversity. The effect was that creating cross-platform gadgets was a significant task, requiring either major rewrites or an isolation layer (like my crossPlatform framework). It also meant that any cross-platform development was limited to the least common denominator of all target APIs, generally leading to less exciting gadgets than one might ideally like.

As web applications mature, however, a number of standards are emerging that directly benefit both of these areas. In this first part of the chapter, I'll cover the current standardization efforts that are most likely to impact widget developers.

HTML 5

As the Web was in its infancy, the HTML specification went through versions 1, 2, and 3 very quickly. However, when the popularity of the Web exploded, the spec basically got stuck at version 4; the browser wars of the mid-90s meant that each vendor was creating its own proprietary extensions, and the priority has been to bring them into some semblance of order rather than to extend the basic specification.

As this book is being written, that stage has generally passed; most of the major browsers now have good standards compliance, and as a result, the standards can begin to progress again. A variety of new browser technologies are now receiving the blessing of the W3C and being widely implemented in current versions. The process isn't yet complete, and there is still some fragmentation on the front lines, but gradually these technologies are coming together under the banner of HTML 5. By the time you read this, they will likely be standardized enough to use in day-to-day development, and they will present you with some exciting new opportunities.

In the next couple of sections, I'll introduce two of the emerging HTML 5 features that I think are of most use to gadget developers. This is far from a full list, because the standard itself is both large and still coalescing, but I hope that this whets your appetite to the possibilities. The W3C is the clearinghouse for the standardization effort; you can find the current spec at `http://w3.org/html/wg/html5`.

Also, full HTML 5 support still isn't universal; most modern browsers support some subset of the features mentioned in the following sections, but few support them all. When you come to implement functionality that could make use of these tools, you'll need to consult the current documentation from the relevant browser vendors to determine which are available to you.

Local Storage

Traditionally, the only technology available for storing data in the browser was the *cookie*, a simple name/value pair really only suitable for small-scale, noncritical usage. So, one major development in HTML 5 is a complete overhaul of this client-side storage environment.

First, the new standard includes cookie replacements that provide more robust and secure techniques for storing basic name/value data. They're also a lot easier to use; storing a string for the duration of the current browser session is as simple as this (contrast with Listing 3-6):

```
sessionStorage.myName = 'my value';
```

Effectively, the `sessionStorage` implementation provides you with a persistent, on-demand namespace; at any later time during the browser session, `sessionStorage.myName` will return `'my value'`. And for name/value storage beyond the current session, the `localStorage` namespace functions equivalently.

When you have need of more sophisticated data storage, HTML 5 also offers a full-featured SQL database accessible from JavaScript. We saw this in action in Chapter 11, where I used this technique to port my `crossPlatform.Storage` class to iPhone. It's a good example of the use that a gadget developer can already make of HTML 5 technologies: when you know that a given platform will use a specific browser and that the browser supports the required technology, you're free to use it.

Although `localStorage` and `sessionStorage` are mostly of interest for being easier to use than cookies, the appeal of SQL databases is that they provide significantly greater functionality. Having local SQL available from JavaScript enables web app developers to create rich applications by storing all data directly in the browser. If a synchronization with server-side data is even necessary, it can be performed in the background via Ajax, invisible to the user. It fundamentally changes what's possible with a web gadget.

For more information on both of these technologies, the HTML 5 storage spec is available at `http://w3.org/TR/webstorage`.

Browser-Based Graphics

Although JavaScript has now brought true application-level functionality into the browser, the corresponding visuals haven't fundamentally changed since the days of Mosaic. Web designers still speak in terms of the *box model* and classify all elements as either `inline` or `block`; HTML 4 web pages are intrinsically rectilinear. This changes with the introduction of the `canvas` element in HTML 5: for the first time, web developers have a standardized way of drawing arbitrary graphics directly onto the page.

The canvas element essentially gives you a blank slate on which to draw whatever you'd like in your web page. Declaring it is extremely easy, because the `canvas` tag by itself doesn't do much of anything; see Listing 13-1.

Listing 13-1. Declaring the canvas Element in HTML

```
<?xml version="1.0" encoding="UTF-8"?>
<!DOCTYPE html PUBLIC "-//W3C//DTD XHTML 1.0 Transitional//EN"
                      "http://www.w3.org/TR/xhtml1/DTD/xhtml1-transitional.dtd">
<html xmlns="http://www.w3.org/1999/xhtml">
  <head>
    <title>Canvas Clock</title>
    <style type="text/css">
      body, body.* {
        margin: 0;
        padding: 0;
      }
    </style>
  </head>
  <body>
    <canvas id="clock" width="200" height="200"></canvas>
    <script type="text/javascript" src="listing_13_02.js"></script>
  </body>
</html>
```

The magic happens in JavaScript, where you issue the actual drawing commands. The complete canvas syntax is beyond the scope of this chapter, but as an example, I'm going to use it to create a simple analog clock gadget entirely in the browser. It uses the HTML of Listing 13-1, and the JavaScript is shown in Listing 13-2.

Listing 13-2. JavaScript for Drawing a Simple Clock with canvas

```
var canvas = document.getElementById('clock');
var context = canvas.getContext('2d');

function drawClock() {
  var now = new Date();
  context.fillStyle = '#eeeeee';
  context.lineCap = 'round';

  // Draw the face and rim
  context.lineWidth = 2;
  context.beginPath();
  context.arc(100, 100, 99, 0, Math.PI*2, true);
  context.fill();
  context.stroke();

  // Draw the hour hand
  var angle = (Math.round(now.getHours()%12) + now.getMinutes()/60) /
              (12 / (Math.PI*2));
  context.lineWidth = 7;
  context.save();
  context.translate(100, 100);
  context.rotate(angle);
  context.beginPath();
  context.moveTo(0, 4);
```

```
    context.lineTo(0, -50);
    context.stroke();
    context.rotate(-angle);
    context.restore();

    // Draw the minute hand
    angle = now.getMinutes() / (60 / (Math.PI*2));
    context.lineWidth = 3;
    context.save();
    context.translate(100, 100);
    context.rotate(angle);
    context.beginPath();
    context.moveTo(0, 10);
    context.lineTo(0, -80);
    context.stroke();
    context.restore();
};
setInterval(drawClock, 1000);
```

After obtaining a handle to the canvas's *context* (its actual drawing surface), I proceed to draw the three elements of the clock—face, hour hand, and minute hand—with a succession of low-level graphical calls to that context. In brief, this entails the following steps:

1. Drawing and filling the face as a complete circular arc

2. Drawing a short, thick line for the hour hand, rotated for the current hour

3. Drawing a longer, thinner line, rotated for the current minute

---

■ **Note** Although the clock example here is a static size, one clear advantage to canvas is that it could easily scale simply by using computed values (rather than numeric literals) for the various dimensions in Listing 13-2.

The entire package is wrapped up in the drawClock function and called once per second via setInterval, ensuring that the clock is always current. Figure 13-1 shows the final result, packaged as an Opera widget.

Figure 13-1. *A simple clock widget, with graphics produced by JavaScript in a canvas element*

Using canvas like this is perfectly safe in this context because Opera has supported it for some time. However, be aware that this code wouldn't yet be usable in a cross-browser gadget, as on iGoogle, because not every browser supports it. The one major holdout at this writing is Internet Explorer—although even there, an alternative is available from http://excanvas.sourceforge.net, an open source project to provide canvas compatibility using Internet Explorer's VML support.

CANVAS VS. SVG

You may recall that in Chapter 8 I used another W3C web graphic standard, SVG, to build backgrounds for my Opera widgets. What's the difference between it and the canvas element?

On the surface, both standards are similar, allowing developers to specify graphics in code (rather than an image file) and deliver them to any standards-compliant browser. But where canvas is an element embedded within an HTML document, SVG is usually a document of its own, able to be used independently or attached to a web page like any other graphic file. Additionally, drawing on a canvas is done in procedural JavaScript, while SVG graphics—specified in XML—are usually static within their document.

To relate the difference to the clock widget example given in this section, SVG could have been used to draw the (static) face and rim and would have scaled to different sizes if so desired. But SVG would not be well suited to drawing the hands, whose position must be recalculated each minute.

In short, the two standards have different uses, even if they do occasionally overlap.

The W3C Widget Specification

Another developing W3C standard that has been mentioned in this book is a non-platform-specific widget specification, which holds the promise of enabling cross-API widgets entirely from the same set of source code—no crossPlatform required. Originally proposed by Opera, a version of the standard has now been adopted by Windows Mobile, and the APIs used by OS X and the Symbian Web Runtime are closely related. Other adherents have also been announced, if not yet released. With every one, the standard gains momentum, and there's additional impetus for new platforms to also follow the spec.

However, it's not all good news. At this writing, it's not yet an established standard, merely a set of Working Drafts covering the various aspects of web gadget support. As a result, there are variations in how each vendor has implemented it. In addition, every platform so far has extended the specification with its own proprietary enhancements. All of this means that the "write once, run anywhere" dream for widgets is still some way off; for the immediate future, each API will still require its own port.

Nonetheless, the W3C specification bears watching. You can find current information from the Web Applications Working Group (which is overseeing the process) at http://w3.org/2008/webapps.

The BONDI Initiative

The last emerging standard I'll cover here isn't a product of the W3C, but it does build upon the widget specification discussed in the previous section. It's called the *BONDI Initiative*, and it's an effort to develop a platform-agnostic mobile API that will give web apps (including gadgets) access to device services, such as messaging, contacts, and camera. You'll recall that such access already exists on many of the device-specific APIs covered in this book, such as Windows Mobile, Symbian Web Run-Time, and T-Mobile Web'n'Walk; the difference here is that BONDI aims to deliver a single API usable on a variety of devices.

BONDI is a project of the Open Mobile Terminal Platform (OMTP) forum, bringing together many major players in the mobile industry, including hardware manufacturers and several international carriers. The stated goal of OMTP is to create and implement standards that encourage interoperability between devices, benefiting the industry as a whole. As part of this mission, BONDI aims to use web gadgets to create a single application platform for the entire smartphone ecosystem, allowing developers full access to device capabilities without needing to rewrite for each.

At this writing, the BONDI Initiative is still in quite an early stage of development. Specifications have been produced, and an open source Reference Implementation is available for Windows Mobile 6.*x*, but as yet no other operating system is supported, nor are any actual devices in the wild able to run BONDI widgets. Assuming it progresses further, the initiative will be of great benefit to gadget developers, and so it merits ongoing attention. For current information, BONDI's web site is located at http://bondi.omtp.org.

THE LG SDK FOR MOBILE WIDGETS

At this writing, the closest thing to a real-world release of BONDI is a gadget API from handset manufacturer LG. It has announced the availability of its SDK for Mobile Widgets and has included in it a subset of version 1.0 of the BONDI specification. However, it has also included LG-specific API classes, somewhat diluting the cross-platform BONDI ideal.

Like BONDI itself, LG's SDK is extremely new and not yet available on any live handsets. On the upside, though, its SDK does include the industry's only emulator specifically for web gadgets, indicating a higher level of commitment to the platform than many others. The SDK and full documentation are available for download from http://developer.lgmobile.com. I encourage you to check on the current status of this project; it has potential, and the techniques of this book should be well applicable to it.

Web-Based Operating Systems

As more of the world's applications are being run on the Web, the nature of operating systems is beginning to change in response. In this second part of the chapter, I'll cover two operating systems with web technologies at their core and examine the implications of each for gadget developers.

Palm webOS

Palm was one of the earliest handset manufacturers, virtually creating the PDA market segment in the days before mobile-phone integration. Its venerable PalmOS never achieved a great smartphone following, however, so in early 2009 Palm announced the overhaul of its handset platform. PalmOS was discontinued, and a new operating system, *webOS*, was introduced in its place.

As its name implies, webOS is built upon web technologies. Where other smartphone platforms use Java or C++ for development, "native" webOS apps are built with HTML, CSS, and JavaScript.[1] Access to device services and the user interface is via Mojo, a JavaScript framework built by Palm as a set of extensions to the Prototype library.

Compared with previous smartphone platforms, it's a radical approach, but faced with dwindling market share, radical change was what was called for at Palm. The intent was to create a platform that would more seamlessly integrate with the new generation of web applications and that could draw upon the large pool of web development talent, not just "mobile developers."

However, webOS has its downsides. For one, the necessary JavaScript abstraction lacks the deep hardware integration required to build some of the more demanding categories of applications, such as media players and fast-paced games.

It also has another, less obvious drawback. Although it uses the *syntaxes* of HTML and JavaScript, it does so within its own application framework and the Mojo API, rather than within the usual context of a web page. Instead, webOS applications are built upon *stages*, rely on *scenes* for their user interface, and use *assistants* and *controllers* for their functionality—terms (and technologies) that are foreign to web development. The source code for these components is indeed web-based, but strictly speaking, the HTML and JavaScript languages are not the same as on the Web. In addition, Mojo's user interface controls replace many standard HTML elements, further widening the gap between webOS and the actual Web.

■ **Note** Palm calls these Mojo user interface elements *widgets*, adding to the confusion—and semantically complicating any future port of a web widget API (like BONDI) to the platform.

The first result is that building webOS applications is not such a shallow learning curve for web developers as one might expect. And the second is perhaps even more surprising: there's no direct route for implementing an existing web app on webOS. Ironically, it's far easier (as you've seen) to port a web app to Android or iPhone than it is to webOS; even Symbian S60 and Windows Mobile, with their widget platforms, are a smoother ride.

---

[1] There is some debate about how truly *native* such webOS applications are; the operating system itself is built on a Linux kernel and clearly isn't executing JavaScript at that level. But like Java on Android in the previous chapter, there is no other, more native API for webOS, so we use the terminology as best we can.

Nonetheless, it is still possible to convert a web gadget's divs and functions into webOS scenes and assistants (see Figure 13-2), though it is beyond the scope of this book. And the webOS platform in general is one to watch; the technology is intriguing, and it is a step in a promising direction.

Figure 13-2. The Moon Phase gadget on webOS

Chrome OS

It's no secret that Google believes that web applications are the way of the future, and indeed, its Android smartphone OS is currently one of the best mobile-gadget platforms. In mid-2009 Google announced its second operating system, Chrome OS, promising a radical departure from any mainstream OS that precedes it. At this writing, Chrome OS is not yet released in any form—but from what is already known, it should have a strong impact on all web applications.

As its name implies, Chrome OS is an operating system based on a browser, and in fact, the vision seems to be that the browser *is* the operating system. A computer running Chrome OS will boot directly into the browser, and all applications "installed" on the system will in fact be web apps. Offline access will be delivered through some combination of HTML 5 techniques and Google's own Gears infrastructure, with the intention being for a seamlessly connected user experience, online or offline. The advent of Chrome OS should propel web applications even further into the mainstream for more users.

For web gadget developers, I anticipate two benefits. First, Google is already well established in the gadget space, with its iGoogle platform integrated into many of its leading services. It wouldn't be at all surprising to see that integration carried over into Chrome OS itself, with the ability for users to install gadgets directly on their computers. Although this is outwardly similar to what Windows and OS X already provide, the fact that web apps will be "native" on Chrome OS means that a closer integration should be possible.

Second, it's not yet clear what categories of device Chrome OS will eventually find its way into. Google has specifically targeted netbooks, but this segment laps over into that of ultra-mobile PCs, and from there it's a short step to true handhelds. Along this continuum, as screen sizes shrink, the line between *web application* and *web gadget* begins to blur. Gadget developers may thus find themselves well positioned to be the leading application providers for smaller Chrome OS devices.

In the end, even if neither of these predictions comes to pass, Chrome OS will unavoidably still be another step toward web technologies pervading the entire user experience.

Summary

The future for web gadgets is bright. Not only are they at home on the newest, fastest-growing smartphone platforms, but other technology trends are working in their favor as well. Several nascent standards (from the W3C and OMTP) will allow a single gadget code base to do more and on more platforms. And with the emergence of web-based operating systems, starting with Palm's webOS and Google's Chrome OS, these platforms will continue to include the most trend-setting devices. There's never been a better time to build a web gadget.

■ ■ ■

Gadget Platform Cross-Reference

This book covers a host of web gadget platforms. Their common trait is that it's feasible to port a generic gadget to any of them, but beyond that, they differ in almost every particular. Those differences are well documented in Chapters 4 through 12, but that's a lot of material to go through if you're looking for a particular figure or comparing platforms.

So, this appendix brings most of the quantifiable data for all relevant platforms together in one place. There's no new material here; it's simply reformatted for easy access.

■ **Note** This material is correct at the time of this writing, but please confirm with the platform vendors before deploying a live gadget, because the material is subject to change.

Packaging

Most platforms *package* the web resources that make up a gadget—its static HTML, CSS, JavaScript, images, and occasional data—for easy distribution to clients and for offline availability. Roughly half the platforms I cover do so as a renamed zip archive, which is a file with its extension changed from `.zip` to something else, but other techniques exist as well. Table A-1 sums up these various approaches.

Table A-1. Gadget Packaging Comparison

Platform	Terminology	Resource Packaging	File Extension	Metadata Location	Packaging Notes
Netvibes	Widget	None		HTML head element	Served directly from the Web
iGoogle	gadget	None		XML `ModulePrefs` element	Cached by Google
Windows Vista/7	Gadget	Zip archive	`.gadget`	`gadget.xml` manifest	Core HTML file name must match value in manifest

Platform	Terminology	Resource Packaging	File Extension	Metadata Location	Packaging Notes
Mac OS X	Widget	OS X bundle	.wdgt	Info.plist (XML)	Initial background image must be named Default.png
Opera (includes Mobile)	Widget	Zip archive	.wgt	config.xml manifest[1]	Core HTML must be named index.html
Windows Mobile	Widget	Zip archive	.widget[2]	config.xml manifest[1]	Core HTML file name must match value in manifest
Symbian Web Runtime	Widget	Zip archive	.wgz	Info.plist (XML)	Core HTML file name must match value in info.plist
iPhone	Web app	None		Web app directory	Served directly from the Web
iPhone	Native app	content folder		Info.plist (XML)	Core HTML must be named index.html
Android	Native app	assets folder	.apk	AndroidManifest.xml	Core HTML file name must match value in Java

Screen Resolutions

Although gadgets are inherently small-screen applications, the actual definition of *small* can itself cover a wide range. In Table A-2, you'll find a reference to available screen sizes in each platform.

- *Fixed* (or a specific pixel size) means that the platform supplies you with a size, and it's up to your gadget to use it.
- *Variable* means you can control the size; the crossPlatform.adjustSize function should fit the gadget's boundaries to your content.

---

[1] Implements a variation of the W3C widget specification (www.w3.org/TR/widgets).

[2] Windows Mobile widgets can also use a .wgt extension, but this may cause confusion with Opera, so I recommend avoiding it.

Table A-2. Screen Resolution Comparison

Platform	Width	Height	Notes
Netvibes	Fixed	Variable	Displayed within columns
iGoogle	Fixed	Variable	Displayed within columns
Windows Vista/7	Variable	Variable	Floating mode
	130px	Variable	Docked mode
Mac OS X	Variable	Variable	
Opera (desktop)	Variable	Variable	
Windows Mobile	Fixed	Fixed	Most commonly 240×320 or 480×640
Opera Mobile	Fixed[3]	Fixed[3]	
Symbian Web Runtime	Fixed[3]	Fixed[3]	
iPhone	320px[3]	480px[3]	As of this writing
Android	Fixed[3]	Fixed[3]	Most commonly 320×480

Icons

Virtually all platforms use *icons* to represent gadgets in menus, directories, or both, but there is essentially no standardization as to size, as shown in Table A-3.

Table A-3. Icon Size Comparison

Platform	Usage	Name	Width	Height
Netvibes	Widget header	In `<link rel="icon" />`	32px	32px
iGoogle	Directory	In `<ModulePrefs />` thumbnail	120px	60px
Windows Vista/7	Picker	In `gadget.xml` manifest	64px	64px

---

[3] Rotatable on at least some clients.

Platform	Usage	Name	Width	Height
Mac OS X	Widget Bar	/Icon.png	75px[4]	75px[4]
Opera (desktop)	Desktop	In config.xml manifest	16px	16px
	Directory	In config.xml manifest	128px	128px
Windows Mobile	Program icon	In config.xml manifest	48px	48px
Opera Mobile	Widgets Manager	In config.xml manifest	64px	64px
T-Mobile Web'n'Walk	T-Mobile Gallery	In config.xml manifest	64px	64px
Symbian Web Runtime	Application icon	/icon.png	88px	88px
iPhone	Application icon	In info.plist (for native app)	57px	57px
	Web apps directory		128px	128px
Android	Application icon	res/drawable/icon.png	48px	48px
	High-DPI app icon	res/drawable_hdpi/icon.png	72px	72px
	Market promo image		180px	120px

Screenshots

For promotion, most platforms allow you to enhance your directory listing with one or more images of your gadget in action. Table A-4 shows the comparative sizes of these *screenshots*; platforms not listed here are not known to support screenshots as of this writing.

- *Variable* height means that the directory will generally display an image of any height you supply for your screenshot.

- *Full size* means that no scaling or cropping is necessary; your gadget's screenshots will display at their native size.

---

[4] 75×75 original icon size; the image will be approximately 81×81 after adding a drop shadow.

Table A-4. *Gadget Screenshot Specifications*

Platform	Width	Height
Netvibes	320px	Variable
iGoogle	280px	Variable
Windows Vista/7	60–100px	60–100px
Mac OS X	Full size	Full size
Opera (includes Mobile)	300px	225px
iPhone (Web Apps)	320px	256px
iPhone (App Store)	320px	480px
Android (Market)	320px	480px
	480px	854px

Description Fields

Like screenshots, gadget *descriptions* usually accompany their directory listings and give you an opportunity to describe your gadget to prospective users before they install it. Table A-5 summarizes the description fields available to you.

- Unless otherwise noted, all descriptions are plain text, though they can usually display special characters by simply inserting their Unicode codes (with the notable exception of iGoogle).

- Although many platforms don't explicitly limit description length (indicated by *none* in Table A-5), they naturally aren't completely open-ended. Use your own discretion.

Table A-5. Description Field Length Comparison

Platform	Usage	Maximum Length
Netvibes	Description	None
iGoogle	Description	None[5]
Windows Vista/7	Summary	208 characters
	Description	1,000 characters
Mac OS X widgets and iPhone web apps	Summary	20 words
	Description[6]	None
Opera (includes Mobile)	Short description	150 characters
	Long description	None
iPhone (App Store)	Description	700 characters[7]
Android (Market)	Description	325 characters
	Promo text	80 characters

---

[5] iGoogle's description field is in an XML attribute and so can't contain line breaks.

[6] Opera's long description field supports the use of HTML formatting.

[7] This is the limit that Apple gives, but it's apparently not strictly enforced.

APPENDIX B

■ ■ ■

The crossPlatform Abstraction Layer

The cornerstone of this book's methodology is the crossPlatform library, a JavaScript middleware layer that isolates your gadget code from the implementation specifics of each platform it runs on. The architecture of crossPlatform, and the rationale behind it, is thoroughly covered in Chapters 2 and 3; in this appendix, you'll find a concise reference to its properties, as well as its complete source code.

crossPlatform works by detecting the gadget platform underlying any installation, setting a crossPlatform.api property accordingly, and then adapting its behavior based on the value of that property. However, crossPlatform.api is also visible to your own JavaScript code, and I encourage you to use it if you need to implement platform-dependent code of your own. Table B-1 lists the value of crossPlatform.api for each platform, along with any other properties that crossPlatform defines for each. Please refer to the appropriate chapter for more information on these additional properties.

Table B-1. *Platform-Dependent Properties*

Platform	.api Value	.emptyPref Value	Other Properties Defined
Netvibes	'netvibes'	undefined	.version, .prefs, .container, .host
iGoogle	'igoogle''	' '	
Windows Vista/7	'windows'	' '	
Mac OS X	'mac'	undefined	
Opera (includes Mobile)	'opera'	' '	
Windows Mobile	'windows_mobile'	null	
Symbian Web Runtime	'wrt'	undefined	
iPhone (native framework)	'iphone'	undefined	.data, .db
Android (native framework)	'android'	null	
Other	'none'	null	

To use the crossPlatform layer, you'll of course need to include it in your own gadgets. The specifics occasionally vary by platform (as covered in the chapters), but in general, you'll simply need a line like this in your HTML:

```
<script type="text/javascript" src="platform.js"></script>
```

Of course, you'll also need the JavaScript source, as shown in Listing B-1. For your convenience, this same code is available for download at http://sterlingudell.com/app_b/listing_b_01.js; simply save it to your own system and deploy it with your gadgets. This is the platform.js referred to in gadget listings throughout the book.

■ **Note** Any bug fixes found after this book goes to press will be included in the downloadable listing_b_01.js.

Listing B-1. *The Complete Source for crossPlatform*

```
/* Directives for the JSLint JavaScript verifier at jslint.com */
/*jslint browser: true, onevar: true, plusplus: true, eqeqeq: true, bitwise: true,
        nomen: false */
/*global window: false, gadgets: false, _IG_Prefs: false, _args: false,
        widget: false, openDatabase: false, System: false,
        _IG_FetchXmlContent: false, UWA: false, _IG_FetchContent: false,
        ActiveXObject: false,_IG_AdjustIFrameHeight: false */

// The crossPlatform namespace.
var crossPlatform = window.crossPlatform || {};

// addHandler: Attach a function as a handler to a DOM event
crossPlatform.addHandler = function (element, event, handler) {
  if (!!element.addEventListener) {
    // W3C DOM Level 2 compliant
    element.addEventListener(event, handler, false);
  } else {
    // Other browsers
    var oldHandler = element['on' + event];
    element['on' + event] = function() {
      if (!!oldHandler) {
        oldHandler();
      }
      handler();
    };
  }
};

// Initialize the platform variables

// iGoogle API (actually two APIs in one, or one API with two distinct versions)
if (!!window.gadgets && !!window.gadgets.util) {
  crossPlatform.api     = 'igoogle';
  crossPlatform.version = 'gadgets.*';
  crossPlatform.prefs   = new gadgets.Prefs();
```

```
} else if (!!window._gel) {
  crossPlatform.api     = 'igoogle';
  crossPlatform.version = 'legacy';
  crossPlatform.prefs   = new _IG_Prefs();
}
if (crossPlatform.api === 'igoogle') {
  crossPlatform.emptyPref = '';
  // iGoogle gadgets can be hosted in many places. Try to figure out where we are.
  crossPlatform.host = '';
  if (window._args instanceof Function) {
    crossPlatform.container = _args().synd || _args().container;
  }
  switch (crossPlatform.container) {
    case 'calendar':     break;
    case 'spreadsheets': break;
    case 'ig':           crossPlatform.container = 'igoogle';  break;
    case 'gm':           crossPlatform.container = 'mail';     break;
    case 'mpl':          crossPlatform.container = 'maps';     break;
    case 'gd':           crossPlatform.container = 'desktop';  break;
    case 'myaolgrs':     crossPlatform.container = 'my.aol';   break;
    case 'gasp2':
      crossPlatform.container = 'start';
      crossPlatform.host      = _args().pid;
      break;
    case 'enterprise':
      crossPlatform.container = 'sites';
      crossPlatform.host      = document.referrer.split('/').splice(0, 2).join('/');
      break;
    default:
      if (/^navclient/.test(crossPlatform.host)) {
        // Catches any 'navclient_xx' hosts, known (ff, ie) or unknown
        crossPlatform.container = 'toolbar';
      } else {
        // Catches blank container strings, 'blogger', 'open', and any new ones
        crossPlatform.container = (crossPlatform.container || 'unknown');
        crossPlatform.host      = document.referrer.split('/')[2];
      }
  }
} else if (!!window.UWA) {
  // Netvibes Universal Widget API
  crossPlatform.api = 'netvibes';
  crossPlatform.emptyPref = undefined;
} else if (!!window.System) {
  // Windows Desktop API
  crossPlatform.api = 'windows';
  crossPlatform.emptyPref = '';
} else if (!!window.widget) {
  // Several platforms use a widget.* namespace
  if (!!widget.getAttention) {
    // Opera, could be either desktop or mobile
    crossPlatform.api = 'opera';
    crossPlatform.emptyPref = '';
  } else if (!!widget.menu) {
```

```
        // Windows Mobile built-in widgets
        crossPlatform.api = 'windows_mobile';
        crossPlatform.emptyPref = null;
      } else {
        if (!!window.menu) {
          // Symbian S60 Web Run-Time
          crossPlatform.api = 'wrt';
        } else {
          // Mac OS X Dashboard
          crossPlatform.api = 'mac';
        }
        crossPlatform.emptyPref = undefined;
      }
    } else if (!!window.isIPhone) {
      // iPhone native app framework
      crossPlatform.api = 'iphone';
      crossPlatform.emptyPref = undefined;
      crossPlatform.data = {};
      crossPlatform.db = openDatabase('crossPlatform', '1.0', '', 65535);
      crossPlatform.db.transaction(
        function(transaction) {
          transaction.executeSql('create table if not exists cpStorage ' +
            '(name varchar(255) not null primary key, value text null);', []);
          transaction.executeSql('select name, value from cpStorage', [],
            function (transaction, results) {
              for (crossPlatform.i = 0; crossPlatform.i < results.rows.length;
                  crossPlatform.i += 1) {
                crossPlatform.data[results.rows.item(crossPlatform.i).name] =
                  results.rows.item(crossPlatform.i).value;
              }
          });
      });
    } else if (!!window.isAndroid) {
      // Android native app framework
      crossPlatform.api = 'android';
      crossPlatform.emptyPref = null;
    } else {
      // No known gadget platform
      crossPlatform.api = 'none';
      crossPlatform.emptyPref = null;
    }

    // Declare the persistent Storage class for name/value data
    crossPlatform.Storage = function (name, defaultValue) {
      var myName = name,
          myValue;

      switch (crossPlatform.api) {
        case 'igoogle':   myValue = crossPlatform.prefs.getString(name);      break;
        case 'netvibes':  myValue = widget.getValue(name);                    break;
        case 'mac':
        case 'wrt':
        case 'windows_mobile':
```

```
      case 'opera':       myValue = widget.preferenceForKey(name);              break;
      case 'windows':     myValue = System.Gadget.Settings.readString(name); break;
      case 'iphone':      myValue = crossPlatform.data[name];                   break;
      default:            myValue = crossPlatform.getCookie(name);
    }
    if (myValue === crossPlatform.emptyPref) {
      myValue = defaultValue.toString();
    }

    // Retrieve the value
    this.get = function () {
      return myValue;
    };

    // Save a value
    this.set = function (value) {
      if (myValue !== value) {
        myValue = value.toString();
        switch (crossPlatform.api) {
          case 'igoogle': crossPlatform.prefs.set(myName, myValue);             break;
          case 'netvibes': widget.setValue(myName, myValue);                    break;
          case 'mac':
          case 'wrt':
          case 'windows_mobile':
          case 'opera':      widget.setPreferenceForKey(myValue, myName);       break;
          case 'windows':    System.Gadget.Settings.writeString(myName, myValue); break;
          case 'iphone':
            crossPlatform.db.transaction(
              function(transaction) {
                transaction.executeSql(
                  'insert into cpStorage (name, value) values (?, ?)',
                  [name, value],
                  null,
                  function (transaction) {
                    transaction.executeSql(
                      'update cpStorage set value = ? where (name = ?)',
                      [value, name]);
                  });
              });
            break;
          default:             crossPlatform.setCookie(myName, myValue);
        }
      }
    };
};

// setCookie and getCookie: Save/retrieve a cookie by name
crossPlatform.setCookie = function (name, value) {
  var mSecPerYear = 1000 * 60 * 60 * 24 * 365,
      cookieExpire;

  if (!value) {
    // Delete the cookie by setting an expiration date in the past
```

```
        cookieExpire = 'Sun, 24-Apr-05 00:00:00 GMT';
    } else {
        // Upsert the cookie by setting an expiration date one year from now
        cookieExpire = (new Date(Number(new Date()) + mSecPerYear)).toUTCString();
    }

    document.cookie = name + '=' + value + ';expires=' + cookieExpire +
                        ';path=' + window.location.pathname;
};
crossPlatform.getCookie = function (name) {
    var cookies = document.cookie.split(';'),
        thisCookie,
        c;

    // Iterate through the cookie list, returning the value associated with "name"
    name = name + '=';
    for (c = 0; c < cookies.length; c += 1) {
        thisCookie = cookies[c].replace(/^\s+/, '');
        if (thisCookie.indexOf(name) === 0) {
            return thisCookie.substring(name.length, thisCookie.length);
        }
    }
    // Target "name" not found
    return null;
};

//fetchXML: Retrieve an XML document from url and pass it to callback as a DOM
crossPlatform.fetchXML = function (url, callback) {
    switch (crossPlatform.api) {
        case 'igoogle':
            if (crossPlatform.version === 'legacy') {
                _IG_FetchXmlContent(url, callback);
            } else {
                gadgets.io.makeRequest(url, function (response) {callback(response.data);},
                    {'CONTENT_TYPE': gadgets.io.ContentType.DOM});
            }
            break;
        case 'netvibes':
            UWA.Data.getXml(url, callback);
            break;
        default:
            crossPlatform.fetch(url, callback, 'responseXML');
    }
};
// fetchText: Retrieve a text document from url and pass it to callback as a string
crossPlatform.fetchText = function (url, callback) {
    switch (crossPlatform.api) {
        case 'igoogle':
            if (crossPlatform.version === 'legacy') {
                _IG_FetchContent(url, callback);
            } else {
                gadgets.io.makeRequest(url, callback);
            }
```

```
      break;
    case 'netvibes':
      UWA.Data.getText(url, callback);
      break;
    default:
      crossPlatform.fetch(url, callback, 'responseText');
  }
};

// Helper code for content-fetching routines
crossPlatform.fetch = function (url, callback, propertyName) {
  var xhrFetcher = crossPlatform.getFetcher();
  if (!xhrFetcher) {
    // We were unable to create the XHR object
    callback(null);
  } else {
    xhrFetcher.open('GET', url, true);
    xhrFetcher.onreadystatechange = function () {
      if (xhrFetcher.readyState === 4) {
        // Retrieval complete
        if (!!xhrFetcher.timeout) {
          clearTimeout(xhrFetcher.timeout);
        }
        if (xhrFetcher.status >= 400) {
          // Returned an HTTP error
          callback(null);
        } else {
          // Returned successfully
          callback(xhrFetcher[propertyName]);
        }
        // We're done with this fetcher object
        crossPlatform.fetchers.push(xhrFetcher);
      }
    };
    xhrFetcher.timeout = setTimeout(callback, 60000);
    xhrFetcher.send(null);
  }
};
crossPlatform.fetchers = [];
crossPlatform.getFetcher = function () {
  if (!!crossPlatform.fetchers.length) {
    return crossPlatform.fetchers.pop();
  } else {
    if (!!window.XMLHttpRequest) {
      return new XMLHttpRequest(); // Most browsers
    } else if (!!window.ActiveXObject) {
      return new ActiveXObject('Microsoft.XMLHTTP'); // Some IE
    } else {
      return null;  // Really old browser
    }
  }
};
```

```
//nodeValue: Extract the text value of a DOM node
crossPlatform.nodeValue = function(node) {
  return (node.innerText || node.text || node.textContent ||
          node.childNodes.length ? node.childNodes[0].data : null);
};

crossPlatform.getWidth = function (element) {
  if (element === window) {
    return document.body.offsetWidth || document.body.parentNode.clientWidth;
  } else {
    return element.offsetWidth || element.innerWidth;
  }
};
crossPlatform.getHeight = function (element) {
  if (element === window) {
    return document.body.offsetHeight || document.body.parentNode.clientHeight;
  } else {
    return element.offsetHeight || element.innerHeight || element.clientHeight;
  }
};
crossPlatform.adjustSize = function () {
  switch (crossPlatform.api) {
    case 'igoogle':
      try {
        if (crossPlatform.version === 'legacy') {
          _IG_AdjustIFrameHeight();
        } else if (!!gadgets.window) {
          gadgets.window.adjustHeight();
        }
      } catch (e) {}  // .adjustHeight is unreliable on some Google containers
      break;
    case 'mac':
    case 'opera':
      window.resizeTo(crossPlatform.getWidth(window),
                      crossPlatform.getHeight(window));
      break;
    case 'windows':
      var adjuster = function () {
        document.body.style.height = document.body.scrollHeight + 'px';
      };
      setTimeout(adjuster, 100);
      break;
  }
};

// escapeHTML: Make a string safe for display within page content
crossPlatform.escapeHTML = function (text) {
  if (!!text) {
    text = String(text).replace(/'/g, '&apos;').replace(/"/g, '&quot;');
    text = text.replace(/&/g, '&amp;').replace(/</g, '&lt;').replace(/>/g, '&gt;');
  }
  return text;
};
```

APPENDIX C

■ ■ ■

The Moon Phase Gadget

This book demonstrates the process of designing a gadget, implementing it, and then porting it across platforms with a single example, following it through its entire life cycle from initial idea to cross-platform deployment. The purpose of this approach is to lend continuity to the process by examining each step in the context of a known gadget. But necessarily, the code for the actual gadget has been presented in pieces, along with the stage of the process to which each piece relates. In this appendix, the entirety of the example gadget code is brought together to serve as a single reference; this should also aid you in following along with the examples in the book, giving you working code upon which each can be based.

The gadget in question is Moon Phase, a simple web app that displays the current phase of the moon, along with the time to the nearest full and new moons (Figure C-1). It's a simple example but reasonably representative of the sorts of tasks gadget developers face: it has several content blocks to be arranged on its surface for different screen layouts, including an image loaded dynamically based on user preferences. It obtains its data via Ajax at runtime, as is common in gadgets; consequently, its functionality and code are divided between client (the web browser) and server (a web host).

Figure C-1. The basic Moon Phase gadget

■ **Note** If you're implementing the examples in this book or simply want to refer to the code, remember that it's available at `http://sterlingudell.com/pwg/appendix_c`.

In the following sections you'll find the complete source code for the core Moon Phase gadget, on which all the platform-specific versions in this book are based.

Client

The client side of Moon Phase is a basic but complete web application; it is built around a single web page, with all changes to content achieved via JavaScript. Accordingly, the HTML is fairly simple, as shown in Listing C-1.

Listing C-1. The HTML for Moon Phase

```
<?xml version="1.0" encoding="UTF-8"?>
<!DOCTYPE html PUBLIC "-//W3C//DTD XHTML 1.0 Transitional//EN"
                      "http://www.w3.org/TR/xhtml1/DTD/xhtml1-transitional.dtd">
<html xmlns="http://www.w3.org/1999/xhtml">
  <head>
    <meta http-equiv="Content-Type" content="text/html;charset=UTF-8" />
    <meta name="description"
          content="Shows the current phase of the moon on a field of stars." />
    <meta name="viewport" content="width=device-width, height=device-height" />
    <title>Moon Phase</title>
    <link href="moon_32.png" type="image/png" rel="icon" />
    <link href="phase.css"   type="text/css"  rel="stylesheet" />
  </head>
  <body class="moonPhase">
    <div id="main">
      <div id="main_icons">
        <a id="config_icon" class="control_icon" title="Settings"
           onclick="moonPhase.showConfig();"></a>
      </div>
      <p id="last" class="text"></p>
      <p id="image_container">
        <img id="moon" alt="Current Moon Image Unavailable" width="176" height="176"
             src="http://daylightmap.com/moon/images/luna_north_small.jpg" />
      </p>
      <p id="next" class="text"></p>
      <p id="credit" class="text">
        by <a target="_top" href="http://www.daylightmap.com">DaylightMap</a>
      </p>
    </div>

    <div id="config" style="display: none">
      <p><strong>Moon Phase Settings</strong></p>
      <p>
        <label for="size">Size:</label>
        <select id="size" name="size">
          <option value="small">Small</option>
          <option value="large">Large</option>
          <option value="auto">Auto</option>
        </select>
      </p>
      <p>
```

```
      <label for="text">Show Text:</label>
      <select id="text" name="text">
        <option value="yes">Yes</option>
        <option value="no">No</option>
        <option value="auto">Auto</option>
      </select>
    </p>
    <p>
      <label for="hemisphere">View From:</label>
      <select id="hemisphere" name="hemisphere">
        <option value="north">Northern Hemisphere</option>
        <option value="south">Southern Hemisphere</option>
      </select>
    </p>
    <p id="config_buttons">
      <input type="submit" value="Save" id="save_button"
             onclick="moonPhase.saveConfig(); return false;" />
      <input type="button" value="Cancel" id="cancel_button"
             onclick="moonPhase.hideConfig();" />
    </p>
  </div>

  <script src="platform.js" type="text/javascript"></script>
  <script src="phase.js"    type="text/javascript"></script>
  </body>
</html>
```

The content is structured into two divs, main and config, for the gadget's primary view and settings pane, respectively; the latter is simply a form containing the configuration controls. The visibility of these panes is alternately toggled in JavaScript; initially, main is visible, and config is hidden.

This beginning state, along with the rest of the Moon Phase's presentation, is coded into the gadget's single CSS file (Listing C-2), phase.css. Again, it's relatively simple, in keeping with the gadget itself. At a high level, it's structured into basic presentational style for the gadget as a whole, absolute positioning for the main view's elements, and normal-flow layout for the configuration pane.

Listing C-2. *The CSS for Moon Phase*

```
/* Body element style, referenced by class instead */
.moonPhase {
  margin: 0;
  padding: 0;
  overflow: hidden;
  font-family: sans-serif;
  color: #cccccc;
  background: black url(http://daylightmap.com/moon/images/stars_large.jpg) center;
}

/* Styling for the full content area and moon image */
.moonPhase #main {
  position: relative;
  left: 0;
  top: 0;
  width: 100%;
```

```css
    font-size: 11px;
}
.moonPhase #image_container {
  margin: 0 10px;
  padding: 10px;
  text-align: center;
}

/* Presentation of the auxiliary text blocks */
.moonPhase a,
.moonPhase a:visited {
  color: #cccccc;
  text-decoration: none;
}
.moonPhase a:hover {
  color: #ffffff;
  text-decoration: underline;
  cursor: pointer;
}
.moonPhase .text {
  width: 30%;
  position: absolute;
  line-height: 1.1em;
  margin: 5px;
}
.moonPhase #last {
  text-align: left;
  left: 0;
  top: 0;
}
.moonPhase #next {
  text-align: right;
  right: 0;
  bottom: 0;
}
.moonPhase #credit {
  text-align: left;
  left: 0;
  bottom: 0;
}

/* Control icons on the main pane */
.moonPhase #main_icons {
  opacity: 0;
  display: block;
  position: absolute;
  right: 0px;
  top: 0px;
  height: 18px;
  width: 18px;
  z-index: 99999;
  overflow: visible;
}
```

```css
.moonPhase .control_icon {
  overflow: hidden;
  position: absolute;
  right: 2px;
  height: 16px;
  width: 16px;
  border: none;
  background: no-repeat 0 0 transparent;
  cursor: pointer;
}
.moonPhase #config_icon {
  top: 2px;
}
.moonPhase #main:hover #main_icons {
  opacity: 0.5;
}
.moonPhase #main #main_icons:hover {
  opacity: 1.0;
}

/* Configuration pane */
.moonPhase #config {
  display: none;
  padding: 3%;
  font-size: 12px;
  max-width: 250px;
  margin: auto;
  background-color: black;
}
.moonPhase #config p {
  margin: 0 0 0.8em 0;
}
.moonPhase #config p {
  padding-left: 3px;
}

.moonPhase label {
  float: left;
  clear: left;
  width: 6em;
}
.moonPhase input {
  vertical-align: top;
  color: black;
}
.moonPhase #config_buttons {
  text-align: right;
}
.moonPhase #config_buttons input {
  height: 20px;
  width: 50px;
  font-size: 11px;
}
```

Making the client side of the gadget function, of course, is JavaScript. This is divided into two source files: `platform.js`, the `crossPlatform` library detailed in Chapter 3 (with code in Appendix B); and `phase.js`, with functionality specifically for this gadget (Listing C-3). For safety, all code in `phase.js` is namespaced under a single top-level object named `moonPhase`. Within it, you'll find functions for initializing the gadget, loading its settings, retrieving and displaying its dynamic content, and controlling the configuration pane.

Listing C-3. *The JavaScript for Moon Phase*

```
/*jslint browser: true, onevar: true, plusplus: true, eqeqeq: true, bitwise: true,
        forin: true  */
/*global crossPlatform */

// The moonPhase namespace
var moonPhase = window.moonPhase || {};

// Declare module-level variables
moonPhase.nextLast = null;
moonPhase.timeout  = null;
moonPhase.elements = {
    'main':         null,
    'config_icon':  null,
    'moon':         null,
    'last':         null,
    'next':         null,
    'credit':       null,
    'config':       null,
    'size':         null,
    'text':         null,
    'hemisphere':   null
};
moonPhase.prefs = {
  'text':         'auto',
  'size':         'auto',
  'hemisphere':  'north'
};

// Stub to be overridden in platforms with a generic content proxy
moonPhase.proxify = moonPhase.proxify || function (url) {return url;};

//init: Initialize the gadget
moonPhase.init = function () {
  var id, name;

  // Attach links to HTML elements
  for (id in moonPhase.elements) {
    moonPhase.elements[id] = document.getElementById(id);
  }

  // Create preference objects
  for (name in moonPhase.prefs) {
    moonPhase.prefs[name] =
      new crossPlatform.Storage(name, moonPhase.prefs[name]);
  }
```

```
// Set the wrench icon for the config button
  moonPhase.elements.config_icon.style.backgroundImage =
    'url(' + moonPhase.proxify('http://daylightmap.com/moon/wrench_16.png') + ')';

  // Attach (and call) the resize handler to load content
  crossPlatform.addHandler(window, 'resize', moonPhase.load);
  moonPhase.load();

//  _IG_Analytics('UA-1556555-7', '/moon/' + platform + '/test');
};
crossPlatform.addHandler(window, 'load', moonPhase.init);

//load: Load the visible content appropriate for the current size of the gadget
moonPhase.load = function () {
  var width, showText, size, hemisphere, imgSrc, now;

  // Get the screen width
  width = crossPlatform.getWidth(window);

  if (moonPhase.prefs.text.get() === 'auto') {
    showText = (width > 220);
  } else {
    showText = (moonPhase.prefs.text.get() === 'yes');
  }

  if (showText) {
    // Show the ancillary text
    moonPhase.elements.last.style.display = 'inline';
    moonPhase.elements.next.style.display = 'inline';

    if (!moonPhase.nextLast ||
        (Number(new Date()) > moonPhase.nextLast.next.when)) {
      // Retrieve the next/last data
      crossPlatform.fetchXML('http://daylightmap.com/moon/next_last.xml.php',
          moonPhase.receiveNextLast);
    } else {
      // No retrieval necessary, just show it
      moonPhase.showText();
    }
  } else {
    // Hide the ancillary text
    moonPhase.elements.last.style.display = 'none';
    moonPhase.elements.next.style.display = 'none';
  }

  if ((moonPhase.prefs.size.get() === 'small') ||
      ((moonPhase.prefs.size.get() === 'auto') &&
      (width < 180))) {
    size = 'small';
  } else if (width < 800) {
    size = 'medium';
  } else {
    size = 'large';
```

```
    }

  hemisphere = moonPhase.prefs.hemisphere.get();

  if (size === 'large') {
    // Large display (for full-sized monitors)
    imgSrc = 'luna_' + hemisphere + '_large.jpg';
    document.body.style.overflow = 'auto';
    moonPhase.elements.moon.height = 625;
    moonPhase.elements.moon.width  = 625;
  } else {
    // Ordinary gadget-sized siaplay
    imgSrc = 'luna_' + hemisphere + '_small.jpg';
    document.body.style.overflow = '';

    if (size === 'small') {
      // Small display
      moonPhase.elements.moon.height = 88;
      moonPhase.elements.moon.width  = 88;
    } else {
      // Medium-sized display
      moonPhase.elements.moon.height = 176;
      moonPhase.elements.moon.width  = 176;
    }
  }

  // Add a cache-control parameter to ensure the hourly moon image is fresh
  now = new Date();
  imgSrc += '?cache=' + now.getUTCMonth() + now.getUTCDate() + now.getUTCHours();

  // Set the source for the main moon image
  moonPhase.elements.moon.src =
    moonPhase.proxify('http://daylightmap.com/moon/images/' + imgSrc);

  crossPlatform.adjustSize();
};
// receiveNextLast: Callback for the next/last XML retrieval
moonPhase.receiveNextLast = function (responseXML) {
  var nodes;
  if (!responseXML) {
    // Error retrieving the data - try again, using exponential back-off
    moonPhase.delay = moonPhase.delay || 5 * 1000;
    // Give up after 4 failures.
    if (moonPhase.delay <= 40 * 1000) {
      moonPhase.delay *= 2;
      window.setTimeout(moonPhase.load, moonPhase.delay);
    }
  } else {
    // Cache the retrieved data into a JS variable and show it on screen
    nodes = responseXML.getElementsByTagName('phase');
    try {
      moonPhase.nextLast = {
```

```
      'last': {'type': crossPlatform.escapeHTML(nodes[0].getAttribute('type')),
               'when': crossPlatform.nodeValue(nodes[0])},
      'next': {'type': crossPlatform.escapeHTML(nodes[1].getAttribute('type')),
               'when': crossPlatform.nodeValue(nodes[1])}
    };
  } catch (e) {
    moonPhase.nextLast = null;
  }
  moonPhase.showText();
  }
};


// showText: Extract the next/last data from the local cache to the visible HTML
moonPhase.showText = function () {
  if (!!moonPhase.nextLast) {
    // Cache has been filled - go ahead!
    moonPhase.elements.last.innerHTML = moonPhase.nextLast.last.type + ' moon ' +
      moonPhase.timeDelta(moonPhase.nextLast.last.when) + ' ago';
    moonPhase.elements.next.innerHTML = moonPhase.nextLast.next.type + ' moon in ' +
      moonPhase.timeDelta(moonPhase.nextLast.next.when);

    // Refresh the text display in 1 hour
    if (!!moonPhase.timeout) {
      window.clearTimeout(moonPhase.timeout);
    }
    moonPhase.timeout = window.setTimeout(moonPhase.load, 60 * 60 * 1000);
  }
};

// timeDelta: Generate a human-readable string showing the difference between the
//            current time and the given JS Date object, as in "3 days, 22 hours"
moonPhase.timeDelta = function (date)
{
  var days = Math.abs(date - Number(new Date())) / (24 * 60 * 60 * 1000),
      hours = Math.round((days - Math.floor(days)) * 24),
      result = '';

  if (Math.floor(hours) === 24) {
    days += 1;
    hours = 0;
  }

  if (days >= 1) {
    result = result + Math.floor(days) + ' day';
    if (days >= 2) {
      result = result + 's';
    }
    result = result + ', ';
  }

  result = result + Math.floor(hours) + ' hour';
  if (hours !== 1) {
```

```
    result = result + 's';
  }

  return result;
};

// saveConfig: Save settings from the config panel to their preferences objects
moonPhase.saveConfig = function () {
  var name, selector;

  try {
    for (name in moonPhase.prefs) {
      selector = moonPhase.elements[name];
      moonPhase.prefs[name].set(selector.options[selector.selectedIndex].value);
    }

    moonPhase.load();
  } catch (e) {
    alert('Unable to save settings: ' + e.message);
    if (!!window.console && !!console.log) {
      console.log(e.message);
    }
  }
  moonPhase.hideConfig();
};

// loadConfig: Load settings into the config pane
moonPhase.loadConfig = function () {
  var name, value, selector, s;

  for (name in moonPhase.prefs) {
    value = moonPhase.prefs[name].get();
    selector = moonPhase.elements[name];
    for (s = 0; s < selector.length; s += 1) {
      selector.options[s].selected = (selector.options[s].value === value);
    }
  }
};

// showConfig: Display the configuration pane
moonPhase.showConfig = function () {
  moonPhase.loadConfig();
  moonPhase.elements.main.style.display   = 'none';
  moonPhase.elements.config.style.display = 'block';
  crossPlatform.adjustSize();
};

// hideConfig: Switch display from the configuration pane back to the default
moonPhase.hideConfig = function () {
  moonPhase.elements.config.style.display = 'none';
  moonPhase.elements.main.style.display   = 'block';
  crossPlatform.adjustSize();
};
```

Server

Moon Phase uses two types of dynamic content: XML-based data for the times of new and full moons, and a simulated live image of the current moon. Accordingly, the server-side code is divided into two areas.

XML

Generating the XML time data is actually surprisingly complex; the moon has a somewhat eccentric orbit, and of course its phase is dependent on both its orbital position relative to the earth and the earth's position relative to the sun. Because of this, computing accurate moon phase times requires computing (or numerically approximating) the elements for both of these orbits and then combining them. Detailing this process is beyond the scope of this chapter; if you're interested in implementing it, the best reference I know of is at http://stjarnhimlen.se/comp/ppcomp.html.

However, it's possible to produce a reasonable approximation of the moon's phase without going to these lengths. Although the actual orbits are complicated, the end result is that the moon's apparent phase is on a roughly 29.5-day cycle; if you're satisfied with accuracy within 13 hours or so, a simple algorithm based on this raw cycle length will suffice. This is the approach, known as *mean full moon*, which you'll find implemented in Listing C-4; for purposes of trying the examples in this book, it's more than adequate. Use it as the next_last.xml.php server called from phase.js.

Listing C-4. PHP Code for Returning Mean Full and New Moon Times As XML

```php
<?php
  // Constants
  define('CYCLE_LENGTH', 29.530588853);
  define('SECS_PER_DAY', 24 * 60 * 60);

  function get_phase($when) {
    // Find the phase of the moon (as a percentage of its cycle) for the given date
    //   0 == new moon
    $new_time = gmmktime(7, 55, 0, 1, 26, 2009);
    $moon_age = ($when - $new_time) / (CYCLE_LENGTH * SECS_PER_DAY);
    return $moon_age - floor($moon_age);
  }

  // Get the current time and phase
  $now = mktime();
  $phase = get_phase($now);

  // Determine which half of the phase we're in
  if ($phase < 0.5) {
    // Waxing
    $last_name = 'New';
    $next_name = 'Full';
    $last_delta = $phase * CYCLE_LENGTH;
    $next_delta = (0.5 - $phase) * CYCLE_LENGTH;
  } else {
    // Waning
    $last_name = 'Full';
    $next_name = 'New';
    $last_delta = ($phase - 0.5) * CYCLE_LENGTH;
```

```
    $next_delta = (1 - $phase) * CYCLE_LENGTH;
}

// Calculate time of the next & last events
$last_time = round(($now - ($last_delta * SECS_PER_DAY)) * 1000);
$next_time = round(($now + ($next_delta * SECS_PER_DAY)) * 1000);

// Output the results as XML
header('Content-Type: text/xml');
echo "<?xml version=\"1.0\" encoding=\"UTF-8\"?>
<moon>
    <phase type=\"$last_name\">$last_time</phase>
    <phase type=\"$next_name\">$next_time</phase>
</moon>";
?>
```

Obviously, it's implemented in PHP, but even if you don't know the language, you should be able to get an idea of what's going on. There's a single subroutine, get_phase, that simply subtracts the time of a known new moon (January 26, 2009, at 07:55 GMT) from the current time and then divides the difference by the mean length of the moon cycle. With that result in hand, it's a simple matter to determine whether the moon is waxing or waning and then return appropriate XML for the result.

Listing C-5 shows a sample of the XML output; it simply gives the types and Unix timestamps of the next and last lunar events. This is the format expected by phase.js, which parses the data and formats it for display in the gadget's HTML. If you were to replace Listing C-4 with the full-accuracy orbital-mechanics version, you'd simply need to ensure that its XML output was in the same format as shown here, and it would power the Moon Phase gadget with no trouble.

Listing C-5. Full and New Moon Data As XML

```
<?xml version=\"1.0\" encoding=\"UTF-8\"?>
<moon>
    <phasetype="New">1250761608910</phase>
    <phasetype="Full">1252037330350</phase>
</moon>
```

Imagery

The other server-side functionality for Moon Phase is live imagery, and for this, I turn to the open source Xplanet project. Originally for Unix X terminals (which is where its name comes from), Xplanet will generate all manner of high-resolution real-time planetary imagery, from day/night maps of the earth to full simulations of the solar system. Of course, this includes current moon images, which is what Moon Phase requires.

From the client side, the architecture is simple. The HTML contains a single img tag for the moon image, and phase.js simply assembles a URL based on current settings, such as luna_north_small.png, and then dynamically sets the src of the img to it. On the client, there's nothing relating the image to the *current* phase; it relies on the server to always have the current image at that URL.

So, on the server side, it's up to Xplanet to generate that current image. Like the moon phase XML data, there are two ways to approach this; the easier way is to simply call Xplanet to directly create each image. An Xplanet call looks like this:

```
./xplanet -num_times 1 -body moon -origin earth -transpng luna_north_small.png ~CCC
  -geometry 176x176
```

The options are fairly straightforward: you want 1 image of the moon, as viewed from earth, with the output going to an alpha-transparent .png of the given name and size. In theory, this is all you need, and if you're simply testing the code in this book, it is sufficient. Schedule an Xplanet command like this to run periodically on your server, and you'll have your imagery.

However, there are some issues. First, to generate the source imagery for the different client options, you'll need to run Xplanet several times—and generating the southern-hemisphere versions is somewhat challenging. Second, Xplanet doesn't antialias its images, and with high-contrast monochrome moon source photos, this produces a noticeable loss of quality. So, my actual Moon Phase server code addresses these problems by wrapping the Xplanet call in the PHP shown in Listing C-6.

Listing C-6. The PHP Code to Generate Moon Phase Imagery

```php
<?php
  function save_image($image, $file_name) {
    if (file_exists($file_name))
      unlink($file_name);
    imagejpeg($image, $file_name);
  }

  // Generate current moon image with xplanet

  $file_name = 'luna_xlarge.png';
  if (file_exists($file_name))
    unlink($file_name);

  $xplanet = '/usr/local/bin/xplanet/xplanet';
  $xplanet .= ' -num_times 1 -body moon -origin earth -transpng '.$file_name.
              ' -geometry 1024x1024';

  exec($xplanet, $output, $return);
  if ($nReturn != 0) {
    echo "exec command failed with error $return <br />\n$xplanet";
    die;
  }

  // Prepare to generate images

  $source = imagecreatefrompng('luna_xlarge.png');
  imagesavealpha($source, true);
  $source_size = imagesx($source);

  $stars = imagecreatefromjpeg('stars_large.jpg');

  // Generate images in various sizes for both hemispheres

  $sizes = array('small' => 176, 'large' => 625);
  foreach ($sizes as $size_name => $dest_size) {
    $dest = imagecreatetruecolor($dest_size, $dest_size);
    imagecopy($dest, $stars, 0, 0, 5, 0, $dest_size, $dest_size);
```

```
    // Northern hemisphere
    imagecopyresampled($dest, $source, 0, 0, 0, 0, $dest_size, $dest_size,
                       $source_size, $source_size);
    fvSaveImage($dest, 'luna_north_'.$size_name.'.jpg');

    // Southern hemisphere
    $imDest = imagerotate($dest, 180, imagecolorallocate($dest, 0, 0, 0));
    fvSaveImage($dest, 'luna_south_'.$size_name.'.jpg');

    imagedestroy($dest);
  }

  // Cleanup
  imagedestroy($source);
  imagedestroy($stars);
?>
```

My approach is as follows: I call Xplanet once to generate a single, high-resolution (1024px) image, and I then use PHP's built-in image* functions to resize it (with antialiasing) and rotate it for the southern hemisphere view, saving each version to the appropriate name.

■ **Note** Since Listing C-6 creates files from code, you may need to adjust permissions on the target directory accordingly, using chmod (or other command appropriate to your operating system).

With this script in hand, all that's left is to schedule it for regular execution. On my Linux-based web host, this is most easily accomplished with crontab, where I have an entry like this:

```
0 * * * * lynx -dump http://daylightmap.com/moon/images/listing_c_06.php
```

Without going into the intricacies of crontab, the summary is that this command will run the Xplanet PHP script every hour on the hour. It uses the built-in Lynx browser to run the script through the Apache server, which is the easiest way to invoke a PHP script in a predictable fashion.

Of course, the Xplanet calls could be wrapped in other languages—the logic of Listing C-6 is not difficult—and the scheduling can be accomplished in other ways and on other operating systems. However, for a basic Linux web server, the code here should be sufficient to get you started.

Index

▓ H

▓ I